Racing & Foc...

FLAT RACING
GUIDE 2018

Interviews • Statistics • Results
Previews • Training centre reports

Contributors: Richard Birch, James Burn, Steffan Edwards, Jack Haynes, Dylan Hill, Bruce Jackson, Tony Jakobson, Justin O'Hanlon, John O'Hara, Ed Quigley, Colin Russell, Mark Storey, James Thomas, Nick Watts

Designed and edited by Nick Watts and Dylan Hill

Published in 2018 by Raceform Ltd
27 Kingfisher Court, Hambridge Road, Newbury RG14 5SJ

Copyright © Raceform Ltd 2018

A catalogue record for this book is available from the British Library.

ISBN 978-1-910497-60-9

Printed by CPI Group (UK) Ltd, Croydon, CRO 4YY

RACING & FOOTBALL OUTLOOK

Est. 1909

Contents

Introduction		4
Profiles for punters	Iain Jardine	6
	Richard Spencer	12

2018 Preview

Pedigrees for punters	17
Ante-post preview	20
Racing & Football Outlook's 30 horses to follow	35
Aborigine	43
Jerry M	48
Downsman	52
Borderer	56
Hastings	60
Southerner	64
John Bull	67
Ed Quigley	70
Richard Birch	73
Time Test	76

2017 Review

Group 1 Review	80
Two-year-old Review	92

Statistics, Races and Racecourses

Comprehensive stats for ten top trainers	113
Jockey & trainer standings	153
Group 1 records	159
Big handicap records	172
Fixtures	181
Big-race dates	188
Track facts for all Britain's Flat courses	191

Final furlong

Picture quiz	233
Betting guide & Rule 4 deductions	236
Horse index	238

Est. 1909

RACING & FOOTBALL OUTLOOK

Editor's introduction

WE'LL admit there have been harder introductions to write than this one. Having written last year about the brilliance of Aidan O'Brien, we could pretty much copy and paste the same words after a stunning year that saw O'Brien hit even greater heights.

The Ballydoyle maestro ended 2017 with an astonishing 28 Group 1 winners,

ENABLE: five-time Group 1 winner

bettering the record of 25 held previously by Bobby Frankel. Saxon Warrior's Racing Post Trophy success had seen him surpass that mark before further wins for Mendelssohn at the Breeders' Cup and Highland Reel in the Hong Kong Vase confirmed O'Brien's status as a man who gets his horses to deliver across the globe.

Somewhat predictably, we're tipping O'Brien for plenty more success in 2018 but our ante-post guru Steffan Edwards goes even further and is backing Saxon Warrior to do a Camelot and win the Guineas-Derby double. And who knows, if that were to happen maybe there would still be a desire among those at Coolmore to settle old scores and go one better than Camelot could manage in the St Leger. That really would be something special.

In the face of such power at Ballydoyle, John Gosden deserves enormous credit for standing up in the heat of battle and arguably finding the two outstanding three-year-olds of the year in Enable and Cracksman – and equally deserving of credit is the decision of connections to keep both in training this year.

It's also noteworthy that the pair are by different sires who could throw up long-term challenges to Coolmore's dominance in Frankel and Nathaniel.

A daughter of Gosden's Nathaniel, who actually came closer than anyone to beating the great Frankel during his own stellar racing career, Enable won five successive Group 1 contests and twice beat the boys in the King George and the Arc, proving in a different league to her rivals both times.

Such was her brilliance that Gosden even decided against bothering with the

AIDAN O'BRIEN: all smiles after Saxon Warrior's Racing Post Trophy success

Arc with arguably the best three-year-old colt in training and, indeed, the best of Frankel's progeny to date, the Prix Niel and Great Voltigeur winner Cracksman instead dropping in trip for the Champion Stakes before his own intended Arc swansong in 2018.

Imagine the reaction of owner Anthony Oppenheimer, then, when Gosden said that Enable would stay in training as well. It's hard to believe that went down well!

Still, it's fantastic news for racing that we get to see more of Enable, hopefully going head to head with her stablemate this time, and her ongoing success could be vital given last year's disappointments with Minding and Almanzor – who won just one race between them as four-year-olds – might put connections off keeping the best horses in training.

So what will 2018 have in store for us? O'Brien and Gosden will be hoping it's more of the same, but there are plenty of other trainers hoping to make their mark and we've spoken to loads of them, kicking off with Ebor winner Iain Jardine and rising star Richard Spencer in our bumper stable tours before we move into our regional reports, in which our local correspondents have scoured their areas for all the key horses.

Pedigree expert James Thomas looks at the first-season sires who should make an impact, while Nick Watts has searched far and wide for his list of 30 horses to follow.

As well as that, we have invaluable stable insight from Ed Quigley and Richard Birch; Time Test brings you all the key speed figures; and Dylan Hill guides you through last season's leading form.

Then there are the stats, reams and reams of winner-finding numbers detailing the top trainers and jockeys also broken down course by course so you know who to follow at your local track.

Once again we have every base covered for a year packed with bumper profits, and don't forget to buy your copy of the RFO every week for the very latest news and tips.

Profiles for punters
Iain Jardine

IAIN JARDINE: proud to be part of a golden period for Scottish trainers

Profile by John O'Hara

RACING in Scotland has rarely been in better shape, as wins in the Grand National and the Ebor testified last year, and Iain Jardine played a big part in that with Nakeeta's success in the big York handicap.

The Ebor is the most prized race in the north, yet Jardine is hardly one to focus solely on events close to home as he then took his stable star to the other side of the world to pick up a six-figure cheque for finishing fifth in the Melbourne Cup.

The Flemington experience certainly whetted his appetite for more of the same.

"It was a great trip over," he says. "They certainly know how to treat visiting connections as we were looked after brilliantly. Nakeeta proved he can travel as he lost relatively little weight going over and but for a terrible draw, in stall 19, his jockey felt he would have been in the first three.

"The aim will be to head to Australia again this autumn, but before then we have what I believe is the best team I have had since taking out a licence to aim at the Flat season."

That is only to be expected as Jardine's career since taking up training has been on an upward curve, with more winners each year than the one before.

In 2016 he doubled his best year to 36 and the last campaign saw him bag 52 Flat winners and more than double the prize-money for his owners up to £639,020.

The big leap forward in recent times has been helped by a move to Len Lungo's old base at Hetland Hill in Carrutherstown, Dumfries, which took Jardine back to his roots in many ways as he had started his career in racing as a jockey for Lungo.

Having hung up his riding boots, he started breaking horses and also looking after a few in pre-training. That evolved into training point-to-pointers for three years, which inevitably led to him taking out a licence under rules.

"It was a natural progression really," says the trainer.

"I initially trained in Hawick in the Borders at a very small yard, but after things went better than we had anticipated we had to move on. It came to a point where I either stayed there and accepted that would be my lot or I could take the step to move to a bigger yard. With the way things had gone, it was an easy decision.

"Len kept this place in immaculate condition after he retired and it has been a joy to train horses here."

The first year at Hetland Hill was the 2016 campaign when Jardine's tally doubled, but it was an itch that Nakeeta was denied success at the Ebor meeting in a tight finish. From that moment the plan was to come back a year later and put that right – this time in the big one.

"It was great to see him run so well, but it was also a disappointment to get so close and not win. It told us he could go well there, though, and from that moment the Ebor was the race we wanted. We gave him three runs beforehand and got him there in top form. Before the race we also sat down and watched lots of videos of previous runnings and I noticed you didn't need to be handy to win. We felt he should be given time to get into a rhythm and then make his run when he was ready. Callum [Rodriguez] followed my instructions to the letter and it was such a thrill. When I saw it was one of Sir Mark's [Prescott, trainer of Flymetothestars] we got the better of, that made it all the more special as I am a huge fan of his."

It's not just the surroundings that have enabled Jardine to make it on the big stage. Naturally, he also puts it down to attracting a better class of horse.

He explains: "I knew coming here to Carrutherstown we would need to attract better horses and I genuinely believe we have. This year we start off with the strongest team I've had and on top of that we've had a productive winner with a good number of winners over jumps. Although our main strength is Flat racing, I do see myself as a dual-purpose trainer.

"I'm particularly looking forward to getting my two-year-olds out as we have more than ever this season (16) and some are showing plenty of early speed, most notably an unnamed son of Gregorian who looks very useful at this early stage. If anyone is interested we still have a handful of them left to sell."

Jardine is confident he has the horses to improve again on last season's total.

"Of course Nakeeta will be the standard bearer but we have a strong group of promising horses who are going to improve on last year. I couldn't pinpoint one and say he'll be the next stable star as that would be the kiss of death on the poor unfortunate horse, but there are a good number capable of climbing the ladder."

Jardine is proud of his Scottish roots and, if the team do live up to expectations, he will be delighted to be part of the success being enjoyed by his compatriots.

He enthuses: "There are a lot of good trainers up here and it has become very competitive. Lucinda Russell won the Grand National and is doing very well, while Keith Dalgleish's career is on an upward curve and Jim Goldie continues to send out the winners. It is all about keeping our names up in lights."

The horses

Atkinson Grimshaw 4yo gelding
Rio De La Plata – Cosabawn

I have a lot of time for this horse. He won twice for Andrew Balding this year and we bought him for 35,000gns. He has no ground issues and should be fine over any trip from 1m4f upwards. He'll be out around May or June and I expect him to give us a lot of fun this year.

Edge Of Sanity 9yo gelding
Invincible Spirit – Saor Sinn

He beat Quest For More at the Ebor meeting in 2014 when he was trained by Brian Ellison, but he's hardly run since as he's had tendon issues and has been difficult to train. We got him out twice last season and he was third at York first time out, but he had problems again. However, he'll

be back for the second half of the season and he has the ability to win a decent long-distance handicap.

Jabbaar 5yo gelding
Medicean – Echelon

He's a nice horse who is progressing with racing. He came back from a break better than ever and has already won on the all-weather this year. He's also a dual winner on turf and I think he'll do well again this summer.

Kyllachy Dragon 3yo gelding
Dragon Pulse – Lafayette

He's a really nice horse who did all but win last year. On the last of his four runs he was beaten a neck in a 17-runner nursery at York, which was frustrating. We've

EDGE OF SANITY (right): has had tendon issues since this big York win in 2014

NAKEETA (far side): gets up to beat Flymetothestars in the Ebor

given him plenty of time to mature over the winter and I expect him to do us proud this year over sprint trips.

L'Inganno Felice 8yo gelding
Librettist – Final Overture

He was clobbered by the handicapper for winning twice on the all-weather at the start of last year and is still at the wrong end of the weights. However, he still has plenty of ability if the handicapper does relent and he acts on almost any ground.

Marnie James 3yo gelding
Camacho – Privy Garden

He was a very decent juvenile last season, winning twice at York and Musselburgh. He was also second to Unfortunately, who later on win two the Prix Morny. He's a very quick horse and we should have a lot of fun in sprints with him this year as there's certainly more to come.

Mayleaf Shine 4yo filly
Mayson – Let Me Shine

I've been very sweet on this filly since she first arrived here and I know she's much better than her record - two wins from 16 races - suggests. She's had a long winter break and I think this could be the year she repays our faith as she's really thrived and looks so much stronger. She's rated 92 and I'd be very disappointed if she wasn't in three figures by the end of the year. Speed is her forte and we'll look for a stiff 5f or easy 6f for her.

Miss Dd 3yo filly
Dandy Man – Dynaperformer

We got her out of Tom Dascombe's stable at the end of last season and I think she could be a dark horse to follow this year. She was a winner over 6f at Pontefract for Tom and looks a nice addition to the string.

Nakeeta 7yo gelding
Sixties Icon – Easy Red

He's been a superstar for us and there's more to come. He needed time when he came here in 2014 and has since got better with every year, obviously peaking last season when he won the Ebor and was fifth in the Melbourne Cup. I think we got everything right down in Australia and the only problem we faced was the draw [stall 19 of 23] which meant he had to sit and

9

TOR (left): winning under Jamie Gormley at Musselburgh last year

suffer, but he ran an amazing race. Having won the Ebor off 103, he's now on 108 and I think we'll start to look at Group and Listed races, possibly starting off in something like the Yorkshire Cup. However, we'll also consider the Ebor again and ultimately his big target will be another crack at the Melbourne Cup. He looks very well for his break and if we can eke out a little more improvement again he could even top last year.

Restive 5yo gelding
Rip Van Winkle – I Hearyou Knocking

He's had his issues but he had a terrific second half of last season, winning three of his last five races. He' still on a competitive mark and should continue to do well.

River Icon 6yo mare
Sixties Icon – River Alder

I'd suggest readers keep an eye out for her. She's lightly raced on the Flat but has already won, as well over hurdles, and we'll continue to campaign her in both codes. I love her stallion, Sixties Icon, as

he passes on versatility to his progeny. She's a hardy individual with more to offer.

Sfumato 4yo gelding
Bated Breath – Modern Look

He won as a two-year-old for Roger Charlton in 2016 but has lost his way a little since then. He did better on his first run for us after coming here midway through last year, finishing second at Ripon, but two runs after that were disappointing again so we gave him a long break and it seems to have done him good. Once we get his head in front it could be the making of him as it would give him the confidence he needs. He must have a fast-run sprint because otherwise he gets too keen.

She's Pukka 4yo filly
Makfi – Chieftess

She's run only twice and is better than she's shown despite winning on her debut at Carlisle. The ground was heavy that day and she didn't really enjoy it, so she should improve on quicker ground. I made a mistake next time by running her on the all-weather as she didn't like it. She'll also be better over 1m4f and could be very progressive this year.

Shrewd 8yo gelding
Street Sense – Cala

He's been a terrific horse, winning nine times, but unfortunately he sustained a tendon injury in last year's Cesarewitch and we don't know his future at the moment. We're taking thing slowly with him and hopefully we'll get him back at some point.

Smugglers Creek 4yo gelding
Medicean – Crystany

He joined us from Mick Halford having won a Dundalk claimer over 7f. We have to teach him how to race properly, but once we do that he's definitely capable of winning more races.

Stone The Crows 4yo gelding
Cape Cross – Stars In Your Eyes

He was a winner for Roger Charlton before we paid 75,000gs for him at the Tattersalls Autumn Sales and I'm hoping he could be a very smart addition to the team. We gave him a break and he's filled out a lot as he was only a frame of a horse last year. I couldn't be happier with him. He needs at least 1m4f and possibly further.

Tor 4yo gelding
Orientor – Dance In The Sun

He's a grand little horse who is as tough as old boots. He did well last season, winning three times on sharp tracks like Chester and Musselburgh. I think he's probably as high as he wants to be in the handicap, but I use my good claimer Jamie Gormley to claim 5lb off him. He'll definitely be winning again.

Yes You 4yo filly
Choisir – Mexican Milly

She won three times from August to October last year, all over sprint distances. She's effective over a stiff 5f and an easy 6f and I think we can get a little more improvement out of her again.

YES YOU (centre): won three times last year and can improve again

Profiles for punters
Richard Spencer

RICHARD SPENCER: stunning success with his first batch of two-year-olds

Profile by Dylan Hill

THE Premier League is a good example of the fact that, where big sums of money are involved, people want a pretty instant return on their investment.

Richard Spencer delivered just that for his landlord Phil Cunningham last season when Rajasinghe won the Coventry Stakes at Royal Ascot in Spencer's second season as a trainer.

The 29-year-old had been entrusted by Cunningham to turn around his fortunes at Albert House in Newmarket, an historic yard that had been all but forgotten until Essex businessman and owner/breeder Cunningham, who famously won the 2,000 Guineas with Cockney Rebel, pumped in more than £1.5 million to return the 23-box establishment to its former glories.

After a brief spell under the tenure of Dave Morris, Albert House needed a new trainer and Spencer answered the call.

"I'd already met Phil when I was working for Barry Hills and he had horses there," says Spencer. "I was working for Michael Bell at the time that I saw the job advertised in the Racing Post. I decided to apply for it and it went from there."

Getting the job meant realising a long-held ambition for Spencer.

"I wanted to be a trainer from when I was a young child," he explains. "I came from a farming background and did pony club, hunting and showjumping, but my weight meant I was never going to make it as a jockey. My family bred a couple of horses and had them in training with Martin Pipe, which gave me the racing bug. As soon as I left school I went to work for Peter Bowen at the age of 16."

From there Spencer's journey took him to Lambourn, where he worked for Barry Hills for five years and then two more under Barry's son Charlie, before moving on to Bell's yard in Newmarket.

"I learned a lot from all of them," he says. "It gave me the perfect grounding for what I do now."

Spencer understandably struggled in his first season given he was the first of many yards in Newmarket to get hit with a virus, managing just three winners.

However, he always felt he would be better judged on his second season at the helm and he duly stepped up to the plate with ten winners, the most notable of which by far came on a magical day in June.

"Last year was the first time I had a part in actually buying the yearlings, so I was working with horses that I'd personally chosen. We also broke them in ourselves for the first time.

"Myself, Phil and our bloodstock agent Bobby O'Ryan buy them as a team. The three of us make a list of what we like the look of and we see where our lists cross over and go from there."

Rajasinghe was the horse who was quickly at the top of everyone's list of horses to follow once he started working.

Spencer explains: "From February he was a standout. I remember saying to a couple of people all the way back then that he was an Ascot horse and thank goodness it all worked out. You dream about that sort of thing and never think you could

PHIL CUNNINGHAM: leading in Cockney Rebel after the Guineas

be so lucky for it to happen so quickly, but it came off."

Rajasinghe's victory is all the more remarkable given he came from a group of just eight two-year-olds and Spencer has theoretically given himself a better chance of finding another juvenile star this time around with a bigger team.

"We've done the same again this year at the sales but we've got more ammunition now," he says. "We've doubled in size and I hope to be up to 50 horses by the time the turf season kicks off. I'm also attracting outside owners now."

The increase in numbers also means the operation is outgrowing Albert House, but Spencer also has 30 boxes at nearly Cadland House.

Asked which of the two-year-olds could be the next Rajasinghe, Spencer picks out a Swiss Spirit two-year-old called Cobweb Catcher, while his enthusiasm for unraced three-year-old Handsome Sansom and smart handicapper Keyser Soze is similarly infectious.

The horses

Bernardo O'Reilly 4yo gelding
Intikhab – Baldovina

He won by six lengths on his debut at Lingfield last year, but he was always a shell of a horse and he struggled after that. The upside is that he's come down in the handicap to a mark of 77 and he should be able to pick up a few sprints this year as he was always going to be better as a four-year-old.

Club Tropicana 3yo filly
Helmet – Twenty Seven

She showed some good form last year but has done well over the winter and should be even better this time around. We should be able to win a maiden with her and then we'll see how she gets on in handicaps.

Dragstone Rock 4yo gelding
Dragon Pulse – Rock Exhibition

He's a half-brother to Justice Day and I understand he was held in high regard at one point, but he must have had some issues because we managed to pick him up unraced at £5,000 for a new syndicate. He's fine now and should be ready to run in April. I hope he'll give his new owners plenty of fun.

Flux Capacitor 3yo colt
Society Rock – Mahela

He's a big horse and a late developer who has needed plenty of time, so he's still unraced. I couldn't tell you just how much ability he has because we couldn't even do any fast, serious work him last year, but all three of his siblings have won, including his stablemate Gustavo Fring, and he looks a similar type.

Gustavo Fring 4yo gelding
Kodiac – Mahela

We got a couple of runs into him on the all-weather late last year and he managed

KEYSER SOZE: winning at Kempton, where he posted some "freakish" splits

to win at Southwell. I'm sure he'll be just as good on turf, but we just wanted to win a maiden with him before the end of the year. Unfortunately he then had a little setback, but he should be back for the middle of the season.

Handsom Sansom 3yo colt
Nathaniel – Factice

He's a half-brother to Cockney Rebel by Nathaniel who could be very good. He's in the Derby and we're definitely not writing it off at this stage. He was too backward to run last year but should be ready for a maiden in April.

Keyser Soze 4yo gelding
Arcano – Causeway Queen

He's a really nice horse. He won twice last spring and the furlong splits when he won at Kempton were freakish. We then took him to Royal Ascot thinking he had a real chance of winning the Britannia, but nothing went to plan. Looking back he probably didn't have the best draw and the occasion maybe got to him. He hasn't run since then, but there was nothing wrong with him. We didn't want to overrace him because he was just a shell of a horse, so we gave him a good break. He's done very well physically and has come back a much bigger and stronger horse. We'll start him off in some top handicaps.

Movie Set 6yo gelding
Dubawi – Short Skirt

He'll be running on the Flat again this summer having gone hurdling over the winter. We got him off Godolphin and he was pretty talented on the Flat a few years ago, winning a maiden at Ascot and finishing a neck second on his only other run. I think we can have some fun with him.

Patty Patch 3yo filly
Big Bad Bob – Cockney Dancer

She was well beaten in three maidens last year, but they were good races every time.

MOVIE SET: once with Godolphin, he could give his followers some fun

She's been given a mark of 62 and I'd like to think that's workable. She can win a handicap.

Philamundo 3yo gelding
Sir Prancealot – Rublevka Star

He ran well on his handicap debut on his final run last year at Wolverhampton and was unlucky not to finish closer, but he's not the easiest of rides. His last three runs were on the all-weather, but he'll have no problem switching back to turf and seems pretty versatile. He should be capable of winning.

Rajasinghe 3yo colt
Choisir – Bunditten

He was amazing for us last year when winning the Coventry and I'm very much looking forward to getting him back on the track because I still think he has a lot to offer. It's easy to say he was disappointing after Ascot, but I don't think so. He was below-par only once in the Middle Park and that was his first run for a long time as he'd scoped badly just when we were getting him ready for the Prix Morny. He was

15

RAJASINGHE: with his overjoyed connections after the Coventry

third in the July Stakes and it's never easy to carry a penalty in that race. Then we took him to the Breeders' Cup and he was drawn 14 of 14 on the sharpest track you'll ever see. He also got no run at all, but he was still beaten less than five lengths and you couldn't say he didn't get the mile. We'll start off by thinking in terms of that trip for the 2,000 Guineas, but I think he's versatile regarding trip and anything from a stiff 6f should be fine. My only concern is that he needs good ground or quicker.

Rebel Cause 5yo gelding
Cockney Rebel – Happy Go Lily

Last season wasn't easy for him as he'd been off for a year, but he gradually improved and I thought his last run in an amateurs' race at Doncaster was much better than it looked. He just didn't quite stay the 1m2f trip ridden the way he was, so we need to hold him up if he goes that far again. He's shown us more at home this year and I'm looking forward to getting him back on track. We might mix and match hurdling and Flat races.

Rebel Surge 5yo mare
Kodiac – Face The Storm

She's a really solid mare who pays her

way and doesn't mind any ground or trip. She ran 14 times last season and very rarely runs a bad race. We might keep her fresher this year, though, and see if that helps her. She can win races off her sort of mark and I'd also love to get some black type with her, although it's very difficult.

Sea Of Flames 5yo gelding
Aqlaam – Hidden Fire

He was bought off David Elsworth to act as a lead horse for Rajasinghe. He's not run for a long time because he had a setback last year, but he's ready for the spring. Most of his form has come on the all-weather, but he's not had enough of a chance on turf, with most of his runs coming in top-class races, so I'm sure he can be effective anywhere.

Thistimenextyear 4yo gelding
New Approach – Scarlet Empire

He won a maiden on soft ground last year and you can forget his last two runs as conditions were too bad for him at Ffos Las and he's also disappointed twice now on the all-weather. He's come down to a mark of 77 and I think we can have some fun with him off that. He could also run over hurdles.

Est. 1909
RACING & FOOTBALL **OUTLOOK**

Pedigrees for punters by James Thomas

THE 2018 turf season looks sure to provide the answers to many of the big questions in bloodstock. Can Frankel, who supplied his first European Group 1 winner with Cracksman, continue his rapid ascent of the stallion ranks? Will Camelot's progeny follow in their sire's footsteps during their own Classic campaign? Can anyone lay a glove on Galileo?

While there is still plenty to learn about the more established names, we will, of course, get our first look at the progeny of some of the more recent retirees to stud, the most notable of whom are discussed below.

Australia
Galileo – Ouija Board (Cape Cross)

A very smart juvenile, Australia developed into an outstanding middle-distance three-year-old, winning the Derby and the Irish Derby before adding the Juddmonte International in the manner of a colt right out of the very top drawer.

His top-class race record is backed up by a flawless pedigree, being by the all-conquering Galileo – whose sire sons include Frankel, Nathaniel and New Approach – and out of the incomparable Ouija Board, a globetrotting daughter of Cape Cross who landed seven top-flight events during her racing career.

Given his profile, it is hardly surprising that his stock have proved popular in sales rings around the world, finding favour with many of the game's top judges.

His first crop includes 30 yearlings who fetched six-figure prices at public auction, including a half-brother to Rekindling who fetched 525,000gns from MV Magnier, Mayfair Speculators and Peter and Ross Doyle during the prestigious Book 1 at Tattersalls.

He covered 172 mares in his first book, meaning he should have plenty of ammunition, most likely for the middle to backend of the turf season. His debut book also contained 45 per cent stakes performers, meaning there is a considerable amount of quality as well as quantity among his debut juveniles.

Kingman
Invincible Spirit – Zenda (Zamindar)

High-class and unbeaten at two, Kingman atoned for a near miss in the 2,000 Guineas by going on to land four Group 1s in a row to mark himself down as one of the finest milers of recent times.

Bred by Prince Khalid Abdullah's Juddmonte operation – the breeder of Frankel, no less – Kingman is by Invincible Spirit, the sire of 15 Group 1 winners and a noted influence for speed and precocity, and out of French 1,000 Guineas winner Zenda, a Zamindar half-sister to another successful Juddmonte stallion, Oasis Dream.

A total of 39 Kingman yearlings changed hands at public auction in 2017 at an average price of 236,255gns, over four times

17

his covering fee of £55,000, a sum that made him the priciest retiree among this year's freshman sires.

The most expensive of those was the half-sister to Abingdon bought by Moyglare Stud for 1.7 million guineas, while a half-sister to Derby hero Wings Of Eagles was snapped up by David Redvers and Meridian International for €750,000 in France and is reportedly in training with John Gosden.

Kingman covered 143 mares during his first breeding season at Banstead Manor Stud, where his debut book contained 59 per cent black-type performers, including 20 Group winners. Among the well-related two-year-olds set to represent Kingman in 2018 are siblings to Poet's Word (named Incharge), La Collina (Fox Chairman), Workforce (Strelka), Reckless Abandon (Wild Abandon), Time Test (Tempus) and Zebedee (Cozi Bay).

No Nay Never
Scat Daddy – Cat's Eye Witness
(Elusive Quality)

A precocious son of US sire sensation Scat Daddy, who has been responsible for the likes of Lady Aurelia, Caravaggio and Acapulco, No Nay Never went unbeaten at two, winning a Keeneland maiden special weight before running away with the Norfolk Stakes and the Group 1 Prix Morny.

He trained on at three to win a Keeneland Grade 3 before going down narrowly to Bobby's Kitten in the Breeders' Cup Turf Sprint.

Despite being introduced to breeders at just €20,000, No Nay Never's first yearlings fetched up to 850,000gns – with JS Company forking out that price for a half-brother to The Wow Signal, while other notable purchasers include Kerri Radcliffe of Phoenix Thoroughbreds, who went to €480,000 for a colt in France, and Al Shaqab, who parted with 420,000gns for a colt at Tattersalls.

No Nay Never covered 144 mares, which should give him plenty of ammunition for the season, and given how precocious he was himself it would be a surprise if his progeny couldn't get on the board early in the season.

Charm Spirit
Invincible Spirit – L'Enjoleuse (Montjeu)

Charm Spirit was high-class at two, with his best effort that season coming when

CHARM SPIRIT (left): has a half-sister to Qemah bought by Shadwell

OLYMPIC GLORY (blinkers): has proved a popular addition to stallion ranks

third behind Karakontie in the Group 1 Prix Jean-Luc Lagardere over 7f.

He could finish only fifth, albeit not beaten far by Night Of Thunder, in the 2,000 Guineas, but from that point on he never looked back. He won his last four starts, including a hat-trick of Group 1s in the Prix Jean Prat, Prix du Moulin and the QEII.

He is a son of Invincible Spirit and shares his damsire, Montjeu, with the likes of Journey, Legatissimo, Mahsoob and Parish Hall.

Charm Spirit had 56 yearlings sell at an average of 66,385gns, including a half-sister to Qemah bought by Shadwell for €500,000 in France and a colt bought by MV Magnier for 210,000gns. Among Charm Spirit's other noteworthy debut juveniles are siblings to Sovereign Debt (Lyndon B), Al Wukair, Side Glance and Steps.

Olympic Glory
Choisir – Acidanthera (Alzao)

Olympic Glory was a top-class juvenile, winning four races at two including the Superlative and Vintage Stakes before rounding off his campaign with a Group 1 win in the Prix Jean-Luc Lagardere.

He came agonisingly close to adding a second top-flight success during his three-year-old season when touched off by a short-head by Moonlight Cloud in the Jacques Le Marois, but he gained due reward at four when winning the Lockinge

Stakes and then the Prix de la Foret on his final outing.

Olympic Glory is the highest-rated son of crack Australian sprinter Choisir and is from the family of Queen Mary winner Amaranda, so expect his progeny to have inherited their share of precocity.

A total of 65 Olympic Glory yearlings changed hands at auction last year at an average of 50,515gns. The most expensive of those was the colt out of Alpen Glen bought by Al Shaqab for 180,000gns.

Others to note

July Cup and Diamond Jubilee hero **Slade Power** also welcomes his first runners in 2018, among whom are a pair of colts who fetched 260,000gns during Book 1 of the Tattersalls October Yearling Sale.

Another son of Dutch Art among this year's first-season sires is Cheveley Park Stud's **Garswood**, who got better with age himself but was still precocious enough to land a 5f Listed event at two.

Runaway Coventry and Dewhurst Stakes winner **War Command** – a son of War Front, the sire of Air Force Blue, US Navy Flag and Roly Poly, among others – also looks to hold solid claims of getting plenty of juvenile winners during his debut season with runners.

Among those whose progeny should display promise this year before improving with time are Coral-Eclipse winner **Mukhadram** and Derby winner **Ruler Of The World**.

Est. 1909
RACING & FOOTBALL OUTLOOK

Ante-post preview by Steffan Edwards

2,000 Guineas

AIDAN O'BRIEN has sent out eight of the last 20 winners of the 2,000 Guineas and has the first three in the betting this year. However, there's no short-priced favourite as we've grown accustomed to, with the bookmakers going 8-1 the field, and this is a rare opportunity to get with what should be the stable's flag-bearer this season at decent odds.

SAXON WARRIOR is probably better bred for the Derby than the Guineas, being by Deep Impact out of a Galileo mare, but that mare was Maybe, who had the speed to win over 6f on her debut and excelled over 7f at two.

For all that Saxon Warrior did all his racing over a mile last year, the main quality he showed was pace, quickening up from behind to win impressively on his debut, then doing his rivals for speed in a steadily run Group 2 at Naas. Finally, in the Racing Post Trophy, he travelled strongly into the lead before finding extra when headed.

O'Brien was quoted afterwards saying that Ryan Moore was adamant that the colt had a miler's pace and would have no problem being a Guineas horse, which confirms the visual impression, and I'll be very surprised if he's not Moore's pick of the Ballydoyle runners at Newmarket.

It has to be said that Guineas winners without form over shorter than a mile at two are rare, Camelot being the only one in the last 30 years, but Saxon Warrior strikes me as a type who can also do the Guineas-Derby double.

Gustav Klimt is next in the betting but I'm not so keen on his chances. I thought he got a bit too much credit for rallying to win the Superlative Stakes after being hampered. Even if he'd had a clear run and beaten Nebo by a more comfortable margin, that wouldn't have been any more than several other horses achieved last year.

Of course he was absent afterwards as well, missing the National Stakes because of a stone bruise and the Dewhurst due to a torn muscle. O'Brien said after the Dewhurst that we'd next see him in the Guineas, but he'll be short of experience and of course those comments were made before Saxon Warrior won at Doncaster.

US Navy Flag stepped in to win the Dewhurst for the stable, following up his Middle Park success a fortnight earlier, and he seems very much in the same mould as his sister Roly Poly, who was also heavily raced over sprint distances at two yet found improvement upped in trip.

It's easy to put a line through his run on dirt at the Breeders' Cup and it wouldn't be a shock to see him run well in the Guineas, but at similar prices I prefer the claims of Saxon Warrior, who will appreciate taking a lead from his strong-galloping, front-running stablemate.

The disappointment of the Dewhurst was undoubtedly **Expert Eye**, who was sent off 4-7 on the back of an impressive success in the Vintage Stakes. He travelled powerfully and bounded clear at Goodwood, but after a dirty scope ruled him out of the National Stakes he was beaten a fair way from home at Newmarket, racing keenly and dropping away to finish last. Although he was initially reported to have finished lame, he later trotted up sound and nothing seemingly came to light afterwards.

He clearly has something to prove now, not least his stamina given he's by Acclamation, whose best progeny have tended to excel over distances short of a mile.

Emaraaty also failed to live up to expectations in the Dewhurst, but it was a big step up in class for him from a Newbury maiden and perhaps it was all a bit much at that stage of his career.

John Gosden had hinted after Newbury that he might start out this year in the Greenham, so he has the potential to get back in the picture and he's certainly bred to be top-class, being a 2.6 million guineas half-brother to Izzi Top and Jazzi Top.

Gosden has another bullet to fire with **Roaring Lion**, who was deemed unlucky by many not to win the Racing Post Trophy. It certainly seemed that had Oisin Murphy timed his challenge perfectly the colt would have beaten Saxon Warrior, but it wasn't the first time he'd hung left when coming through to challenge as he did the same in his previous two wins and ultimately he was outbattled.

As smart as he is, it seems he has a quirk or two and maybe that will hold him back. Just like Saxon Warrior, he didn't run over shorter than a mile at two so also has that uncomfortable stat to overcome.

Elarqam won both his starts over 7f at two, seeing his races out in the style of a colt who is going to be suited by a step up to a mile. A 1.6 million guineas son of Frankel out of his trainer Mark Johnston's

SAXON WARRIOR: could emulate Camelot with the Guineas/Derby double

VERBAL DEXTERITY: has something to prove on good ground or faster

1,000 Guineas winner Attraction, he has plenty of scope and appeals as the type to improve considerably from two to three.

Johnston clearly thinks highly of him and, aware of the expectation around the colt, admitted after the Tattersalls Stakes that it was the most nervous he had been for years. The colt got warm beforehand at Newmarket and raced a shade keenly and he wouldn't want to do that in the Guineas, but he does hold good credentials.

Charlie Appleby has a couple of interesting contenders.

Masar was a bit too keen on unsuitably soft ground when only third in the Lagardere and got too far back before finishing fast at the Breeders' Cup. We probably haven't seen the best of him yet, but whether he goes for the Guineas or heads down the Derby trial route remains to be seen.

Appleby's other one to keep an eye on is **Glorious Journey**, who won both his starts last year, including a French

Group 3. A 2.6 million guineas purchase, he has a miler's pedigree (by Dubawi out of a Coronation Stakes winner) and would be an interesting contender if turning up, especially given his sire's stunning record in the race with the few runners he's had. From only four runners, Dubawi has had two winners – at 33-1 and 40-1 – and placed horses at 33-1 and 16-1. The other son of Dubawi in the reckoning at the moment is Gosden's Emaraaty. **Ghaiyyath** is also by Dubawi but looks more of a Derby candidate on paper.

After winning the National Stakes, Jim Bolger described **Verbal Dexterity** as "the real deal" and "as good as any of the two-year-olds I've had."

The Dewhurst, which he's won five times in the last 12 years, was going to be the colt's next assignment, but he scoped dirty and had to swerve the race. Instead, he ran in the Racing Post Trophy a fortnight later. Although a solidly backed 5-2 second-favourite, he was uncharacteristically chased along early and never really travelled. Despite that, he was first to tackle the winner before dropping away to finish fourth.

Bolger later blamed himself for the disappointing performance, stating that the colt seemed in good form at home and that he took a chance in running him but in hindsight wished he hadn't. He went on to say that Verbal Dexterity would go straight to the Guineas next.

It might be worth forgiving that run at Doncaster and it wouldn't come as a surprise to see him in the shake-up at Newmarket, especially given his trainer's record in the race this century (a winner and two placed horses from six runners – five genuine contenders if you don't count Dawn Approach's pacemaker).

However, it's a concern that he's yet to encounter good ground or faster and, while his trainer is of the opinion that won't be a problem for him, it's worth noting that his sire Vocalised ran his best races in the mud as well.

Wootton veered left and right through greenness on his debut but still won by 6l. He then followed up in a Listed race by 5l, looking far more professional. He looks an exciting prospect, but outside of the odd Ascot runner his trainer Henri-Alex Pantall hasn't made a habit of bringing his horses over to Britain. It remains to be seen whether his purchase by Godolphin before his second start changes things.

Sacred Life was impressive in the Prix Thomas Bryon, but he's another more likely to stay in France given his connections. I expect the Lagardere runner-up **Olmedo** to do likewise.

Stamina could be an issue for **Sioux Nation**, **James Garfield** and Richmond Stakes winner **Barraquero**, while Karl Burke has said that **Raydiance** is ground dependent, needing plenty of give to be seen at his best.

A dirty scope prevented **Wells Farhh Go** from contesting the Racing Post Trophy and Tim Easterby said afterwards that the Acomb winner might return in a conditions race at Newcastle before heading to the Dante, so it looks like he's seen as more of a middle-distance prospect.

I'd say **The Pentagon**, **Nelson**, **James Cook** and **Amedeo Modigliani** look like Derby horses in the making, while **Kenya** might fall between two stools.

Mendelssohn, who could be aimed at the Kentucky Derby, is a May foal, while **Family Tree** and **Herculean** are late April foals, so are all younger than ideal – Dawn Approach, who was very experienced at two, is the only winner in the last 25 years to have been born after the first week in April.

With lightly raced colts, it's pretty important that they prove themselves up to the task of competing in the Guineas by taking in a trial. There are several who have the potential to do that.

Flavius, a comfortable winner of a Leopardstown maiden in October, was pencilled in for a Guineas trial by Dermot Weld afterwards. He's by War Front out of a Dynaformer mare, so the quicker the ground the better for him.

MENDELSSOHN: would be very rare as a May foal to win the Guineas

23

Richard Hughes looks to have a decent colt on his hands in **Glendevon**, who beat a subsequent winner by five lengths at Kempton in October. A son of Scat Daddy, he'll surely take his chance in a trial to see where he stands.

Willie John won in good style at Yarmouth first time out. He's by Dansili out of dual 1m2f Group 1 winner Izzi Top and could be anything.

Without Parole bolted up on his debut at Newcastle in December, but that was over a mile and on the balance of his pedigree this son of Frankel might need a bit further to show his best.

Henry Candy suggested that **Thrave**, a winner at Newmarket on his second start, would start this year off in a Guineas trial. Although he's a son of Sir Percy and has plenty of stamina on the dam's side of his pedigree, Candy was adamant that he won't get beyond 1m2f and is a miler in the making.

A few other nice colts might be ones for later in the season: **Key Victory**, who got up late to win a good novice at Newmarket first time up; **Regal Reality**, who won a slowly run Yarmouth maiden on his debut; and **Tabdeed**, who won impressively at Leicester in August but finished lame and wasn't seen out again.

THRAVE: among a few who could announce themselves in a trial

2,000 Guineas

Newmarket, 5 May

	Bet365	Betfred	Coral	Hills	Lads	PPower	SkyBet	188Bet
Saxon Warrior	7	7	7	6	6	7	7	**8**
Gustav Klimt	6	7	**8**	6	7	**8**	7	7
US Navy Flag	7	8	8	7	8	**9**	8	7
Expert Eye	**10**	9	7	8	8	**10**	8	**10**
Roaring Lion	**10**	8	8	7	**10**	**10**	9	**10**
Wootton	14	14	12	12	14	**16**	**16**	14
Elarqam	**16**	14	14	12	12	**16**	**16**	14
The Pentagon	14	**20**	16	16	16	16	16	16
Mendelssohn	16	**20**	12	16	14	14	16	14
Verbal Dexterity	16	16	**20**	14	**20**	16	16	·16
Masar	**25**	20	20	16	20	20	20	20
Herculean	**25**	**25**	20	**25**	20	**25**	**25**	**25**
Emaraaty	**33**	**33**	25	**33**	25	**33**	**33**	25
Barraquero	**33**	**33**	**33**	**33**	**33**	**33**	**33**	**33**

each-way 1/4 odds, 1-2-3

Others on application, prices correct at time of going to press

1,000 Guineas

OF the 15 daughters of Galileo to have contested the 1,000 Guineas, ten have been placed, including two winners. That confirms the market has this right with **Clemmie** and **Happily** holding strong claims.

Both are both sisters to 2,000 Guineas winners – Churchill and Gleneagles respectively – so couldn't be better bred for the job and they also both won at Group 1 level at two, Clemmie becoming Galileo's first Group 1 winner over 6f when taking the Cheveley Park Stakes while Happily added to her Moyglare victory by beating the colts in the Prix Jean-Luc Lagardere.

Perhaps the greater improvement will come from Clemmie as she moves up to a distance more in keeping with her pedigree, but I can also see Happily improving for getting on quicker ground, which she had only once last year at the Breeders' Cup when getting no sort of run. The only issue with both of them is the price.

Another Galileo filly, **Magical**, beat Happily in the Debutante Stakes but couldn't quite confirm the form in the Moyglare and was then fourth in her last two starts in Group 1 company. She wouldn't need to improve a great deal to be a player, but like her sister Rhododendron she might improve for going a bit further than a mile. She's also a May foal, which is a negative when it comes to the Guineas.

At the end of the season Coolmore also bought **Different League** at the sales for 1.5 million guineas. They have had great success pairing up speedy mares with Galileo and presumably that's the plan with her down the line, but in the meantime she's to stay in training at Ballydoyle.

When it comes to the Guineas, though, the pace she showed in the Cheveley Park (last off the bridle but outstayed by Clemmie) makes me think the Commonwealth Cup might become her priority. She showed she acts over the course and distance when taking the Albany Stakes and could be a fair bet for the Royal Ascot race at around 14-1.

O'Brien's other potential contender at this stage is **September**, who is by Deep Impact out of Irish Oaks winner Peeping Fawn and a sister to a 1m4½f winner, so she's bred to improve for middle distances this year. She was staying on strongly over a mile in her final two starts last year and might just find one or two a bit sharp for her in the Guineas.

The Ballydoyle stable is also full of fillies who were lightly raced last year or seemingly exposed as no better than Listed/Group 3 class, but one of them could take a jump over the winter and show that in the Leopardstown Trial. Three of the last six Guineas winners warmed up in this race and each one came from leftfield –Homecoming Queen, Legatissimo and Winter – as did Virginia Waters in 2005, so it'll be worth treating seriously anything that does well in it and heads to Newmarket.

The main possibility is **Snowflakes**, who ran a fine race for one so inexperienced when eighth (fourth on her side and one place behind Clemmie) in the Albany on the back of a down-the-field effort on her debut in a Curragh maiden. She missed the rest of the season but as a sister to Winter she could still be anything.

While the O'Brien team will be hard to beat, I think the forgotten horse of the race is **ALPHA CENTAURI** and she's the each-way value.

Jessica Harrington's filly impressed in winning her first two races at Naas, including a five-length win over subsequent Group 3 winner Actress second time out. She was sent off favourite for the Albany and lost little in defeat, beaten a neck into second by Different League and pulling three lengths clear of the third with Clemmie back in seventh.

It was in the Moyglare at the Curragh next time out that the wheels came off. Again sent off favourite, she was last off the bridle but just couldn't pick up in the testing ground and dropped out to finish fifth.

I think we can put a line through that and it's easy to see her bouncing back on a

ALPHA CENTAURI: the forgotten horse in the 1,000 Guineas

sounder surface. She was quite a sizeable two-year-old and is open to improvement this year, with a mile likely to suit her well given that she's by Mastercraftsman out of a Rahy mare. Her trainer has said the aim is the Guineas and I think she's well worth chancing at a big price.

Alpha Centauri's owner also has **Liquid Amber** as a possible for the race. A five-length winner of a Group 3 at the Curragh on her second start, she's American-bred and may well improve for quicker ground, but I expect Willie McCreery to prepare her for the Irish Guineas.

Going back more than 30 years prior to Ghanaati's Guineas victory in 2009, every winner had Group race form at two. However, in the eight years since she won, another three – Blue Bunting, Legatissimo and Winter – have overcome that hurdle so it looks very much like the times have changed and a line can no longer be put through the inexperienced fillies.

John Gosden's **Nawassi** was well backed but clueless on her debut and trailed in last, but she came back from a break in November to show her true ability, running out a clear winner of a 7f nov-ice at Newmarket.

By Dubawi out of a Guineas third, she's bred for the race, and is just the type who could leap into contention, like Daban last year, via a prominent showing in one of the trials.

Veracious, trained by Sir Michael Stoute, is another lightly raced filly capable of becoming a player. A daughter of Frankel and half-sister to Group 2 winner Mutakayyef, she improved from her debut in a conditions race at Newbury to take a maiden at Newmarket by four lengths from the Godolphin filly Winter Lightning, who has since shown smart form in Dubai. Again, given her lack of experience, it would no doubt aid her cause if she took in a trial before the Guineas.

Magnolia Springs, who was a surprise but impressive winner of the aforementioned conditions race at Newbury, was held in Listed company next time. She has the scope to make a better three-year-old, but the Guineas might come a bit soon and on breeding she might need middle distances to show her best.

Teppal impressed in winning both her starts over 7f last year. David Simcock doesn't make a habit of having first-time-out two-year-old winners, but on her debut at Lingfield she comfortably beat a William Haggas-trained filly who won her next two starts and then she quickened up impressively to defy a penalty at Kempton.

She has plenty of pace and it's possible a mile will stretch her, while she's a May foal which is a negative, but it'll be interesting to see if she returns in the Fred Darling.

Karl Burke has said that the Prix de Diane is a big option for the Fillies' Mile winner **Laurens**. As a French-bred she qualifies for owners' premiums, so there's an understandable temptation to travel. She might well take in a Guineas on the way but which one is open to question.

The Freddy Head-trained **Polydream** beat Laurens in a French Group 3 before finishing second in the Boussac, so her form is right up there, but given her connections the likelihood has to be that she stays at home for the Pouliches.

Wind Chimes has looked something special in her two starts to date and a mile should suit her perfectly, but she's owned by the Coolmore 'lads' and, with so many options for Newmarket among the fillies at Ballydoyle, it would make sense for this Andre Fabre-trained filly to also remain in France for the Pouliches.

Godolphin appear a little light on genuine contenders, as their best fillies, **Magic Lily** and **Wild Illusion**, who are both trained by Charlie Appleby, look likelier types for the Oaks. Appleby has said that Wild Illusion may take in the Guineas first but only because he sees it as the best trial for the Oaks.

A stiff mile might just stretch the stamina of Albany third **Take Me With You** and the trip would also have to be a concern for the likes of **Threading**, **Juliet Capulet** and **Madeline** as well. In contrast, **Contingent** and **Sarrocchi** look likely to thrive over further.

Nyaleti was a precocious May foal and found rivals improving past her later in the season. We might already have seen the best of her.

On the other hand, the Oh So Sharp first and second, **Altyn Orda** and **Gavota**, are potential improvers. The winner, trained by Roger Varian, came home strongly on the stands' side and can surely only do better over a mile, while Gavota, trained by Roger Charlton, was a little unlucky to be mugged after seeing off her rivals up the centre of the track. This came on the heels of another luckless run in the Rockfel and she should also be suited by the Guineas trip.

1,000 Guineas

Newmarket, 6 May

	Bet365	Betfred	Coral	Hills	Lads	PPower	SkyBet	188Bet
Clemmie	3	5-2	9-4	11-4	9-4	3	5-2	3
Happily	5	5	5	6	6	5	5	5
September	10	6	12	10	12	10	12	8
Wild Illusion	16	16	16	14	14	16	16	14
Polydream	16	20	-	16	-	20	20	16
Laurens	14	20	20	14	20	20	20	14
Veracious	25	20	16	16	20	20	20	-
Different League	16	20	20	20	20	20	25	20
Magic Lily	16	-	-	25	-	20	20	20
Magical	16	20	25	16	25	25	25	20
Alpha Centauri	20	25	20	20	20	33	25	25
Threading	25	33	25	33	33	33	25	25
Nyaleti	33	33	33	33	33	33	25	33
Poetic Charm	40	-	40	33	50	33	20	33

each-way 1/4 odds, 1-2-3
Others on application, prices correct at time of going to press

Derby

SINCE the turn of the century, the record of Guineas winners and runners-up in the Derby has been fantastic. From the ten to go on to Epsom, five have won, two winning both races. Another two finished second in the Derby and only three were unplaced. This sample does not even include 2014 Derby winner Australia, who 'won' the race on his side in a Guineas decided by the draw but finished only third overall, beaten less than a length.

I fully expect **SAXON WARRIOR** to try to emulate his stablemate Camelot and do the double.

His credentials for Epsom are strong in that he's already shown a high level of form but is bred to improve for middle distances. He's not short of pace, but it's hard to imagine that, being by Deep Impact out of a Galileo mare who finished a close fifth in the Oaks, he isn't going to stay 1m4f and indeed we've yet to see him on good ground or faster, which he's very much bred to appreciate.

He's a worthy Derby favourite, and on the basis that I believe he's going to run at Newmarket first, and run well, it's worth chancing a little on him doing the double. Bet365 offer 25-1 and most bookmakers will offer a special double price on request.

Let's not forget, Australia was sent off 11-8 for his Derby after finishing third in the Guineas, while Camelot landed odds of 8-13 when completing the double two years earlier, so if Saxon Warrior wins or even just places in the Guineas he's likely to go off very short for the Derby.

If that's the case, then Aidan O'Brien may not run as many stablemates as is normally the case. When Camelot won he was accompanied by one pacemaking stablemate, whereas last year, in a very open looking race with no standout contender, O'Brien ran six. Therefore other Ballydoyle contenders may be relying on Saxon Warrior not coming up to scratch.

Chief among those is **The Pentagon**, who ran with great credit in the Racing Post Trophy, finishing third despite having been off the track since July. He was weak in the market and entitled to be a bit rusty, so it was an encouraging run and the trip won't be an issue as he's bred to stay well.

Amedeo Modigliani justified cramped odds in style second time out at Galway in August, quickening up to win easily. The form can certainly be crabbed, but he'd shaped well behind Gustav Klimt on his debut and is clearly well regarded.

Gustav Klimt himself is not bred to stay and is more likely to be a miler, while there would have to be stamina doubts about **Kenya** as well.

Family Tree is at least bred to stay and overcame greenness to make a winning debut at Gowran Park, though the form doesn't amount to much.

Kew Gardens and **Delano Roosevelt** look a notch below the class required, but **Nelson** could well be up to the task. He ran Roaring Lion close in the Royal Lodge

LATROBE (left): catches the eye behind James Cook at Leopardstown

despite arriving at the course late after travel disruption. There are no stamina doubts either as he's closely related to Derby runner-up US Army Ranger.

The choice of the Royal Lodge for him is slightly off-putting, though, as it's not a race O'Brien has tended to send his top-notchers to contest.

James Cook is a brother to Found so has every chance of getting 1m4f. He stayed on well to win in a good time on his second start at Leopardstown in October and is open to plenty of improvement.

However, it's the runner-up from that race who really caught my eye and is the one I'm going to take a flyer on.

LATROBE was making his debut and was sent off 16-1. He was slowest away and ran green in the early stages but then made a big move around the outside on the turn. It would have been understandable had he weakened from there, but instead he found extra in the straight to go in pursuit of the more experienced James Cook. He was edging closer with every stride as the line approached and, while he came up short, he shaped like the best horse in the race.

A son of Camelot, whose first crop are now three, he looks a sure-fire improver for middle distances and getting off the mark in a maiden before stepping into a trial shouldn't be difficult.

His trainer Joseph O'Brien, who saddled subsequent Melbourne Cup winner Rekindling for the same owner in last year's Derby, looks like he's got another talented colt on his hands.

In Latrobe's maiden there was also promise from fellow debutant **Gardens Of Babylon**, who didn't get the clearest of runs before staying on to be third. He's also by Camelot and could develop into a candidate.

Roaring Lion hasn't had the opportunity to run on fast ground and John Gosden expects improvement for that, while it's also reasonable to assume he'll stay 1m4f on breeding, but given that he's tended to hang left in the closing stages of previous races I just wonder whether Epsom will be his ideal track. I wouldn't be shocked if he skipped the race.

THE PENTAGON: a strong second string for Ballydoyle but may not run if Saxon Warrior comes up to scratch

Enable made her debut in a winter maiden on the Tapeta at Newcastle and it's possible Gosden introduced another Classic prospect there in December.

Without Parole was sent off a short price and quickened away to win by an eased-down six lengths from a couple of fair rivals. It's hard to be sure what his trip will be, though, as he's related to some milers, including Breeders' Cup Dirt Mile winner Tamarkuz. That said, he's by a stouter sire in Frankel and should get at least 1m2f.

Charlie Appleby has a couple of obvious contenders, but the Prix du Jockey Club looks the likelier landing spot for **Masar**, who was quick enough to win over 6f at two and might be better suited to the 1m2½f at Chantilly than 1m4f at Epsom.

It's therefore likely that the Autumn Stakes winner **Ghaiyyath** is the stable's main Derby hope. A strong, galloping type, he should relish the trip and it's not hard to see this him being a player.

Stamina is unlikely to be an issue for **Setting Sail** or **Brundtland**, who both won over 1m2f on their debuts, or **Cross Counter**, who notched a double on the all-weather over the winter, but all three will have to prove their value in better company first.

Near Gold will surely stay in France for the Prix du Jockey Club, but it's possible the Andre Fabre-trained **Cascadian** might make the trip to Epsom. He's owned by Godolphin and was impressive in winning two of his three starts last year (given too much to do second time out).

He was due to run in the Group 1 Criterium International before the meeting was abandoned, so we didn't get to see him run at the top level, but it's clear he's well regarded, and his pedigree – by New Approach out of a UAE Oaks winner – gives hope on the stamina front.

Highclere have a couple of possible contenders.

The Ralph Beckett-trained **Occupy** was an unconsidered 25-1 shot on his debut but won in good style at Kempton in November. He's by Declaration Of War out of a half-sister to Telescope so has decent prospects of getting the Derby trip.

The Mark Johnston-trained **Showroom** galloped on strongly to win by five lengths

at Goodwood on his debut. He was being considered for the Royal Lodge or Lagardere afterwards, which says something about the regard in which he's held, and as a half-brother by Motivator to a 1m4f French Group 2 winner he should be well suited by middle distances this year.

Given his connections, the Dante might be **Wells Farhh Go**'s Derby, but of course a good run at York will certainly put him in the Derby picture.

Perfect Illusion beat little but won by 12 lengths on his debut over the Derby trip at Lingfield in January. Along with other maiden/novice winners such as **My Lord And Master**, **Bombyx** and Jessica Harrington's pair **Whirling Dervish** and **The King**, we'll know more once he's taken in a trial.

There are stamina concerns for the likes of **Emaraaty**, **Glorious Journey**, **Mendelssohn**, **Herculean**, **Wadilsafa** and **Elarqam**, while the trip might also stretch **Willie John**'s stamina. **Thrave** is at least bred to stay, but his trainer Henry Candy is convinced he won't get beyond 1m2f.

In contrast, **Photographer** may be more of a Leger type. He won over 1m2f on his debut in November and is closely related to Leger runner-up Midas Touch.

Derby

Epsom, 2 June

	Bet365	Betfred	Coral	Hills	Lads	PPower	SkyBet	188Bet
Saxon Warrior	4	4	4	4	7-2	4	4	4
The Pentagon	8	8	10	10	10	8	10	10
Roaring Lion	12	14	12	12	12	14	14	14
Amedeo Modigliani	16	14	12	14	12	12	14	14
Gustav Klimt	16	16	14	-	12	16	16	14
Ghaiyyath	25	20	25	25	20	20	25	20
Kenya	20	-	20	-	25	20	25	20
Verbal Dexterity	20	16	-	25	-	25	20	25
Kew Gardens	25	20	25	25	25	25	25	25
Nelson	25	25	25	20	25	33	25	25
Delano Roosevelt	33	33	25	33	25	33	25	33
Without Parole	40	-	33	-	33	33	33	-
Latrobe	50	-	-	-	-	-	-	-
Wells Farhh Go	50	-	-	-	-	66	50	-

each-way 1/4 odds, 1-2-3
Others on application, prices correct at time of going to press

BYE BYE BABY: could improve past higher-rated stablemates this season

Oaks

THERE are four Ballydoyle fillies towards the head of the Oaks market, but I think they can all be taken on, especially Clemmie, who very much looks a miler in the making.

On breeding it's likely that **Happily** may well stay 1m2f, but whether she'll get another quarter-mile on top of that is open to question. She's a sister to two Guineas winners, Gleneagles and Marvellous, and it's worth remembering that the latter was sent off favourite for the Oaks after winning the Irish Guineas but could finish only sixth behind Taghrooda and was again well held in the Irish Oaks.

Magical has better prospects of staying the trip as she's a sister to Rhododendron, who finished second to Enable in last year's Oaks. She was only fourth in the Fillies' Mile but raced away from the favoured stands' rail, so it might be wise not to judge her too harshly on the bare form.

However, her best efforts all came on soft ground, including her win in the Debutante Stakes when she handled testing conditions much better than Happily and September. She's out of a Pivotal mare and perhaps needs cut to be seen at her very best.

On paper **September** looks best bred for the job. She's by Deep Impact out of Irish Oaks winner Peeping Fawn, so stamina shouldn't be any concern, and the way she was finishing her races last year backs up the thinking that she should improve over middle distances. The concern with her is that she's not very big, so there has to be a chance that scopier rivals improve past her over the winter.

At bigger odds it wouldn't come as a surprise if **Bye Bye Baby** improved past one or two of her higher-rated stablemates as she steps up in trip. She progressed with every start, rounding off the season by winning a Listed race at Navan and

SARROCCHI (centre): swoops late to make a winning debut last year

finishing third in the Group 3 Killavullan Stakes, but she's bred to do much better over middle distances at three, being by Galileo out of Oaks runner-up Remember When.

That said, the one from the Ballydoyle stable who interests me most is a bit of a dark horse. Aidan O'Brien had only seven first-time-out two-year-old winners last year and it's worth noting what they did afterwards. Saxon Warrior and September went on to prove themselves at Group 1 level, Seahenge won the Group 2 Champagne Stakes, Delano Roosevelt went on to finish runner-up in the Beresford Stakes and I Can Fly was third in the Oh So Sharp Stakes second time out.

Family Tree didn't run again and neither did **SARROCCHI**, but this filly made a striking impression on her debut in a backend Leopardstown maiden and looks to have any amount of potential.

Despite being poorly drawn and held up in a race that was otherwise contested by those ridden prominently, she overcame greenness to come home strongly and win with a bit in hand.

Five days earlier she was in the sales at Goffs as a result of China Horse Club and Coolmore dissolving their partnership, but after topping the sale at €215,000 she was soon back at Ballydoyle. Those in the yard clearly knew she had plenty of ability and

she was backed to justify it – from 10-1 to 7-2 – becoming the only one of the stable's seven debut winners to be sent off outright favourite.

Her pedigree is encouraging with the Oaks in mind. By Galileo, she's out of an Oasis Dream mare who ran her best race over the longest trip she tried – a 1m1½f Group 3 in the French provinces. She's also a sister to a French filly who stays beyond 1m4f, albeit at a low level.

Open to any amount of improvement, she has a decent chance of overtaking a few of her better-known stablemates once the trials come round.

I can also see **I Can Fly** developing into a candidate. She was impressive at Dundalk first time out and lost little in defeat up in class in the Oh So Sharp. Her pedigree (by Fastnet Rock out of a Montjeu mare) would give plenty of confidence that she'll make up into a middle-distance filly, but that is tempered by the fact that her half-brother Viscount Barfield has shown all his best form short of a mile.

Looking outside of the Ballydoyle yard, **CONTINGENT** takes my eye.

Her trainer Dermot Weld had a disappointing 2017 as a result of a virus which lingered in the stable for some time, but her late-season success in a Leopardstown maiden was a bright spot. Drawn in the outside stall, she was caught wide throughout but still found a good turn of foot to come through and win decisively from Hamdan Al Maktoum's well-related Alghabrah, with more than five lengths back to the rest.

A daughter of Frankel out of Prix Marcel Boussac winner Proportional, she's bred to be high-class and, while her trainer suggested she could be quick enough to go the Guineas route to begin with, she's a half-sister to 1m4f Listed winner Variable, who was also trained by Weld, and it's likely that it's over the Oaks trip that we'll see the best of her.

I could find only six Weld runners who ran in the Oaks, but they include 1981 winner Blue Wind, 2014 runner-up and subsequent Group 1 winner Chinese White, so Weld will make the trip if he thinks Contingent has a live chance.

Charlie Appleby holds a strong hand with **Wild Illusion** and **Magic Lily**, both of whom come with strong Group 1 juvenile form and are bred to excel over middle distances at three.

The Boussac winner Wild Illusion is by Dubawi out of a mare who won at up to 2m, while Magic Lily, who ran so well for one so inexperienced when third in the Fillies' Mile, is by New Approach out of Oaks winner Dancing Rain. It's unlikely either will be done for stamina, so it's just a

case of whether they build on their juvenile promise. For now, it's hard to argue with their prominent positions in the market.

The Fillies' Mile winner **Laurens** is currently being pointed towards the Prix de Diane rather than the Oaks, while that's likely to be the target for the Freddy Head-trained **Luminate** as well.

Toujours, who's trained by Andre Fabre and won nicely on her debut over 1m1f, is better bred for the Oaks – she's by Galileo out of a 1m4f Group 3 winner – but as she's owned by the Coolmore crew she might only make the trip if the fillies from Ballydoyle fail to come up to the standard required.

The Flame of Tara Stakes winner **Liquid Amber** has prospects of getting 1m4f. She's a half-sister to a mile winner, but her sire and dam won at up to 1m4f, albeit both spent most of their careers racing over shorter.

Stream Song took a while to get the hang of things, but when she got off the mark third time out at Newmarket she beat a couple of decent rivals in Sheikha Reika and Hadith (Listed winner since) and her trainer John Gosden was complimentary afterwards, saying she'd reappear in an Oaks trial. A half-sister by Mastercraftsman to Group 1 winner Journey, she'll have no problem with trip, which might even turn

CONTINGENT: could a rare runner in the Oaks for Dermot Weld

out to be a minimum for her.

Gosden's other candidate at this stage looks to be **Highgarden**, who justified good support when winning comfortably on her debut in soft ground at Newbury. However, being by Nathaniel out of a Green Desert mare who won over a mile, she wouldn't be as certain to get 1m4f and the knee action she showed at Newbury suggests she might always need give in the ground to be at her best.

Another daughter of Nathaniel, **Perfect Clarity**, overcame greenness to make a winning debut at Nottingham in August. Her trainer Clive Cox clearly thinks a bit of her as he had her entered in the Fillies' Mile and, while she skipped the race, she retains plenty of potential.

Similar comments apply to the David Simcock-trained **Lady Of Shalott**, who also held the Group 1 entry but swerved the race. She travelled strongly and quickened up well to win on her debut at Yarmouth and, being by Camelot out of a 1m4f winner, the Oaks trip should be right up her street.

Eve Johnson Houghton's **Magnolia Springs** was another who impressed first time out and on pedigree she should be suited by at least 1m2f.

Portfolio

2,000 Guineas

Saxon Warrior 1pt 8-1
(188Bet)

Saxon Warrior to win Guineas-Derby double 1pt 25-1
(bet365)

1,000 Guineas

Alpha Centauri 1pt 33-1
(Paddy Power)

Derby

Saxon Warrior 2pts 4-1
(generally available)

Latrobe 1pt 50-1
(bet365)

Oaks

Contingent 1pt 25-1
(generally available)

Sarrocchi 1pt 25-1
(bet365)

Oaks

Epsom, 1 June

	Bet365	Betfred	Coral	Hills	Lads	PPower	SkyBet	188Bet
Happily	7	6	5	6	5	6	6	6
September	10	8	10	10	10	8	8	8
Wild Illusion	16	16	12	14	12	16	16	14
Magic Lily	14	16	16	16	16	14	14	14
Laurens	14	16	16	14	16	-	16	-
Clemmie	10	16	12	-	10	20	14	12
Magical	16	16	25	14	20	25	25	14
Highgarden	25	16	25	20	25	25	25	-
Contingent	20	25	25	25	25	20	25	-
Bye Bye Baby	25	-	-	-	-	-	25	-
Sarrocchi	-	-	-	-	-	-	25	-
Liquid Amber	-	-	-	33	-	33	25	-
Conquest	33	33	-	-	-	50	33	33
Ballet Shoes	33	-	-	33	-	33	66	33

each-way 1/4 odds, 1-2-3
Others on application, prices correct at time of going to press

RACING & FOOTBALL OUTLOOK

Est. 1909

Nick Watts's horses to follow

AMAZING RED 5 b g
Teofilo – Artisia (Peintre Celebre)
3691924-

He's a half-brother to the great Red Cadeaux, who got better with age, so this could be the season when Amazing Red takes off. He's shown promise so far, winning twice including at Newmarket in August, and I now expect him to progress past his rating of 89. He ended last season with two good efforts at Doncaster and Haydock (ground may have been a touch heavy for him on the latter occasion) and is still lightly raced with only nine starts to his name.

Ed Dunlop, Newmarket

ARCH VILLAIN 9 b g
Arch – Barzah (Darshaan)
48-

Going for the Ebor first time out at the age of eight is quite a bold move, but that is what Amanda Perrett did with Arch Villain last season and it worked quite well as he finished a good fourth behind Nakeeta. That shows the ability remains and he could be interesting in staying handicaps on the turf and the all-weather as he has proved in the past that he handles both. His career win ratio of ten from 28 starts is very good and indicates that when he gets a winning chance he can make the most of it. He is effective from 1m4f to 2m.

Amanda Perrett, Pulborough

BATTAASH 4 b g
Dark Angel – Anna Law (Lawman)
11141-

This horse was a revelation last season and it was just a pity we didn't see the real Battaash turn up in the Nunthorpe. He got stirred up before the race, went way too fast and never got close to Marsha and Lady Aurelia. However, he showed that performance to be all wrong when going to France for the Abbaye on his final start of the campaign and hosing up, beating Marsha by four lengths with an explosive display of speed. Look forward to more of the same this season.

Charlie Hills, Lambourn

35

BATTLE OF JERICHO 3 b c
War Front – Together (Galileo)
34127-

Battle Of Jericho was one of the less heralded Ballydoyle juveniles last season with only a Leopardstown maiden win to his name, but it could have been better than that. He followed up his win with a good second in a Listed race at Dundalk before turning up at Newmarket for the Cornwallis. That was surprising as he was dropping from 7f to 5f, but it looked as though the move would come off as he travelled strongly early on. It all went wrong from there, however, as he never got a clear run and had to coast home for seventh, beaten three lengths. He's better than that.

Aidan O'Brien, Ballydoyle

BLESS HIM 4 b c
Sea The Stars – Happy Land (Refuse To Bend)
213515-

Bless Him had his day in the sun at Royal Ascot when getting in as a reserve for the Britannia and winning at 25-1. The application of a hood and a step back up to a mile seemed to work the oracle there and he looked useful. Although beaten on his next start in the Supreme Stakes, he was back down to 7f again and his rider said he was outpaced, while it was also his second poor run at Goodwood so maybe he doesn't handle it there. Over a mile, on a conventional track, a Group success should be within his remit this summer.

David Simcock, Newmarket

CHIARA LUNA 3 br f
War Front – Princess Highway (Street Cry)
1-

Chiara Luna comes from a family Dermot Weld knows well, with her dam, Princess Highway, having won the Ribblesdale for him at Royal Ascot in 2012. She just made it to the track once last season, at Leopardstown in August, and it was a winning appearance over 6f. That trip would be short of her best and predictably she was very strong in the closing stages. She will do much better this season when upped in trip. She is in the Irish 1,000 Guineas, which is a start, but it would be a surprise if she didn't stay middle distances in time.

Dermot Weld, Co Kildare

CLEMMIE 3 b f
Galileo – Meow (Storm Cat)
37111-

Things didn't look too exciting for Clemmie after she was beaten on her first two starts, including in the Albany at Royal Ascot. However, she didn't look back after that, reeling off three wins in a row culminating in an easy win in the Cheveley Park at Newmarket in September. All her runs thus far have been over 6f, but she is a full sister to last year's 2,000 Guineas winner Churchill and it would be a shock if she didn't stay a mile. She is favourite for the 1,000 Guineas and it is hard to think of anything that can stop her at this stage.

Aidan O'Brien, Ballydoyle

CRACKSMAN 4 b c
Frankel – Rhadegunda (Pivotal)
132111-

John Gosden said a few times last year that Cracksman would be a better four-year-old so what an exciting time we could have in store. Defeat in two Derbys seemed to back up Gosden's words, but in the latter half of the season he took off, annexing the Voltigeur, Prix Foy and Champion Stakes in successive races. He wasn't hard pressed to win any of them and showed pace in the Champion that people didn't think he had. Effective between 1m2f and 1m4f, he may well win the the King George and the Arc this season.

John Gosden, Newmarket

CROSS COUNTER 3 b c
Teofilo – Waitress (Kingmambo)
1-1

You're much more likely to see a Classic contender strut their stuff on the all-weather early on than you once were and Cross Counter could be the latest. He has no fancy entries at this stage, but he has been twice to Wolverhampton – in December and January – and hosed up both times, the latest by eight lengths. It will be fascinating to see how he gets on when racing on turf, but there is no reason to suspect he won't go on it. Offspring of Teofilo normally stay well, so middle distances look a viable option for him.

Charlie Appleby, Newmarket

CRYSTAL OCEAN 3 b c
Sea The Stars – Crystal Star (Mark Of Esteem)
13312-

Crystal Ocean was mooted for the Derby at one stage, but Sir Michael Stoute exercised his famed patience with this horse, shunning Epsom and leaving him off until the King Edward at Royal Ascot. That decision didn't immediately bear fruit as he was beaten by Permian, but he went on to land the Gordon Stakes at Goodwood and ran a cracker in the St Leger when going down by just half a length to Capri. Stoute is brilliant with those he keeps in training at four, so expect another surge of improvement from this horse during the summer. Group 1 success awaits.

Sir Michael Stoute, Newmarket

DEE EX BEE 3 b c
Farhh – Dubai Sunrise (Seeking The Gold)
16312-

Permian excelled in these colours last season and Dee Ex Bee might have a similar path in store. He has already won at Epsom, winning a race that guaranteed automatic entry into the Derby this year. Therefore it's easy to imagine him going for the Investec Derby Trial prior to June – a race in which Permian was just touched off by Cracksman last season. Like his sire, Farhh, he seems to enjoy cut in the ground, but he showed on his final start in the Zetland Stakes that he also handles good going.

Mark Johnston, Middleham

EXPERT EYE 3 b c
Acclamation – Exemplify (Dansili)
119-

If you're a great believer, as I am, in the old adage that horses aren't machines and deserve the benefit of the doubt after a poor run, then you must agree that Expert Eye still has a lot to offer this season. He was awful in the Dewhurst, but it's a measure of his ability that he was sent of at 4-7 to win that. And he went off so short because on his previous start in the Group 2 Vintage Stakes at Goodwood he looked out of the top drawer, slamming Zaman with future winners Mildenberger, James Garfield and Seahenge all further behind. Stick with him!

Sir Michael Stoute, Newmarket

FRONTIERSMAN 5 br h
Dubawi – Ouija Board (Cape Cross)
41223616-3

Quirky – that is probably the best way to describe this hugely talented but sometimes frustrating entire. Two wins last season showed that he does know how to win, but there were a few less than convincing displays thrown in as well. Perhaps his most eyecatching effort came in the Coronation Cup when, despite not appearing to handle Epsom at all, he finished a good second behind Highland Reel. That run in Group 1 company came straight after him winning a Newmarket handicap so he can hack it at the top table if his mind is right.

Charlie Appleby, Newmarket

HARRY ANGEL 4 b c
Dark Angel – Beatrix Potter (Cadeaux Genereux)
212114-

It's a curious thing that all of Harry Angel's defeats have come at Ascot, but it's equally hard to say that he doesn't act there with form figures of 2224 including a great run when beating all bar Caravaggio in the Commonwealth Cup at the royal meeting. What can be said with more certainty is that he loves Haydock, where he is two from two including an easy win in the Group 1 Sprint Cup in September. He'll definitely be back there again, but Clive Cox would love him to break that Ascot hoodoo at some stage and I'm backing him to do it.

Clive Cox, Lambourn

HIGHGARDEN 3 b f
Nathaniel – Regalline (Green Desert)
1-

Nathaniel really came of age as a sire last season with the emergence of the champion filly Enable and, in Highgarden, he has another daughter who could achieve great things. She was made favourite for her debut in a Newbury maiden in October and justified her starting price of 13-8 with an easy win by upwards of two lengths. That came over a mile on soft ground, so middle distances will be no problem for her this season and an Oaks trial might be on the cards in the early part of the season. There's much more to come.

John Gosden, Newmarket

IL PRIMO SOLE 3 b c
Raven's Pass – Sweet Alabama (Johannesburg)
123-

After two defeats, Il Primo Sole's 2,000 Guineas entry might appear a little bold, but he should still be capable of making his presence felt as a three-year-old. He started off in the best way possible, hacking up in a maiden at Yarmouth to win by nearly five lengths. It may not have been the strongest race, but he was very stylish in victory and it was a shame to see him fail to back up that impression next time at Sandown. A subsequent defeat at Lingfield can be written off, though, as he should have won) that day. On fast ground this year he can exploit his rating of 93.

John Gosden, Newmarket

JAMES GARFIELD 3 b c
Exceed And Excel – Whazzat (Daylami)
3314210-

What a horse to get so early on in your training career. Third in the Windsor Castle on his second start before getting off the mark at Doncaster, James Garfield held his form well throughout the summer for his rookie handler George Scott and put in his best performance at Newbury in September when taking the Group 2 Mill Reef Stakes. An unsuccessful foray to the Breeders' Cup shouldn't be held against him and he will now start off in the Greenham at Newbury before it is decided whether he is a miler or a sprinter.

George Scott, Newmarket

KENYA 3 b c
Galileo – Tender Morn (Dayjur)
311-

There won't be many horses left with Dayjur in their pedigree, but this son of Galileo has him as his broodmare sire and looks a useful prospect. Third on debut at Naas, he then went to Cork and won by eight lengths before taking the inevitable step up to Group 3 company for his final start of the campaign at Leopardstown. He won that as well, beating Mcmunigal by a length, and confirmed he handles dig in the ground very well. He might be one who comes to the fore early on but I fancy him for the Irish Classics rather than Newmarket or Epsom.

Aidan O'Brien, Ballydoyle

MAGIC LILY 3 ch f
New Approach – Dancing Rain (Danehill Dancer)
13-

If you want a live Oaks contender they don't come much better bred than this horse. By a Derby winner, out of an Oaks winner, she didn't make her debut until late September when she turned a Newmarket maiden into a procession, winning by eight lengths. She was then thrown in at the deep end for the Group 1 Fillies' Mile on her next start and acquitted herself very well indeed, beaten less than a length in third behind the more experienced Laurens. She will love stepping up in trip and may well uphold the family name at Epsom.

Charlie Appleby, Newmarket

MIRAGE DANCER 4 b c
Frankel – Heat Haze (Green Desert)
4334-

Mirage Dancer was unable to win from four starts last season, but he showed promise in a light campaign and is one with whom Sir Michael Stoute may do well with now he is a four-year-old. He did put in some encouraging displays last season – he was fourth in the Dee Stakes on his return, not beaten far, and then he ran a cracker in the Hampton Court Stakes at Royal Ascot to finish third behind Benbatl. He was disappointing on his final start at Doncaster, but that came on soft ground which may have been too much for him. Faster ground will suit a lot better.

Sir Michael Stoute, Newmarket

MONARCHS GLEN 4 b g
Frankel – Mirabilis (Lear Fan)
144211-

Monarchs Glen was in grave danger of becoming disappointing by midsummer, hamstrung by a tendency to pull too hard and not see out his races. However, a gelding operation in June transformed him as in three subsequent runs he finished 211, which included wins in Listed and Group 3 company. On his final start he beat the useful Robin Of Navan comfortably and, with another year on his back, I'd imagine he will be even calmer and more tractable now. Further Group success surely awaits.

John Gosden, Newmarket

NELSON 3 b c
Frankel – Moonstone (Dalakhani)
62112-

Nelson caught they eye on his debut at Leopardstown before getting off the mark at the same track two starts later. Aidan O'Brien saw enough to run him on Irish Champions Weekend in a Group 3 and he made all the running to beat Kew Gardens comfortably. His last start came in the Royal Lodge, in which he fought out a superb finish with Roaring Lion, going down by a neck, and the form was then franked after Roaring Lion put in a superb run in the Racing Post Trophy. He will be suited by 1m4f in due course and is sure to be running in a Derby trial in the spring.

Aidan O'Brien, Ballydoyle

ONE MASTER 4 b f
Fastnet Rock – Enticing (Pivotal)
311-

One Master comes from a family William Haggas knows very well, going back on the dam's side to Superstar Leo. She didn't hit the track until last August but made big progress in a short space of time, winning her maiden in September before going for a Listed race at Ascot the following month. An unfancied 20-1 shot, and the lowest-rated, she beat Bletchley comfortably, surprising her trainer. Bearing in mind he thought she needed time, it is encouraging what she has achieved already and a Group success is definitely possible.

William Haggas, Newmarket

ORION'S BOW 7 ch g
Pivotal – Heavenly Ray (Rahy)
6403500070-

Just looking at last season's form figures, you may wonder what Orion's Bow is doing here, but he could just be the best-handicapped horse in training. He started off the season on a mark of 105 but is now 16lb lower after a winless campaign. He still showed promise on occasions, though, as when third at Newcastle in June and fifth behind Danzeno at Ascot on his next start. Bearing in mind he won his last race off 97, a mark of 89 is almost definitely exploitable and it would be no surprise if he roared back to his very best this season.

Tim Easterby, Great Habton

ORDER OF ST GEORGE 6 b h
Galileo – Another Storm (Rahy)
2121141-

Possibly the new Iron Horse. Order Of St George took another tough campaign really well, with his best effort coming when beating Torcedor by nine lengths in the Irish St Leger, a race he'd been beaten in the previous year. His second to Big Orange in the Ascot Gold Cup was a monumental effort, as was his courageous display when he landed the Long Distance Cup on his final start. If he is ridden a bit closer to the pace this year then there is no reason why he can't regain his Gold Cup crown he so narrowly lost last year.

Aidan O'Brien, Ballydoyle

RAID 3 b c
Havana Gold – Remarkable Story (Mark Of Esteem)
1-

A half-brother to Grendisar, this £135,000 two-year-old made a very late entrance last season, not reaching the track until November at Doncaster. Apparently it was down to a few niggling issues such as sore shins, but he was ready for the run as he won comfortably over 6f, handling the prevailing soft ground really well. His trainer thinks 7f will be his limit this season and added that "he has got a bit of talent". Soft ground may always be important to him, but when he gets it he could prove very handy.

David Simcock, Newmarket

THE PENTAGON 3 b c
Galileo – Vadawina (Unfuwain)
6113-

The Pentagon didn't look much on his debut but took off after after that, winning two races in quick succession including the Group 3 Tyros Stakes at Leopardstown. He had a problem after that and didn't reappear until the Racing Post Trophy in October, when he was noticeably weak in the market, but he ran a cracker in the race itself, finishing third behind Saxon Warrior and Roaring Lion. Bearing in mind his troubled preparation, it was an excellent effort and he will definitely be a Derby contender this season.

Aidan O'Brien, Ballydoyle

TOCCO D'AMORE 3 b c
Raven's Pass – Spirit Of Tara (Sadler's Wells)
11-

Just two races, one at the start of the season, one at the end, but with the same result – easy victory. Unraced as a two-year-old, Tocco D'Amore won at Naas in April, beating Clongowes by six lengths, but then wasn't seen out again until November when she took in a Listed event, again at Naas, and saw off Lagostovegas quite comfortably. It's a great pity we didn't see more of her as a three-year-old as she appears to possess plenty of talent. However, after only two starts in her life, she could start making up for lost time this season as long as she stays free of injury.

Dermot Weld, Co Kildare

UAE KING 4 b c
Frankel – Zomaradah (Deploy)
5211133-

Plenty of Frankel's progeny stay very well and UAE King is perhaps the most extreme example. A half-brother to Dubawi, he started off life over a mile but has gradually been upped in trip and now is perfectly at home over two miles, his form improving the longer the distance he's been asked to race over. He broke his maiden tag over 1m3½f at Haydock, then went up to 1m6f to win at Sandown, and completed the hat-trick over 2m at Ascot. A couple of defeats thereafter haven't put me off him – he is a smart stayer.

Roger Varian, Newmarket

ZILARA 3 bb f
Big Bad Bob – Celtic Slipper (Anabaa)
40-

A real dark horse but one who, on breeding, may come into her own this season. Zilara ran twice as a juvenile and performed well on the first of those at Goodwood when fourth in a maiden behind Roulette. She was very green then but ran on well when the penny dropped. Unfortunately she got a bit lost in a big field at York on her only subsequent run and finished down the field. However, this half-sister to smart stayer Moonrise Landing is worth persevering with, particularly as her trainer Ralph Beckett is so adept with fillies.

Ralph Beckett, Kimpton

Top ten horses

Battle Of Jericho	**Kenya**
Clemmie	**Monarchs Glen**
Cracksman	**Orion's Bow**
Expert Eye	**The Pentagon**
Highgarden	**UAE King**

ENABLE: superstar filly could drop in trip, with the Juddmonte a likely target

Newmarket
by Aborigine

NABLE and **Cracksman** head *JOHN GOSDEN*'s power-packed 2018 taskforce and could end up taking each other on in the Prix de l'Arc de Triomphe.

Gosden tells me he is delighted with the way Enable has wintered and the four-year-old will be trained with the Arc in mind. It is easy to understand Gosden's thinking as she put in such an impressive display to win the prestigious French race last year.

Few will forget the confidence that Frankie Dettori oozed as he bounced her out of the stalls to counter what was considered by some to be a bad draw. The Nathaniel filly answered every question he asked, coasting home two and a half lengths clear of Cloth Of Stars.

Her form in the run up to that race was hardly shabby either as she had picked up five wins, four at the top level with the Oaks, Irish and Yorkshire Oaks along with the King George at Ascot.

Gosden, in typical fashion, says that Enable herself will tell him when she is ready to reappear in public. However, he feels that the Juddmonte at York is likely to be on the itinerary. That would mean a drop in trip to 1m2f, but she has the speed to prove sufficiently versatile.

Cracksman finished third at Epsom and

43

second in the Irish Derby before rounding his season off with a brilliant effort in landing the Champion Stakes at Ascot.

Talking of Ascot, it is understandable that owner/breeder Anthony Oppenheimer would like to have a tilt at the King George as his family firm, De Beers, sponsored the Ascot showpiece for many years.

On the Classic front, Gosden singled out **Roaring Lion** as a potentially serious contender. Looking at his juvenile form, it is easy to share the view as he won three of his four starts, including the Royal Lodge, and was a fine second in the Racing Post Trophy.

The Kitten's Joy colt started off with a maiden win on the July course before taking in a novice race at Kempton in September. With the experience gained, Gosden was then happy to step him up into Pattern company and the move met with immediate success in the Royal Lodge, in which he beat Aidan O'Brien's Nelson by a neck, before it took a strong late run from Saxon Warrior to deny him at Doncaster.

Gosden is looking at a tilt at the 2,000 Guineas here at Newmarket as there is no guarantee that he will get the Derby trip.

WILLIAM HAGGAS has a promising three-year-old in **Al Muffrih**.

This Sea The Stars colt had just one run last season, finishing third behind Knight To Behold over a mile at Newmarket.

Being out of a Peintre Celebre mare, this 260,000gns yearling will improve with both age and distance so he should not be long in losing his maiden tag.

Give And Take has already made her mark, landing her only start as a juvenile by four and a half lengths from Lady Of Aran at Lingfield. Haggas intends to saddle her for an Oaks trial and believes she will get better with age.

On the Haggas handicapping front, there is a lot to like about **Reverend Jacobs**. After three seconds, he won a modest maiden at Ascot and figures on a rating that looks very commercial. He could easily graduate to Pattern races.

ROGER VARIAN's **Defoe** is one of the most exciting prospects in the town even though he blotted his copybook in the St Leger.

He went into the race as one of the market

DEFOE (centre): disappointed in the Leger but can bounce back this year

ALTYN ORDA (far side): won the Oh So Sharp and is a Guineas horse

leaders because of his progressive profile having won his first four races, including the Geoffrey Freer, but sadly he ran no sort of a race and had clearly gone over the top.

The signals he is giving out on the heath confirm his sparkle has returned, though, and the John Porter Stakes at Newbury is a likely starting point before a possible step back up into Group 1 company.

Stablemate **Sharjah Bridge** is also on the up and this Lincoln entry looks set to eventually be better than a handicapper.

Among Varian's three-year-olds, the Group 3 Oh So Sharp winner **Altyn Orda** strikes me as a natural for the 1,000 Guineas, while **Masaar** recorded an exceptionally fast time for the final two furlongs when winning at Lingfield in November. Keep the New Approach colt on your side.

JAMES TATE has quickly made a name for himself and believes that **Invincible Army** will be his flag-bearer at the highest level this season.

This Invincible Spirit colt has clearly inherited his sire's speed. After sound seconds in the Molecomb and the Gimcrack, he gave Tate his first Group 3 win in the Sirenia Stakes and was then unlucky in the

Group 2 Mill Reef Stakes at Newbury on his final start when checked in his finishing run and forced to settle for second place behind James Garfield.

Tate is pleased with his winter progress and is aiming him at the Commonwealth Cup at Royal Ascot.

Tate also has enterprising plans for **Hey Gaman**, who made a rapid impact as a juvenile when winning three of his five races, most significantly in the Listed Washington Singer Stakes at Newbury, although his best performance came in defeat when he found only the Irish challenger Seahenge too good in the Group 2 Champagne Stakes at Doncaster.

Tate believes he favours easy ground, which is why he is being aimed at the Irish 2,000 Guineas.

MARCO BOTTI continues to saddle a steady stream of winners and the affable Italian has likely money-spinners in **Aljazzi**, **Dark Acclaim** and **Artieshow**.

It is worth noting that Aljazzi was the first horse to spring to mind when I quizzed him on the heath.

The five-year-old contributed to her keep with several sound performances last year and was unlucky in running when ninth to Roly Poly in the Sun Chariot. That run earned her a trip to the States and she underlined her durability by keeping on to be seventh to Kitten's Row in the Goldikova Stakes at Del Mar.

Botti is delighted with the way she looks and she goes for the Duke Of Cambridge Stakes at Royal Ascot, a race in which she was second to the French raider Qemah last year.

On the three-year-old front, Botti likes Dark Acclaim, who won at Doncaster in July. His sights were raised with a couple of efforts resulting in places in Listed races at Haydock and Pontefract.

There is no doubt that he is a stronger individual with the winter behind him and will figure prominently in the top races at around a mile.

Another member of the Prestige Stables team to wait for is Artieshow, who took a long time to come to hand but gained his first win on his third start when beating Mary Elise at Kempton in January. He won with such authority that I share Botti's belief he will finish up in far better company.

PETER CHAPPLE-HYAM has Classic aspirations with **Just Brilliant**.

The Lope De Vega colt cost 115,000gns as a yearling – a reasonable price as Chapple-Hyam saddled his half-brother Marcel to win the Group 1 Racing Post Trophy.

Just Brilliant made a favourable impression when he followed some smart work on the heath with a smooth debut win over Silver Quartz in a hot Newmarket maiden and the plan is to return to the Rowley Mile for the Craven Stakes, a potential launching pad to the 2,000 Guineas.

Chapple-Hyam also has a high opinion of **Lubinka**. The Mastercraftsman filly showed promise in her first two starts when placed in decent maidens at Ascot and Doncaster and her work encouraged her trainer to raise her sights for the Fillies' Mile here at Newmarket, in which she was slowly into stride but made significant late progress into sixth behind Laurens.

There is ample stamina in her pedigree and her trainer told me she would go for a Classic trial on the way to a bid for Oaks glory.

46

RICHARD SPENCER is one of the new kids around town and is delighted to have a Classic contender **Rajasinghe** so early in his career, but **Keyzer Soze** could be particularly worth noting.

The Arcano gelding won twice early on but was sidelined after being down the field in the Britannia Handicap at Royal Ascot. He's well handicapped.

TOM CLOVER is another young trainer on the up and gave us a couple of horses to follow in **Go Fox** and **Balgair**. He reckons both are weighted to pay their way.

Former Newcastle striker *MICK QUINN* has soldiered on with mainly moderate horses that he has handled with skill and could now have his first potential Group performer in **Princess Harley**.

The daughter of Dark Angel signed off with a highly encouraging effort on our Rowley Mile in the autumn. Though she never looked like troubling the easy winner Bye Bye Baby, she kept on to be third and Quinn is keen to get her into action early as she enjoys give underfoot.

St Leger-winning *MARK TOMPKINS* is one of the Newmarket's longest-established trainers and has a couple of handicappers to follow. I particularly like **Topapinion**, who is from a family he knows well and landed some significant bets at Lingfield on his handicap bow.

The way **Velvet Voice** and **Ginger Lady** are working indicates they will also pay their way.

PAUL D'ARCY has always held a high opinion of **Spring Loaded** and that faith was rewarded when he made short work of smart handicappers to land a gamble and Aborigine's 12-1 nap in the Portland.

Sadly he has had tendon trouble that means he may miss Lingfield's Good Friday bonanza, but if so D'Arcy hopes to ready him for the Wokingham at Royal Ascot.

Hot off the Heath
Altyn Orda
Cracksman
Keyser Soze

TONY JAKOBSON

RED-HOT NEWMARKET
INSIDE INFO EVERY DAY

I spend my time on the gallops and found winners at huge prices last year so ring my daily service!

Call 0906 911 0232

BT UK calls cost £1 per minute. ROI call 1560 719 760 (Eircom calls €1.25/min). Calls from mobiles and other networks will vary.

Ireland
by Jerry M

A YEAR ago we were thinking that *AIDAN O'BRIEN* might not have the same strength in depth among his three-year-olds that he had in 2016. So much for that theory!

O'Brien, of course, went on to break the record for Group 1 wins in a calendar year and the three-year-olds were the bedrock as only the performances of Enable at Epsom and the Curragh prevented him form walking away with a clean sweep of the British and Irish Classics.

KEW GARDENS: could be a Leger horse and is 25-1 for Doncaster

It seems that you can never underestimate the three-year-olds at Ballydoyle and this year O'Brien seems to have even more of an embarrassment of middle-distance riches than normal.

Saxon Warrior went into winter quarters as favourite for the Derby having won all three starts in 2017, culminating in a gutsy victory in the Racing Post Trophy at Doncaster in October. That effort seemed to point the way to him being more of a Derby than a Guineas horse, but if the Guineas is a realistic option then going straight to Newmarket looks the most likely plan.

The Pentagon could be a very viable alternative for Epsom. His form was solid throughout the year and the step up to a mile, when a strong-staying third after meeting interference in the Racing Post Trophy, was very encouraging regarding his propensity to step up to middle distances this year.

Amedeo Modigliani is short enough in the Derby betting considering what he has done, but the manner of his victory in a maiden at Galway in the summer was supremely impressive and he really could be anything.

Nelson's form is rock-solid. He beat Kew Gardens convincingly on Champions Weekend at Leopardstown and his narrow defeat by Roaring Lion in the Royal Lodge puts him pretty close to Saxon Warrior.

Kew Gardens went on to win the Zetland Stakes at Newmarket and may well end up being one of the main St Leger hopes, while the nicely progressive Killavullan Stakes winner **Kenya** is another to note.

As for the Guineas, depth is provided by the very promising **Gustav Klimt** and it would be a detriment to the race if he did not manage to get there.

Winner of two of his three starts, he overcame a lot of adversity to narrowly land the Superlative Stakes at Newmarket last July

CLEMMIE: the Cheveley Park winner will be very hard to beat in the Guineas

and a setback prevented him from being seen out again.

There is little doubt that he would have improved further as the season goes on and, if getting to Newmarket in rude health, he could well rate as one of the likelier winners.

Possibly no Ballydoyle juvenile colt from last season improved as much as **Mendelssohn** and it will be interesting to see if he fits into the Guineas picture.

His progress followed the application of blinkers and his convincing victory in the Breeders' Cup Juvenile Turf suggested a mile this season is likely to suit him well.

For the third year in a row, the top-rated Ballydoyle colt is one who appears to be more at home as a potential sprinter as **US Navy Flag** didn't appear to get the mile in the Breeders' Cup Juvenile.

Still, the strides he made in the second half of last season was nothing short of astonishing. The application of blinkers and the switch to front-running tactics was the catalyst and culminated in him being among a select band of horses to land both the Middle Park and the Dewhurst.

He had perhaps gone over the top by the time he went to the US, but I suspect there's every chance he will be among the top sprinters if training on.

Fleet Review has a lot of the same qualities having shown all his best form over 6f and been beaten only half a length in the Middle Park Despite there being 7lb between them on ratings, the gap could indeed be much closer.

You can also throw Phoenix Stakes winner **Sioux Nation** into this mix as well as he is likely to be campaigned at sprint trips. He did not get the run of the race in the Middle Park and looks capable of getting much closer.

O'Brien looks to have a considerable stranglehold when it comes to three-year-old fillies, with Churchill's sister **Clemmie** looking as though she will be very hard to beat in the 1,000 Guineas.

Anyone unconvinced by her in the first half of the season must have had their

49

IDAHO: the Hardwicke winner could be a major force in the staying division

doubts dispelled by the manner of her victory in the Cheveley Park and, despite the fact that she has not raced beyond six furlongs, the way she came home that day and her pedigree would seem to suggest that she might even improve at a mile.

Stablemates **Happily** and **Magical** fought out a couple of good battles on soft ground last summer and might be this year's equivalent of Hydrangea and Rhododendron with very little between them.

The early-season hype surrounding **September** took a little bit of a summer dent, but on better ground in the autumn she did not get her just desserts in the Fillies' Mile at Newmarket or the Breeders' Cup Juvenile Fillies Turf. She did get a mile very well, though, and could well be the stable's main hope of landing the Oaks.

Among the older brigade, established stars such as Highland Reel, Roly Poly, Churchill, Winter and Melbourne Cup runner-up Johannes Vermeer will not be returning, but Irish Derby and St Leger winner **Capri** could be the one to spearhead the team.

The aforementioned fillies **Hydrangea** and **Rhododendron** will also be back for another season, as is champion stayer

Order Of St George, but that division looks very competitive indeed and one of the bigger challengers could lay within in **Idaho**.

It is not easy to know where the domestic competition will lie, but *GER LYONS* had the best season of his career and was obviously instrumental in helping Colin Keane to win his first jockeys' title.

Among his three-year-olds, **Gobi Desert** can do some good in the sprinting division after winning two of his three starts, including a Listed contest at Navan.

The filly **Lethal Steps** could also be interesting. She did well on good ground last year and will get a mile well.

The main hope for *JIM BOLGER* would appear to be **Verbal Dexterity**, one of last season's best two-year-olds, although it did appear that soft ground was a must for him. How he will be campaigned will be interesting as he did not appear to see out the mile of the Racing Post Trophy in the autumn.

The impeccably bred and unbeaten **Goldrush** will be embarking on a four-year-old career and we have yet to see the best of her.

How *DERMOT WELD* will come back from a desperately disappointing 2017 campaign is a conundrum.

His two-year-olds came alive at the backend of the year, though, and there is plenty of optimism surrounding Curragh maiden winner **Chiara Luna** and Leopardstown maiden winners **Contingent** and **Flavius**. All three won their only starts and will be prepared for Classic trials.

Of the older horses at Rosewell, do not be surprised if quite a few waves are made by the filly **Tocco D'Amore**, unbeaten in two starts last year and a very convincing winner of a 1m4f Listed race at Naas on the second of them.

JESSICA HARRINGTON carried all before her in the early part of last season and a couple of her stars from that time are still worth bearing in mind.

The imposing filly **Alpha Centauri** looked very smart and could well scale further heights as she has plenty of scope, while **Brother Bear** could bounce back despite disappointing after an unlucky defeat in the Coventry.

Torcedor beat Order Of St George once last season and almost repeated the dose at Ascot in the autumn. He is going to be one of his main challengers for top staying honours.

JOSEPH O'BRIEN will have plenty of winners this season, but undoubtedly the class act will be Melbourne Cup winner **Rekindling**, who is likely to make a return trip to Flemington in November. Before that, though, he should be a major contender for the Cup races.

WILLIE McCREERY will have slept soundly over the winter in the knowledge that he has a potentially exciting filly in **Liquid Amber**, impressive winner of the Flame of Tara Stakes on her second start.

Invincible Irish
Clemmie
Gustav Klimt
Tocco D'Amore

GOLDRUSH: we have yet to see the best of Jim Bolger's unbeaten filly

Berkshire by Downsman

L AST year was another fruitful one for *CLIVE COX*, who cemented his reputation has one of the most capable trainers around.

Although there has been transition over the winter at his Sheepdrove stable with My Dream Boat, Profitable and Priceless retired, the 2018 squad promises plenty.

Headlining the bill is **Harry Angel**, who became the world's top sprinter thanks to wins in the July Cup and the Sprint Cup.

Those races are likely to be on the agenda again for the four-year-old, who has wintered well and should be even better this term when he is likely to kick off in the Duke of York Stakes in May.

Harry Angel's four defeats have come at Ascot, but that is not a worry for Cox.

Tis Marvellous was not far behind his stablemate on a couple of occasions last year and is another Cox is hoping to have fun with, while the classy miler **Zonderland** has good races in him on fast ground.

Of the three-year-olds, **Connect** is described as an interesting prospect and is from a family the trainer knows well. He could start in a Classic trial.

So could the sizeable **Perfect Clarity**, a Nottingham novice winner who was then given time to fill her frame.

Queen Mary heroine **Heartache** has also had a good winter and the Commonwealth Cup is her main early-season aim, while **Snazzy Jazzy** is another connections have fairly high expectations for.

Like Cox, *CHARLIE HILLS* has a brilliant sprinter on his hands in **Battaash**, whose Prix de l'Abbaye triumph stamped him down as a horse of rare talent.

That ability does need harnessing, but Hills and his team did a great job of that.

He could return in Haydock's Temple Stakes and might be tried over an extra furlong in the July Cup, which would mean a mouthwatering clash with Harry Angel.

Consistent older horses **Magical Memory**, **Dutch Connection** and **Jallota** will

ZONDERLAND (right): has good races in him when the ground is quick

MASSAAT: the Lockinge could be an option if the ground is on the easy side

continue to pay their way and strike in the right conditions.

Horris Hill winner **Nebo** could start in the Greenham, leading a capable bunch of three-year-olds that includes **Rock Of Estonia**, who is two from two, as well as **Wafy** and **Bartholomeu Dias**, who could both thrive when stepped up in trip.

Chrisellaine, closely related to the yard's Breeders' Cup winner Chriselliam, could run in a 1,000 Guineas trial, which is also an option for the well-regarded **Juliet Foxtrot**.

Equilateral and **Ripley** are others held in high regard by Hills, while **Mutakatif** is a nice horse who could be well handicapped and **Arthenia** may improve over further.

OWEN BURROWS is another trainer eagerly anticipating the turf campaign and it is easy to see why.

He built on a solid debut season last year and has a good blend of older horses and three-year-olds among his 90-odd string for 2018.

Hungerford Stakes winner **Massaat** looks a leading player for Burrows, who is eyeing top mile races on easy ground

for the son of Teofilo with the Lockinge an option.

Laraaib, who is three from four, is another of the older brigade to keep on your side.

Among last year's juvenile team, Burrows really rates **Shabaaby** and describes **Wadilsafa**, who should appreciate decent conditions, as a "lovely horse".

Tabdeed, impressive on his only start at Leicester last year, is another well-regarded three-year-old, while **Enjazaat** has had a winter wind operation after his Mill Reef defeat.

Mutaaqeb also has potential, as does **Oriental Song**, who is thought more than capable of achieving some black type.

ED WALKER's move to Lambourn from Newmarket at the end of 2016 resulted in by far his most prolific campaign and the trainer is not resting on his laurels this spring.

He is convinced we did not see the best of **Stormy Antarctic**, who was gelded towards the end of last term and is felt to have a big race in him, especially on testing ground. International races will be on his agenda.

Stewards' Cup runner-up **Aeolus** will go into bat in valuable sprint handicaps and could be on a workable mark, while **Dark Pearl** and **Tuff Rock** are considered useful stayers in the making.

Among the youngsters, **Desert Doctor** is developing into a smart sprinter but Derby entry **Stephensons Rocket** is the one Walker is dreaming of turning into a Classic horse. Not short of speed, he is rated an appealing prospect who could start in a trial.

That is certainly the objective for *HARRY DUNLOP*'s **Knight To Behold**, who created a fine impression when second on his debut at Newbury before going one better at Newmarket in a race that has worked out well. His camp are getting excited about his claims for Epsom glory.

Stablemate **Fighting Irish**, a Group 2 winner in France last year, will return there for the Prix Djebel as his front-running style is thought to be well suited to racing in the country.

Similarly, **Robin Of Navan** has May's

CODE RED: on the comeback trail

Prix d'Ispahan, in which he was second last spring, as his main goal, while **Flight Of Fantasy** is another Windsor House inmate worth following.

MARK USHER, entering his 35th year with a licence, also hopes to pocket some euros on his raids to France this season, with **Miracle Of Medinah**, a winner at Deauville last summer, the horse pencilled in for more raids.

Dreamboat Annie, a brilliant worker according to Usher, is open to improvement now she has strengthened.

The canny *JOE TUITE* has been busy at the sales. **Shabbah**, formerly with Sir Michael Stoute, has races in him over a trip and the trainer also thinks the ex-Hills **Redgrave** has more to offer, with fast-run 7f/1m handicaps on easy ground likely to bring out the best in him if he relaxes.

Of the old guard, Tuite is convinced **Machine Learner** will flourish in staying handicaps and is on a fair mark, while **Surrey Hope** – potentially the best horse the trainer has had – is thought up to winning a good race somewhere, particularly on fast ground.

Those conditions seemed to suit *ROGER TEAL*'s **Tip Two Win** when he landed a conditions race in Qatar over Christmas and the three-year-old will be entered in the 2,000 Guineas.

The Newmarket Classic could also be the target for **Glendevon**, who has pleased trainer *RICHARD HUGHES* with how he has matured over the winter.

The three-time champion jockey is leaning towards running his Scat Daddy youngster in the Craven at Newmarket.

This time last year, *WILLIAM MUIR* thought **Phijee** would be a Guineas horse, but injury hold-ups limited him to just one run. However, Muir reports he is on his way back and still rates him extremely highly. He could run at the Craven meeting.

Cuttin' Edge, who missed all of last term, is back after a niggling problem and another for whom Muir has loads of time.

Code Red, described by his trainer as "a class act", is another on the comeback trail and the "magnificent" **Hollander** is reportedly a different animal after being gelded.

SALOUEN (far right): one of the best from Sylvester Kirk's Lambourn yard

Six-year-olds **Limato** and **Chain Of Daisies** will remain flagbearers for *HENRY CANDY*, whose promising Casamento colt **Blazing Tunder** has been bought by Qatar Racing.

A once-raced Nottingham winner, he might not be rushed anywhere too deep too soon, but Candy believes he will be a nice horse.

JONATHAN PORTMAN's hopes rest with **Mrs Danvers**, who was too good for Battaash in the 2016 Cornwallis but was not right last term suffering from hind-leg lameness.

Portman reports the four-year-old to be sound heading into the spring and aims to have her ready for a Listed contest in April.

Derby-winning trainer *PAUL COLE* still retains all his enthusiasm and has acquired **Port Douglas** for big-spending Leicester City chairman Vichai Srivaddhanaprabha. The 2015 Beresford winner, fifth in the following year's Derby behind Harzand, could be interesting over a trip.

Musical Art appears good enough to win a black-type race and **Plunger** is another to note for the Whatcombe trainer.

East Ilsley-based *HUGHIE MORRISON* has a second trip down under on his mind for **Marmelo**, who was ninth in November's Melbourne Cup. The Hardwicke

at Royal Ascot may be his main summer objective.

The progressive **Star Rock**, who won three of her five starts in 2017, should be effective at a range of trips and decent stayers **Nearly Caught**, **Fun Mac** and **Sweet Selection** are also still around.

EVE JOHNSON HOUGHTON's Blewbury yard continues to go from strength to strength and she reckons she has assembled her strongest ever team for 2018.

On To Victory could develop into an Ebor horse and **Ice Age** can make a splash in the top sprint handicaps.

Accidental Agent will contest Pattern races and that is also the hope for young filly **Magnolia Springs**, who has wintered well and returned looking great.

Finally, **Salouen**, **Gawdawpalin**, **Music Society**, **She Believes** and **Bubble And Squeak** are the pick of the names on duty for *SYLVESTER KIRK*.

The North by Borderer

THERE have been only two Classic winners trained in the north this century, but the two trainers responsible for those successes have realistic chances again this year.

In 2002 Bollin Eric powered home under Kevin Darley to land the St Leger for *TIM EASTERBY*, who reckons he has another horse of the same calibre in **Wells Farrh Go**.

With two wins from two starts last season, the colt certainly shaped as though he is another who could go right to the top.

Bought for just 16,000gns as a yearling, he was sent off at 16-1 for his debut at York last July and proved very green, but he still came from last to first to win going away.

On his next start in the more competitive Group 3 Acomb Stakes, Wells Farrh Go scored again, getting up in the last stride to beat James Garfield by a nose, the runner-up franking the form by winning the Mill Reef on his next start.

The plan after that had been for him to go for the Racing Post Trophy, but he wasn't quite right during the autumn so his trainer decided not to run him again.

Although he has never raced beyond 7f, Wells Farhh Go, who is a half-brother to the winning chaser Hills Of Dubai, is sure to get middle-distances and may well end up in the St Leger, although he could start in the 2,000 Guineas first.

Two years after Bollin Eric's Doncaster victory, Attraction provided *MARK JOHNSTON* with his latest Classic victory and the Middleham trainer had a strong team of juveniles last season, with Elarqam emerging as the best.

Elarqam is a daughter of Attraction by the mighty Frankel and was bought by

WELLS FARHH GO (left): could have Classic pretensions for Tim Easterby

DEE EX BEE (left): has guaranteed himself a shot at the Derby already

Sheikh Hamdan Al Maktoum for 1.6 million guineas in October 2016, so he had made headlines even before setting foot on the racecourse.

He proved a hit on the track as well, though, winning a York novice in fine style on his debut – the three who followed him home all won next time – before going on to add the Group 3 Tattersalls Stakes at Newmarket.

Although he has yet to be seriously tested, Elarqam looks a smart prospect and a live Classic contender, with the 2,000 Guineas his priority.

Frankel seems to inject plenty of stamina into his stock, however, and it would be no surprise were he to go for the Dante and perhaps on to Epsom after that.

This is likely to be a highly significant year for Johnston who sent out the 4,000th winner of his career last autumn and is a virtual certainty to beat Richard Hannon Snr's record total of 4,194 winners at some point during 2018.

As usual he will mix quality with quantity, with **Threading** and **Cardsharp** other class acts who are likely to contribute to his tally.

Threading made an impressive winning debut at Glorious Goodwood and confirmed the promise she showed that day by following up in York's Group 2 Lowther Stakes before disappointing in the Cheveley Park.

She is by no means certain to stay a mile but should find plenty more winning opportunities.

Dee Ex Bee was another Johnston juvenile to make a winning debut at Goodwood's big meeting last season and, though he never quite fulfilled that promise, he earned himself a free entry for the Investec Derby by winning a conditions event at Epsom on testing ground in October.

A colt with plenty of scope, he could well improve markedly from two to three and might be the surprise package among the Johnston three-year-olds.

Dominating, who gave Johnston his 4,000th winner when scoring over 2m2f at Pontefract in October, is a four-year-old who should progress during the season. Stamina is his forte and, though he has some way to go yet, he could well make up into a Cup horse this season.

Johnston has nominated **Lucky Deal** as one worth following this season. Having

57

LAURENS: set for the Prix de Diane

won a four-runner conditions event over 1m2f at Chelmsford on his second outing in November, he'll start off in handicaps and should be a real moneyspinner in that sphere before graduating to conditions events.

In what could be a fine year for northern yards, *KARL BURKE*'s **Laurens** could make her mark in races like the Oaks.

It is one of Burke's ambitions to train a Classic winner. He didn't quite make it back in 2013 when Libertarian finished runner-up to Ruler Of The World in the Derby having previously become the first Yorkshire-trained winner of the Dante Stakes for more than 70 years.

Laurens could be the one to realise the trainer's ambition as she won three of her four races in 2017 and has emerged as a live contender for the fillies' Classics.

Bought by her owner John Dance

for £220,000 at the 2016 Goffs St Leger yearling sales, she overcame greenness to make a winning debut in a 7f maiden at Doncaster in July and then her trainer pitched her straight into Pattern races.

Although only second to the smart Polydream in the Prix du Calvados in August, she went on to land two of the top juvenile races of the year for staying fillies, the May Hill Stakes at Doncaster's St Leger meeting and the Group 1 Fillies' Mile at Newmarket in which she held the late run of the Aidan O'Brien-trained September by a nose.

Her programme this year is by no means set in stone. Soft ground would make the 1,000 Guineas more likely, but her dam is a stayer who won over the St Leger trip and Burke reckons she will really come into her own when stepped up in trip, so he is considering the Prix de Diane. She might well prove to be ideally suited by going even further in time.

Whichever route she goes down, Laurens looks a smart prospect and it will be disappointing if she doesn't capture at least one top-class race this year.

Burke enjoyed a magnificent season with his juveniles in 2017, also sending out the first two home in the Group 1 Prix Morny with **Unfortunately** beating Havana Grey, the winner having previously landed the Group 2 Prix Robert Papin at Maisons-Laffitte.

Subsequently bought by Cheveley Park Stud, Unfortunately was disappointing in the Middle Park on his only run in those colours, but he can be forgiven one below-par run and looks just the sort to make up into a top-class three-year-old sprinter, with the Commonwealth Cup at Royal Ascot high on his agenda.

Havana Grey is a real speedster and, though he did well to hang on to second in the Morny on his only run over 6f, he is likely to be kept to the minimum trip this year.

Ellthea is another interesting three-year-old filly form Burke's Spigot Lodge yard. She wasn't easy to train last season as she was continually in season through the summer, but she came back in the autumn to win a Doncaster nursery and a

LORD GLITTERS (right): could be up to Group company this season

Group 3 at Naas before an honourable fifth to Laurens in the Fillies' Mile. She is pretty smart and there will be plenty of opportunities for her this season.

Two others to note in the Burke yard are the progressive **Raydiance**, who wasn't seen out after winning an Ascot Listed race last July, and the useful 7f handicapper **Mjjack**.

RICHARD FAHEY has lost his stable star Ribchester, but **Sands Of Mali** looked a class act when running away with York's Gimcrack Stakes in August. He didn't back that up in either the Middle Park or the Breeders' Cup Juvenile Turf a mile but should prove a decent sprinter.

The one to note in *DAVID O'MEARA*'s powerful string is **Lord Glitters**. He was bought for €270,000 in France in July and proved a shrewd buy as he won the valuable Balmoral Handicap at Ascot on

Champions Day before finishing second in a Listed contest at Newmarket. Best with some cut in the ground, he looks up to winning in Group company.

Keep an eye on **Hey Jonesy** from the *KEVIN RYAN* yard. Considered a backward sort last year, he got off the mark in his second race when landing a York novice in July and, though he didn't win again, he ran particularly well when fourth in the Middle Park. He is another with plenty of scope and is expected to do even better this year.

The West
by Hastings

THIS time last year we discussed a change of emphasis at *RICHARD HANNON*'s yard as he looked more towards horses with long-term potential instead of focusing on nippy two-year-olds and that certainly bore fruit over 2017.

Not only did Hannon edge back up towards the 200-winner mark, but he also did it with more than half of his victories coming from those aged three or older for the very first time.

The leading light was Barney Roy, who won the St James's Palace Stakes and the Coral-Eclipse. Hannon would have loved the chance to keep him in training as a four-year-old as he was just the type to improve again with age, but Godolphin have taken the decision to retire him to the paddocks.

His absence leaves a big hole at the top level, but **Danehill Kodiac** beat a proper Group 1 horse in Waldgeist when winning the Cumberland Lodge Stakes at Ascot last October and is improving all the time.

Indeed, his progress has taken his owners by surprise – he was bought to go hurdling, like their popular stayer Lil Rockerfeller, but those plans are very much on hold now.

Having progressed nicely in handicaps, Danehill Kodiac showed far more resolution than the runner-up when winning by a neck at Ascot and ran well when third in the St Simon Stakes next time given he was too keen off a steady early gallop. He could continue to surprise people.

Fellow five-year-old **Tabarrak** is another who may well have more to offer as he is very lightly raced for his age having

DANEHILL KODIAC: won the Cumberland Lodge and is on the upgrade

OLIVER REED (right): a dark horse worth following from Richard Hannon's yard

missed nearly all of his three-year-old season in 2016.

Tabarrak won two Listed races last season, including his final outing at Newbury in September, and the form of that win looks red-hot given the runner-up Accidental Agent went on to win a big handicap at Ascot.

The handicapper left Tabarrak alone on a mark of 110 and that could make him interesting in some big mile handicaps – he should be more streetwise than when fifth in last season's Royal Hunt Cup off 1lb higher – while he isn't far off winning at Group level either.

Khafoo Shememi was another dual Listed winner last season, both in mile races at Sandown, and he is another with more to offer, while **Oh This Is Us** is back down to the mark off which he came second in last season's Lincoln.

Euginio wasn't quite up to that sort of level last season, but he is really expected to flourish this time around.

The four-year-old has been slow to come to hand, but he signed off with a second handicap success at Doncaster's St Leger meeting even though the tacky ground was against him. He went up just 2lb to a mark of 104 for that success and Hannon thinks he could be a Group 3 horse.

Among the three-year-olds, Hannon has a couple of lovely middle-distance fillies in **Tajaanus** and **Billesdon Brook**.

Both disappointed when well fancied for the May Hill Stakes, but Billesdon Brook wasn't suited by the slow pace given she looks a strong stayer and Tajaanus had already proved herself much better than that by winning the Sweet Solera Stakes.

Oliver Reed is more of a dark horse to follow. Hannon really liked this colt last year, but he was just beaten at Newbury and was rubbed off for the year after a fair fifth in a red-hot Glorious Goodwood maiden. He is a surefire winner.

Fellow Wiltshire trainer *ROGER CHARLTON* gave a reminder of his training genius last season when pulling off a masterful coup to win the Cesarewitch with **Withhold**.

WITHHOLD: spreadeagles the Cesarewitch field and will win plenty more

The five-year-old was bought for 170,000gns in October 2016 after winning a 2m handicap at Haydock for Charlie Hills and the Cesarewitch was the plan from that moment.

Charlton gave him just a single prep run, when an encouraging third over an inadequate trip at Newbury, and Withhold then delivered in style on the day that mattered under a remarkably positive ride from Silvestre de Sousa, who left nothing to chance as he stretched the field for the final mile and came home clear.

Connections clearly knew he had a ton in hand off his mark of 87 and, while starting the season 12lb higher, it would be no surprise to see another big staying handicap come his way.

Blakeney Point and **Second Step** are other older horses who are sure to pay their way again, while it will be fascinating to see how **Atty Persse** gets on.

Considered a Derby horse at the start of last season, he never made it to Epsom but underlined his potential with a runaway win in the King George V Stakes at Royal Ascot.

Two disappointments followed at Group level, but those performances were too bad to be true and he can do better.

As for this year's Classic hopes, **Herculean** is the horse who has Charlton dreaming this time around.

The son of Frankel was an impressive winner of his only run last year in a 7f maiden at Ascot and was aimed at the Royal Lodge Stakes after that only to miss out because of a last-minute setback.

A big, imposing colt, he should do much better now he's had the chance to strengthen into his frame and could be a contender for top mile races, perhaps even the 2,000 Guineas if Charlton can get him there.

Gavota leads Charlton's team of three-year-old fillies. She twice looked unlucky in Group races at Newmarket last season and can certainly strike at that level.

Charlton's neighbour *BRIAN MEEHAN* is very excited about his Richmond Stakes winner **Barraquero**.

The Zebedee colt was the apple of Meehan's eye since the spring and, although only third on his debut – albeit behind Expert Eye – he duly won his next two races impressively, including his Glorious Goodwood triumph.

Barraquero suffered a minor shin injury

that day and didn't recover in time for the Middle Park, but it hasn't held him up at all as Meehan prepares him for the 2,000 Guineas.

It remains to be seen whether he will get the mile, but either way his trainer is convinced he is a Group 1 horse and it would be no surprise to see him win the Commonwealth Cup at Royal Ascot.

At the other end of the distance scale, **Raheen House** leads Meehan's team of older horses. He disappointed in the St Leger but was otherwise progressive throughout last season, especially when stepped up beyond 1m4f to win the Bahrain Trophy and the Noel Murless Stakes – awarded the race having been a close second past the post.

Meehan describes him as "a proper stayer with a huge, huge future".

MARTYN MEADE is a new arrival in Manton this year. Unfortunately his Group 1 winner Aclaim hasn't made the journey from Newmarket with him having been retired to stud, but there have long been high hopes that **Eminent** can break through at the highest level.

Last season began most promisingly when he won the Craven, but he clearly found a mile too sharp against the best in the 2,000 Guineas and didn't appear to quite get home when not beaten far in fourth in the Derby.

Back at 1m2f, which should be his optimum trip, he disappointed in the Eclipse when looking in need of time to strengthen but was much better after a break in the autumn and won at Deauville before a fine third in the Irish Champion Stakes.

He should be much better as a four-year-old and could be a real force to be reckoned with in 1m2f Group 1 races, of which there are plenty.

ROD MILLMAN is the leading light in Devon and has worked wonders in recent seasons with **Master Carpenter**, who won the John Smith's Cup in 2015 and added another big handicap at his beloved York at last year's Dante meeting.

Unfortunately the handicapper took that five-length win literally and whacked him up 10lb – he was simply one of few horses to act on desperate ground – but he is down to the same mark now and will be highly competitive again.

Millman also has a budding handicap star in **Duke Of Bronte**, who ran well in several good races last season and has more to come.

Western wonders
Danehill Kodiac
Eminent
Withhold

EMINENT (right): has more good races in him this season

The South
by Southerner

ANDREW BALDING enjoyed his best prize-money haul domestically last year when banking more than £2.5 million and the good news is that the Kingsclere trainer has almost all the top earners back in 2018.

Here Comes When will have his season built around a repeat bid for the Qatar Sussex Stakes at Goodwood on August 1, which he won last year when a 20-1 outsider and holding off Ribchester by a diminishing neck.

Beat The Bank is another with more Group 1 assignments as his trainer has the Lockinge and Queen Anne in mind for the four-year-old, who failed to run his race in the QEII at Ascot on Champions Day after looking a rising star with a Group 3 win at Goodwood followed by a romp in the Group 2 Joel Stakes at Newmarket.

The older division as usual looks strong from sprinting up to the staying division.

Balding picked out **Count Octave** as having done well over the winter and, along with **Duretto**, he will be expected to make his presence felt in the Cup races.

South Seas, a top two-year-old who was a Group 1 second at Saint-Cloud, ran only twice last year, ending well beaten in the French 2,000 Guineas in May. He has been gelded and done well for his long break to suggest he can make up for lost time off a mark of 107.

Horseplay, who won the Listed Pretty Polly at Newmarket to earn her Oaks place and came fourth to Enable, is another to have done well over the winter to raise hopes of more black type.

Brorocco, a tearaway in his younger days, started to repay all the work put in on him at home last season with two big handicap wins and a good run in the Cambridgeshire. Balding reports: "He's definitely improving and will start in handicaps."

Isomer, second to Churchill in the Chesham two years ago, disappointed last year but has been gelded and could be a sprinter to note.

Dancing Star, who took on the best in the first half of last year after winning the Stewards' Cup in 2016 before being ruled out for the second half, is also back and remains a high-class sprinter.

The autumn sales also brought two interesting additions from Newmarket stables in Listed winner and Group-placed **Morando**, who will contest similar races, and **Zwayyan**, another useful miler who will be aimed at some of the top handicaps.

Danzan, second in the big-money sales race at Doncaster and eighth in the Middle Park, has been first of the three-year-olds into action this year and will contest the Good Friday 6f final.

Crossing The Line, a debut winner who was taken off her feet in the Cheveley Park, has physical scope and is expected to add black type sooner rather than later.

Fortune's Pearl is another filly expected to step up this year having done very well for the winter break, while **Whitefountainfairy**, second in the Prestige at Goodwood after leaving Jessica Harrington, and maidens **Foxtrot Lady** and the gelded **Rebel Streak** are others to keep in mind.

RALPH BECKETT had a frustrating 2017 with illness making it a stop-start time through the height of the summer, although the final annual score would not confirm such a difficult time.

The two-year-olds were most affected by the low-grade virus and then an outbreak of ringworm and as a consequence it was not until the early all-weather season that some potential stars emerged.

Cecchini announced herself a talent when breaking the two-year-old mile track record at Kempton in November and

DANCING STAR: a high-class sprinter and will prove the point this season

her trainer, who has won two of the last ten Oaks with Look Here and Talent, is mapping out an Oaks trial for her start on turf.

Another all-weather winner, **Kinaesthesia**, is pencilled in for an Oaks trial as well, possibly the Listed Pretty Polly at Newmarket early in May.

Occupy surprised Beckett with his debut win at Kempton, where he was sent off at 25-1, but he was another to record a quick time and win in some style.

Podemos had to settle for second on his debut at Kempton after making the running, run down late by Bow Street, the 2-7 Godolphin winner.

This big son of Shamardal is expected to improve more than most for that run and will stay further.

Twice Over's half-brother **Breath Caught** won his third and final start as a juvenile after taking time to learn his job and, with his form working out well, he could thrive from an opening mark of 84.

Park Hill winner Alyssa has gone to the paddocks, but Beckett still has a strong hand in the older division and **Chemical Charge**, winner of the Group 3 September Stakes last year, is set to start his year in Qatar with a $1m target in the Emir Trophy.

He needs to race right-handed, which limits his opportunities, but the Hardwicke at Royal Ascot, in which he was third to Idaho last year, is his likely summer target again.

Mount Moriah, not disgraced in fourth behind Order Of St George in the Long Distance Cup at Ascot, could make up into a Cup horse this year, although with a proviso that the four-year-old is at his best with some give in the ground.

As such, Beckett will target one of the early staying races such as the Sagaro or the Henry II Stakes to test his Gold Cup aspirations.

Mountain Bell is another useful stayer in the stable. The five-year-old mare is on course to run in the Betway Marathon at Lingfield on Good Friday having won a fast-track qualifier.

DEAN IVORY is still walking on air after his first Group 1 success with Librisa Breeze in the Champions Sprint at Ascot last October after so many near misses with Tropics.

Librisa Breeze is set to start his season in Dubai having been invited for the Al Quoz Sprint on World Cup night and, with his Group 1 status, his programme is mapped out with the Diamond Jubilee at Royal Ascot providing a return to the scene of his big win.

Ivory still believes the four-year-old is

HARBOUR LAW: a late-season campaign is the idea for him

best at 7f and even a mile, which would open up more opportunities both home and abroad.

Eirene, who won the 6f Listed St Hugh's Stakes at Newbury before finishing sixth to Clemmie in the Cheveley Park, has wintered well and her owner has given her a 1,000 Guineas entry.

A Classic trial therefore beckons this spring to test whether this Declaration Of War filly will get the mile.

DAVID MENUISIER is another trainer who had a stop-start year in 2017 with illness in his yard.

Thundering Blue was the stable's flag-bearer, with a hat-trick of 1m2f wins before finding the Cambridgeshire on the sharp side. A return to further beckons, although he was given a "tentative" Lincoln entry in case he showed more speed in his training.

Contrapposto may be more of a miler. The four-year-old is over the pulled hamstring he suffered while running in the Dante at York last year and nearly made it back to the track at the end of last season before being given a holiday.

Vintager, one of the stable to have an interrupted year after an impressive debut success in a strong Newmarket maiden, has wintered very well, but Menuisier ruled

out any Classic aspirations for the Master-craftsman colt.

He had given mixed messages about his stamina with his two 7f runs, not looking to stay in the Solario before keeping on after hitting a flat spot in the Horris Hill.

Harbour Law, the 2016 St Leger hero, was expected back with his Epsom trainer *LAURA MONGAN* this spring having recovered from the tendon injury that ended his year after running third to Big Orange and Order Of St George in the Ascot Gold Cup last June.

As such, connections will be looking towards a late-season campaign on his favoured easier ground.

GARY MOORE is best known for his exploits over jumps, but he also keeps things ticking over on the Flat and has picked out an unnamed two-year-old by Slade Power as one for readers to follow.

Midlands
by John Bull

MICK APPLEBY again came close to a first century of winners last season – his tally of 91 was just three off his peak from 2015 – and he has another strong team this year, led by **Big Country**.

The imposing five-year-old finished a close second to Ballet Concerto in the John Smith's Cup at York last year and remains open to improvement.

Appleby is hoping the son of High Chaparral will be mixing the leading handicaps with potential Group-race assignments.

He said: "Big Country has wintered really well and is doing nicely. We'll aim him at the Lincoln at the start of the turf campaign and it should suit him. We'll see how he gets on there before deciding on our next step, but I'd hope he'll be up to contesting Group races during the season."

Big Country's owners, The Horse Watchers, also own **The Great Wall**, an emphatic Southwell maiden winner in the winter who pulled a muscle when defeated at the track the following week, and **Hakam**, who is best suited by cut in the ground, likes Ascot and will be contesting fair sprint handicaps.

Yard favourite **Danzeno** has been plying his trade in Dubai in the winter but is another sprinter likely to return to Berkshire over the summer.

Appleby said: "We'll be looking to mix and match handicaps and Group races with him. He loves Ascot and won the heritage handicap there last summer, so we'll head back there with him for all the major sprint handicaps."

Appleby has a number of intriguing new recruits, most notably **Moonraker**, a 22,000gns purchase whom he feels

DANZENO (right): Mick Appleby's old warrior will be back for more this season

"arrives on a good mark", and **Cape Cova**, a 45,000gns buy who will be aimed at the Northumberland Plate and the Cesarewitch.

Willoughton trainer *JAMES GIVEN* is another trainer looking forward to the Lincoln and hopes the early-season handicap will remain in the race title's county with stable star **Sands Chorus**.

He improved 16lb on official ratings on turf last year, most notably finishing second to Dolphin Vista in the Betfred Cambridgeshire at Newmarket in September.

Given said: "I always thought he would improve with time as even now he's still not greatly furnished – that's just him – but I couldn't have said I expected him to improve to such an extent last year.

"He's tough as teak and ran a fantastic race in the Cambridgeshire and, with the Lincoln a similar type of big-runner handicap, that will be his early-season aim with another crack at the Cambridgeshire planned for the autumn."

Improving three-year-olds **Gift In Time** and **Cool Spirit** are set to be contesting some decent sprint handicaps, with the former gelded over the winter and described by the trainer as an "honest citizen". He expects the pair to progress through the year.

Tawny Port, a four-time winner as a two-year-old, ran just once last year at three but has recovered from a knee injury, which the trainer believes the son of Arcano sustained when avoiding a faller at Chester in September 2016, and is cantering ahead of a return on the turf in the spring.

Given said: "We're delighted to have Tawny Port back in for this campaign and I'm looking forward to him getting back on the track. He's had an excellent recovery and looks magnificent.

"The way he put a strong field to bed in a nursery at Ayr on his final win at two suggested he's talented and we haven't been able to find out just how good he is.

"He's a strong type who looks a sprinter and showed plenty of speed at two, but his breeding suggests he'll get at least a mile, so we have plenty of options to explore with him."

Given has the highest ever percentage of his yard filled by two-year-olds with over 50 per cent of his string set for their juvenile campaigns, including a daughter of Showcasing and a "very exciting" Zebedee filly who are showing plenty early on, plus relations to former yard favourites Sign Of The Kodiac and Mistress Of Venice.

Wiseton-based *IVAN FURTADO* enjoyed his best year in 2017 and has high hopes for the forthcoming turf campaign with several progressive types.

Sword Exceed has won three races for the yard since joining from Charlie Appleby for £18,000 in November 2016, benefiting for the step up to 7f when scoring at Lingfield in January.

The smooth-travelling son of Exceed And Excel is suited by a fast pace and may well be ideally suited to the hustle and bustle of a big-field handicap.

Furtado said: "He's a nice type and when a race pans out for him he's a decent horse. He's not the most straightforward and needs a good pace, but he has a great turn of foot and he's done nothing wrong for us so far.

"There's plenty of stamina on his dam's side and there should be more improvement to come from him over 7f – we may even try him over a mile in time. He'll be contesting some nice races in the summer."

TAWNY PORT: back for more

SAUNTER (left): won the November Handicap for the Ian Williams team

Furtado claimed **Malaspina** for €12,000 after she defeated his Intensical at Saint-Cloud on heavy ground in September and she soon proved a revelation, winning twice at the end of last year.

Furtado said: "She's done really well for us and it was a tactical race which didn't really work out for her when her winning run came to an end at Newcastle in January.

"Although she wouldn't want too fast ground, she should be able to translate her form to turf as she has won on the Flat in France.

"We'll have plenty of fun with her – she's still improving and it'll be interesting to see how far she can go."

Sir Ottoman has been dropping down the weights since joining from Mohamed Moubarak last autumn and Furtado feels there are races to be won with the five-year-old.

He said: "We're still trying to find the key to him. He has some fair bits of form and there are certainly races in him when he's in the right grade. He works like a nice horse and a step up in trip to 7f and possibly beyond may well suit him."

Of his handicappers at a slightly lower level, Furtado is hopeful of improvement from **Huddersfilly Town** and **Frank's Legacy** on the turf.

Roger Charlton's former assistant also has his largest team of two-year-olds for this campaign, with 14 in training including a particularly forward colt by Sir Prancealot who cost £20,000 at the Goffs UK Premier Yearling Sale and is catching the eye.

Dual-purpose trainer *IAN WILLIAMS* enjoyed a fine year on the Flat in 2017 with 51 winners and a number of last year's stars may be worth following again.

Listed winner **Speedo Boy** will win more good races when he gets his preferred soft ground, while **Saunter** also relished those conditions when landing the November Handicap.

New recruit **Michael's Mount** has the potential to rise through the ranks in handicaps this year.

Est. 1909
RACING & FOOTBALL OUTLOOK

Tipping Point
Ed Quigley

Six hitters to give you punters a profit this summer

THE last Flat season felt like Groundhog Day in many respects as Aidan O'Brien took his own extremely high standards to new levels when eclipsing Bobby Frankel's world record for Group/Grade 1 wins in a season.

O'Brien ended with a total of 28 victories at the highest level, setting a barometer few will ever be likely to match – even he himself may struggle to overhaul that astonishing record in the years to come.

However, not everything was about the Ballydoyle battalions as John Gosden set the season alight with his superstars Enable and Cracksman.

It took a while for many to latch on to just how good Enable was and I hope plenty of you took my advice to back her at 12-1 for

Prix de l'Arc de Triomphe after her victory in the Oaks. Indeed, she actually managed to beat the boys twice, winning the King George before her Chantilly romp.

Calls for the majestic Cracksman to lock horns with her that day failed to materialise, with the colt instead rerouted to the Champion Stakes, in which he pulverised the opposition.

The two of them are bound to meet at some point this year – a marketing dream and a contest which will set the pulse racing once the stalls open.

There is a lot to look forward to once again – the only thing now will be to hope for some warm weather!

Whatever you back this season, the very best of luck and I hope you have a profitable and enjoyable summer. Here are a few selections below whom I think could be worth following.

Big Country 5yo gelding
11418205-   (Mick Appleby)

Big Country was a consistent handicapper last season, scooping a couple of big pots.

The five-year-old's form tailed off to an extent towards the end of a long season, so with that in mind it may be best to catch him once again in the early part of the campaign.

Often a strong traveller who likes to settle off a sound gallop, it has been mooted that he could drop back in trip to a mile and tackle contests such as the Lincoln.

There should be more to come from him off a mark of 100 and he could easily bridge the gap into Pattern company.

Expert Eye 3yo colt
119- (Sir Michael Stoute)

When Expert Eye romped home in the Vintage Stakes, my post-race analysis was one word – wow. Not much more explaining was needed.

However, the wheels came off in equally spectacular fashion as his unbeaten record went up in smoke when he trailed home last of nine finishers in the Dewhurst. Initial reports he was lame weren't backed up, but either way it was too bad to be true and you can put a line through it.

With the Greenham at Newbury pencilled in for his comeback, Sir Michael Stoute's colt can put himself back in the picture for the 2,000 Guineas. He still has real potential and, based on that Goodwood effort, I think redemption awaits.

Kew Gardens 3yo colt
71241- (Aidan O'Brien)

Kew Gardens looked like a horse with lots of stamina in his locker when he won the Zetland Stakes at Newmarket in October.

He galloped through the line and gives the visual impression he will only get better the further he goes.

Clearly Ballydoyle won't be short of options for the the top middle-distance contests, but it has already been mentioned by connections that he will be aimed towards the Derby so he is clearly held in high regard there.

In the longer term, though, he looks just the type who could make up into a St Leger candidate and we may not see the best of him until we get into the backend of the season.

Laurens 3yo filly
1211- (Karl Burke)

The Karl Burke-trained Laurens got the better of some more fancied rivals when producing a very game performance to win the Fillies' Mile at Newmarket. That took her tally to three wins from four starts.

She has demonstrated her ability over a mile and if conditions were soft the 1,000 Guineas would come into the equation.

However, with plenty of stamina on the dam's side it will be no surprise to see her

BIG COUNTRY (in front): consistent handicapper with more races in him

flourish when tackling middle distances. The Oaks would be a possibility, though her long stride may not be ideal for the contours of Epsom and the Prix de Diane has been highlighted by connections as the potential big target for the season.

She is tough, genuine and finds a way to win and should have plenty of success in her three-year-old campaign.

Roaring Lion 3yo colt
1112- (John Gosden)

There is no doubting Roaring Lion's immense ability, but he also brings a quirkiness, making him fun to watch.

Admittedly it wouldn't have been much fun for his backers in the Racing Post Trophy, in which he travelled all over his rivals, including Classic favourite Saxon Warrior. As he hit the front inside the final furlong it looked just a matter of how far he would win by, but he hung left and Saxon Warrior battled back to land the odds.

However, he could be devastating this season, perhaps with exaggerated hold-up tactics.

The 2,000 Guineas looks an obvious major target for the first half of the season, but there is also the possibility we could see him and Expert Eye meet in the Greenham, which would be a race to savour.

It will take an abundance of skill from the jockey who has the task of delivering his challenge at the crucial moment, but whatever he ends up doing this year it should be exciting to watch.

Stradivarius 4yo colt
121133- (John Gosden)

There should be more to come from the lightly-raced Stradivarius when tackling marathon trips.

The Sea The Stars colt showed some smart form last term, winning the Queen's Vase at Royal Ascot before seeing off Big Orange and company when stepped up to Group 1 level against his elders in the Goodwood Cup.

Narrow defeats in the Leger and on Champions Day on ground softer than ideal underlined his ability and he looks as though he should have a fruitful campaign in all the top staying events.

Granted quick ground, the Ascot Gold Cup looks ideal for him and there is every chance he can get his revenge on Order Of St George.

STRADIVARIUS (second left): Ascot Gold Cup looks the ideal race for him

Est. 1909
RACING & FOOTBALL OUTLOOK

Richard Birch

Read Richard every week in the RFO

Bin Suroor's juveniles could shine but these ten will be better value

THE biggest certainty of the 2018 Flat turf season is that Saeed Bin Suroor will have an army of early two-year-olds ready for Royal Ascot.

Remember the Godolphin row last year which led to the resignation of John Ferguson after Bin Suroor complained that most of the team's sharp juveniles were with Charlie Appleby?

It's no offers that situation won't arise this time, but I doubt punters will get rich by backing them all.

Let's concentrate, as usual, on a selection of ten handicappers who are likely to pay their way throughout the spring, summer and autumn months, headed by the Kevin Ryan-trained **Laughton**.

Gelded at the end of a successful three-year-old campaign in 2016, which included a fluent victory off a mark of 79 at Glorious Goodwood, this sprinter surprisingly drew a blank last season.

However, the end result is that Laughton begins his five-year-old career rated just 68, having been dropped a total of 10lb for his last three defeats, which were all on

ground he detested.

Ideally suited by being produced fast and late over 5f on a good to firm surface, Laughton should get plenty of opportunities in the early part of the campaign and, once he has got his confidence back, I expect him to make up into the 85 horse he once looked like being.

Regular readers of my Get It Ready! column will know that I can't wait to see **Give It Some Teddy** in 2018.

Totally unexposed in handicap company after just one start for Tim Easterby over 7f at Newmarket last backend, this lightly raced four-year-old failed by three-quarters of a length to peg back Yellow-hammer, who was landing her fourth consecutive race.

Give It Some Teddy had previously unleashed a fantastic turn of foot to win a modest Redcar maiden over 6f and looks just the type to make considerable improvement when stepped up to a mile.

The 2018 Royal Hunt Cup is likely to come too soon in his career, but I have little doubt he could make up into that type of horse in due course. He looks a proper

73

money-spinner off a mark of 74.

Magic Circle must be one of the most unlucky horses in training when it comes to getting his preferred ground conditions.

That's two years running now that this soft-ground lover has seen his Cesarewitch chance ended by unseasonably fast terrain. Pulled out of the race in 2016, he could finish only 13th last October, performing with credit despite loathing the ground.

If Magic Circle is to bid for the Cesarewitch again this year it will be for new connections since he was sold out of Ralph Beckett's stable for 70,000gns at Tattersalls in November.

Ian Williams will now map out the six-year-old gelding's campaign and I will be surprised if it doesn't involve repeat bids for the Chester Cup and the Cesarewitch.

Is it too late for Magic Circle to develop into the Group horse I have always believed was his destiny? We'll have to see.

Paul Midgley is a dab hand with sprinters and I am more than hopeful he will get **Giant Spark** firmly back on track this year.

His profile is not too dissimilar to Laughton's in that he missed out a season last year after excelling in 2016.

A huge horse who has taken a long time to physically mature, he needs soft or heavy ground and will probably be best in the autumn.

An Ayr Gold Cup bid could be firmly on the cards at that time because, while he starts the year on 82, he kicked off last spring with a rating of 95 and could soon feature on an even higher mark.

Kaeso, one of the most progressive low-grade handicappers in the north last season, is another emphatically to keep on the right side of in 2018.

Well placed by Nigel Tinkler to rattle off a four-timer in 6f handicaps at Thirsk, Redcar, Ripon and Doncaster, he starts his new campaign still rated only 70 and there could be further improvement to come when stepped up to 7f.

A really likeable sort with a high cruising speed and a good turn of foot, he should be plying his trade at major meetings such as York by late summer.

MAGIC CIRCLE: looks a good recruit for the Ian Williams yard

LUXFORD: could easily develop into a Brighton specialist

Fantasy Keeper, who goes particularly well at Nottingham, was gelded last winter after a successful 2017. It looked then as if there was even better to come in 6f handicaps when there is plenty of cut in the ground and he is another to follow.

So, too, is David Simcock's **Free Forum**, likely to improve considerably this year when stepped up to 1m6f and 2m after a sole success over 1m2f at Yarmouth in 2017.

He won with far more in hand than the official margin suggests under Silvestre de Sousa that afternoon and things didn't really fall for him in three subsequent starts. A mark of 67 gives his shrewd handler plenty to work with.

I also like **Sheriff Garrett**, a Tim Easterby horse who promises to stay really well as he learns to settle better. There could be plenty of opportunities at Pontefract for him this campaign.

Briyouni is another to note. Now with Ralph Beckett, he has always promised more than he has delivered, but it may prove profitable to trust his new handler to get the best out of him.

Briyouni boasts some excellent form at Doncaster and I would love to see him venture to Town Moor off his current mark of 76 for a big-field 7f handicap on fast ground at some stage this season.

I cannot sign off without a horse to follow for lovers of all things Brighton like myself. Essaka, Roy Rocket and Pour La Victoire should all win races there this season, but the biggest money-spinner there could be the John Best-trained **Luxford**.

She won twice at the Sussex track last year and gives the impression she could well develop into a Roy Rocket-type Brighton specialist.

A mark of 59 means there will be ample opportunities for her.

Est. 1909
RACING & OUTLOOK
FOOTBALL

Time Test
speed figures

Clock flags up Navy as still being underrated

W E tend to like our two-year-olds unblemished, which helps to explain the luke-warm reaction to **US Navy Flag**'s autumn wins in the Middle Park and Dewhurst.

When the son of War Front lined up in the Middle Park he had already been beaten six times and was easy to back at 10-1. A fortnight later, though, he had won two Group 1 races at Newmarket – and his Time Test figures suggest there was no fluke about it.

His rating of 83, earned for winning the Dewhurst by two and a half lengths from Mendelssohn, was the best by a juvenile in 2017 and maintained his steady pro-gress since disappointing in the Coventry Stakes at Royal Ascot on his fourth start.

A maiden success in first-time blinkers got things rolling and the curve has been upward since, with a figure of 64 for fin-ishing second in Newmarket's July Stakes

shattered in the Middle Park and improved upon again in the Dewhurst on his first try at 7f.

A blowout on the dirt in the Breeders' Cup Juvenile ended the season on a downbeat note, but that does not detract from the overall sense that the hardy US Navy Flag, crowned European champion two-year-old, could still go into the new campaign underestimated.

The figure of 75 posted by fellow Aidan O'Brien-trained inmate **Mendelssohn** in defeat in the Dewhurst was enough to put him in the top six juveniles of the season and his subsequent win in the Breeders' Cup Juvenile Turf also supports that lofty assessment of the race.

Unbeaten stablemate **Saxon Warrior** matches the more conventional blueprint for an exciting two-year-old and his Time Test figure of 78 for winning the Racing Post Trophy justifiably has him to the fore in 2,000 Guineas ante-post lists.

It has been six years since a Racing Post Trophy winner followed up at Newmarket, but this was another strong race on the clock with runner-up Roaring Lion also running a cracker.

Way behind US Navy Flag in the Dewhurst was **Expert Eye**, the odds-on favourite running far too freely on his first start for two months and finishing lame, but he shouldn't be forgotten either as his daz-zling win in the Vintage Stakes at Glorious Goodwood was also supported by a good time figure.

US NAVY FLAG: the clock shows there was no fluke about his Group 1 wins

Among the sprinters, Prix Morny winner **Unfortunately** is much better than he showed in the Middle Park, but fellow Newmarket flop Sioux Nation looks too short in the Commonwealth Cup. Though he also won the Phoenix Stakes, he has yet to better the perch of 64 established when winning the Norfolk Stakes at Royal Ascot.

Another one from Aidan O'Brien's yard not getting the clock whirring is Moyglare winner **Happily**, who has been high up lists for the 1,000 Guineas since earning the accolades for beating the colts in the Group 1 Prix Jean-Luc Lagadere on Arc day.

But that win, in receipt of 4lb, failed to trouble her Time Test mark of 67 from the Moyglare and she has plenty of catching up to do to worry stablemate **Clemmie**, who seized favouritism for the Guineas when winning the Cheveley Park.

The daughter of Galileo has notched an improved time figure with each run, turning around the form of her Albany Stakes defeat to **Different League** in securing a rating of 81 at Newmarket, a rating only bettered by US Navy Flag among the juveniles.

She promises to be better stepped up to a mile and could prove hard to overcome in the first fillies' Classic.

Wild Illusion is a Group 1 winner sailing more under the radar, her win in the Prix Marcel Boussac not seizing the headlines it perhaps deserved.

Having been beaten in a Group 3, the Charlie Appleby-trained daughter of Dubawi was sent off a 25-1 chance at Chantilly, but her defeat of the fancied **Polydream**, a previous conqueror of Fillies' Mile winner **Laurens**, in first-time cheekpieces earned a Time Test mark of 76 to suggest a bright 2018.

BATTAASH: Goodwood romp marked him out as something special

Four more good reasons to get excited about the 2018 Flat season are that the quartet topping the Time Test rankings for three-year-olds have all stayed in training.

Battaash, **Lady Aurelia**, **Cracksman** and **Enable** rate quite a foursome, comprising two of the most devastating sprinters around and the first two in the betting for the Prix de l'Arc de Triomphe.

Getting gelded has been the making of Battaash – on the racecourse at least – and the only surprise last season was that it took him until the Abbaye in October to win his first Group 1.

His glorious front-running destruction of the King George Stakes field at Goodwood marked him out as something special and one capable of producing an outstanding Time Test mark given the chance.

That explosive talent needs to be brought to the boil at the right moment, which is why his defeat behind Marsha after getting worked up at the start of the Nunthorpe could be forgiven.

In turning the tables on Marsha at Chantilly, the son of Dark Angel notched a figure of 93, the best of 2017, and lit the fires for what promises to be a scintillating 2018.

Waiting to clash over the minimum trip in the King's Stand at Royal Ascot is Lady Aurelia, whose mark of 86 when getting inched out by Marsha in the Nunthorpe bettered her 2016 peak by a point.

Topped in Godolphin blue like Battaash, **Harry Angel** captured the imagination with victories against his elders in the July Cup and Haydock's Sprint Cup, but he has more to prove on the clock.

Top two-year-old colts of 2017

	Horse	Speed rating	Distance in furlongs	Going	Track	Date achieved
1	**US Navy Flag**	**83**	**7**	**GD**	**Newmarket**	**Oct 14**
2	Saxon Warrior	78	8	GS	Doncaster	Oct 28
3	Roaring Lion	77	8	GS	Doncaster	Oct 2
4	Mendelssohn	75	7	GD	Newmarket	Oct 14
5	Expert Eye	73	7	GD	Goodwood	Aug 1
5	Havana Grey	73	5	GS	Doncaster	Sep 15
5	James Garfield	73	6	GD	Newbury	Sep 23
5	Unfortunately	73	6	GD	Deauville	Aug 20
9	Cardsharp	71	6	GD	Newmarket	Jul 13
9	Fleet Review	71	6	GS	Newmarket	Sep 30

Top two-year-old fillies of 2017

	Horse	Speed rating	Distance in furlongs	Going	Track	Date achieved
1	**Clemmie**	**81**	**6**	**GS**	**Newmarket**	**Sep 30**
2	Wild Illusion	76	8	SFT	Chantilly	Oct 1
3	Different League	74	6	GS	Newmarket	Sep 30
4	Heartache	72	5	GS	Doncaster	Sep 15
4	Nyaleti	72	6	GS	Ascot	Jul 29
4	September	72	7	GF	Ascot	Jun 24
7	Laurens	71	8	GD	Newmarket	Oct 13
7	Polydream	71	8	SFT	Chantilly	Oct 1
9	Mission Impassible	70	8	SFT	Chantilly	Oct 1
10	Magical	69	8	SFT	Chantilly	Oct 1

His highest mark of 80 came when finishing only fourth behind the Dean Ivory-trained **Librisa Breeze** in the Champions Sprint Stakes, a red-hot contest that saw the winner produce the highest mark by any older horse in 2017 and seemed to find Harry Angel wanting.

Cracksman's mark of 82 in the Great Voltigeur exceeded what he achieved when third in the Derby and the sense there was more to come was fulfilled with a swaggering Champion Stakes performance that earned him a rating of 90.

The measure of that display, when he took up the running three furlongs out to power clear, was that the mark surpassed anything achieved by Oaks and Arc winner Enable. That said, her consistency was amazing, with three Time Test figures of 85 or more – the peak figure of 87 coming in her defeat of Ulysses in the King George.

The form of the St Leger also looks strong and the first three home – **Capri**, **Crystal Ocean** and **Stradivarius** – all stay in training as well.

Capri and Stradivarius are rightly prominent in the Gold Cup betting, while Crystal Ocean will be dropping back to contest top 1m4f races and shouldn't be underestimated even in such a red-hot division.

Est. 1909

RACING & FOOTBALL OUTLOOK

Group 1 review by Dylan Hill

1 **Qipco 2,000 Guineas Stakes (1m)**
Newmarket May 6 (Good To Firm)

1	**Churchill** 3-9-0	Ryan Moore
2	**Barney Roy** 3-9-0	James Doyle
3	**Al Wukair** 3-9-0	Gregory Benoist

6/4F, 7/2, 11/2. 1l, nk. 10 ran. 1m 36.61s
(A P O'Brien).

A tactical masterclass from the Ballydoyle team enabled **Churchill** to graduate from champion two-year-old to Classic winner despite having his limitations exposed later in the season. With two stablemates dictating a steady gallop, Churchill was ideally placed throughout and swept into a decisive lead as the pacemakers eased aside for him, with **Barney Roy** and **Al Wukair** coming from too far back to bridge the gap. Barney Roy also stumbled badly over a furlong out and looked a particularly unlucky loser, while early leader **Lancaster Bomber** stuck on well enough for fourth ahead of **Dream Castle** and **Eminent**, who needed further.

2 **Qipco 1,000 Guineas Stakes (Fillies)**
(1m)
Newmarket May 7 (Good To Firm)

1	**Winter** 3-9-0	Wayne Lordan
2	**Rhododendron** 3-9-0	Ryan Moore
3	**Daban** 3-9-0	Frankie Dettori

9/1, 5/4F, 5/1. 2l, nk. 14 ran. 1m 35.66s
(A P O'Brien).

The emergence of a new star as **Winter** gained the first of her four Group 1 wins, helped by a woeful lack of top-class British-trained fillies. Winter was always in command as her stablemate **Rhododendron**, probably better over further anyway, found all sorts of

trouble behind, eventually doing well to get up for second ahead of Nell Gwyn winner **Daban**. **Talaayeb** was a good fourth, with another Ballydoyle filly, **Hydrangea**, the most notable disappointment behind.

3 **Al Shaqab Lockinge Stakes (1m)**
Newbury May 20 (Soft)

1	**Ribchester** 4-9-0	William Buick
2	**Lightning Spear** 6-9-0	Oisin Murphy
3	**Breton Rock** 7-9-0	Andrea Atzeni

7/4F, 9/2, 25/1. 3¾l, 2½l. 8 ran. 1m 43.00s
(Richard Fahey).

Easy pickings for **Ribchester**, who had very little to beat and managed to destroy the opposition even on ground that would subsequently prove his undoing. Ribchester made all the running and powered away from **Lightning Spear**, who had improved throughout 2016 to get to within a length of Ribchester in the QEII but would prove far more inconsistent as a six-year-old. **Galileo Gold** was the other proven Group 1 performer in the field, but a tame fifth precipitated his retirement and **Aclaim** was also well below his best in sixth.

4 **Tattersalls Irish 2,000 Guineas (1m)**
Curragh (IRE) May 27 (Yielding)

1	**Churchill** 3-9-0	Ryan Moore
2	**Thunder Snow** 3-9-0	C Soumillon
3	**Irishcorrespondent** 3-9-0	Shane Foley

4/9F, 5/1, 7/1. 2½l, 4½l. 6 ran. 1m40.46s
(A P O'Brien).

This was desperately short of depth with **Churchill** facing only pacemakers **Lancaster Bomber** and **Spirit Of Valor** among the Newmarket field, but he at least dealt with his one serious rival, **Thunder Snow**, with impressive ease. Thunder Snow led briefly 2f out, but Churchill quickened past him and won well, with the pair pulling 4½l clear of **Irishcorrespondent** in third.

5 Tattersalls Irish 1,000 Guineas (Fillies) (1m)
Curragh (IRE) May 28 (Yielding)

1	**Winter** 3-9-0	Ryan Moore
2	**Roly Poly** 3-9-0	Seamie Heffernan
3	**Hydrangea** 3-9-0	P B Beggy

8/13F, 14/1, 7/1. 4¾l, hd. 8 ran. 1m39.78s (A P O'Brien).

The second leg of **Winter**'s Group 1 four-timer and the first of two in which she would beat stablemates **Roly Poly** and **Hydrangea**, who would go on to score five times at the top level between them to underline the winner's quality. Always going well, Winter took over in front 2f out and stayed on strongly for a comprehensive victory. Roly Poly did well to get up for second on ground softer than ideal ahead of the front-running Hydrangea and **Intricately**.

6 Tattersalls Gold Cup (1m2f110y)
Curragh (IRE) May 28 (Yielding)

1	**Decorated Knight** 5-9-3	Andrea Atzeni
2	**Somehow** 4-9-0	Seamie Heffernan
3	**Deauville** 4-9-3	Ryan Moore

7/2F, 4/1 ,4/1. 1¼l, 2¼l. 8 ran. 2m18.03s (Roger Charlton).

A good opportunity for **Decorated Knight** with **Somehow** and **Deauville** hardly representing Aidan O'Brien's A team and he made the most of it. Always travelling strongly, Decorated Knight kept on well enough to comfortably hold off the late thrust of Somehow as the pair pulled 2¼l clear of Deauville.

7 Investec Oaks (Fillies) (1m4f6y)
Epsom June 2 (Good)

1	**Enable** 3-9-0	Frankie Dettori
2	**Rhododendron** 3-9-0	Ryan Moore
3	**Alluringly** 3-9-0	Seamie Heffernan

6/1, 8/11F, 16/1. 5l, 6l. 8 ran. 2m 34.13s (John Gosden).

This was supposed to be all about **Rhododendron**, but instead the 1,000 Guineas runner-up had the misfortune to run into a second great filly as **Enable** produced an outstanding performance. The stage looked set for a terrific duel as Enable and Rhododendron locked horns in the straight, but Enable was much too good and powered clear in hugely impressive fashion. Rhododendron did little wrong, keeping on well enough to pull 6l clear of **Alluringly** in third with **Coronet** beaten nearly 16l in fifth.

8 Investec Coronation Cup (1m4f6y)
Epsom June 2 (Good)

1	**Highland Reel** 5-9-0	Ryan Moore
2	**Frontiersman** 4-9-0	James Doyle
3	**Hawkbill** 4-9-0	William Buick

9/4F, 9/1, 11/2. 1¾l, 3½l. 10 ran. 2m 33.34s (A P O'Brien).

One of the most consistent Group 1 performers of recent times, **Highland Reel** gained another

CHURCHILL (right): tactical masterclass sparked a soft Guineas double

big success in a race that magnified his qualities by their contrast with runner-up **Frontiersman**. Still admirably straightforward despite a travel nightmare for his yard, Highland Reel made most of the running and regained the initiative after a battle with **Hawkbill**. Frontiersman ran on for second despite appearing to hate the track as he hung down the camber, but he proved equally awkward in other races.

9 Investec Derby (1m4f6y)
Epsom June 3 (Good)

1 **Wings Of Eagles** 3-9-0   P B Beggy
2 **Cliffs Of Moher** 3-9-0   Ryan Moore
3 **Cracksman** 3-9-0   Frankie Dettori
40/1, 5/1, 7/2F. ¾l, nk. 18 ran. 2m 33.02s
(A P O'Brien).

A shock winner of a moderate Derby as **Wings Of Eagles** upset his better-fancied stablemate **Cliffs Of Moher** with **Cracksman**, the one genuine superstar in the field but still very much a work in progress, only third. Wings Of Eagles, retired after just one more run, seemed to benefit from being held up well off a very strong gallop and produced a storming run down the outside to sweep past Cliffs Of Moher, who didn't quite last home but just came up short in the top races over 1m2f anyway, as did **Eminent** after his close fourth. Cracksman finished in between that pair, with **Benbatl** and **Capri** next.

10 Queen Anne Stakes (1m)
Ascot June 20 (Good To Firm)

1 **Ribchester** 4-9-0   William Buick
2 **Mutakayyef** 6-9-0   Jim Crowley
3 **Deauville** 4-9-0   Ryan Moore
11/10F, 5/1, 12/1. 1¼l, nk. 16 ran. 1m 36.60s
(Richard Fahey).

Ribchester rarely got genuinely quick ground during his career and won plenty of good races on soft, but this was perhaps his best performance as he proved in his element on good to firm. Always well placed and left in front early as the pacemakers faded, Ribchester didn't put the race to bed in the same manner as the Lockinge against far stronger opposition, but he was always holding dual Summer Mile winner **Mutakayyef** and had the field well strung out behind. **Deauville**, relishing a strongly run mile, ran a cracker in third ahead of German challenger **Spectre** and that quartet pulled 3¼l clear of **Kaspersky**, who proved this was no fluke when second to easy winner Mutakayyef in the Summer Mile, while **Lightning Spear** was among the also-rans.

11 King's Stand Stakes (5f)
Ascot June 20 (Good To Firm)

1 **Lady Aurelia** 3-8-9   John R Velazquez
2 **Profitable** 5-9-4   James Doyle
3 **Marsha** 4-9-1   Luke Morris
7/2, 14/1, 11/4F. 3l, hd. 17 ran. 57.45s
(Wesley A Ward).

Twelve months after a sensational victory in the Queen Mary, **Lady Aurelia** proved she was still a monster as a three-year-old as she stormed to a remarkably comfortable victory. Always going well close to the pace, Lady Aurelia quickened clear of the 2016 winner **Profitable**, who ran another terrific race against a better rival than he had faced that year, and favourite **Marsha**, against whom she was arguably a shade unlucky not to add another Group 1 in the Nunthorpe.

12 St James's Palace Stakes (7f213y)
Ascot June 20 (Good To Firm)

1 **Barney Roy** 3-9-0   James Doyle
2 **Lancaster Bomber** 3-9-0   D O'Brien
3 **Thunder Snow** 3-9-0   C Soumillon
5/2, 12/1, 6/1. 1l, hd. 8 ran. 1m 37.22s
(Richard Hannon).

An eagerly awaited rematch between **Churchill** and **Barney Roy** proved a bit of a damp squib with the dual Classic winner well below his best, allowing Barney Roy to come out on top. Barney Roy still made hard work of victory and would prove even better when he stepped up in trip for the Eclipse, but he did enough to wear down the pacemaker **Lancaster Bomber** and subsequent Prix Jean Prat winner **Thunder Snow**. It was another 3¼l back to Churchill in fourth.

13 Prince of Wales's Stakes (1m1f212y)
Ascot June 21 (Good To Firm)

1 **Highland Reel** 5-9-0   Ryan Moore
2 **Decorated Knight** 5-9-0   Andrea Atzeni
3 **Ulysses** 4-9-0   Jim Crowley
9/4, 10/1, 9/2. 1¼l, shd. 8 ran. 2m 5.04s
(A P O'Brien).

With an outstanding 1m2f horse yet to emerge, this race didn't take a huge amount of winning and **Highland Reel** took full advantage to strike over a trip short of his best. Highland Reel was always prominent and got on top close home to gain only his second Group 1 victory over 1m2f – the first having come back in 2015 in the Secretariat Stakes – among seven in total by the end of the year. **Ulysses**, the horse who would go on to fill the void in the division, went for home too soon, with his subsequent Eclipse and Juddmonte

RIBCHESTER: most potent on quick ground in the Queen Anne

wins confirming just how late he needed to be delivered, and even lost second to **Decorated Knight**. **Queen's Trust** was just behind them in fourth and little over 5l covered all of the eight runners.

14 Gold Cup (2m3f210y)
Ascot June 22 (Good To Firm)
1 **Big Orange** 6-9-2   James Doyle
2 **Order Of St George** 5-9-2   Ryan Moore
3 **Harbour Law** 4-9-0   Jim Crowley
5/1, 5/6F, 33/1. shd, 6l. 14 ran. 4m 22.40s
(Michael Bell).

A wonderful duel saw the 2016 winner **Order Of St George** lose his crown to the brilliantly courageous **Big Orange**. Order Of St George was probably the best horse in the race and just given too much to do – he managed to beat Big Orange's subsequent Goodwood conqueror Stradivarius when winning the Long Distance Cup on Champions Day – but the winning horse and jockey deserve massive credit, Big Orange bravely pulling out more in the final 100 yards under a brilliant front-running ride. The pair pulled 6l clear of **Harbour Law** and **She Is No Lady**, with Long Distance Cup runner-up **Torcedor** only fifth on much quicker ground.

15 Commonwealth Cup (6f)
Ascot June 23 (Good To Firm)
1 **Caravaggio** 3-9-3   Ryan Moore
2 **Harry Angel** 3-9-3   Adam Kirby
3 **Blue Point** 3-9-3   William Buick
5/6F, 11/4, 9/2. ¾l, ½l. 12 ran. 1m 13.49s
(A P O'Brien).

This brought together three hugely exciting young sprinters, but the pre-race billing perhaps led to too much being made of the result, with **Caravaggio** proving a hugely overrated winner. Instead **Harry Angel** was the one to take out of the race, but he was much too keen and finished weakly – by the end of the season his record at Ascot was also 0-4 compared to 5-5 elsewhere – allowing Caravaggio, having been outpaced, to come through and pick up the pieces. Harry Angel held on for second ahead of **Blue Point**, with that trio 3l clear of US raider **Bound For Nowhere**.

16 Coronation Stakes (Fillies) (7f213y)
Ascot June 23 (Good To Firm)
1 **Winter** 3-9-0   Ryan Moore
2 **Roly Poly** 3-9-0   Seamie Heffernan
3 **Hydrangea** 3-9-0   P B Beggy
4/9F, 12/1, 16/1. 2¼l, nk. 7 ran. 1m 39.39s
(A P O'Brien).

A repeat of the Irish 1,000 Guineas one-two-three as Winter again beat Group 1-winning stablemates **Roly Poly** and **Hydrangea** with an outstanding performance, this time in a more exacting test of her credentials. Roly Poly had quick ground in her favour while Hydrangea seemed to benefit from a slightly more patient ride, but Winter had too much speed as she quickened into the lead early in the straight before staying on as strongly as ever. Roly Poly and Hydrangea kept on well to fill the places ahead of Fred Darling winner **Dabyah**, who ran a big race but just failed to see out the extra furlong.

17 Diamond Jubilee Stakes (6f)
Ascot June 24 (Good To Firm)
1 **The Tin Man** 5-9-3   Tom Queally
2 **Tasleet** 4-9-3   Jim Crowley
3 **Limato** 5-9-3   Ryan Moore
9/2, 7/1, 2/1F. nk, ¾l. 19 ran. 1m 12.02s
(James Fanshawe).

A moderate renewal with the three-year-olds soon putting these older sprinters in their place, but **The Tin Man** took his chance to claim a second Group 1 over his favourite course and distance. The Tin Man was briefly stopped in his run but quickened up smartly to beat **Tasleet** and **Limato**, who wasn't quite

CAPRI (left): proved his Derby running all wrong when winning at the Curragh

at his best on his first run since an unhappy trip to Dubai. **Librisa Breeze** was another to be short of room but finished well in fourth, pointing to his subsequent win on Champions Day.

18 Dubai Duty Free Irish Derby (1m4f)
Curragh (IRE) July 1 (Good)
1 **Capri** 3-9-0   Seamie Heffernan
2 **Cracksman** 3-9-0   Pat Smullen
3 **Wings Of Eagles** 3-9-0   Ryan Moore
6/1, 3/1, 2/1F. nk, shd. 9 ran. 2m 35.45s
(A P O'Brien).

A terrific three-way battle in which **Capri** and **Cracksman** reversed the Derby form with **Wings Of Eagles**, Capri in particular proving his Epsom running all wrong by grinding out a narrow victory. Ridden more prominently and making full use of the stamina that would later see him add the St Leger, Capri was in front early in the straight and battled hard to hold on. Cracksman, still a long way short of his subsequent form, got going too late as he got up for second ahead of Wings Of Eagles, who at least did enough to show his Derby win was no fluke with a close third. Prix du Jockey Club runner-up **Waldgeist**, representing what proved a poor bunch of French three-year-olds, was 1½l back in fourth.

19 Pretty Polly Stakes (Fillies & Mares) (1m2f)
Curragh (IRE) July 2 (Good)
1 **Nezwaah** 4-9-8   Andrea Atzeni
2 **Rain Goddess** 3-8-12   Ryan Moore
3 **Turret Rocks** 4-9-8   Ronan Whelan
13/2, 6/1, 25/1. 3¼l, 1½l. 11 ran. 2m 6.19s
(Roger Varian).

A desperately weak renewal without any Group 1-winning three-year-olds and leading older horse **Journey** running no sort of race, but **Nezwaah** at least dealt with her rivals in suitably dismissive fashion. Unsuited by soft ground on her next two runs before flopping in the Breeders' Cup, Nezwaah was able to unleash her stunning turn of foot on this occasion, storming clear of **Rain Goddess**.

20 Coral-Eclipse (1m1f209y)
Sandown July 8 (Good To Firm)
1 **Ulysses** 4-9-7   Jim Crowley
2 **Barney Roy** 3-8-11   James Doyle
3 **Desert Encounter** 5-9-7   Sean Levey
8/1, 9/4, 50/1. nse, 3½l. 9 ran. 2m 3.49s
(Sir Michael Stoute).

A real thriller as **Ulysses** edged out **Barney Roy** by a nose. The tightness of the finish meant agony for Barney Roy, who relished the step up in trip as he finished strongly and would have got up in another yard, but that hid the fact that Ulysses was much the best horse, nearly throwing away victory as he again did very little once hitting the front despite being ridden with more patience than at Royal Ascot. **Desert Encounter** was third ahead of **Cliffs Of Moher**, who endured a rough passage but would probably have finished only a well-held third anyway on a line through **Eminent** in fifth. **Decorated Knight** was next ahead of **Lightning Spear**.

21 Tattersalls Falmouth Stakes (1m) Newmarket (July) July 14 (Good To Firm)
1 **Roly Poly** 3-8-12   Ryan Moore
2 **Wuheida** 3-8-12   William Buick
3 **Arabian Hope** 3-8-12 Josephine Gordon
6/4F, 3/1, 13/2. 1¼l, ½l. 7 ran. 1m 36.01s
(A P O'Brien).

Roly Poly made the most of the chance to step out of Winter's shadow as she comfortably won what was admittedly a desperately weak Group 1, lacking a single 1,000 Guineas runner and any serious older challengers. Roly Poly made all the running and was always in command from the subsequent Breeders' Cup heroine **Wuheida**, who was having her first run of the season, and **Arabian Hope**.

22 Darley July Cup (6f) Newmarket (July) July 15 (Good To Firm)
1 **Harry Angel** 3-9-0   Adam Kirby
2 **Limato** 5-9-6   Harry Bentley
3 **Brando** 5-9-6   Tom Eaves
9/2, 4/1, 28/1. 1¼l, ½l. 10 ran. 1m 11.25s
(Clive Cox).

Harry Angel came of age as he stormed to a spectacular victory. Settling much better than at Royal Ascot, which caused the pace to be far more modest, Harry Angel was able to show a stunning turn of foot which took him clear of **Limato** and **Brando**, both of whom would frank the form by winning Group 1 races in France later in the year. The steady gallop allowed early leader **Intelligence Cross** to stick on for fifth, but it didn't play to **Caravaggio**'s strengths as he was made to look quite slow and struggled to get past his pacemaker into fourth. **The Tin Man** was well beaten, while **Tasleet** raced much too freely.

23 Darley Irish Oaks (Fillies) (1m4f) Curragh (IRE) July 15 (Good To Firm)
1 **Enable** 3-9-0   Frankie Dettori
2 **Rain Goddess** 3-9-0   Seamie Heffernan
3 **Eziyra** 3-9-0   Pat Smullen
2/5F, 7/1, 20/1. 5½l, 2l. 9 ran. 2m 32.13s
(John Gosden).

The quickest ground **Enable** has faced since suffering her sole defeat in April but it couldn't stop her, albeit in a race in which she was never likely to be fully tested. Always prominent, Enable easily quickened clear of **Rain Goddess** while **Eziyra**, a subsequent dual Group 3 winner at the trip, and Ribblesdale winner **Coronet** were done no favours by being held up too far off the moderate gallop.

24 King George VI and Queen Elizabeth Stakes (Sponsored by Qipco) (1m3f211y)
Ascot July 29 (Good To Soft)
1 **Enable** 3-8-7   Frankie Dettori
2 **Ulysses** 4-9-7   Jim Crowley
3 **Idaho** 4-9-7   Seamie Heffernan
5/4F, 9/1, 8/1. 4½l, ¾l. 10 ran. 2m 36.22s
(John Gosden).

Enable stepped out of fillies' races and her own age group to establish her superstar status in magnificent fashion, storming to a remarkably easy victory. In what was becoming trademark fashion, Enable was always close to the pace and showed a brilliant turn of foot early in the straight before staying on strongly. There wasn't much depth behind, with the testing ground adding to **Ulysses**'s stamina deficiencies and conditions very much against **Highland Reel**, but Ulysses had already been unable to live with Enable's turn of foot before just holding off **Idaho** for second. Highland Reel was 4l adrift in fourth ahead of **Benbatl**, with another 6l back to **Desert Encounter**.

25 Qatar Goodwood Cup (2m) Goodwood August 1 (Good)
1 **Stradivarius** 3-8-8   Andrea Atzeni
2 **Big Orange** 6-9-7   Frankie Dettori
3 **Desert Skyline** 3-8-8   David Probert
6/1, 6/4F, 14/1. 1¾l, 3½l. 14 ran. 3m 25.47s
(John Gosden).

As a dual winner fresh from taking the staying crown at Ascot, **Big Orange** looked to have plenty in his favour, but the weight-for-age concession to a top three-year-old in **Stradivarius** proved too much. Big Orange made a typically valiant bid from the front, but the good gallop also played into the hands of the strong-staying Stradivarius, who weaved his way through the pack with a sustained run in the straight and won going away. **Desert Skyline**, another three-year-old to excel in top staying events as he went on to land the Doncaster Cup, was third ahead of **Wicklow Brave** and **She Is No Lady**.

26 Qatar Sussex Stakes (1m)
Goodwood August 2 (Soft)

1 **Here Comes When** 7-9-8   Jim Crowley
2 **Ribchester** 4-9-8   William Buick
3 **Lightning Spear** 6-9-8   Oisin Murphy
20/1, 8/13F, 8/1. nk, ¾l. 7 ran. 1m 46.11s
(Andrew Balding).

Torrential rain turned conditions upside-down and led to a big upset as the veteran **Here Comes When**, exposed as well below this level in general, took advantage of a below-par performance from **Ribchester** and the late withdrawal of Churchill. Ribchester made the running but was slow to pick up on the soft ground, so much so it looked briefly like he would be swamped, before running on again close home. It was too late to reel in Here Comes When, who relished the conditions, while **Lightning Spear** was third in a blanket finish.

27 Qatar Nassau Stakes (Fillies & Mares) (1m1f197y)
Goodwood August 3 (Soft)

1 **Winter** 3-8-13   Ryan Moore
2 **Blond Me** 5-9-7   Oisin Murphy
3 **Sobetsu** 3-8-13   William Buick
10/11F, 16/1, 6/1. 1½l, nk. 6 ran. 2m 11.79s
(A P O'Brien).

A fourth Group 1 win for **Winter** but probably the least impressive of the lot as she battled home in workmanlike fashion. Expected to appreciate the step up in trip – and even tried over further in the Arc – Winter struggled to show her usual turn of foot, perhaps affected by the conditions, but still saw off **Blond Me**, who was far more at home given she went on to win a Grade 1 in Canada on soft ground. **Sobetsu**, having dictated a steady gallop, stuck on well for third ahead of **Hydrangea**.

28 Juddmonte International Stakes (1m2f56y)
York August 23 (Good To Soft)

1 **Ulysses** 4-9-6   Jim Crowley
2 **Churchill** 3-8-13   Ryan Moore
3 **Barney Roy** 3-8-13   James Doyle
4/1, 5/2F, 11/4. 2l, nk. 7 ran. 2m 12.11s
(Sir Michael Stoute).

Ulysses finally showed his true potential when delivered late off a strong gallop, extending his Sandown superiority over **Barney Roy** as **Churchill** split the pair in a terrific race. Ulysses was always travelling strongly and found plenty when asked to quicken, drawing clear in the final furlong as Churchill also stayed on well on this step up in trip but was just outclassed. Barney Roy wasn't aided by racing too close to the strong pace but ran a brave race and did much better than the front-running **Cliffs Of Moher**, who may have found the ground softer than ideal as he finished another 4½l back in fourth ahead of **Decorated Knight**, who was found to have

MARSHA (left): takes advantage as Lady Aurelia hangs to her left

pulled muscles.

29 Darley Yorkshire Oaks (Fillies & Mares) (1m3f188y)
York August 24 (Good To Soft)
1 **Enable** 3-8-12		Frankie Dettori
2 **Coronet** 3-8-12		Olivier Peslier
3 **Queen's Trust** 4-9-7		Jim Crowley

1/4F, 16/1, 12/1. 5l, ¾l. 6 ran. 2m 35.79s (John Gosden).

More of the same from **Enable**, who made all the running with her versatility regarding the ground emphasising her superiority over fellow Group 1 winners **Queen's Trust** and **Nezwaah**, both of whom could have done with a quicker surface. With that pair below-par, **Coronet** plugged on for second but again found Enable in a different league.

30 Coolmore Nunthorpe Stakes (5f)
York August 25 (Good)
1 **Marsha** 4-9-8		Luke Morris
2 **Lady Aurelia** 3-9-6		Frankie Dettori
3 **Cotai Glory** 5-9-11		Silvestre De Sousa

8/1, 10/11F, 50/1. nse, 3¾l. 11 ran. 57.97s (Sir Mark Prescott).

A significant upset at the time and an even more puzzling one in retrospect given **Marsha** managed to beat not only **Lady Aurelia** but also the subsequent wide-margin Abbaye winner **Battaash**. Marsha finished strongly to pip Lady Aurelia on the line, clearly a much-improved filly from her previous Royal Ascot meeting and much better suited by good ground than when twice thrashed by Battaash on soft. However, Lady Aurelia probably threw away the race by hanging towards the unfavoured far side and the headstrong Battaash was clearly a long way below his best in fourth having boiled over in the preliminaries, his Chantilly demolition job confirming him as the outstanding horse of the year over this trip whereas he even finished behind stablemate **Cotai Glory** here. **Priceless** and **Profitable** were next, also done no favours by being drawn on the far side.

31 32Red Sprint Cup (6f)
Haydock September 9 (Heavy)
1 **Harry Angel** 3-9-1		Adam Kirby
2 **Tasleet** 4-9-3		Jim Crowley
3 **The Tin Man** 5-9-3		Tom Queally

2/1F, 9/2, 11/2. 4l, 1½l. 11 ran. 1m 13.90s (Clive Cox).

An even more stunning performance from **Harry Angel**, who tore through the heavy ground to storm clear of a good field. Harry Angel made all but was always travelling within himself and quickened up superbly at the furlong pole, drawing clear of **Tasleet**, who bounced back to his best in second. **The Tin Man** was next ahead of **Blue Point**.

32 Qipco Irish Champion Stakes (1m2f)
Leopardstown (IRE) September 9 (Good)
1 **Decorated Knight** 5-9-7		Andrea Atzeni
2 **Poet's Word** 4-9-7		James Doyle
3 **Eminent** 3-9-1		Frankie Dettori

25/1, 10/1, 3/1. ½l, 1¾l. 10 ran. 2m 8.36s (Roger Charlton).

Just an ordinary race for the grade, with **Churchill** odds-on despite never having won over the trip, and **Decorated Knight** proved good enough in a race that seemed to favour those delivered late down the outside. Sent off at 25-1 because of two disappointing runs, Decorated Knight bounced back to form as he stormed from last to first, just overhauling another fast finisher in the progressive **Poet's Word**. **Eminent** did well to hold on for third having made the running, although **Cliffs Of Moher** looked very unlucky not to get placed at least as he was repeatedly denied a run and Churchill was a long way below his best in seventh.

33 Coolmore Fastnet Rock Matron Stakes (Fillies & Mares) (1m)
Leopardstown (IRE) September 9 (Good)
1 **Hydrangea** 3-9-0		Wayne Lordan
2 **Winter** 3-9-0		Ryan Moore
3 **Persuasive** 4-9-5		Frankie Dettori

20/1, EvensF, 6/1. hd, ¾l. 10 ran. 1m 41.89s (A P O'Brien).

A stunning demonstration of the strength in depth at Ballydoyle as, even with **Winter** a below-par second, Aidan O'Brien still took the prize with **Hydrangea**. O'Brien's fourth string according to the betting, Hydrangea showed tremendous courage to get up on the line after Winter had failed to put the race to bed when driven to the front at the furlong pole. Subsequent QEII heroine **Persuasive** didn't have her favoured soft ground but was still a fair third ahead of **Wuheida**, while **Roly Poly** and **Rhododendron** were well beaten.

34 Comer Group International Irish St Leger (1m6f)
Curragh (IRE) September 10 (Soft)
1 **Order Of St George** 5-9-10		Ryan Moore
2 **Torcedor** 5-9-10		Colm O'Donoghue
3 **Mount Moriah** 3-9-1		Harry Bentley

2/5F, 14/1, 14/1. 9l, 4½l. 10 ran. 3m 7.82s (A P O'Brien).

A demolition job from **Order Of St George**, the second time he has run away with this race – the gap had been 11l in 2015 – over a course and distance that clearly brings out the very best in him. Ridden far more positively than in the Gold Cup, Order Of St George was in front 3f out and powered clear of **Torcedor**, who stayed on for a clear second ahead of **Mount Moriah** and **Wicklow Brave**.

35 William Hill St Leger Stakes (1m6f115y)
Doncaster September 16 (Good To Soft)

1 **Capri** 3-9-1		Ryan Moore
2 **Crystal Ocean** 3-9-1		Jim Crowley
3 **Stradivarius** 3-9-1		James Doyle

3/1F, 5/1, 9/2. ½l, shd. 11 ran. 3m 4.04s
(A P O'Brien).

It's not often any Derby winner steps up in trip these days, but **Capri** showed he had the stamina to go with his class and won what looked a strong St Leger. Even against top stayers like **Stradivarius** and Melbourne Cup winner **Rekindling**, the Ballydoyle team set out to make this a real test and Capri answered every question, staying on strongly. It proved just too much for **Crystal Ocean**, who was still a fine second, with Stradivarius also just run out of it. Rekindling was next ahead of **Coronet** and **Count Octave** before an 11l gap back to the rest, who included the bitterly disappointing Geoffrey Freer winner **Defoe**.

36 Qatar Prix de l'Arc de Triomphe (1m4f)
Chantilly (FR) October 1 (Soft)

1 **Enable** 3-8-9		Frankie Dettori
2 **Cloth Of Stars** 4-9-5	Mickael Barzalona	
3 **Ulysses** 4-9-5		Jim Crowley

10/11F, 20/1, 9/1. 2½l, 1¼l. 18 ran. 2m 28.69s
(John Gosden).

Enable crowned her astonishing campaign with a fifth Group 1 win as she stormed to a remarkably straightforward victory. Always handy, Enable quickened into the lead early in the straight and stayed on strongly, proving herself clearly the best horse in the race. That said, her superiority was perhaps exaggerated by a massive draw bias that saw the nine horses drawn in double figures fill eight of the last nine places, the exception being Prix Foy winner **Dschingis Secret** in a commendable sixth. **Cloth Of Stars** also did well having failed to make the most of his good draw before running on late into second, while **Ulysses** and **Order Of St George** were handy throughout before finishing third and fourth ahead of Prix du Jockey Club winner

Brametot. **Idaho** and **Winter** finished in mid-division, with **Capri** tailed off.

37 Kingdom of Bahrain Sun Chariot Stakes (1m)
Newmarket October 7 (Good)

1 **Roly Poly** 3-9-0		Ryan Moore
2 **Persuasive** 4-9-3		Frankie Dettori
3 **Nathra** 4-9-3		Jimmy Fortune

4/1, 9/4F, 20/1. 1¼l, 1¼l. 13 ran. 1m 34.88s
(A P O'Brien).

Roly Poly continued to defy the doubters as she put her poor run in the Matron behind her to claim a third Group 1 win. Quick to grab the favoured ground on the stands' side, Roly Poly made most of the running and stayed on strongly when pressed in the closing stages, beating **Persuasive**, who again found the ground quicker than ideal. **Nathra** was next ahead of **Usherette**, who was the best of a disappointing trio of French hopes.

38 Qipco British Champions Sprint Stakes (6f)
Ascot October 21 (Soft)

1 **Librisa Breeze** 5-9-2	Robert Winston	
2 **Tasleet** 4-9-2		Jim Crowley
3 **Caravaggio** 3-9-1		Ryan Moore

10/1, 10/1, 9/2. 1¼l, ¾l. 12 ran. 1m 16.78s
(Dean Ivory).

Soft ground, a strong gallop and a stiff headwind brought stamina to the fore and that enabled **Librisa Breeze**, arguably most effective over 7f, to pull off an upset as he stayed on strongly past **Tasleet** with the red-hot favourite **Harry Angel** only fourth. Still, Tasleet's proximity in second having been beaten so comprehensively at Haydock emphasises the extent to which Harry Angel was below his best as he tied up badly in the final 100 yards having been committed for home too soon, his apparent dislike of Ascot perhaps also playing a part. **Caravaggio** seemed to run his race in third, with **The Tin Man** fifth ahead of **Brando**.

39 Qipco British Champions Fillies & Mares Stakes (1m3f211y)
Ascot October 21 (Soft)

1 **Hydrangea** 3-8-13		Ryan Moore
2 **Bateel** 5-9-5	Pierre-Charles Boudot	
3 **Coronet** 3-8-13		Olivier Peslier

4/1, 7/4F, 11/2. 2l, 1¾l. 10 ran. 2m 40.82s
(A P O'Brien).

Stepping up in trip saw **Hydrangea** take her form to an even higher level as she showed terrific reserves of stamina to see off **Bateel** and **Coronet** in a really strong contest. Always prominent and in front turning for home, Hydrangea looked to be struggling when joined by Prix Vermeille winner Bateel before the furlong pole, but she battled hard and forged clear in the final 100 yards. Coronet was the only other horse to finish within 8½l of Hydrangea as the field finished well strung out, with the 2016 winner **Journey** among the also-rans.

40 Queen Elizabeth II Stakes (Sponsored by Qipco) (1m)

Ascot October 21 (Soft)

1	**Persuasive** 4-9-1	Frankie Dettori
2	**Ribchester** 4-9-4	William Buick
3	**Churchill** 3-9-1	Ryan Moore

8/1, 2/1F, 9/2. 1l, ½l. 15 ran. 1m 46.13s (John Gosden).

Persuasive had soft ground in her favour for the first time all season and finally landed a Group 1 on her last run before retirement. Held up early, Persuasive produced a smart turn of foot and was always in command in the final furlong, certainly enjoying the conditions far more than **Ribchester**, who ran a similar race to the Sussex Stakes as he couldn't find the required turn of foot when in front 2f out but still stayed on gamely in second. **Churchill** also plugged on well to take third from **Nathra**, with that quartet 4½l clear of **Sea Of Grace** and **Lightning Spear**.

41 Qipco Champion Stakes (1m1f212y)

Ascot October 21 (Soft)

1	**Cracksman** 3-9-1	Frankie Dettori
2	**Poet's Word** 4-9-5	Andrea Atzeni
3	**Highland Reel** 5-9-5	Ryan Moore

13/8F, 7/1, 17/2. 7l, nk. 10 ran. 2m 11.75s (John Gosden).

This didn't have a field befitting its massive prize fund but certainly produced a champion performance as **Cracksman** absolutely destroyed his rivals. A wide-margin winner of the Great Voltigeur and the Prix Niel since his near misses at Epsom and the Curragh, Cracksman easily coped with the drop in trip, helped by the ground and a strong gallop that had the field well strung out, as he hit top gear turning for home and strode further and further clear in a stunning time. Irish Champion runner-up **Poet's Word** filled the same spot ahead of **Highland Reel**, who had conditions against him but was enterprisingly ridden to get the best of the ground out wide and stayed on well. **Recoletos** and **Desert Encounter** were close behind them before another 5l gap back to **Brametot** and **Cliffs Of Moher**, who failed to handle the conditions. **Barney Roy** also hated the ground.

PERSUASIVE: signs off in style with victory in the QEII on Champions Day

Group 1 index

All horses placed or commented on in our Group 1 review section, with race numbers

Aclaim 3
Al Wukair 1
Alluringly 7
Arabian Hope 21
Barney Roy 1, 12, 20, 28, 41
Bateel 39
Battaash 30
Benbatl 9, 24
Big Orange 14, 25
Blond Me 27
Blue Point 15, 31
Bound For Nowhere 15
Brametot 36, 41
Brando 22, 38
Breton Rock 3
Capri 9, 18, 35, 36
Caravaggio 15, 22, 38
Churchill 1, 4, 12, 28, 32, 40
Cliffs Of Moher 9, 20, 28, 32, 41
Cloth Of Stars 36

Coronet 7, 23, 29, 35, 39
Cotai Glory 30
Count Octave 35
Cracksman 9, 18, 41
Crystal Ocean 35
Daban 2
Dabyah 16
Deauville 6, 10
Decorated Knight 6, 13, 20, 28, 32
Defoe 35
Desert Encounter 20, 24, 41
Desert Skyline 25
Dream Castle 1
Dschingis Secret 36
Eminent 1, 9, 20, 32
Enable 7, 23, 24, 29, 36
Eziyra 23
Frontiersman 8
Galileo Gold 3
Harbour Law 14

CORONET (right): won the Ribblesdale and ran well at Group 1 level

LIGHTNING SPEAR: now 0-12 in Group 1 races but has twice won the Celebration Mile the last two times he's dropped below the top level

Harry Angel 15, 22, 31, 38
Hawkbill...8
Here Comes When..........................26
Highland Reel.......................8, 13, 41
Hydrangea 2, 5, 16, 27, 33, 39
Idaho 24, 36
Intelligence Cross 22
Intricately...5
Irishcorrespondent.............................4
Journey 19, 39
Kaspersky 10
Lady Aurelia 11, 30
Lancaster Bomber...................1, 4, 12
Librisa Breeze 17, 38
Lightning Spear..........3, 10, 20, 26, 40
Limato...17, 22
Marsha 11, 30
Mount Moriah 34
Mutakayyef.......................................10
Nathra...37, 40
Nezwaah 19, 29
Order Of St George..............14, 34, 36
Persuasive...........................33, 37, 40
Poet's Word...............................32, 41
Priceless...30
Profitable 11, 30
Queen's Trust.............................13, 29

Rain Goddess 19, 23
Recoletos 41
Rekindling 35
Rhododendron......................2, 7, 33
Ribchester 3, 10, 26, 40
Roly Poly 5, 16, 21, 33, 37
Sea Of Grace....................................40
She Is No Lady...........................14, 25
Sobetsu...27
Somehow 6
Spectre..10
Spirit Of Valor 4
Stradivarius 25, 35
Talaayeb..2
Tasleet.........................17, 22, 31, 38
The Tin Man 17, 22, 31, 38
Thunder Snow...............................4, 12
Torcedor.....................................14, 34
Turret Rocks............................,.......19
Ulysses....................13, 20, 24, 28, 36
Usherette...37
Waldgeist 18
Wicklow Brave............................25, 34
Wings Of Eagles 9, 18
Winter 2, 5, 16, 27, 33, 36
Wuheida 21, 33

Est. 1909
RACING & FOOTBALL OUTLOOK

Two-year-old review by Dylan Hill

1 Langleys Solicitors British EBF Marygate Fillies' Stakes (Listed) (5f)
York May 19 (Soft)
1 **Main Desire** 2-8-12   Daniel Tudhope
2 **Neola** 2-8-12   Graham Lee
3 **Mistress Of Venice** 2-8-12   Luke Morris
4/1J, 4/1J, 16/1. ½l, ½l. 10 ran. 1m 1.70s
(Michael Bell).

Main Desire unfortunately missed the rest of the season with a setback, but this win worked out well enough to suggest she could still have a bright future. Main Desire shook off **Neola**, who had increasingly patchy form but won a Goodwood nursery off 89 back on soft ground and also ran well at Royal Ascot, as did **Mistress Of Venice**. Maggies Angel was another to frank the form after finishing fourth.

2 Coventry Stakes (Group 2) (6f)
Ascot June 20 (Good To Firm)
1 **Rajasinghe** 2-9-1   Stevie Donohoe
2 **Headway** 2-9-1   Pat Cosgrave
3 **Murillo** 2-9-1   Ryan Moore
11/1, 33/1, 8/1. hd, nk. 17 ran. 1m 12.39s
(Richard Spencer).

Amid a clamour for the Coventry to be upgraded to a Group 1, this race did the argument few favours as **Rajasinghe** won a desperate renewal in which the first seven remarkably failed to win another race between them all season. Looking short of pace subsequently, Rajasinghe appreciated a proper test at the trip and held off **Headway**, **Murillo** and **Brother Bear** in a tight finish, with **Aqabah** just ¾l back in fifth. **Nebo** and **US Navy Flag** proved the best of those behind.

3 Windsor Castle Stakes (Listed) (5f)
Ascot June 20 (Good To Firm)
1 **Sound And Silence** 2-9-3   William Buick
2 **Roussel** 2-9-3   James Doyle
3 **James Garfield** 2-9-3   Harry Bentley
16/1, 12/1, 25/1. nk, 1¼l. 20 ran. 59.20s
(Charlie Appleby).

One of the most tough and consistent juveniles of the year, **Sound And Silence** showcased his courage with a terrifically game victory in a strong race. Sound And Silence was just too strong for **Roussel**, with subsequent Mill Reef winner **James Garfield**, who got going too late on his only run over 5f, and Cornwallis third **Mokaatil** next.

4 Queen Mary Stakes (Group 2) (Fillies) (5f)
Ascot June 21 (Good To Firm)
1 **Heartache** 2-9-0   Adam Kirby
2 **Happy Like A Fool** 2-9-0   Ryan Moore
3 **Out Of The Flames** 2-9-0   Oisin Murphy
5/1, 10/11F, 14/1. 2½l, ½l. 22 ran. 59.63s
(Clive Cox).

Wesley Ward's US fillies have become increasingly hard to stop in this race, but **Heartache** claimed the notable scalp of **Happy Like A Fool** with an outstanding performance. Heartache had the ability to track the typically strong pace set by Happy Like A Fool and then eased clear in the final furlong as the American held off **Out Of The Flames** and **Now You're Talking** for second, with **Neola** next.

5 Norfolk Stakes (Group 2) (5f)
Ascot June 22 (Good To Firm)
1 **Sioux Nation** 2-9-1   Ryan Moore

DIFFERENT LEAGUE (right): wins at Royal Ascot and is now with Aidan O'Brien

2 **Santry** 2-9-1   Jim Crowley
3 **Cardsharp** 2-9-1   James Doyle
14/1, 13/2J, 8/1. ½l, 1½l. 17 ran. 1m 0.88s
(A P O'Brien).

A controversial result with several trainers feeling overwatering had reversed an apparent draw bias, helping **Sioux Nation** to victory with two others in his small far-side group of just four finishing in the first five. Still, that pair happened to be future Group 2 and Listed runners-up in **Frozen Angel** and **It Dont Come Easy**, with Sioux Nation's own Phoenix win also showing he was a high-class juvenile. **Santry**, who sadly died in August before getting the chance to prove the point, was perhaps unlucky, beating subsequent Group 2 winner **Cardsharp** on the near side, with **Havana Grey** only tenth.

6 Albany Stakes (Group 3) (Fillies) (6f)
Ascot June 23 (Good To Firm)
1 **Different League** 2-9-0   Antoine Hamelin
2 **Alpha Centauri** 2-9-0   Colm O'Donoghue
3 **Take Me With You** 2-9-0   Gerald Mosse
20/1, 2/1F, 20/1. nk, 3l. 19 ran. 1m 14.60s
(Matthieu Palussiere).

A red-hot race which produced the first three in the Cheveley Park, yet Newmarket runner-up **Different League** and **Alpha Centauri** proved utterly dominant. Alpha Centauri, seemingly dependent on this quick ground, ran a stormer but just couldn't get to the French raider. The pair raced away from their nearest rivals on the far side, but **Clemmie**, who would go on to prove the year's outstanding juvenile filly, was next in their group and beaten nearly 5l, suggesting it would be wrong to make too much of the draw. However, there was depth all over the race, with Cheveley Park third **Madeline** and Group 3 winner **Actress** prominent on the near side behind **Take Me With You** and **Mistress Of Venice**.

7 Chesham Stakes (Listed) (7f)
Ascot June 24 (Good To Firm)
1 **September** 2-8-12   Ryan Moore
2 **Nyaleti** 2-8-12   J F Egan
3 **Masar** 2-9-3   William Buick
11/8F, 10/1, 3/1. 2¼l, shd. 15 ran. 1m 26.70s
(A P O'Brien).

Three very smart juveniles were vastly superior to the rest, most notably **September**. Relishing the quick ground, September quickened past a rock-solid yardstick in **Nyaleti**, who perhaps did just too much in front but still managed to hold off the subse-

HAVANA GREY: won two Listed races at Sandown, where he seems to excel

quent Solario winner **Masar** for second. That trio were 3½l clear of **Bartholomeu Dias**, with **Hey Gaman** only ninth.

8 Betway Empress Fillies' Stakes (Listed) (6f)
Newmarket (July) July 1 (Good To Soft)
1 **Dance Diva** 2-9-0   William Buick
2 **Maggies Angel** 2-9-0   Gerald Mosse
3 **So Hi Society** 2-9-0   Robert Winston
3/1F, 8/1, 10/1. 1¼l, 1l. 11 ran. 1m 11.73s
(Richard Fahey).

A good Listed race even though the winner, **Dance Diva**, didn't quite hit the heights expected of her. Dance Diva saw off **Maggies Angel** with subsequent Lowther fourth **So Hi Society** next, that trio pulling 3¾l clear of the rest. **Tajaanus** didn't get a clear run behind and came home sixth.

9 GAIN Railway Stakes (Group 2) (6f)
Curragh (IRE) July 1 (Good To Yielding)
1 **Beckford** 2-9-3   Declan McDonogh
2 **Verbal Dexterity** 2-9-3   Kevin Manning
3 **Murillo** 2-9-3   Ryan Moore
11/2, 100/30, 6/4F. 1l, 1¼l. 8 ran. 1m 11.71s
(Gordon Elliott).

Even with Coventry third **Murillo** found wanting, this still produced a terrific clash as **Beckford** claimed a big scalp in **Verbal Dexterity**, with the trip playing far more to his strengths. Unable to win again but with excuses more than once, Beckford had too much speed for

the subsequent National Stakes winner, with Murillo only third.

10 Grangecon Stud Stakes (Group 3) (Fillies) (6f)
Curragh (IRE) July 2 (Good)
1 **Clemmie** 2-9-0   Ryan Moore
2 **Butterscotch** 2-9-0   Seamie Heffernan
3 **Mamba Noire** 2-9-0   Shane Foley
6/4F, 3/1, 25/1. 2¾l, ¾l. 8 ran. 1m 11.87s
(A P O'Brien).

Clemmie got back on track after her Royal Ascot effort with a tremendously smooth victory. Clemmie was ridden clear of her front-running stablemate **Butterscotch** in the final furlong, while **Mamba Noire**, twice third at a higher level later in the season, was next.

11 Allied World Dragon Stakes (Listed) (5f10y)
Sandown July 7 (Good To Firm)
1 **Havana Grey** 2-9-5   P J McDonald
2 **Roussel** 2-9-2   James Doyle
3 **To Wafij** 2-9-2   Andrea Atzeni
3/1, 5/4F, 12/1. 1¼l, nk. 7 ran. 1m 0.59s
(K R Burke).

Havana Grey had disappointed at Royal Ascot, but the return to Sandown, where he had won the National Stakes, saw him land a second Listed success. Havana Grey gave 3lb and a comfortable beating to a smart rival in **Roussel**, who just held off **To Wafij** for second with that trio 5l clear of the rest.

12 Arqana July Stakes (Group 2) (6f)
Newmarket (July) July 13 (Good)
1 **Cardsharp** 2-9-0 — James Doyle
2 **US Navy Flag** 2-9-0 — Ryan Moore
3 **Rajasinghe** 2-9-3 — Stevie Donohoe
8/1, 10/1, 100/30. 1¾l, ¾l. 11 ran. 1m 11.75s
(Mark Johnston).

Probably not helped by the draw at Royal Ascot, **Cardsharp** stepped up over an extra furlong to storm to a terrific win over **US Navy Flag**, who was still very much a work in progress at this stage. **Rajasinghe** got going too late, finishing fast to snatch third from a rock-solid yardstick in **Invincible Army**, and that quartet pulled 2l clear of **Alba Power** and **Enjazaat** with **It Dont Come Easy**, **Sound And Silence** and **Hey Gaman** further back.

13 Duchess of Cambridge Stakes (Sponsored by bet365) (Group 2) (6f)
Newmarket (July) July 14 (Good To Firm)
1 **Clemmie** 2-9-0 — Ryan Moore
2 **Nyaleti** 2-9-0 — William Buick
3 **Mamba Noire** 2-9-0 — Andrea Atzeni
11/8F, 7/4, 20/1. 1¾l, ½l. 7 ran. 1m 10.34s
(A P O'Brien).

Another excellent win from **Clemmie**, who was probably racing well within herself as she drew clear of **Nyaleti**. The front-running Chesham runner-up seemed better suited to this shorter trip for now, but she was still no match for **Clemmie**, who had **Mamba Noire** finish closer to her in third than she had at the Curragh. **Mistress Of Venice** and **Out Of The Flames** were also close behind, the latter not quite getting home, with **So Hi Society** sixth.

14 bet365 Superlative Stakes (Group 2) (7f)
Newmarket (July) July 15 (Good To Firm)
1 **Gustav Klimt** 2-9-1 — Ryan Moore
2 **Nebo** 2-9-1 — Jim Crowley
3 **Great Prospector** 2-9-1 — Paul Hanagan
5/6F, 10/1, 12/1. hd, ½l. 10 ran. 1m 25.39s
(A P O'Brien).

A spectacular win from **Gustav Klimt**, who lost his place when badly hampered 2f out but picked up again in stunning fashion to nail **Nebo** on the line. That said, Gustav Klimt wasn't seen again to back this up – he missed the National Stakes with a stone bruise and then suffered a muscle tear – and may have beaten nothing given how badly the form worked out. Nebo went on to win the Horris Hill, albeit after four more defeats, but among the rest of the field, tenth-placed

Maksab's nose win in a nursery off 83 was the only success later in the season, with six runs in Group races seeing them beaten further every time.

15 Jebel Ali Silver Jubilee Anglesey Stakes (Group 3) (6f63y)
Curragh (IRE) July 15 (Good To Firm)
1 **Actress** 2-9-0 — Seamie Heffernan
2 **Theobald** 2-9-3 — Kevin Manning
3 **Brother Bear** 2-9-3 — Colm O'Donoghue
7/1, 100/30, 9/10F. 1¾l, ½l. 5 ran. 1m 14.26s
(A P O'Brien).

Beaten at odds-on by Sirici in a 5f Listed race at Tipperary on her previous start, **Actress** relished a much longer trip as she ran out a comfortable winner. The only filly in the line-up, Actress saw off **Theobald** with Coventry fourth **Brother Bear** a disappointing third.

16 JRA Tyros Stakes (Group 3) (7f)
Leopardstown (IRE) July 27 (Good)
1 **The Pentagon** 2-9-3 — Ryan Moore
2 **Theobald** 2-9-3 — Kevin Manning
3 **Would Be King** 2-9-3 — Colin Keane
4/11F, 4/1, 8/1. 1¾l, ½l. 6 ran. 1m 28.05s
(A P O'Brien).

The Pentagon, sent off at 4-11 after a stunning maiden win at the Curragh, duly made the step up to Pattern level, although the subsequent Racing Post Trophy third did no more than he was entitled to do in victory. The Pentagon had to be strongly ridden before asserting close home to beat **Theobald** by the same margin as Actress had managed in the Anglesey, with **Berkeley Square** among those behind.

17 Longines Irish Champions Weekend EBF Stallions Star Stakes (Listed) (7f)
Sandown July 27 (Good To Soft)
1 **Tajaanus** 2-9-0 — Jim Crowley
2 **Capomento** 2-9-0 — Richard Kingscote
3 **Billesdon Brook** 2-9-0 — Sean Levey
8/1, 14/1, 5/2J. nse, nk. 10 ran. 1m 30.76s
(Richard Hannon).

A fiercely competitive contest with three fillies who would score at a higher level involved, including the victorious **Tajaanus**. **Billesdon Brook**, another subsequent Group 3 winner, perhaps paid the price for committing too soon as she was reeled in close home by Tajaanus and **Capomento**, but the winner was improving fast and proved better again in the Sweet Solera. **So Hi Society** was fourth ahead of **Whitefountainfairy** and **Ellthea**.

18 Princess Margaret Juddmonte Stakes (Group 3) (Fillies) (6f)

Ascot July 29 (Good To Soft)

1 **Nyaleti** 2-9-0		Ryan Moore
2 **Dance Diva** 2-9-0		Paul Hanagan
3 **Musical Art** 2-9-0		Fran Berry

2/1F, 9/4, 12/1. 5l, 1¾l. 6 ran. 1m 14.62s (Mark Johnston).

After two fine runs in defeat behind September and Clemmie, **Nyaleti** gained a much-deserved victory and even seemed to improve for encountering some cut in the ground. Nyaleti stayed on strongly and drew clear of **Dance Diva**, who in turn beat the rest well with **Rebel Assault**, **Neola** and **Mistress Of Venice** among those behind.

19 Qatar Vintage Stakes (Group 2) (7f)

Goodwood August 1 (Good)

1 **Expert Eye** 2-9-1		Andrea Atzeni
2 **Zaman** 2-9-1		William Buick
3 **Mildenberger** 2-9-1		James Doyle

7/4F, 8/1, 7/2. 4½l, ¾l. 10 ran. 1m 26.97s (Sir Michael Stoute).

A special performance from **Expert Eye** at first glance and, even after flopping in the Dewhurst, the form of those behind suggests this was indeed as good as it looked. Cruising to the front 2f out, Expert Eye soon had a strong field in trouble and powered clear in the final furlong. Runner-up **Zaman** had been one of those made to look like trees by Gustav Klimt in the Superlative, but he didn't get another chance to prove himself an improved colt and the next three – **Mildenberger**, **James Garfield** and **Seahenge** – all franked the form in their subsequent races.

20 Bombay Sapphire Molecomb Stakes (Group 3) (5f)

Goodwood August 2 (Soft)

1 **Havana Grey** 2-9-1		P J McDonald
2 **Invincible Army** 2-9-1		Martin Harley
3 **To Wafij** 2-9-1		Andrea Atzeni

7/2, 5/2F, 8/1. 1¾l, nse. 10 ran. 1m 0.89s (K R Burke).

Very impressive in two wins at Sandown on good to firm ground, **Havana Grey** proved just as effective on soft as he stormed to another commanding victory. Havana Grey made all the running and was going away from **Invincible Army** at the line, with **To Wafij**, third behind the winner previously, doing even better in third again. That trio pulled 4½l clear of the rest, including **It Dont Come Easy** in sixth.

21 Qatar Richmond Stakes (Group 2) (6f)

Goodwood August 3 (Soft)

1 **Barraquero** 2-9-0		William Buick
2 **Nebo** 2-9-0		Jim Crowley
3 **Cardsharp** 2-9-3		James Doyle

4/1, 3/1, 2/1F. 1¼l, 2¼l. 7 ran. 1m 15.42s (Brian Meehan).

Not a particularly competitive Group 2 with heavy rain turning the ground against a couple of leading contenders, but **Barraquero** coped with the conditions well. Ruled out for the rest of the season with a minor shin injury, Barraquero quickened up smartly from the rear and beat **Nebo**, who was dropping back from 7f after his Superlative second. **Cardsharp** was one of those most inconvenienced by the ground in third, with **Headway** another to run below-par in sixth.

22 german-thoroughbred.comSweet Solera Stakes (Group 3) (Fillies) (7f)

Newmarket (July) August 12 (Good To Soft)

1 **Tajaanus** 2-9-0		Dane O'Neill
2 **Juliet Capulet** 2-9-0		Robert Tart
3 **Capla Temptress** 2-9-0		Harry Bentley

10/1, 20/1, 5/1. 1l, 1l. 9 ran. 1m 26.35s (Richard Hannon).

A clearcut win for **Tajaanus**, aided by a brilliant ride from Dane O'Neill as he made all the running up the rail while all but one of the other riders went up the centre. That main group was led home by two leading juveniles in subsequent Rockfel winner **Juliet Capulet** and Canadian Grade 1 heroine **Capla Temptress**, with Tajaanus perhaps flattered to beat that pair so well, though she was still 4½l clear of a useful filly in **Mamba Noire** on her side. **Ertiyad** was fourth ahead of the favourite **Poetic Charm**, with **Dance Diva** a non-stayer behind.

23 Keeneland Phoenix Stakes (Group 1) (6f)

Curragh (IRE) August 13 (Good To Firm)

1 **Sioux Nation** 2-9-3		Ryan Moore
2 **Beckford** 2-9-3		Declan McDonogh
3 **Actress** 2-9-0		Seamie Heffernan

2/1, 15/8F, 5/1. ½l, 1½l. 8 ran. 1m 11.72s (A P O'Brien).

A terrific battle between **Sioux Nation** and **Beckford**, with the Norfolk winner seeing out the extra furlong well to come out on top. Held up early, Sioux Nation produced a strong run to lead inside the final furlong and was always holding Beckford. The rest finished in a heap behind, led by **Actress**, who again did well taking on the colts, from **US Navy Flag**, **Frozen Angel** and **Romanised**.

24 Denford Stakes (Listed) (formerly the Washington Singer Stakes) (7f)

Newbury August 19 (Soft)

1 **Hey Gaman** 2-9-1   Martin Harley
2 **Red Mist** 2-9-1   Silvestre De Sousa
3 **Another Batt** 2-9-1   Robert Winston
100/30, 9/4F, 9/2. shd, 1¾l. 6 ran. 1m 28.79s (James Tate).

Hey Gaman had twice come up short when highly tried earlier in the season, but he was making giant strides at this time and won a good Listed race. Hey Gaman made all and just held off the favourite **Red Mist**, while **Another Batt**, beaten just a neck by Raydiance at this level at Ascot in July, was third ahead of **Learn By Heart**.

25 Galileo Irish EBF Futurity Stakes (Group 2) (7f)

Curragh (IRE) August 20 (Yielding To Soft)

1 **Rostropovich** 2-9-3   Ryan Moore
2 **Coat Of Arms** 2-9-3   Donnacha O'Brien
3 **Berkeley Square** 2-9-3 Seamie Heffernan
11/8F, 7/1, 4/1. shd, 1¾l. 5 ran. 1m 29.29s (A P O'Brien).

A desperately weak Group 2 in which **Rostropovich**, put firmly in his place in the National Stakes, beat a trio of colts who were all beaten significantly further on their other ventures into Group company. Rostropovich needed all his stamina to edge past the front-running **Coat Of Arms**, while **Berkeley Square** just pipped **Camelback** for third.

26 Breast Cancer Research Debutante Stakes (Group 2) (Fillies) (7f)

Curragh (IRE) August 20 (Soft)

1 **Magical** 2-9-0   Donnacha O'Brien
2 **Happily** 2-9-0   Ryan Moore
3 **Mary Tudor** 2-9-0   W J Lee
11/1, 6/4, 12/1. 1¼l, 1¼l. 8 ran. 1m 29.64s (A P O'Brien).

A really strong contest thanks to Aidan O'Brien unveiling his big guns as the first two also went on to dominate the Moyglare, although this time **Magical** got the better of **Happily**. That owed much to a fine front-running ride as Magical set a steady pace that caused several rivals to race keenly, including Happily, before quickening up smartly to put the race to bed. **Mary Tudor** ran a cracker to finish a clear third ahead of **September**, who failed to act on the soft ground.

27 Qatar Racing and Equestrian Club Curragh Stakes (Group 3) (5f)

Curragh (IRE) August 20 (Soft)

1 **Treasuring** 2-9-0   Colin Keane
2 **Goodthingstaketime** 2-9-0   Chris Hayes
3 **Sirici** 2-9-0   Pat Smullen

HEY GAMAN (near side): a big improver in the second half of the season

THREADING: Lowther win still reads well despite her Cheveley Park flop

3/1, 9/4F, 9/2. ½l, ½l. 6 ran. 1m 2.35s
(G M Lyons).

This race lacked a star and battle-hardened **Treasuring**, who would later move to the US, put her experience to good use in holding off **Goodthingstaketime**. **Sirici**, a surprise Listed winner over Actress in June but regarded as nothing more than an early two-year-old by her trainer, fared better than some expected in third but couldn't match her best form on softer ground.

28 Darley Prix Morny (Group 1) (6f) Deauville (FR) August 20 (Good)

1 **Unfortunately** 2-9-0   Tony Piccone
2 **Havana Grey** 2-9-0   P J McDonald
3 **Different League** 2-8-10 Antoine Hamelin
57/10, 31/5, 4/1. 1¼l, shd. 7 ran. 1m 8.92s
(K R Burke).

A one-two for the British raiders, with **Unfortunately** beating **Havana Grey**. Progressive in his five previous runs, culminating in victory in the Prix Robert Papin at Maisons-Laffitte, Unfortunately improved again and comfortably quickened clear, though his task was made easier by Havana Grey not quite seeing out this step up in trip. French fillies **Different League** and **Zonza** were just behind him, with **Nyaleti** and the favourite **Tantheem** both disappointing.

29 Tattersalls Acomb Stakes (Group 3) (7f)

York August 23 (Good To Soft)
1 **Wells Farhh Go** 2-9-1   David Allan
2 **James Garfield** 2-9-1   Frankie Dettori
3 **Lansky** 2-9-1   Gerald Mosse
10/1, 10/1, 8/1. nse, 3¾l. 11 ran. 1m 26.32s
(Tim Easterby).

A thrilling finish involving **Wells Farhh Go** and **James Garfield**, with the staying power of Wells Farhh Go just taking him past his speedier rival. James Garfield showed a good turn of foot to quicken clear, but he would need to drop back to 6f to make his Pattern breakthrough and was nailed on the line as Wells Farhh Go got going just in time. The pair pulled well clear of **Lansky**, who would also return to 6f, while **Dee Ex Bee** was only sixth.

30 Goffs Premier Yearling Stakes (6f)

York August 24 (Good To Soft)
1 **Tangled** 2-8-11   Sean Levey
2 **Great Prospector** 2-8-11   Paul Hanagan
3 **Hey Jonesy** 2-9-0   Kevin Stott
15/2, 9/2, 3/1F. nk, ½l. 19 ran. 1m 12.23s
(Richard Hannon).

By far the strongest two-year-old sales race of the season, dominated by three smart colts. **Tangled**, close at Group 3 level later in the season, came out on top and subsequent

Middle Park fourth **Hey Jonesy**, who was perhaps undone by a high draw, was third, with **Great Prospector**, the only disappointment among them when a beaten favourite in a similar race won by Laugh A Minute at Doncaster, doing really well to split that pair. **Alba Power** was fourth and there was a 3l gap back to **Darkanna**.

31 Sky Bet Lowther Stakes (Group 2) (Fillies) (6f)

York August 24 (Good To Soft)

1	**Threading** 2-9-0	James Doyle
2	**Madeline** 2-9-0	Andrea Atzeni
3	**Mamba Noire** 2-9-0	Shane Foley

9/2, 7/2, 25/1. 1¾l, ¾l. 9 ran. 1m 12.48s (Mark Johnston).

The flop of the favourite **Actress** and **Happy Like A Fool**'s failure to stay made this far more winnable, but there was still plenty of depth to the race and **Threading** produced a smart performance in victory over Cheveley Park third **Madeline**. Threading went on to disappoint in that race herself, but this was much better as she produced a storming run to draw clear of Madeline, who was second ahead of **Mamba Noire**, **So Hi Society** and **Special Purpose**. Happy Like A Fool faded into sixth, with Actress tailed off in ninth.

32 British Stallion Studs EBF Stonehenge Stakes (Listed) (1m)

Salisbury August 25 (Good)

1	**Mildenberger** 2-9-1	Franny Norton
2	**Albishr** 2-9-1	Dougie Costello
3	**Tigre Du Terre** 2-9-1	Sean Levey

11/10F, 28/1, 7/2. nse, ¾l. 7 ran. 1m 42.15s (Mark Johnston).

A drop in grade for **Mildenberger** and he just about took advantage, edging out **Albishr** by a nose. Albishr ran a long way above all of his other form, but **Tigre Du Terre** would prove a solid performer at this level and that trio pulled 8l clear of the rest to suggest this was a decent race.

33 Al Basti Equiworld Gimcrack Stakes (Group 2) (6f)

York August 26 (Good)

1	**Sands Of Mali** 2-9-0	Paul Hanagan
2	**Invincible Army** 2-9-0	Martin Harley
3	**Cardsharp** 2-9-3	James Doyle

14/1, 9/2C, 5/1. 2¾l, 1l. 10 ran. 1m 11.16s (Richard Fahey).

A hard result to work out, with **Sands Of Mali** storming to a comprehensive success but one at odds with the rest of his form. Sands Of Mali made all and drew clear in the final furlong when pressed, but he failed to back up this run in two subsequent outings and there are other reasons to question the form, with the fifth, **Staxton**, beaten much further by Invincible Army in the Mill Reef and twice held in Listed races while **Nebo** scoped badly after his sixth. That suggests **Invincible Army** may well have been below his best despite running on into second ahead of dead-heaters **Cardsharp**, who was carrying a penalty, and **Headway**.

34 Julia Graves Roses Stakes (Listed) (5f)

York August 26 (Good)

1	**Sound And Silence** 2-9-3	James Doyle
2	**Abel Handy** 2-9-0	Tom Eaves
3	**Out Of The Flames** 2-8-9	Martin Lane

9/2, 10/1, 9/1. ½l, nk. 10 ran. 59.19s (Charlie Appleby).

A strong Listed sprint and **Sound And Silence** did really well to defy a penalty and run down his subsequent Cornwallis conqueror **Abel Handy**. **Out Of The Flames** bounced back to form in her optimum conditions with a fine third ahead of **Bengali Boys**, who had won the Super Sprint by six lengths but found this tougher company just too much.

35 Grosvenor Sport Prestige Stakes (Group 3) (Fillies) (7f)

Goodwood August 26 (Good)

1	**Billesdon Brook** 2-9-0	Sean Levey
2	**Whitefountainfairy** 2-9-0	Oisin Murphy
3	**Miss Bar Beach** 2-9-0	Shane Kelly

4/1, 10/1, 33/1. ¾l, ¾l. 10 ran. 1m 26.55s (Richard Hannon).

A modest race for the grade and **Billesdon Brook** managed to win despite plenty going against her. Stuck wide throughout without cover, Billesdon Brook still did enough to beat **Whitefountainfary**, who finished closer to her than she had previously at Sandown. The next two, **Miss Bar Beach** and **Quivery**, were both found out subsequently, while **Ertiyad** was below her best in sixth ahead of **Izzy Bizu**.

36 Flame Of Tara Irish EBF Stakes (Group 3) (Fillies) (1m)

Curragh (IRE) August 27 (Yielding)

1	**Liquid Amber** 2-9-0	W J Lee
2	**Ballet Shoes** 2-9-0	Ryan Moore
3	**Sometimesadiamond** 2-9-0	K Manning

10/1, 2/7F, 14/1. 5l, 2l. 7 ran. 1m 39.17s (W McCreery).

A terrific performance from **Liquid Amber** as she put 2-7 favourite **Ballet Shoes** firmly in her place, quickening clear in hugely impressive fashion. Ballet Shoes, who had easily won a Listed race at Tipperary, admittedly took less beating than seemed likely at the time, with **Sometimesadiamond** continuing to come up short after her third place and **Bye Bye Baby** yet to reach her subsequent Listed-winning form on just her second start, but Liquid Amber put big gaps into them and beat Ballet Shoes by further than several other smart fillies later in the season.

37 Longines Irish Champions Weekend EBF Ripon Champion 2YO Trophy (Listed) (6f)
Ripon August 28 (Good)
1 **Enjazaat** 2-9-3   Jim Crowley
2 **Tip Two Win** 2-9-3   Tom Marquand
3 **Lake Volta** 2-9-3   Franny Norton
7/2, 16/1, 5/4F. 2l, ¾l. 7 ran. 1m 11.79s
(Owen Burrows).

Enjazaat twice flopped in stronger company, but this confirmed his credentials as a very smart colt as he comfortably saw off a couple of useful rivals. Enjazaat was pushed out to beat **Tip Two Win** and **Lake Volta**, with the runner-up really doing his bit for the form subsequently, and the rest were well strung out.

38 BetBright Solario Stakes (Group 3) (7f)
Sandown September 2 (Good)
1 **Masar** 2-9-1   James Doyle
2 **Romanised** 2-9-1   Shane Foley
3 **Arbalet** 2-9-1   Ryan Moore
11/8F, 7/1, 14/1. 2l, 1¼l. 7 ran. 1m 27.89s
(Charlie Appleby).

An impressive victory from **Masar**, who comfortably saw off a decent yardstick in **Romanised**, though the form would hardly set the world alight. **Arbalet** was third ahead of **Purser**, who couldn't get a clear run in the closing stages, with **Vintager** next before a big gap back to **Connect** as he faded after going off too fast in front.

39 Bathwick Tyres Dick Poole Fillies' Stakes (Group 3) (6f)
Salisbury September 7 (Good)
1 **Anna Nerium** 2-9-0   Tom Marquand
2 **Eirene** 2-9-0   Adam Kirby
3 **Special Purpose** 2-9-0 Oisin Murphy
40/1, 7/2C, 7/2C. nk, shd. 12 ran. 1m 15.30s
(Richard Hannon).

This looked a solid Group 3 with two of the co-favourites – **Eirene**, who had won a Listed race at Newbury and went on to finish sixth

in the Cheveley Park, and Lowther fifth **Special Purpose** – to the fore, yet it produced a big surprise as 40-1 shot **Anna Nerium** pipped both of them. Anna Nerium was outpaced, but she had already won over 7f and a strong gallop saw her greater stamina prove decisive at the death, with a subsequent flop in the Oh So Sharp leaving questions over whether the race simply fell into her lap. **Izzy Bizu** was among the also-rans.

40 totepool Sirenia Stakes (Group 3) (6f)
Kempton (AW) September 9 (Standard To Slow)
1 **Invincible Army** 2-9-1   Martin Harley
2 **Corinthia Knight** 2-9-1 Oisin Murphy
3 **Lake Volta** 2-9-1   Franny Norton
11/8F, 11/4, 10/1. 1½l, 3¾l. 8 ran. 1m 11.02s
(James Tate).

Close in a number of Group races over the season, **Invincible Army** was found a more straightforward opportunity and took full advantage with what looked an improved performance. Invincible Army comfortably quickened past **Corinthia Knight**, who also did well to pull 3¾l clear of **Lake Volta** in third.

41 32Red Casino Ascendant Stakes (Listed) (1m37y)
Haydock September 9 (Heavy)
1 **Chilean** 2-9-2   Silvestre De Sousa
2 **Learn By Heart** 2-9-2   Jim Crowley
3 **Dee Ex Bee** 2-9-2   Adam Kirby
6/1, 4/1, 3/1F. 3½l, ½l. 7 ran. 1m 47.73s
(Martyn Meade).

A terrific performance from **Chilean**, who was keen early but produced a powerful run to draw clear of some decent rivals and went on to acquit himself well in a red-hot Racing Post Trophy. **Learn By Heart**, **Dee Ex Bee** and **Dark Acclaim** filled the next three places and were all beaten further than in other Listed races over the season.

42 Willis Towers Watson Champions Juvenile Stakes (Group 3) (1m)
Leopardstown (IRE) September 9 (Good To Yielding)
1 **Nelson** 2-9-3   Donnacha O'Brien
2 **Kew Gardens** 2-9-3   Seamie Heffernan
3 **Delano Roosevelt** 2-9-3 Ryan Moore
11/2, 10/1, 11/10F. 3l, ¾l. 10 ran. 1m 47.35s
(A P O'Brien).

An excellent performance from a top-class colt in **Nelson**, who made nearly all the running and stormed clear of a strong field. **Kew Gardens** and **Delano Roosevelt** were never

MASAR: impressive in the Solario but the form hardly set the world alight

in a position to challenge, though Kew Gardens had been pushed along from shortly after halfway as he struggled to match Nelson's gallop. That pair stayed on past **Riyazan** and **Camelback**, who was beaten much further than he had been in the Futurity.

43 Goffs Vincent O'Brien National Stakes (Group 1) (7f)
Curragh (IRE) September 10 (Soft To Heavy)
1 **Verbal Dexterity** 2-9-3   Kevin Manning
2 **Beckford** 2-9-3   Pat Smullen
3 **Rostropovich** 2-9-3   Ryan Moore
5/2, 6/4F, 7/1. 3½l, 2¾l. 7 ran. 1m 27.32s
(J S Bolger).

An extra furlong helped **Verbal Dexterity** to comfortably reverse Railway Stakes form with **Beckford**. Verbal Dexterity relished the longer distance and stayed on strongly in very testing conditions, although Beckford's failure to last home meant there was little meaningful opposition. **Rostropovich** was left as the Aidan O'Brien number one when Gustav Klimt suffered a setback but had his limitations exposed in third despite extending his Futurity superiority over **Coat Of Arms** and **Berkeley Square**, while **Brother Bear** was another to struggle.

44 Moyglare Stud Stakes (Group 1) (Fillies) (7f)
Curragh (IRE) September 10 (Soft To Heavy)
1 **Happily** 2-9-0   Donnacha O'Brien
2 **Magical** 2-9-0   Ryan Moore
3 **September** 2-9-0   Seamie Heffernan
13/2, 9/4, 4/1. shd, 3¾l. 8 ran. 1m 26.93s
(A P O'Brien).

A very similar race to the Debutante, but **Happily** managed to reverse the form with **Magical** in a more truly run contest. Again ridden close behind the front-running Magical, who went a little quicker this time even on softer ground, Happily just proved the strongest in the closing stages, getting up in the final strides in a thriller. The pair were again clear of **September**, who hated the conditions but showed a bit more zip in third, while **Alpha Centauri** failed to cope in fifth with **Ballet Shoes** behind.

45 William Hill May Hill Stakes (Group 2) (Fillies) (1m)
Doncaster September 14 (Good To Soft)
1 **Laurens** 2-9-0   P J McDonald
2 **Dark Rose Angel** 2-9-0   Paul Mulrennan
3 **Nyaleti** 2-9-0   James Doyle
11/4F, 14/1, 4/1. hd, hd. 8 ran. 1m 40.06s
(K R Burke).

This didn't look a vintage renewal, but **Laurens** proved much better than the bare form when following up in the Fillies' Mile. Unsuited by a steady gallop, Laurens did well to get up on the line in a blanket finish, just edging out Doncaster maiden winner **Dark Rose Angel** and **Nyaleti**, who dictated the pace and just about saw out a trip that probably stretches her. **Sizzling**, well down the pecking

101

order at Ballydoyle, was nonetheless just a neck further back in fourth ahead of **Billesdon Brook**, who was too keen to do herself justice, the disappointing **Tajaanus** and **Miss Bar Beach**.

46 Wainwrights Flying Childers Stakes (Group 2) (5f3y)
Doncaster September 15 (Good To Soft)
1	**Heartache** 2-8-12	Ryan Moore
2	**Havana Grey** 2-9-1	P J McDonald
3	**May Girl** 2-8-12	Andrea Atzeni

6/4, EvensF, 10/1. ½l, 4½l. 9 ran. 58.73s (Clive Cox).

The 5f juvenile championship produced a great clash between the two outstanding horses over the trip, **Heartache** and **Havana Grey**, with the filly Heartache just too good. Beaten only once when coming back very sore after the Prix Robert Papin, Heartache made light of a layoff when driven past Havana Grey in the final 100 yards. There was little opposition to the front pair, but they pulled 4½l clear of the next two in the market, **May Girl** and **Pursuing The Dream**, with another 3l gap back to the rest.

47 Weatherbys Bank Foreign Exchange Flying Scotsman Stakes (Listed) (7f6y)
Doncaster September 15 (Good To Soft)

1	**Tip Two Win** 2-9-0	Adam Kirby
2	**Tigre Du Terre** 2-9-0	Ryan Moore
3	**Aqabah** 2-9-0	James Doyle

11/2, 15/8F, 7/2. 2l, nk. 8 ran. 1m 25.58s (Roger Teal).

An excellent win from **Tip Two Win**, who had finished a good second to Enjazaat at Ripon and relished this extra furlong. **Tigre Du Terre** stayed on well to take second from **Aqabah**.

48 Howcroft Industrial Supplies Champagne Stakes (Group 2) (7f6y)
Doncaster September 16 (Good To Soft)

1	**Seahenge** 2-9-0	Donnacha O'Brien
2	**Hey Gaman** 2-9-0	Martin Harley
3	**Mythical Magic** 2-9-0	James Doyle

8/1, 6/1, 9/4F. nk, nk. 7 ran. 1m 25.78s (A P O'Brien).

Victory for Aidan O'Brien's second string on jockey bookings in **Seahenge** and, while that is often the case with Ballydoyle, that was the first sign that this would prove a very weak renewal. The Vintage fifth had clearly improved, as had runner-up **Hey Gaman** on a line through **Red Mist** after their Newbury clash, but Seahenge and favourite **Mythical Magic**, a close third, would both prove disappointing subsequently. The trio were 4l clear of Red

HEARTACHE: proved herself the fastest juvenile around in the Flying Childers

Mist, while **Dream Today** and **Mendelssohn** probably found the ground against them.

49 Dubai Duty Free Mill Reef Stakes (Group 2) (6f)
Newbury September 23 (Good)
1 **James Garfield** 2-9-1   Frankie Dettori
2 **Invincible Army** 2-9-1   Martin Harley
3 **Nebo** 2-9-1   Ryan Moore
100/30, 5/2F, 15/2. ¾l, ½l. 9 ran. 1m 10.64s (George Scott).

This race lacked a superstar but there was still plenty of solid Group form on show and Acomb runner-up **James Garfield** stepped up on that near miss over this shorter trip, holding off **Invincible Army**, who may well have gone even closer but for being short of room as the winner made his move. Given this was a new juvenile track record, the first two perhaps benefited from being ridden off the pace and **Nebo** did best of those ridden prominently in third, with **Lansky** also staying on from the rear, albeit another 3½l back, in fourth. **Staxton** dropped out to finish sixth having held every chance, with **Enjazaat** particularly disappointing behind.

50 Juddmonte Beresford Stakes (Group 2) (1m)
Naas (IRE) September 24 (Soft)
1 **Saxon Warrior** 2-9-3   Ryan Moore
2 **Delano Roosevelt** 2-9-3 Seamie Heffernan
3 **Warm The Voice** 2-9-3   Kevin Manning
5/6F, 3/1, 12/1. 2½l, hd. 5 ran. 1m 46.45s (A P O'Brien).

A really strong race with four very useful juveniles, including the subsequent wide-margin Zetland winner **Kew Gardens**, put firmly in their place by the brilliant **Saxon Warrior**, who showed plenty of speed to quicken clear off a steady gallop. Three of those behind had locked horns previously at Leopardstown and **Delano Roosevelt** improved past Kew Gardens and beat **Riyazan** much more comfortably than that day, the latter bringing up the rear but beaten just 4¾l, with the in-form **Warm The Voice**, on a four-timer after two nursery wins, doing well to finish among them in third.

51 C.L. & M.F. Weld Park Stakes (Group 3) (Fillies) (7f)
Naas (IRE) September 24 (Soft)
1 **Ellthea** 2-9-0   Colm O'Donoghue
2 **Sizzling** 2-9-0   Ryan Moore
3 **Ballet Shoes** 2-9-0   Donnacha O'Brien
10/1, 3/1, 6/1. 2¾l, ½l. 9 ran. 1m 30.23s (K R Burke).

Ellthea had flopped when previously stepped up in grade, but she showed her true colours with a convincing triumph and would prove herself again when running much better than the bare form of her Fillies' Mile fifth. Ellthea stayed on strongly to pull clear of **Sizzling** and **Ballet Shoes**, while Debutante Stakes third **Mary Tudor** failed to run up to her best in fourth.

52 Tattersalls Stakes (Group 3) (registered as the Somerville Stakes) (7f)
Newmarket September 28 (Good To Soft)
1 **Elarqam** 2-9-0   Jim Crowley
2 **Tip Two Win** 2-9-0   Adam Kirby
3 **Tangled** 2-9-0   Sean Levey
11/8F, 9/2, 8/1. 2¼l, shd. 9 ran. 1m 25.49s (Mark Johnston).

A hugely impressive victory from **Elarqam** and plenty of substance to go with the style as he beat two very useful rivals. Elarqam made all the running and took command when asked to quicken, easing down to see off Listed winner **Tip Two Win** and **Tangled**, who would get much closer at this level in the Horris Hill. Only two others finished within 10l, with the disappointing **Albishr** among those well strung out.

53 Shadwell Rockfel Stakes (Group 2) (Fillies) (7f)
Newmarket September 29 (Good To Soft)
1 **Juliet Capulet** 2-9-0   Frankie Dettori
2 **Nyaleti** 2-9-0   James Doyle
3 **Gavota** 2-9-0   Jim Crowley
9/1, 2/1F, 5/1. hd, 1½l. 10 ran. 1m 27.23s (John Gosden).

A narrow win for **Juliet Capulet** that was probably more comfortable than the head margin suggests as she landed a strong renewal. Always prominent, Juliet Capulet shook off **Nyaleti**, who had everything in her favour back over her optimum trip, and she just seemed to be idling as the runner-up clawed back at her again late. **Gavota** was unlucky as she couldn't get a clear run, finishing third ahead of subsequent Listed winner **Hikmaa**. It was 2¼l back to **Butterscotch**, who faded late on her first run for three months.

54 Juddmonte Cheveley Park Stakes (Group 1) (Fillies) (6f)
Newmarket September 30 (Good To Soft)
1 **Clemmie** 2-9-0   Ryan Moore
2 **Different League** 2-9-0 Antoine Hamelin
3 **Madeline** 2-9-0   Andrea Atzeni
15/8F, 4/1, 8/1. 1¾l, 1½l. 11 ran. 1m 12.00s (A P O'Brien).

Off since July, **Clemmie** showed that she had continued to progress in leaps and bounds in the meantime as she stormed to victory in an outstanding time. Always close to the fierce gallop, Clemmie was committed early yet still had the strength to go away again at the death, proving too strong for **Different League**, who also ran a terrific race in second. **Madeline** just held off the fast-finishing **Now You're Talking** for third, with **Darkanna** and **Eirene**, who didn't seem to handle the track, next. **Threading** was the big disappointment, finishing a tame seventh.

55 Juddmonte Middle Park Stakes (Group 1) (6f)
Newmarket September 30 (Good To Soft)
1 **US Navy Flag** 2-9-0   Seamie Heffernan
2 **Fleet Review** 2-9-0   Donnacha O'Brien
3 **Cardsharp** 2-9-0   James Doyle
10/1, 25/1, 14/1. ½l, 2¼l. 11 ran. 1m 12.44s
(A P O'Brien).

A slightly baffling result at the time that made more sense after **US Navy Flag**'s Dewhurst win, but he didn't need to run to that level to win this disappointing contest. A six-length winner of an admittedly weak Group 3 on his previous start, US Navy Flag confirmed that apparent improvement by beating his less-fancied stablemate **Fleet Review**, though the pair benefited from a big pace bias that worked against Aidan O'Brien's first string **Sioux Nation** and the favourite **Beckford**, that pair never able to get involved and managing only fifth and sixth. **Rajasinghe** was woefully outpaced, while **Unfortunately** and **Sands Of Mali** were very disappointing.

56 Juddmonte Royal Lodge Stakes (Group 2) (1m)
Newmarket September 30 (Good To Soft)
1 **Roaring Lion** 2-9-0   Oisin Murphy
2 **Nelson** 2-9-0   Ryan Moore
3 **Mildenberger** 2-9-0   James Doyle
11/4, 5/6F, 7/2. nk, 1¾l. 5 ran. 1m 39.56s
(John Gosden).

This brought together two of the best two-year-old colts of the year and resulted in a more authoritative win for **Roaring Lion** than the neck margin suggests. Roaring Lion did well to quicken through from the rear on a track that favoured front-runners all autumn and stayed on strongly despite showing the greenness that would later catch him out in the Racing Post Trophy by wandering left under pressure. **Nelson**, though, had his excuses having only arrived at the track shortly before the race due to travel problems.

Mildenberger was perhaps flattered to finish so close to the first two but still ran a nice race in third ahead of **Petrus**.

57 Total Prix Marcel Boussac – Criterium des Pouliches (Group 1) (Fillies) (1m)
Chantilly (FR) October 1 (Soft)
1 **Wild Illusion** 2-8-11   James Doyle
2 **Polydream** 2-8-11   Maxime Guyon
3 **Mission Impassible** 2-8-11   C Soumillon
25/1, 11/8F, 16/1. 1½l, hd. 7 ran. 1m 37.47s
(Charlie Appleby).

A strong contest featuring five Group winners, including a leading line to the top Irish form in **Magical**, yet one of the exceptions, **Wild Illusion**, made massive improvement to run out a clear winner. Third in a course-and-distance Group 3 on her previous start, the Godolphin filly benefited from positive tactics and first-time cheekpieces as she stayed on strongly. Magical ran another solid race, beaten for second in a three-way photo behind **Polydream** and **Mission Impassible**, with a 3½l gap back to **Zonza**.

58 Qatar Prix Jean-Luc Lagardere (Grand Criterium) (Group 1) (1m)
Chantilly (FR) October 1 (Soft)
1 **Happily** 2-8-10   Ryan Moore
2 **Olmedo** 2-9-0   Cristian Demuro
3 **Masar** 2-9-0   James Doyle
6/5F, 7/2, 7/2. 1¼l, snk. 6 ran. 1m 38.51s
(A P O'Brien).

Shrewd placing from the Coolmore team as the filly **Happily** beat the colts, taking advantage of a woeful lack of decent domestic opposition. Smart prospect **Olmedo** was the only French runner priced in single figures and duly proved Happily's main rival, but the Moyglare winner saw out the extra furlong well and produced a strong run in the straight. **Masar** stepped up on his Solario form in third despite failing to settle on ground softer than ideal, but **Mythical Magic** was well beaten in fifth.

59 Irish Stallion Farms EBF Star Appeal Stakes (Listed) (7f)
Dundalk (AW) (IRE) October 6 (Standard)
1 **Riyazan** 2-9-3   Pat Smullen
2 **Battle Of Jericho** 2-9-3 Seamie Heffernan
3 **Lake Volta** 2-9-3   Kevin Manning
11/4, 7/2, 4/1. ½l, shd. 7 ran. 1m 24.52s
(M Halford).

A competitive contest, albeit involving horses who had come up short at a higher level, and **Riyazan** made the most of his drop in

WILD ILLUSION: had five Group winners behind her in the Prix Marcel Boussac

grade by battling past **Lake Volta. Battle Of Jericho** finished strongly to split the pair and **Lethal Steps** was ½l back in fourth, with a 6l gap to the rest.

60 totepool Two-Year-Old Trophy (Listed) (5f217y)
Redcar October 7 (Good To Soft)

1	**Darkanna** 2-8-11	Barry McHugh
2	**Flying Sparkle** 2-8-4	Hayley Turner
3	**Foxtrot Lady** 2-8-4	Cam Hardie

4/1F, 11/1, 12/1. ½l, 1¾l. 22 ran. 1m 10.49s (Richard Fahey).

Darkanna, a big improver when fifth in the Cheveley Park, stood out on that form and duly made her superiority count, successfully conceding 7lb to **Flying Sparkle** despite a strong challenge from that filly. **Red Roman** wasn't favoured by the weights but ran a fine race in fourth ahead of **Maybride** and **Never Back Down**.

61 Legacy Stakes (Listed) (5f182y)
Navan (IRE) October 8 (Soft)

1	**Gobi Desert** 2-9-3	Colin Keane
2	**Golden Spell** 2-8-12	N G McCullagh
3	**Brick By Brick** 2-9-6	Chris Hayes

3/1, 14/1, 5/1. ½l, 1l. 10 ran. 1m 16.81s (G M Lyons).

Solid Listed form with the first three having already dominated another race in this grade at Fairyhouse the previous month, but in a different order as **Gobi Desert** reversed the placings with **Brick By Brick**. Always best placed having been allowed to dictate a slow gallop that day, Brick By Brick was only third this time as Gobi Desert quickened up well to reel in **Golden Spell**, with **Brother Bear** a disappointing seventh.

62 Staffordstown Stud Stakes (Listed) (1m)
Navan (IRE) October 8 (Soft)

1	**Bye Bye Baby** 2-9-0	Donnacha O'Brien
2	**Coeur D'Amour** 2-9-0	W J Lee
3	**Ballet Shoes** 2-9-3	P B Beggy

5/4F, 10/1, 5/1. 2¼l, 1½l. 7 ran. 1m 53.01s (A P O'Brien).

Progressing all the time having just got off the mark at Newmarket in a maiden at the fourth attempt, **Bye Bye Baby** bridged the gap to Listed level with ease. Bye Bye Baby made virtually all the running and picked up smartly when asked to assert, beating **Coeur D'Amour** and **Ballet Shoes**, who reversed Park Stakes form with **Sizzling** even on 3lb worse terms as that filly felt the impact of a busy time.

63 bet365 Fillies' Mile (Group 1) (1m)
Newmarket October 13 (Good)

1	**Laurens** 2-9-0	P J McDonald
2	**September** 2-9-0	Seamie Heffernan
3	**Magic Lily** 2-9-0	William Buick

GHAIYYATH: produced a tremendous performance to win the Autumn Stakes

10/1, 9/2, 8/1. nse, ¾l. 11 ran. 1m 36.15s (K R Burke).

Laurens stepped up on her May Hill win to just hold off the unlucky September in a real thriller. Quick to ensure there was no dawdling this time, and in the process grabbing the favoured stands rail, Laurens made all the running and prevailed by a nose as **September**, back to form on quicker ground, finished fast having been forced to switch to find room. **Magic Lily**, an eight-length maiden winner over course and distance, ran a cracker in third on only her second start and pulled 3l clear of **Magical**, who wasn't helped by the draw and stuck wide throughout. **Ellthea** held every chance before just failing to get home, while **Nyaleti** looked a more patent non-stayer.

64 Newmarket Academy Godolphin Beacon Project Cornwallis Stakes (Group 3) (5f)
Newmarket October 13 (Good)
1 **Abel Handy** 2-9-1   James Doyle
2 **Sound And Silence** 2-9-4   William Buick
3 **Mokaatil** 2-9-1   Jim Crowley
9/2, 5/2F, 8/1. nk, ½l. 11 ran. 58.65s (Declan Carroll).

A blanket finish with less than 2l covering the first six, including 100-1 rag **Spoof**, and several hard-luck stories, but **Abel Handy** avoided

the trouble in front and battled back bravely when headed to run out a game winner. Abel Handy reversed York form with **Sound And Silence**, who was perhaps unfortunate as he paid the price close home for being keen early but ran another solid race under a 3lb penalty for a Group 3 win at Maisons-Laffitte in September. **Battle Of Jericho**, dropping a long way back in trip, never got a run in seventh, with **Pursuing The Dream** next but still beaten just 3l.

65 Godolphin Lifetime Care Oh So Sharp Stakes (Group 3) (Fillies) (7f)
Newmarket October 13 (Good)
1 **Altyn Orda** 2-9-0   Andrea Atzeni
2 **Gavota** 2-9-0   James Doyle
3 **I Can Fly** 2-9-0   Ryan Moore
25/1, 7/2, 2/1F. nk, 1l. 14 ran. 1m 23.71s (Roger Varian).

This race was packed with proven Group performers and it took a good performance from **Altyn Orda** to win it, though she was perhaps flattered by racing away from the other protagonists on the stands side, which was favoured throughout the meeting. Second in two hot maidens, Altyn Orda stayed on strongly to pip **Gavota**, who was again slightly unlucky given she had the favourite **I Can Fly**, **Butterscotch**, who was much sharper for her Rockfel run, and subsequent Listed winner **Hikmaa** next in her group whereas **Expressiy**, beaten by Hikmaa that day, was next best in Altyn Orda's group ahead of **Herecomesthesun**. **Anna Nerium**, **Special Purpose** and **Dark Rose Angel** were all disappointing.

66 Darley Dewhurst Stakes (Group 1) (7f)
Newmarket October 14 (Good)

1 US Navy Flag 2-9-1		Ryan Moore
2 Mendelssohn 2-9-1		Wayne Lordan
3 Seahenge 2-9-1		Donnacha O'Brien

5/1, 50/1, 9/1. 2½l, 2½l. 9 ran. 1m 22.37s
(A P O'Brien).

A desperately weak Dewhurst as **Expert Eye** scared off much of the opposition only to run an absolute shocker, with **US Navy Flag**, left to set the standard after his Middle Park win, taking advantage. Nonetheless, this was still a much-improved performance from US Navy Flag as he relished the extra furlong and ran out an easy winner over **Mendelssohn**, who franked the form by winning the Breeders' Cup Juvenile Turf. **Seahenge** was a well-beaten third, though he ran better than the bare form after his rider bizarrely switched from the plum inside stall to race down the centre of the track, while **Three-andfourpence** completed Aidan O'Brien's clean sweep of the first four places. **Cardsharp** was best of the rest but didn't quite see out the trip, with **Great Prospector** also weakening late, though they fared better than Expert Eye, who was never travelling, and another leading contender in Newbury novice winner **Emaraaty**.

67 Masar Godolphin Autumn Stakes (Group 3) (1m)
Newmarket October 14 (Good)

1 Ghaiyyath 2-9-1		William Buick
2 Dream Today 2-9-1		P J McDonald
3 Purser 2-9-1		Frankie Dettori

11/4, 10/1, 9/4F. 1¾l, 2½l. 8 ran. 1m 35.92s
(Charlie Appleby).

A tremendous performance from **Ghaiyyath**, who stayed on strongly to leave some useful rivals well strung out despite having had to wait for room to make his challenge. The front-running **Dream Today**, encountering good ground for the only time since a winning debut in the Convivial Maiden at York, ran a cracker to keep the winner honest, finishing a clear second over **Purser**, who got no cover in the centre but still reversed Solario form with **Arbalet** in sixth, with both beaten

considerably further here. **Petrus** was fourth, beaten a similar distance as he had been in the Royal Lodge, with subsequent Group 3 winner **Flag Of Honour** fifth.

68 Godolphin Flying Start Zetland Stakes (Listed) (1m2f)
Newmarket October 14 (Good)

1 Kew Gardens 2-9-2		Ryan Moore
2 Dee Ex Bee 2-9-2		P J McDonald
3 Graffiti Master 2-9-2		James Doyle

13/8F, 7/2, 6/1. 3½l, ½l. 7 ran. 2m 2.76s
(A P O'Brien).

Having run well behind Nelson and Saxon Warrior, this was a much easier challenge for **Kew Gardens** and he duly took advantage. With full confidence in his stamina, Ryan Moore set a solid gallop on Kew Gardens, who drew clear of **Dee Ex Bee** and **Graffiti Master**. That pair were 4l clear of the rest.

69 coral.co.uk Rockingham Stakes (Listed) (6f)
York October 14 (Good)

1 Rebel Assault 2-8-10		Franny Norton
2 It Dont Come Easy 2-9-1		David Nolan
3 Staxton 2-9-1		David Allan

25/1, 12/1, 11/2. 1¼l, ¾l. 11 ran. 1m 11.72s
(Mark Johnston).

This had a surprising but worthy winner in **Rebel Assault**, who did really well to fight back having been headed 2f out and won going away from a decent field. An apparent non-stayer on other runs over this trip, Rebel Assault benefited from better ground and beat **It Dont Come Easy** and **Staxton**, with red-hot favourite **Shabaaby** only fourth. **Pulitzer** and **Daddies Girl** were next ahead of **Dance Diva**, who was below-par on her first run in two months.

70 Killavullan Stakes (Group 3) (7f) Leopardstown (IRE) October 22 (Soft)

1 Kenya 2-9-3		Donnacha O'Brien
2 Mcmunigal 2-9-3		Colin Keane
3 Bye Bye Baby 2-9-0		Seamie Heffernan

7/4F, 4/1, 2/1. 1l, ½l. 7 ran. 1m 35.28s
(A P O'Brien).

An impressive win from the exciting **Kenya**, though he perhaps had little to beat with **Mcmunigal** and **Bye Bye Baby** looking in need of further. Still, Kenya showed plenty of speed for a middle-distance prospect to have that pair in trouble from an early stage and won comfortably as Mcmunigal and Bye Bye Baby, back at 7f after her mile Listed win, stayed on at the death.

71 totepool ebfstallions.com Silver Tankard Stakes (Listed) (1m6y)
Pontefract October 23 (Soft)
1 **Connect** 2-9-3   Adam Kirby
2 **Lisheen Castle** 2-9-3   Jason Hart
3 **Dark Acclaim** 2-9-3   Daniel Muscutt
9/1, 14/1, 7/1. 2¾l, hd. 8 ran. 1m 51.87s
(Clive Cox).

A weak Listed race but a decent winner in **Connect**, who was transformed from the colt well beaten in the Solario when last seen. Ridden far more conservatively this time, Connect showed a fine turn of foot to burst clear of **Lisheen Castle** and **Dark Acclaim**, who reversed recent Haydock form with the below-par **Learn By Heart**. The favourite **Old Persian** was reportedly unsuited by the ground.

72 Racing Post Trophy (Group 1) (1m)
Doncaster October 28 (Good To Soft)
1 **Saxon Warrior** 2-9-1   Ryan Moore
2 **Roaring Lion** 2-9-1   Oisin Murphy
3 **The Pentagon** 2-9-1   Seamie Heffernan
13/8F, 8/1, 10/1. nk, 2½l. 12 ran. 1m 40.12s
(A P O'Brien).

The best two-year-old race of the season in Europe, with loads of good colts well beaten by a couple of real stars in **Saxon Warrior** and **Roaring Lion**. The contrasting qualities of the pair were seen to fascinating effect as Saxon Warrior dug deep in hugely professional fashion to get back past Roaring Lion, who looked to have put the race to bed with a terrific turn of foot only to run green in the final furlong. **The Pentagon** ran a career-best in third despite an interrupted preparation that saw him drift badly on the track, staying on past **Verbal Dexterity**, who perhaps did too much work to get competitive too early after struggling early. **Gabr** ran a fine race in fifth having won no more than a maiden, finishing ahead of **Chilean**, who was in turn 2¼l clear of **Loxton** and the below-par **Seahenge**.

73 Bet Through The Racing Post App Doncaster Stakes (Listed) (6f2y)
Doncaster October 28 (Good To Soft)
1 **Speak In Colours** 2-9-1   Andrea Atzeni
2 **Mutaaqeb** 2-9-1   Jim Crowley
3 **Staxton** 2-9-1   David Allan
6/1, 9/2J, 9/2J. ½l, 1l. 8 ran. 1m 14.09s
(Marco Botti).

A fair Listed race in which two inexperienced colts looked far superior, with **Speak In Colours**, despite being keen early, picking up

strongly to hold off **Mutaaqeb**, who was perhaps unlucky having been short of room at a key time. The pair were too good for **Staxton**, who ran another solid race and comfortably reversed York form with **Rebel Assault** as that colt weakened late on this softer ground. There was another gap back to **Never Back Down**, beaten 3l further than he had been behind Darkanna at Redcar, though he still reversed that form with the disappointing **Red Roman**.

74 Bathwick Tyres Stakes (registered as the Horris Hill Stakes) (Group 3) (7f)
Newbury October 28 (Soft)
1 **Nebo** 2-9-0   Frankie Dettori
2 **Tangled** 2-9-0   Sean Levey
3 **Mythical Magic** 2-9-0   James Doyle
4/1, 15/2, 2/1F. ½l, ¾l. 6 ran. 1m 27.87s
(Charles Hills).

Knocking on the door in good races all season, **Nebo** deservedly landed a Pattern prize as he proved equally effective over 7f having done most of his racing over shorter. Nebo just got the better of **Tangled**, with the favourite **Mythical Magic** again coming up short in third. **Vintager** was fifth and **Dream Today** was last of the six runners, failing to run to form on soft ground.

75 Bathwick Tyres Stakes (registered as the Radley Stakes) (Listed) (7f)
Newbury October 28 (Soft)
1 **Hikmaa** 2-9-0   Adam Beschizza
2 **Shepherd Market** 2-9-0   Adam Kirby
3 **Expressiy** 2-9-0   James Doyle
7/2, 10/1, 6/1. ¾l, ½l. 13 ran. 1m 28.84s
(Ed Vaughan).

Hikmaa was the highest-rated filly in the line-up and didn't need to run to the form of her Rockfel fourth. Down in trip, Hikmaa coped with the soft ground better than her connections had expected and beat **Shepherd Market** and **Expressiy**, with **Daddies Girl** and **Miss Bar Beach** dead-heating for fourth another 1½l back. The favourite **Magnolia Springs** was a disappointing sixth ahead of **Elysium Dream**.

76 TheTote.com Eyrefield Stakes (Group 3) (1m1f)
Leopardstown (IRE) October 28 (Yielding)
1 **Flag Of Honour** 2-9-3   P B Beggy
2 **Giuseppe Garibaldi** 2-9-3 Michael Hussey
3 **Hazapour** 2-9-3   Leigh Roche
2/1F, 14/1, 3/1. 1½l, 2¼l. 9 ran. 2m 4.79s
(A P O'Brien).

Flag Of Honour set the standard on his Autumn Stakes fifth in a much weaker Group 3 – only one rival had won anything more than a maiden and that was a 25-1 also-ran – and he made the most of his opportunity. **Giuseppe Garibaldi** was a promising second on only his second run ahead of **Hazapour**, who didn't seem to get the trip.

77 Irish Stallion Farms EBF "Bosra Sham" Fillies' Stakes (Listed) (6f)
Newmarket November 3 (Good To Firm)
1 **Alwasmiya** 2-9-0   Robert Havlin
2 **Izzy Bizu** 2-9-3   P J McDonald
3 **All Out** 2-9-0   Sean Levey
8/1, 5/1, 3/1F. 3l, nk. 10 ran. 1m 11.78s (Simon Crisford).

A weak contest but a convincing winner in **Alwasmiya**, who showed a smart turn of foot to pull clear. Just 1l covered the sextet from second to seventh behind her, with **Izzy Bizu** doing well to come out on top of that bunch under a 3lb penalty for a Listed win at Deauville, but even she had been found out in much stronger races in Britain.

78 British Stallion Studs EBF Montrose Fillies' Stakes (Listed) (1m)
Newmarket November 4 (Good To Soft)
1 **Hadith** 2-9-0   Adam Kirby
2 **Baroness** 2-9-0   Fran Berry
3 **Herecomesthesun** 2-9-0   Jim Crowley
5/2F, 8/1, 5/1. 1¼l, ¾l. 11 ran. 1m 38.73s (Charlie Appleby).

A straightforward task for the favourite **Hadith**, who made all the running to see off **Baroness**, with **Herecomesthesun**, beaten nearly 7l in the Oh So Sharp, providing the most solid formline with her 2l third. However, the fact that the seventh, **Elysium Dream**, having been 16-1 when well beaten by Hikmaa at Newbury, was halved in price for this race emphasises its lack of depth.

SAXON WARRIOR (right): won the two-year-old race of the season at Donny

Two-year-old index

All horses placed or commented on in our two-year-old review section, with race numbers

Abel Handy..................................34, 64
Actress 6, 15, 23, 31
Alba Power................................12, 30
Albishr 32, 52
All Out...77
Alpha Centauri 6, 44
Altyn Orda 65
Alwasmiya......................................77
Anna Nerium 39, 65
Another Batt 24
Aqabah...2, 47
Arbalet.......................................38, 67
Ballet Shoes 36, 44, 51, 62
Baroness 78
Barraquero 21
Bartholomeu Dias 7
Battle Of Jericho.........................59, 64
Beckford.....................9, 23, 43, 55
Bengali Boys 34
Berkeley Square................16, 25, 43
Billesdon Brook..................17, 35, 45
Brick By Brick................................61
Brother Bear.................2, 15, 43, 61
Butterscotch....................10, 53, 65
Bye Bye Baby....................36, 62, 70
Camelback...................................25, 42
Capla Temptress..............................22
Capomento 17
Cardsharp 5, 12, 21, 33, 55, 66
Chilean 41, 72
Clemmie.................6, 10, 13, 54
Coat Of Arms....................25, 43
Coeur D'Amour 62
Connect....................................38, 71
Corinthia Knight 40
Daddies Girl 69, 75
Dance Diva..................8, 18, 22, 69
Dark Acclaim............................41, 71
Dark Rose Angel 45, 65
Darkanna....................30, 54, 60
Dee Ex Bee 29, 41, 68
Delano Roosevelt.......................42, 50
Different League..................6, 28, 54

Dream Today 48, 67, 74
Eirene...39, 54
Elarqam...52
Ellthea 17, 51, 63
Elysium Dream.........................75, 78
Emaraaty.......................................66
Enjazaat...............................12, 37, 49
Ertiyad.....................................22, 35
Expert Eye.............................19, 66
Expressiy...............................65, 75
Flag Of Honour 67, 76
Fleet Review...................................55
Flying Sparkle 60
Foxtrot Lady 60
Frozen Angel..............................5, 23
Gabr...72
Gavota...............................53, 65
Ghaiyyath.......................................67
Giuseppe Garibaldi 76
Gobi Desert....................................61
Golden Spell 61
Goodthingstaketime.........................27
Graffiti Master.................................68
Great Prospector.................14, 30, 66
Gustav Klimt 14
Hadith...78
Happily....................26, 44, 58
Happy Like A Fool.......................4, 31
Havana Grey 5, 11, 20, 28, 46
Hazapour..76
Headway 2, 21, 33
Heartache...................................4, 46
Herecomesthesun.........................65, 78
Hey Gaman 7, 12, 24, 48
Hey Jonesy 30
Hikmaa................................53, 65, 75
I Can Fly 65
Invincible Army.........12, 20, 33, 40, 49
It Dont Come Easy...........5, 12, 20, 69
Izzy Bizu.........................35, 39, 77
James Garfield.................3, 19, 29, 49
Juliet Capulet 22, 53
Kenya 70

Kew Gardens.........................42, 50, 68
Lake Volta............................37, 40, 59
Lansky...................................29, 49
Laurens.................................45, 63
Learn By Heart....................24, 41, 71
Lethal Steps..................................59
Liquid Amber.................................36
Lisheen Castle...............................71
Loxton...72
Madeline...........................6, 31, 54
Maggies Angel...........................1, 8
Magic Lily......................................63
Magical..........................26, 44, 57, 63
Magnolia Springs...........................75
Main Desire.....................................1
Maksab...14
Mamba Noire.............10, 13, 22, 31
Mary Tudor.............................26, 51
Masar..7, 38, 58
May Girl..46
Mcmunigal.....................................70
Mendelssohn...........................48, 66
Mildenberger.........................19, 32, 56
Miss Bar Beach.....................35, 45, 75
Mission Impassible........................57
Mistress Of Venice...........1, 6, 13, 18
Mokaatil....................................3, 64
Murillo.......................................2, 9
Musical Art....................................18
Mutaaqeb......................................73
Mythical Magic....................48, 58, 74
Nebo..................2, 14, 21, 33, 49, 74
Nelson.....................................42, 56
Neola......................................1, 4, 18
Never Back Down..........................73
Now You're Talking...................4, 54
Nyaleti.........7, 13, 18, 28, 45, 53, 63
Old Persian....................................71
Olmedo...58
Out Of The Flames..............4, 13, 34
Petrus......................................56, 67
Poetic Charm................................22
Polydream.....................................57
Pulitzer...69
Purser......................................38, 67
Pursuing The Dream..................46, 64
Quivery..35
Rajasinghe..........................2, 12, 55

Rebel Assault.....................18, 69, 73
Red Mist.................................24, 48
Red Roman.............................60, 73
Riyazan................................42, 50, 59
Roaring Lion..........................56, 72
Romanised.............................23, 38
Rostropovich...........................25, 43
Roussel......................................3, 11
Sands Of Mali........................33, 55
Santry...5
Saxon Warrior.......................50, 72
Seahenge................19, 48, 66, 72
September.................7, 26, 44, 63
Shabaaby.......................................69
Shepherd Market..........................75
Sioux Nation.........................5, 23, 55
Sirici...27
Sizzling...............................45, 51, 62
So Hi Society...............8, 13, 17, 31
Somestimesadiamond...................36
Sound And Silence............3, 12, 34, 64
Speak In Colours..........................73
Special Purpose...................31, 39, 65
Spoof...64
Staxton....................33, 49, 69, 73
Tajaanus......................8, 17, 22, 45
Take Me With You............................6
Tangled...................................30, 52, 74
Tantheem......................................28
The Pentagon........................16, 72
Theobald..................................15, 16
Threading................................31, 54
Threeandfourpence........................66
Tigre Du Terre......................32, 47
Tip Two Win............................37, 47, 52
To Wafij..................................11, 20
Treasuring.....................................27
Unfortunately.........................28, 55
US Navy Flag...........2, 12, 23, 55, 66
Verbal Dexterity....................9, 43, 72
Vintager..................................38, 74
Warm The Voice.............................50
Wells Farhh Go.............................29
Whitefountainfairy.................17, 35
Wild Illusion..................................57
Would Be King...............................16
Zaman...19
Zonza......................................28, 57

Trainer Statistics

Mark Johnston

By month – 2017

	Overall			Two-year-olds			Three-year-olds			Older horses		
	W-R	%	£1	W-R	%	£1	W-R	%	£1	W-R	%	£1
January	8-51	16	-18.45	0-0	-	+0.00	4-34	12	-18.86	4-17	24	+0.41
February	8-47	17	-13.60	0-0	-	+0.00	4-28	14	-9.43	4-19	21	-4.17
March	12-44	27	+12.80	0-0	-	+0.00	5-21	24	+5.05	7-23	30	+7.75
April	12-81	15	-23.50	1-9	11	-7.56	7-45	16	-10.04	4-27	15	-5.90
May	24-172	14	-58.28	7-36	19	-15.36	14-92	15	-13.17	3-44	7	-29.75
June	37-213	17	-42.26	15-62	24	+15.14	17-119	14	-60.65	5-32	16	+3.25
July	38-203	19	-15.92	22-63	35	+40.16	13-112	12	-52.08	3-28	11	-4.00
August	33-196	17	-23.05	16-66	24	+18.58	13-103	13	-38.63	4-27	15	-3.00
September	17-156	11	-79.09	9-71	13	-41.97	7-64	11	-28.13	1-21	5	-9.00
October	19-133	14	+82.21	7-64	11	+28.83	10-52	19	+49.38	2-17	12	+4.00
November	6-46	13	-11.65	4-31	13	-16.65	1-9	11	+4.00	1-6	17	+1.00
December	0-21	-	-21.00	0-13	-	-13.00	0-2	-	-2.00	0-6	-	-6.00

By month – 2016

	Overall			Two-year-olds			Three-year-olds			Older horses		
	W-R	%	£1	W-R	%	£1	W-R	%	£1	W-R	%	£1
January	5-34	15	-13.70	0-0	-	+0.00	5-23	22	-2.70	0-11	-	-11.00
February	4-23	17	-12.40	0-0	-	+0.00	4-15	27	-4.40	0-8	-	-8.00
March	11-49	22	-10.64	3-3	100	+4.82	4-28	14	-18.45	4-18	22	+3.00
April	12-117	10	-75.76	3-24	13	-15.76	7-68	10	-41.88	2-25	8	-18.13
May	21-168	13	-62.71	11-52	21	+0.25	7-75	9	-38.79	3-41	7	-24.17
June	35-204	17	-33.23	23-74	31	+17.31	8-96	8	-48.04	4-34	12	-2.50
July	38-233	16	+24.03	15-84	18	-28.05	16-109	15	+42.58	7-40	18	+9.50
August	23-178	13	-98.89	12-82	15	-43.36	8-62	13	-36.94	3-34	9	-18.59
September	19-149	13	-4.29	10-67	15	+17.46	7-62	11	-10.00	2-20	10	-11.75
October	14-140	10	+10.41	10-82	12	+28.91	2-43	5	-17.00	2-15	13	-1.50
November	7-64	11	-32.53	5-41	12	-25.03	0-16	-	-16.00	2-7	29	+8.50
December	6-54	11	-7.25	2-31	6	-13.00	3-17	18	-3.25	1-6	17	+9.00

By month – 2015

	Overall			Two-year-olds			Three-year-olds			Older horses		
	W-R	%	£1	W-R	%	£1	W-R	%	£1	W-R	%	£1
January	0-7	-	-7.00	0-0	-	+0.00	0-4	-	-4.00	0-3	-	-3.00
February	2-18	11	+9.91	0-0	-	+0.00	2-11	18	+16.91	0-7	-	-7.00
March	11-41	27	-1.75	3-3	100	+9.75	6-25	24	-2.80	2-13	15	-8.70
April	11-100	11	-29.30	3-22	14	-14.22	5-55	9	-2.50	3-23	13	-12.58
May	30-141	21	+58.48	11-49	22	-1.04	13-66	20	+49.05	6-26	23	+10.48
June	35-183	19	-24.16	18-72	25	-10.29	11-88	13	-35.88	6-23	26	+22.00
July	47-213	22	+36.10	19-88	22	-9.69	22-96	23	+20.29	6-29	21	+25.50
August	24-172	14	-38.65	14-80	18	-18.06	10-70	14	+1.41	0-22	-	-22.00
September	23-148	16	-54.91	12-77	16	-40.32	10-51	20	+2.53	1-20	5	-17.13
October	12-135	9	-68.32	5-87	6	-65.25	4-36	11	-7.73	3-12	25	+4.66
November	5-36	14	-7.47	4-26	15	-2.47	0-6	-	-6.00	1-4	25	+1.00
December	4-14	29	+15.25	3-8	38	+13.25	1-6	17	+2.00	0-0	-	+0.00

By race type – 2017

	Overall			Two-year-olds			Three-year-olds			Older horses		
	W-R	%	£1	W-R	%	£1	W-R	%	£1	W-R	%	£1
Handicap	127-911	14	-230.55	17-107	16	+2.53	75-552	14	-185.17	35-252	14	-47.91
Group	7-49	14	-2.13	4-27	15	-7.13	3-20	15	+7.00	0-2	-	-2.00
Maiden	17-116	15	-28.59	9-44	20	+13.83	8-72	11	-42.42	0-0	-	+0.00

By race type – 2016

	Overall			Two-year-olds			Three-year-olds			Older horses		
	W-R	%	£1	W-R	%	£1	W-R	%	£1	W-R	%	£1
Handicap	101-854	12%	-153.82	19-142	13%	+21.22	55-485	11%	-123.41	27-227	12%	-51.63
Group	4-51	8%	-7.63	4-31	13%	+12.38	0-15	-	-15.00	0-5	-	-5.00
Maiden	41-277	15%	-124.77	30-192	16%	-78.22	11-83	13%	-44.55	0-2	-	-2.00

By race type – 2015

	Overall			Two-year-olds			Three-year-olds			Older horses		
	W-R	%	£1	W-R	%	£1	W-R	%	£1	W-R	%	£1
Handicap	117-721	16	-34.31	21-132	16	-58.47	71-426	17	+25.69	25-163	15	-1.52
Group	2-43	5	-31.67	2-35	6	-23.67	0-4	-	-4.00	0-4	-	-4.00
Maiden	67-358	19	-19.03	54-277	19	-41.15	13-77	17	+26.11	0-4	-	-4.00

By jockey – 2017

	Overall			Two-year-olds			Three-year-olds			Older horses		
	W-R	%	£1	W-R	%	£1	W-R	%	£1	W-R	%	£1
Joe Fanning	64-392	16	-50.66	17-96	18	-49.44	27-192	14	-7.21	20-104	19	+5.99
Franny Norton	41-294	14	-74.62	17-97	18	-6.03	19-147	13	-38.44	5-50	10	-30.15
P J McDonald	35-204	17	+25.44	16-74	22	+67.50	19-108	18	-20.06	0-22	-	-22.00
S De Sousa	21-79	27	+7.97	14-34	41	+23.28	6-32	19	-14.32	1-13	8	-1.00
Jim Crowley	9-32	28	+8.75	3-9	33	+0.25	4-17	24	+2.00	2-6	33	+6.50
James Doyle	6-51	12	-15.00	3-24	13	-6.50	2-23	9	-17.50	1-4	25	+9.00
Ryan Moore	4-13	31	-2.64	2-4	50	+0.62	2-7	29	-1.25	0-2	-	-2.00
Dane O'Neill	4-21	19	-4.09	1-4	25	-2.09	2-11	18	-2.50	1-6	17	+0.50
Richard Oliver	4-30	13	-10.25	0-0	-	+0.00	4-21	19	-1.25	0-9	-	-9.00
R Kingscote	4-33	12	-15.00	1-8	13	-4.25	1-16	6	-9.50	2-9	22	-1.25
J F Egan	3-16	19	+13.50	1-6	17	+11.00	1-8	13	-5.50	1-2	50	+8.00
Harry Bentley	3-17	18	+5.00	1-3	33	+4.00	0-9	-	-9.00	2-5	40	+10.00

By jockey – 2016

	Overall			Two-year-olds			Three-year-olds			Older horses		
	W-R	%	£1	W-R	%	£1	W-R	%	£1	W-R	%	£1
Joe Fanning	73-491	15	-100.76	27-176	15	-19.01	34-221	15	-55.12	12-94	13	-26.63
Franny Norton	46-253	18	-3.72	23-103	22	-11.88	18-110	16	+15.92	5-40	13	-7.75
S De Sousa	15-91	16	-37.96	6-32	19	-8.65	6-35	17	-16.07	3-24	13	-13.25
James Doyle	12-67	18	-22.43	10-30	33	+10.43	1-33	3	-32.36	1-4	25	-0.50
P J McDonald	10-61	16	+21.25	7-32	22	+21.25	1-19	5	-15.00	2-10	20	+15.00
William Buick	8-57	14	-25.66	6-27	22	-9.66	2-27	7	-13.00	0-3	-	-3.00
Paul Mulrennan	5-61	8	-29.00	4-28	14	-9.00	1-27	4	-14.00	0-6	-	-6.00
R Kingscote	4-36	11	-8.00	2-12	17	+5.00	1-16	6	-12.50	1-8	13	-0.50
Andrew Mullen	3-34	9	+0.50	3-24	13	+10.50	0-8	-	-8.00	0-2	-	-2.00

By jockey – 2015

	Overall			Two-year-olds			Three-year-olds			Older horses		
	W-R	%	£1	W-R	%	£1	W-R	%	£1	W-R	%	£1
Joe Fanning	70-397	18	-49.98	29-148	20	-35.13	30-177	17	-4.94	11-72	15	-9.92
S De Sousa	41-182	23	+17.21	19-74	26	-5.32	18-83	22	+14.53	4-25	16	+8.00
Franny Norton	38-279	14	-92.43	14-121	12	-70.68	19-114	17	-6.17	5-44	11	-15.58
William Buick	13-51	25	+22.87	10-36	28	-2.13	2-11	18	+8.00	1-4	25	+17.00
Paul Mulrennan	10-46	22	+0.43	6-21	29	+8.93	3-13	23	-4.00	1-12	8	-4.50
James Doyle	6-33	18	+15.13	5-26	19	+3.13	1-7	14	+12.00	0-0	-	+0.00
Adam Kirby	5-16	31	+14.75	3-9	33	+13.50	0-3	-	-3.00	2-4	50	+4.25
Adrian Nicholls	4-37	11	+13.75	1-15	7	-11.75	3-20	15	+27.50	0-2	-	-2.00
Nicky Mackay	3-9	33	+11.00	0-1	-	-1.00	3-7	43	+13.00	0-1	-	-1.00

By course – 2014-2017

	Overall			Two-year-olds			Three-year-olds			Older horses		
	W-R	%	£1	W-R	%	£1	W-R	%	£1	W-R	%	£1
Ascot	18-199	9	-63.88	6-54	11	-30.88	8-109	7	-54.50	4-36	11	+21.50
Ayr	14-113	12	-58.25	8-49	16	-26.18	4-45	9	-30.40	2-19	11	-1.67
Bath	8-59	14	-21.92	2-13	15	-8.67	5-36	14	-6.25	1-10	10	-7.00
Beverley	43-226	19	-22.53	13-70	19	-23.66	26-125	21	+11.62	4-31	13	-10.50
Brighton	14-67	21	-8.86	5-26	19	-13.45	8-30	27	+7.58	1-11	9	-3.00
Carlisle	20-123	16	-27.18	7-38	18	-12.17	8-55	15	-13.59	5-30	17	-1.42
Catterick	24-121	20	-20.25	13-58	22	-12.60	9-50	18	-4.40	2-13	15	-3.25
Chelmsfd (AW)	36-257	14	-88.21	18-93	19	-6.83	11-112	10	-55.30	7-52	13	-26.08
Chepstow	3-29	10	-21.42	0-7	-	-7.00	3-18	17	-10.42	0-4	-	-4.00
Chester	33-218	15	-59.67	12-64	19	-6.88	18-116	16	-37.29	3-38	8	-15.50
Doncaster	17-137	12	-34.60	8-60	13	+8.26	9-62	15	-27.86	0-15	-	-15.00
Epsom	17-113	15	-22.48	9-25	36	+5.42	3-53	6	-30.00	5-35	14	+2.10
Ffos Las	0-17	-	-17.00	0-6	-	-6.00	0-10	-	-10.00	0-1	-	-1.00
Goodwood	36-238	15	+93.50	12-76	16	+1.75	16-120	13	+36.25	8-42	19	+55.50
Hamilton	34-172	20	-30.37	18-56	32	+18.88	14-91	15	-32.13	2-25	8	-17.13
Haydock	28-188	15	-11.83	11-66	17	-23.00	13-85	15	+16.17	4-37	11	-5.00
Kempton (AW)	28-227	12	-91.04	11-77	14	-36.98	12-96	13	-32.56	5-54	9	-21.50
Leicester	24-117	21	-9.31	8-51	16	-20.81	12-49	24	+8.38	4-17	24	+3.13
Lingfield	4-34	12	-18.75	1-11	9	-4.00	3-16	19	-7.75	0-7	-	-7.00
Lingfield (AW)	50-286	17	-49.49	6-41	15	-3.75	30-152	20	-27.79	14-93	15	-17.95
Musselburgh	41-212	19	-30.77	14-67	21	-8.91	22-108	20	-1.89	5-37	14	-19.97
Newbury	9-69	13	-5.63	4-32	13	-6.50	3-24	13	-1.13	2-13	15	+2.00
Newcastle	6-29	21	+0.13	2-15	13	-2.50	4-8	50	+8.63	0-6	-	-6.00
N'castle (AW)	20-152	13	-13.81	9-71	13	-40.53	8-54	15	+36.57	3-27	11	-9.84
Newmarket	21-199	11	-30.87	13-79	16	+19.03	5-82	6	-26.50	3-38	8	-23.40
Newmarket (J)	38-185	21	+16.27	12-60	20	-6.19	20-101	20	+17.71	6-24	25	+4.75
Nottingham	13-102	13	-40.92	9-51	18	-5.67	4-42	10	-26.25	0-9	-	-9.00
Pontefract	28-157	18	-50.12	12-52	23	-15.65	11-79	14	-29.38	5-26	19	-5.09
Redcar	16-101	16	-9.80	5-38	13	-20.00	6-45	13	-15.00	5-18	28	+26.00
Ripon	29-176	16	-0.13	13-55	24	-15.05	14-81	17	+46.17	2-40	5	-31.25
Salisbury	5-24	21	+12.10	5-14	36	+22.10	0-8	-	-8.00	0-2	-	-2.00
Sandown	12-89	13	-39.54	7-27	26	+5.41	5-47	11	-29.95	0-15	-	-15.00
South'll (AW)	19-112	17	-30.79	3-20	15	-10.67	5-47	11	-9.22	11-45	24	-10.90
Thirsk	4-68	6	-53.60	3-27	11	-16.35	1-29	3	-25.25	0-12	-	-12.00
Warwick	0-1	-	-1.00	0-0	-	+0.00	0-0	-	+0.00	0-1	-	-1.00
Wetherby	2-10	20	+3.10	1-4	25	-1.90	1-5	20	+6.00	0-1	-	-1.00
Windsor	7-47	15	-18.44	4-16	25	-1.07	2-19	11	-12.38	1-12	8	-5.00
Wolves (AW)	71-394	18	-75.03	13-96	14	-31.35	32-193	17	-69.51	26-105	25	+25.83
Yarmouth	11-53	21	+65.77	3-14	21	+58.00	6-33	18	-0.73	2-6	33	+8.50
York	17-214	8	-43.99	10-91	11	-3.49	5-76	7	-13.50	2-47	4	-27.00

Ten-year summary

	Wins	Runs	%	Win prize-money	Total prize-money	£1
2017	214	1363	16	£2,401,913.22	£3,506,059.94	-211.79
2016	195	1413	14	£1,553,727.94	£2,726,246.11	-316.95
2015	204	1208	17	£1,806,254.46	£2,749,132.37	-111.80
2014	207	1344	15	£1,985,940.54	£2,992,111.82	-283.07
2013	216	1557	14	£1,826,629.78	£2,743,581.49	-396.21
2012	215	1344	16	£1,545,130.29	£2,284,275.76	-148.88
2011	179	1311	14	£927,711.46	£1,550,631.62	-270.93
2010	211	1458	14	£1,657,512.68	£2,419,718.15	-377.04
2009	216	1227	18	£1,747,013.96	£2,843,943.25	-139.14
2008	164	1145	14	£1,345,669.48	£2,070,937.14	-200.11

CARDSHARP: on the go for a long time last year but held his form admirably

Richard Fahey

By month – 2017

	Overall			Two-year-olds			Three-year-olds			Older horses		
	W-R	%	£1	W-R	%	£1	W-R	%	£1	W-R	%	£1
January	6-61	10	-27.00	0-0	-	+0.00	4-25	16	-7.00	2-36	6	-20.00
February	8-38	21	+1.38	0-0	-	+0.00	1-14	7	-10.50	7-24	29	+11.88
March	5-35	14	-7.00	0-0	-	+0.00	0-10	-	-10.00	5-25	20	+3.00
April	19-122	16	+14.88	6-17	35	+13.00	4-34	12	+21.00	9-71	13	-19.13
May	27-198	14	-61.18	6-43	14	-22.88	6-70	9	-38.40	15-85	18	+0.10
June	29-232	13	-83.14	13-67	19	+8.16	7-64	11	-31.13	9-101	9	-60.17
July	21-259	8	-85.66	7-93	8	-57.74	10-77	13	-5.17	4-89	4	-22.75
August	18-235	8	-141.06	11-108	10	-37.56	5-53	9	-36.25	2-74	3	-67.25
September	29-233	12	-1.00	12-108	11	-33.08	10-44	23	+37.25	7-81	9	-5.17
October	20-188	11	-81.86	10-83	12	-31.02	6-45	13	-12.00	4-60	7	-38.84
November	5-61	8	-18.13	3-20	15	+8.38	0-15	-	-15.00	2-26	8	-11.50
December	6-43	14	-14.00	1-17	6	-12.50	1-9	11	-3.50	4-17	24	+2.00

By month – 2016

	Overall			Two-year-olds			Three-year-olds			Older horses		
	W-R	%	£1	W-R	%	£1	W-R	%	£1	W-R	%	£1
January	7-48	15	+0.25	0-0	-	+0.00	1-16	6	-9.50	6-32	19	+9.75
February	6-42	14	-13.25	0-0	-	+0.00	3-17	18	+0.50	3-25	12	-13.75
March	6-45	13	-13.30	0-1	-	-1.00	2-20	10	-12.39	4-24	17	+0.08
April	22-130	17	-13.13	3-11	27	+12.23	12-49	24	+2.89	7-70	10	-28.25
May	18-211	9	-67.50	5-38	13	+34.25	5-70	7	-40.13	8-103	8	-61.63
June	35-220	16	+25.23	6-51	12	-19.85	15-84	18	+10.08	14-85	16	+35.00
July	27-278	10	-84.00	10-91	11	-40.63	9-79	11	+7.75	8-108	7	-51.13
August	27-240	11	-46.73	11-90	12	-20.83	11-62	18	+16.60	5-88	6	-42.50
September	19-200	10	-77.85	9-66	14	-14.72	6-50	12	-6.75	4-84	5	-56.39
October	18-171	11	-62.80	10-61	16	-12.80	5-49	10	-8.00	3-61	5	-42.00
November	9-89	10	-28.75	4-30	13	-1.75	3-24	13	-3.00	2-35	6	-24.00
December	4-65	6	-16.00	0-17	-	-17.00	3-24	13	-1.00	1-24	4	+2.00

By month – 2015

	Overall			Two-year-olds			Three-year-olds			Older horses		
	W-R	%	£1	W-R	%	£1	W-R	%	£1	W-R	%	£1
January	5-52	10	-22.50	0-0	-	+0.00	2-19	11	-6.50	3-33	9	-16.00
February	10-38	26	+27.63	0-0	-	+0.00	3-15	20	+5.50	7-23	30	+22.13
March	10-43	23	+16.98	0-1	-	-1.00	2-13	15	-4.40	8-29	28	+22.38
April	23-106	22	+16.43	5-14	36	+9.88	12-50	24	+4.81	6-42	14	+1.75
May	30-209	14	-24.30	7-45	16	-9.34	11-73	15	-4.96	12-91	13	-10.00
June	24-215	11	-97.29	2-45	4	-34.38	15-88	17	-17.79	7-82	9	-45.13
July	23-228	10	-86.11	6-66	9	-15.51	11-91	12	-45.35	6-71	8	-25.25
August	43-249	17	+42.52	19-78	24	+44.19	13-81	16	+16.60	11-90	12	-18.27
September	30-218	14	-3.83	13-86	15	-15.08	8-55	15	+3.25	9-77	12	+5.00
October	21-181	12	-67.99	12-65	18	+2.00	2-50	4	-43.97	7-66	11	-26.02
November	9-86	10	-11.72	3-38	8	-26.25	2-20	10	+14.00	4-28	14	+0.53
December	7-66	11	-17.50	1-28	4	-17.00	2-19	11	-5.00	4-19	21	+4.50

By race type – 2017

	Overall			Two-year-olds			Three-year-olds			Older horses		
	W-R	%	£1	W-R	%	£1	W-R	%	£1	W-R	%	£1
Handicap	106-1128	9	-350.03	13-150	9	-54.25	40-370	11	-93.71	53-608	9	-202.07
Group	3-52	6	-32.15	1-14	7	+1.00	0-10	-	-10.00	2-28	7	-23.15
Maiden	16-92	17	-10.73	6-36	17	+8.75	10-55	18	-18.48	0-1	-	-1.00

By race type – 2016

	Overall			Two-year-olds			Three-year-olds			Older horses		
	W-R	%	£1	W-R	%	£1	W-R	%	£1	W-R	%	£1
Handicap	125-1241	10	-334.48	17-137	12	-27.29	56-446	13	-42.03	52-658	8	-265.17
Group	2-51	4	-37.50	1-13	8	-7.50	1-16	6	-8.00	0-22	-	-22.00
Maiden	33-237	14	-84.87	21-177	12	-77.37	11-56	20	-8.00	1-4	25	+0.50

By race type – 2015

	Overall			Two-year-olds			Three-year-olds			Older horses		
	W-R	%	£1	W-R	%	£1	W-R	%	£1	W-R	%	£1
Handicap	147-1152	13	-104.08	16-103	16	+15.38	60-462	13	-53.33	71-587	12	-66.13
Group	3-28	11	-11.88	2-10	20	+0.63	0-3	-	-3.00	1-15	7	-9.50
Maiden	62-371	17	-96.66	41-290	14	-87.55	20-78	26	-10.61	1-3	33	+1.50

By jockey – 2017

	Overall			Two-year-olds			Three-year-olds			Older horses		
	W-R	%	£1	W-R	%	£1	W-R	%	£1	W-R	%	£1
Paul Hanagan	68-453	15	-29.76	28-148	19	+3.59	10-123	8	-66.07	30-182	16	+32.72
Tony Hamilton	36-383	9	-155.58	16-144	11	-55.50	11-116	9	-28.58	9-123	7	-71.50
A McNamara	22-160	14	-34.50	7-49	14	-7.58	10-32	31	+22.83	5-79	6	-49.75
C Murtagh	12-104	12	-38.52	1-6	17	-3.50	6-35	17	-4.13	5-63	8	-30.90
Jack Garritty	10-114	9	-64.71	5-57	9	-33.13	3-28	11	-11.25	2-29	7	-20.33
Barry McHugh	9-61	15	+2.13	4-31	13	+4.38	3-21	14	-7.25	2-9	22	+5.00
S Woods	6-42	14	+0.50	0-1	-	-1.00	2-10	20	+1.00	4-31	13	+0.50
Sammy Jo Bell	6-77	8	-30.50	1-20	5	-16.00	3-21	14	+14.00	2-36	6	-28.50
William Buick	3-8	38	+0.85	1-1	100	+3.00	0-2	-	-2.00	2-5	40	-0.15
Patrick Mathers	3-54	6	-37.00	1-25	4	-23.00	0-12	-	-12.00	2-17	12	-2.00
David Nolan	3-56	5	-34.00	2-29	7	-12.00	1-8	13	-3.00	0-19	-	-19.00
S De Sousa	2-5	40	+4.00	1-3	33	+2.00	1-2	50	+2.00	0-0	-	+0.00

By jockey – 2016

	Overall			Two-year-olds			Three-year-olds			Older horses		
	W-R	%	£1	W-R	%	£1	W-R	%	£1	W-R	%	£1
Tony Hamilton	66-528	13	-151.07	31-195	16	-21.97	21-175	12	-37.29	14-158	9	-91.80
A McNamara	33-247	13	-61.28	6-32	19	+7.38	11-68	16	-14.53	16-147	11	-54.13
David Nolan	20-143	14	+0.17	3-38	8	-5.50	13-54	24	+30.17	4-51	8	-24.50
P Mathers	14-117	12	+15.25	5-36	14	+0.25	5-47	11	-10.50	4-34	12	+25.50
G Chaloner	14-137	10	-23.78	3-42	7	-20.00	6-30	20	+31.10	5-65	8	-34.88
Paul Hanagan	10-89	11	-4.50	3-24	13	-6.00	2-17	12	-6.00	5-48	10	+7.50
Sammy Jo Bell	7-57	12	-18.89	0-1	-	-1.00	1-17	6	-15.39	6-39	15	-2.50
Jack Garritty	7-117	6	-52.88	2-36	6	+0.88	4-37	11	-15.25	1-44	2	-38.50
Jamie Spencer	6-29	21	-2.04	3-9	33	-1.04	3-13	23	+6.00	0-7	-	-7.00

By jockey – 2015

	Overall			Two-year-olds			Three-year-olds			Older horses		
	W-R	%	£1	W-R	%	£1	W-R	%	£1	W-R	%	£1
Tony Hamilton	82-555	15	-136.59	26-194	13	-56.01	29-187	16	-46.69	27-174	16	-33.89
Jack Garritty	41-256	16	-30.81	14-74	19	-17.57	12-80	15	-26.99	15-102	15	+13.75
Paul Hanagan	24-140	17	+6.76	7-25	28	+11.83	9-52	17	-11.83	8-63	13	+6.75
Sammy Jo Bell	23-148	16	+0.10	0-17	-	-17.00	10-56	18	-6.28	13-75	17	+23.38
P Mathers	14-116	12	+37.03	4-30	13	+30.00	8-51	16	+25.03	2-35	6	-18.00
David Nolan	13-112	12	-42.93	4-38	11	-16.63	6-28	21	+1.95	3-46	7	-28.25
G Chaloner	11-125	9	-28.75	2-27	7	-13.50	4-41	10	+0.00	5-57	9	-15.25
N Hambling	5-24	21	+12.50	0-1	-	-1.00	1-9	11	-1.00	4-14	29	+14.50
Tom Eaves	3-11	27	+3.75	3-7	43	+7.75	0-1	-	-1.00	0-3	-	-3.00

By course – 2014-2017

	Overall			Two-year-olds			Three-year-olds			Older horses		
	W-R	%	£1	W-R	%	£1	W-R	%	£1	W-R	%	£1
Ascot	8-154	5	-49.40	0-20	-	-20.00	2-36	6	-19.00	6-98	6	-10.40
Ayr	25-299	8	-116.74	5-70	7	-43.87	6-85	7	-36.50	14-144	10	-36.38
Bath	2-12	17	+0.00	0-0	-	+0.00	2-7	29	+5.00	0-5	-	-5.00
Beverley	47-283	17	-68.58	20-108	19	-27.53	20-94	21	+1.71	7-81	9	-42.75
Brighton	1-7	14	-3.00	0-2	-	-2.00	1-4	25	+0.00	0-1	-	-1.00
Carlisle	25-207	12	-77.68	9-81	11	-42.71	12-76	16	-24.47	4-50	8	-10.50
Catterick	37-172	22	+4.17	20-69	29	-0.97	5-45	11	-18.67	12-58	21	+23.81
Chelmsfd (AW)	9-113	8	-39.08	3-20	15	-9.25	1-41	2	-39.33	5-52	10	+9.50
Chepstow	0-1	-	-1.00	0-1	-	-1.00	0-0	-	+0.00	0-0	-	+0.00
Chester	52-405	13	-52.63	12-70	17	+2.29	15-103	15	-3.92	25-232	11	-51.00
Doncaster	34-384	9	-91.99	10-110	9	-27.47	9-109	8	-25.03	15-165	9	-39.50
Epsom	11-97	11	-21.63	1-17	6	-12.50	3-25	12	-9.00	7-55	13	-0.13
Ffos Las	1-2	50	+0.50	1-2	50	+0.50	0-0	-	+0.00	0-0	-	+0.00
Goodwood	7-128	5	-63.00	2-25	8	-15.00	3-30	10	-3.00	2-73	3	-45.00
Hamilton	26-221	12	-86.18	6-67	9	-22.75	14-81	17	-13.42	6-73	8	-50.01
Haydock	29-315	9	-142.22	10-81	12	-22.93	14-90	16	+2.21	5-144	3	-121.50
Kempton (AW)	1-81	1	-59.00	0-27	-	-27.00	1-22	5	-11.00	0-32	-	-32.00
Leicester	28-134	21	+30.89	12-52	23	+16.10	9-46	20	+14.03	7-36	19	+0.75
Lingfield	1-10	10	-7.38	1-8	13	-5.38	0-2	-	-2.00	0-0	-	+0.00
Lingfield (AW)	25-198	13	-33.90	3-17	18	-2.25	9-67	13	-19.15	13-114	11	-12.50
Musselburgh	35-159	18	+40.18	12-53	23	-7.53	15-70	21	+60.95	8-68	12	-13.25
Newbury	9-76	12	+23.38	6-35	17	+39.63	0-17	-	-17.00	3-24	13	+0.75
Newcastle	16-102	16	+24.08	5-34	15	-11.25	4-33	12	+6.00	7-35	20	+29.33
N'castle (AW)	30-265	11	-45.00	12-90	13	-6.38	10-70	14	+15.88	8-105	8	-54.50
Newmarket	12-154	8	-58.95	3-43	7	-27.70	5-63	8	-19.50	4-48	8	-11.75
Newmarket (J)	19-148	13	+16.50	5-39	13	+5.00	9-62	15	+11.50	5-47	11	+0.00
Nottingham	32-175	18	+29.92	12-58	21	+3.63	13-76	17	+21.05	7-41	17	+5.25
Pontefract	41-238	17	+16.30	14-77	18	+41.38	17-85	20	-2.01	10-76	13	-23.07
Redcar	44-263	17	+3.27	20-122	16	-6.12	10-75	13	-29.01	14-66	21	+38.41
Ripon	30-270	11	-113.34	9-82	11	-31.54	14-91	15	-18.63	7-97	7	-63.17
Salisbury	1-9	11	-4.50	0-3	-	-3.00	0-4	-	-4.00	1-2	50	+2.50
Sandown	4-35	11	-21.38	2-7	29	+0.25	1-16	6	-12.50	1-12	8	-9.13
South'll (AW)	30-159	19	-18.49	8-34	24	+0.72	10-60	17	-15.39	12-65	18	-3.83
Thirsk	40-241	17	-2.38	13-91	14	-14.52	14-79	18	+26.27	13-71	18	-14.13
Warwick	2-6	33	+10.50	0-2	-	-2.00	2-4	50	+12.50	0-0	-	+0.00
Wetherby	4-19	21	+1.25	2-6	33	-0.25	2-6	33	+8.50	0-7	-	-7.00
Windsor	8-44	18	+15.91	1-9	11	+8.00	3-20	15	-2.00	4-15	27	+9.91
Wolves (AW)	62-495	13	-56.93	8-142	6	-25.50	18-143	13	-34.10	36-210	17	+2.67
Yarmouth	3-28	11	-14.77	2-11	18	-2.27	0-10	-	-10.00	1-7	14	-2.50
York	28-508	6	-213.50	14-166	8	-22.75	4-115	3	-66.50	10-227	4	-124.25

Ten-year summary

	Wins	Runs	%	Win prize-money	Total prize-money	£1
2017	193	1705	11	£2,439,577.60	£4,155,876.15	-503.77
2016	198	1739	11	£1,555,029.70	£3,162,107.98	-397.84
2015	235	1691	14	£2,394,305.99	£3,846,973.63	-227.69
2014	192	1502	13	£1,882,767.02	£2,882,652.01	-119.24
2013	164	1287	13	£1,588,826.54	£2,455,584.17	-236.90
2012	142	1294	11	£1,213,826.13	£1,982,267.62	-294.66
2011	151	1224	12	£980,328.63	£1,650,127.14	-260.88
2010	181	1356	13	£1,325,389.94	£2,075,925.44	-273.54
2009	165	1106	15	£1,123,057.39	£1,657,128.68	+25.22
2008	113	971	12	£753,492.30	£1,247,043.13	-285.77

SANDS OF MALI: winning the Gimcrack for Richard Fahey at the Ebor meeting

Richard Hannon

By month – 2017

	Overall			Two-year-olds			Three-year-olds			Older horses		
	W-R	%	£1	W-R	%	£1	W-R	%	£1	W-R	%	£1
January	4-28	14	+19.88	0-0	-	+0.00	2-20	10	-13.13	2-8	25	+33.00
February	4-17	24	+6.57	0-0	-	+0.00	4-14	29	+9.57	0-3	-	-3.00
March	5-31	16	+13.98	0-0	-	+0.00	5-29	17	+15.98	0-2	-	-2.00
April	20-125	16	-7.84	1-12	8	-9.25	14-87	16	-14.59	5-26	19	+16.00
May	30-173	17	-29.49	10-38	26	-1.32	12-113	11	-45.13	8-22	36	+16.95
June	19-167	11	-56.47	8-58	14	-23.97	10-89	11	-17.50	1-20	5	-15.00
July	27-206	13	+20.63	15-101	15	+38.63	11-91	12	-15.00	1-14	7	-3.00
August	32-198	16	-32.41	18-101	18	-6.72	13-82	16	-14.69	1-15	7	-11.00
September	18-160	11	+2.99	9-88	10	+22.91	7-57	12	-15.92	2-15	13	-4.00
October	17-152	11	-5.98	10-98	10	-9.90	5-41	12	+5.55	2-13	15	-1.63
November	7-49	14	-20.09	6-38	16	-11.97	1-10	10	-7.13	0-1	-	-1.00
December	6-29	21	-1.13	6-21	29	+6.88	0-7	-	-7.00	0-1	-	-1.00

By month – 2016

	Overall			Two-year-olds			Three-year-olds			Older horses		
	W-R	%	£1	W-R	%	£1	W-R	%	£1	W-R	%	£1
January	8-28	29	+13.82	0-0	-	+0.00	7-23	30	+13.82	1-5	20	+0.00
February	2-18	11	-7.00	0-0	-	+0.00	2-17	12	-6.00	0-1	-	-1.00
March	2-19	11	-11.63	0-1	-	-1.00	1-12	8	-9.13	1-6	17	-1.50
April	13-110	12	-41.26	4-18	22	-9.31	8-73	11	-17.46	1-19	5	-14.50
May	36-196	18	+68.61	15-56	27	+17.08	20-118	17	+60.53	1-22	5	-9.00
June	20-191	10	-71.97	9-75	12	-28.63	11-97	11	-24.34	0-19	-	-19.00
July	31-223	14	-9.35	15-103	15	-13.50	15-91	16	+31.15	1-29	3	-27.00
August	24-170	14	-47.07	19-102	19	-4.40	5-56	9	-30.67	0-12	-	-12.00
September	9-178	5	-119.92	7-112	6	-64.25	2-50	4	-39.67	0-16	-	-16.00
October	17-145	12	+3.75	10-101	10	+0.00	6-34	18	+9.25	1-10	10	-5.50
November	7-44	16	+26.00	4-31	13	+16.00	3-10	30	+13.00	0-3	-	-3.00
December	4-35	11	-7.92	4-23	17	+4.08	0-12	-	-12.00	0-0	-	+0.00

By month – 2015

	Overall			Two-year-olds			Three-year-olds			Older horses		
	W-R	%	£1	W-R	%	£1	W-R	%	£1	W-R	%	£1
January	1-18	6	-15.75	0-0	-	+0.00	1-10	10	-7.75	0-8	-	-8.00
February	1-13	8	-10.50	0-0	-	+0.00	1-6	17	-3.50	0-7	-	-7.00
March	8-28	29	+17.50	0-1	-	-1.00	6-19	32	+16.13	2-8	25	+2.38
April	15-100	15	-0.75	4-14	29	+0.62	9-71	13	-16.87	2-15	13	+15.50
May	33-177	19	-16.72	10-47	21	-10.37	20-105	19	+9.24	3-25	12	-15.59
June	32-198	16	-42.14	17-81	21	-26.39	14-103	14	-13.75	1-14	7	-2.00
July	34-234	15	-52.13	21-127	17	-22.13	12-93	13	-19.25	1-14	7	-10.75
August	30-209	14	-57.38	23-124	19	-10.13	6-67	9	-32.50	1-18	6	-14.75
September	18-200	9	-111.04	16-138	12	-69.04	1-48	2	-40.00	1-14	7	-2.00
October	11-126	9	-52.17	10-83	12	-14.67	1-33	3	-27.50	0-10	-	-10.00
November	6-37	16	+5.00	4-24	17	+7.50	2-13	15	-2.50	0-0	-	+0.00
December	5-42	12	-15.80	3-36	8	-19.90	2-6	33	+4.10	0-0	-	+0.00

By race type – 2017

	Overall			Two-year-olds			Three-year-olds			Older horses		
	W-R	%	£1	W-R	%	£1	W-R	%	£1	W-R	%	£1
Handicap	83-700	12	-129.34	16-124	13	-14.04	53-474	11	-125.50	14-102	14	+10.20
Group	7-54	13	+30.00	3-24	13	+33.00	2-13	15	-6.00	2-17	12	+3.00
Maiden	22-178	12	-24.44	8-73	11	+15.41	14-105	13	-39.85	0-0	-	+0.00

By race type – 2016

	Overall			Two-year-olds			Three-year-olds			Older horses		
	W-R	%	£1	W-R	%	£1	W-R	%	£1	W-R	%	£1
Handicap	66-636	10	-116.18	13-140	9	-41.00	51-408	13	-4.68	2-88	2	-70.50
Group	6-74	8	-43.75	4-29	14	-6.75	1-26	4	-22.50	1-19	5	-14.50
Maiden	52-381	14	-40.77	40-275	15	+6.68	12-106	11	-47.45	0-0	-	+0.00

By race type – 2015

	Overall			Two-year-olds			Three-year-olds			Older horses		
	W-R	%	£1	W-R	%	£1	W-R	%	£1	W-R	%	£1
Handicap	62-549	11	-91.19	22-138	16	+0.40	36-337	11	-62.59	4-74	5	-29.00
Group	8-113	7	-63.50	3-41	7	-30.50	2-38	5	-18.00	3-34	9	-15.00
Maiden	93-541	17	-139.93	68-412	17	-105.34	25-129	19	-34.60	0-0	-	+0.00

By jockey – 2017

	Overall			Two-year-olds			Three-year-olds			Older horses		
	W-R	%	£1	W-R	%	£1	W-R	%	£1	W-R	%	£1
Sean Levey	54-368	15	-23.19	26-174	15	-8.51	24-157	15	-2.18	4-37	11	-12.50
Tom Marquand	33-275	12	-18.55	18-130	14	+28.60	13-125	10	-32.77	2-20	10	-14.38
Hollie Doyle	20-124	16	+12.04	6-47	13	-12.29	11-64	17	+12.33	3-13	23	+12.00
Jim Crowley	12-46	26	+3.39	4-15	27	+4.67	6-24	25	-4.78	2-7	29	+3.50
Dane O'Neill	10-35	29	+53.43	7-21	33	+35.92	3-14	21	+17.50	0-0	-	+0.00
Ryan Moore	10-73	14	-30.81	4-38	11	-27.81	4-25	16	-9.00	2-10	20	+6.00
Rossa Ryan	9-61	15	+14.33	2-16	13	-5.00	4-36	11	+8.63	3-9	33	+10.70
Pat Dobbs	7-79	9	-42.80	1-14	7	-12.39	4-53	8	-33.42	2-12	17	+3.00
S De Sousa	6-17	35	+3.22	2-6	33	+2.30	4-10	40	+1.92	0-1	-	-1.00
Kieran O'Neill	6-80	8	-15.20	2-30	7	+13.00	4-43	9	-21.20	0-7	-	-7.00
Timmy Murphy	5-29	17	+25.63	3-13	23	+2.63	1-14	7	-1.00	1-2	50	+24.00
Frankie Dettori	5-33	15	-20.36	3-16	19	-9.36	1-12	8	-9.00	1-5	20	-2.00

By jockey – 2016

	Overall			Two-year-olds			Three-year-olds			Older horses		
	W-R	%	£1	W-R	%	£1	W-R	%	£1	W-R	%	£1
Sean Levey	44-371	12	-96.99	21-185	11	-44.76	22-154	14	-25.23	1-32	3	-27.00
Tom Marquand	26-209	12	+11.53	15-100	15	+27.28	10-95	11	-14.75	1-14	7	-1.00
Pat Dobbs	20-233	9	-91.95	14-109	13	-39.95	6-95	6	-23.00	0-29	-	-29.00
Kieran O'Neill	18-152	12	-34.22	6-62	10	-16.00	11-69	16	-1.72	1-21	5	-16.50
Hollie Doyle	10-60	17	+2.50	3-19	16	+3.00	7-35	20	+5.50	0-6	-	-6.00
Frankie Dettori	9-43	21	-2.67	6-24	25	+3.58	3-14	21	-1.25	0-5	-	-5.00
Timmy Murphy	7-22	32	+16.67	5-15	33	+6.83	2-7	29	+9.83	0-0	-	+0.00
Megan Nicholls	5-23	22	+39.50	1-3	33	+10.00	4-19	21	+30.50	0-1	-	-1.00
Gary Mahon	5-31	16	-15.19	3-12	25	-2.60	2-13	15	-6.59	0-6	-	-6.00

By jockey – 2015

	Overall			Two-year-olds			Three-year-olds			Older horses		
	W-R	%	£1	W-R	%	£1	W-R	%	£1	W-R	%	£1
Sean Levey	42-277	15	-29.62	26-142	18	-2.79	14-112	13	-14.21	2-23	9	-12.63
R Hughes	38-185	21	-21.50	16-75	21	-21.72	19-95	20	+5.06	3-15	20	-4.84
Pat Dobbs	29-253	11	-124.38	24-141	17	-51.63	3-88	3	-64.00	2-24	8	-8.75
Cam Hardie	17-121	14	-10.09	6-48	13	+10.00	11-66	17	-13.09	0-7	-	-7.00
Kieran O'Neill	12-86	14	-1.80	7-49	14	-7.40	4-31	13	-14.40	1-6	17	+20.00
Frankie Dettori	11-57	19	-13.62	3-21	14	-15.60	8-35	23	+2.98	0-1	-	-1.00
Tom Marquand	11-122	9	-35.13	6-55	11	-14.00	4-49	8	-15.13	1-18	6	-6.00
Ryan Moore	7-32	22	+2.50	4-18	22	+1.13	3-10	30	+5.38	0-4	-	-4.00
Paul Hanagan	6-26	23	+3.38	4-16	25	+2.13	2-10	20	+1.25	0-0	-	+0.00

By course – 2014-2017

	Overall			Two-year-olds			Three-year-olds			Older horses		
	W-R	%	£1	W-R	%	£1	W-R	%	£1	W-R	%	£1
Ascot	25-298	8	-124.95	15-103	15	+13.00	6-120	5	-81.50	4-75	5	-56.45
Ayr	2-19	11	-4.00	1-13	8	-6.00	1-4	25	+4.00	0-2	-	-2.00
Bath	26-146	18	-35.96	13-68	19	-24.19	12-74	16	-11.77	1-4	25	+0.00
Beverley	2-5	40	+0.17	2-4	50	+1.17	0-1	-	-1.00	0-0	-	+0.00
Brighton	26-117	22	+3.72	15-56	27	-0.50	11-60	18	+5.22	0-1	-	-1.00
Carlisle	0-1	-	-1.00	0-0	-	+0.00	0-1	-	-1.00	0-0	-	+0.00
Catterick	0-5	-	-5.00	0-2	-	-2.00	0-3	-	-3.00	0-0	-	+0.00
Chelmsfd (AW)	26-204	13	-58.30	13-91	14	-11.13	13-99	13	-33.17	0-14	-	-14.00
Chepstow	25-132	19	-33.96	15-53	28	-5.21	8-69	12	-36.25	2-10	20	+7.50
Chester	11-81	14	-24.61	9-36	25	+2.89	2-37	5	-19.50	0-8	-	-8.00
Doncaster	33-243	14	-5.40	14-118	12	-50.50	14-90	16	+46.23	5-35	14	-1.13
Epsom	12-81	15	-23.54	7-30	23	+0.38	4-42	10	-26.92	1-9	11	+3.00
Ffos Las	6-28	21	-3.00	5-18	28	-1.00	1-9	11	-1.00	0-1	-	-1.00
Goodwood	40-338	12	-101.60	21-142	15	-44.70	16-137	12	-6.00	3-59	5	-50.90
Hamilton	1-2	50	+7.00	0-0	-	-1.00	1-1	100	+8.00	0-0	-	+0.00
Haydock	21-182	12	-39.15	9-76	12	-10.02	8-74	11	-32.75	4-32	13	+3.63
Kempton (AW)	57-498	11	-156.43	29-253	11	-79.51	23-203	11	-86.17	5-42	12	+9.25
Leicester	25-165	15	-37.08	14-79	18	-5.13	10-70	14	-20.45	1-16	6	-11.50
Lingfield	19-116	16	-0.12	8-48	17	+4.15	9-60	15	-4.27	2-8	25	+0.00
Lingfield (AW)	59-332	18	+22.07	22-99	22	-13.02	33-188	18	+49.60	4-45	9	-14.50
Musselburgh	0-1	-	-1.00	0-0	-	+0.00	0-1	-	-1.00	0-0	-	+0.00
Newbury	45-422	11	-123.30	25-232	11	-81.18	16-144	11	-14.75	4-46	9	-27.38
N'castle (AW)	1-8	13	-6.67	1-4	25	-2.67	0-4	-	-4.00	0-0	-	+0.00
Newmarket	34-278	12	-20.96	13-120	11	-53.46	18-124	15	+44.50	3-34	9	-12.00
Newmarket (J)	45-331	14	-43.78	32-182	18	+7.38	12-132	9	-38.17	1-17	6	-13.00
Nottingham	21-133	16	-19.78	11-63	17	+6.19	8-60	13	-26.47	2-10	20	+0.50
Pontefract	4-16	25	-3.25	1-8	13	-5.38	3-6	50	+4.13	0-2	-	-2.00
Redcar	6-21	29	+30.58	3-10	30	+23.58	3-10	30	+8.00	0-1	-	-1.00
Ripon	4-14	29	+2.83	1-4	25	+2.50	3-7	43	+3.33	0-3	-	-3.00
Salisbury	49-330	15	-17.29	32-163	20	+28.34	14-146	10	-49.25	3-21	14	+3.63
Sandown	32-241	13	-29.00	16-98	16	-0.21	13-116	11	-20.29	3-27	11	-8.50
South'll (AW)	8-31	26	+5.75	2-12	17	-1.50	5-15	33	+6.25	1-4	25	+1.00
Thirsk	3-5	60	+4.88	1-2	50	+3.50	1-2	50	+0.38	1-1	100	+1.00
Warwick	1-8	13	-6.20	1-3	33	-1.20	0-5	-	-5.00	0-0	-	+0.00
Wetherby	0-2	-	-2.00	0-0	-	+0.00	0-2	-	-2.00	0-0	-	+0.00
Windsor	49-327	15	-85.69	27-143	19	-65.96	18-147	12	-3.83	4-37	11	-15.89
Wolves (AW)	33-201	16	-58.35	14-89	16	-3.92	19-101	19	-43.44	0-11	-	-11.00
Yarmouth	2-10	20	-4.09	0-7	-	-7.00	1-2	50	-0.09	1-1	100	+3.00
York	9-115	8	-26.63	5-60	8	-21.63	3-41	7	-4.00	1-14	7	-1.00

Ten-year summary

	Wins	Runs	%	Win prize-money	Total prize-money	£1
2017	189	1335	14	£1,820,484.01	£2,957,106.43	-89.36
2016	172	1357	13	£1,562,891.35	£2,809,779.05	-211.92
2015	195	1382	14	£2,050,242.78	£3,606,069.97	-348.38
2014	206	1404	15	£2,729,648.95	£4,749,469.60	-366.41
2013*	235	1412	17	£3,137,720.00	£4,532,464.69	-306.32
2012*	218	1367	16	£1,767,369.39	£2,821,469.49	-165.90
2011*	218	1408	15	£2,283,589.58	£3,726,396.80	-46.12
2010*	210	1341	16	£2,054,058.90	£3,218,574.92	-203.61
2009*	188	1371	14	£1,751,642.04	£2,814,384.49	-193.61
2008*	189	1406	13	£1,884,767.33	£2,982,090.39	-283.60

*Richard Hannon Sr training

BARNEY ROY: flew the flag at the top level for Richard Hannon

William Haggas

By month – 2017

	Overall			Two-year-olds			Three-year-olds			Older horses		
	W-R	%	£1	W-R	%	£1	W-R	%	£1	W-R	%	£1
January	6-10	60	+8.24	0-0	-	+0.00	6-10	60	+8.24	0-0	-	+0.00
February	2-3	67	+7.44	0-0	-	+0.00	1-1	100	+8.00	1-2	50	-0.56
March	4-7	57	+1.56	0-0	-	+0.00	3-5	60	+2.23	1-2	50	-0.67
April	10-32	31	+5.95	0-1	-	-1.00	5-21	24	+2.54	5-10	50	+4.41
May	18-70	26	+5.89	3-9	33	+3.80	9-42	21	-13.84	6-19	32	+15.93
June	18-85	21	-24.10	4-16	25	-4.49	11-53	21	-16.44	3-16	19	-3.17
July	29-92	32	+36.89	7-15	47	+2.59	16-55	29	+33.13	6-22	27	+1.17
August	17-86	20	+0.73	2-30	7	-8.50	13-41	32	+14.66	2-15	13	-5.43
September	18-80	23	-19.39	7-29	24	-5.04	8-34	24	-15.60	3-17	18	+1.25
October	19-72	26	+16.10	10-40	25	-6.50	6-20	30	+23.60	3-12	25	-1.00
November	12-35	34	+2.38	8-22	36	+1.06	2-8	25	-0.56	2-5	40	+1.88
December	3-10	30	+4.73	3-9	33	+5.73	0-1	-	-1.00	0-0	-	+0.00

By month – 2016

	Overall			Two-year-olds			Three-year-olds			Older horses		
	W-R	%	£1	W-R	%	£1	W-R	%	£1	W-R	%	£1
January	3-15	20	+0.20	0-0	-	+0.00	1-12	8	-10.80	2-3	67	+11.00
February	0-3	-	-3.00	0-0	-	+0.00	0-0	-	+0.00	0-3	-	-3.00
March	4-8	50	+8.25	0-0	-	+0.00	2-5	40	+0.50	2-3	67	+7.75
April	7-30	23	-10.36	0-0	-	+0.00	6-25	24	-10.36	1-5	20	+0.00
May	10-60	17	-15.97	0-4	-	-4.00	9-44	20	-11.97	1-12	8	+0.00
June	15-71	21	-15.72	2-11	18	-3.75	11-51	22	-10.72	2-9	22	-1.25
July	21-102	21	-25.32	6-25	24	-9.89	13-62	21	-21.93	2-15	13	+6.50
August	20-86	23	-30.63	6-28	21	-10.22	14-48	29	-10.41	0-10	-	-10.00
September	36-104	35	+42.88	12-39	31	+18.95	21-54	39	+18.43	3-11	27	+5.50
October	13-80	16	-25.40	8-47	17	-20.65	2-21	10	-10.50	3-12	25	+5.75
November	6-24	25	-0.33	4-19	21	-2.00	2-4	50	+2.67	0-1	-	-1.00
December	2-13	15	-7.89	2-10	20	-4.89	0-1	-	-1.00	0-2	-	-2.00

By month – 2015

	Overall			Two-year-olds			Three-year-olds			Older horses		
	W-R	%	£1	W-R	%	£1	W-R	%	£1	W-R	%	£1
January	0-5	-	-5.00	0-0	-	+0.00	0-4	-	-4.00	0-1	-	-1.00
February	1-5	20	-1.25	0-0	-	+0.00	0-3	-	-3.00	1-2	50	+1.75
March	0-4	-	-4.00	0-0	-	+0.00	0-2	-	-2.00	0-2	-	-2.00
April	3-20	15	-9.88	0-0	-	+0.00	3-20	15	-9.88	0-0	-	+0.00
May	12-48	25	+7.70	3-6	50	+10.30	9-33	27	+6.40	0-9	-	-9.00
June	14-63	22	-21.25	3-16	19	-11.87	11-39	28	-1.38	0-8	-	-8.00
July	24-82	29	-14.14	10-24	42	+5.05	11-44	25	-16.77	3-14	21	-2.42
August	20-85	24	-0.73	9-33	27	+4.03	10-38	26	+3.24	1-14	7	-8.00
September	15-87	17	-42.48	7-43	16	-20.13	6-33	18	-17.23	2-11	18	-5.13
October	10-77	13	-36.17	7-44	16	-15.38	3-28	11	-15.79	0-5	-	-5.00
November	6-35	17	-12.02	5-21	24	+0.25	1-11	9	-9.27	0-3	-	-3.00
December	8-22	36	+12.10	4-13	31	+0.48	2-5	40	+9.00	2-4	50	+2.63

By race type – 2017

	Overall			Two-year-olds			Three-year-olds			Older horses		
	W-R	%	£1	W-R	%	£1	W-R	%	£1	W-R	%	£1
Handicap	59-238	25	+26.72	5-15	33	+20.70	35-152	23	+0.10	19-71	27	+5.92
Group	2-57	4	-40.43	0-12	-	-12.00	0-19	-	-19.00	2-26	8	-9.43
Maiden	44-122	36	+30.19	7-29	24	-10.49	35-91	38	+39.14	2-2	100	+1.54

By race type – 2016

	Overall			Two-year-olds			Three-year-olds			Older horses		
	W-R	%	£1	W-R	%	£1	W-R	%	£1	W-R	%	£1
Handicap	54-241	22	-16.18	4-30	13	-15.59	41-158	26	-6.09	9-53	17	+5.50
Group	6-45	13	-16.93	2-12	17	-5.50	1-16	6	-14.43	3-17	18	+3.00
Maiden	63-244	26	-45.34	26-118	22	-19.52	37-126	29	-25.82	0-0	-	+0.00

By race type – 2015

	Overall			Two-year-olds			Three-year-olds			Older horses		
	W-R	%	£1	W-R	%	£1	W-R	%	£1	W-R	%	£1
Handicap	29-201	14	-70.99	4-28	14	-1.47	21-137	15	-49.73	4-36	11	-19.79
Group	8-52	15	-12.38	4-20	20	-3.88	3-16	19	+3.50	1-16	6	-12.00
Maiden	58-222	26	-45.78	31-136	23	-29.09	27-84	32	-14.70	0-2	-	-2.00

By jockey – 2017

	Overall			Two-year-olds			Three-year-olds			Older horses		
	W-R	%	£1	W-R	%	£1	W-R	%	£1	W-R	%	£1
Pat Cosgrave	26-134	19	-36.76	8-36	22	-9.72	14-71	20	-17.78	4-27	15	-9.25
Ryan Moore	17-46	37	+16.70	4-13	31	-5.63	10-24	42	+16.08	3-9	33	+6.25
Jim Crowley	13-58	22	-8.16	5-18	28	-4.61	4-20	20	-8.40	4-20	20	+4.85
Georgia Cox	11-50	22	+6.28	2-13	15	-2.30	4-18	22	+2.75	5-19	26	+5.83
Daniel Tudhope	10-27	37	+0.36	6-16	38	+2.38	3-9	33	-1.58	1-2	50	-0.43
James Doyle	9-17	53	+9.45	3-7	43	+0.05	4-7	57	+6.78	2-3	67	+2.63
Martin Harley	8-25	32	+19.54	3-12	25	-3.55	4-11	36	+20.58	1-2	50	+2.50
Paul Hanagan	6-14	43	+8.78	0-0	-	+0.00	2-8	25	+0.00	4-6	67	+8.78
Joe Fanning	5-16	31	+3.38	1-5	20	-1.25	4-8	50	+7.63	0-3	-	-3.00
Ben Curtis	5-19	26	+1.37	1-4	25	-2.00	4-15	27	+3.37	0-0	-	+0.00
R Kingscote	4-8	50	+4.21	3-5	60	+5.54	1-2	50	-0.33	0-1	-	-1.00
Robert Winston	4-13	31	+1.00	0-4	-	-4.00	4-9	44	+5.00	0-0	-	+0.00

By jockey – 2016

	Overall			Two-year-olds			Three-year-olds			Older horses		
	W-R	%	£1	W-R	%	£1	W-R	%	£1	W-R	%	£1
Pat Cosgrave	57-218	26	+20.37	17-75	23	-0.07	30-107	28	+2.19	10-36	28	+18.25
Ben Curtis	13-32	41	+14.23	7-16	44	+2.78	5-13	38	+2.45	1-3	33	+9.00
Frankie Dettori	12-28	43	+7.72	5-8	63	+7.91	6-15	40	-1.69	1-5	20	+1.50
G Gibbons	7-30	23	-6.26	0-4	-	-4.00	7-25	28	-1.26	0-1	-	-1.00
Ryan Moore	7-32	22	-10.29	3-9	33	+1.13	4-17	24	-5.42	0-6	-	-6.00
Georgia Cox	7-37	19	-11.26	0-8	-	-8.00	6-22	27	-3.26	1-7	14	+0.00
Paul Hanagan	6-43	14	-30.00	1-14	7	-12.39	5-20	25	-8.61	0-9	-	-9.00
Jim Crowley	4-18	22	-5.63	0-6	-	-6.00	4-12	33	+0.38	0-0	-	+0.00
Dane O'Neill	3-17	18	+7.50	0-5	-	-5.00	1-8	13	-5.00	2-4	50	+17.50

By jockey – 2015

	Overall			Two-year-olds			Three-year-olds			Older horses		
	W-R	%	£1	W-R	%	£1	W-R	%	£1	W-R	%	£1
Pat Cosgrave	39-201	19	-65.97	17-94	18	-36.71	19-81	23	-16.26	3-26	12	-13.00
Paul Hanagan	14-51	27	+0.40	4-12	33	-1.34	7-29	24	+0.16	3-10	30	+1.58
Joe Fanning	8-18	44	+15.05	4-6	67	+9.75	4-12	33	+5.30	0-0	-	+0.00
G Gibbons	8-24	33	+3.99	6-14	43	+8.64	2-8	25	-2.65	0-2	-	-2.00
Harry Bentley	7-31	23	+0.33	2-8	25	+0.13	5-19	26	+4.20	0-4	-	-4.00
Frankie Dettori	4-10	40	+1.62	1-4	25	+1.00	3-5	60	+1.62	0-1	-	-1.00
Seb Sanders	4-10	40	+4.32	0-1	-	-1.00	3-6	50	+4.57	1-3	33	+0.75
Tom Queally	4-13	31	+14.00	3-9	33	+14.00	1-1	100	+3.00	0-3	-	-3.00
Graham Lee	4-14	29	-4.56	2-2	100	+2.29	2-8	25	-2.85	0-4	-	-4.00

By course – 2014-2017

	Overall			Two-year-olds			Three-year-olds			Older horses		
	W-R	%	£1	W-R	%	£1	W-R	%	£1	W-R	%	£1
Ascot	21-161	13	-32.69	4-30	13	+2.13	12-81	15	-5.14	5-50	10	-29.68
Ayr	3-8	38	+6.57	2-4	50	+9.00	1-2	50	-0.43	0-2	-	-2.00
Bath	7-28	25	-10.73	3-6	50	+2.78	3-20	15	-13.42	1-2	50	-0.09
Beverley	10-26	38	+4.04	3-8	38	+5.44	7-17	41	-0.40	0-1	-	-1.00
Brighton	5-24	21	-9.68	1-10	10	-8.64	4-13	31	-0.04	0-1	-	-1.00
Carlisle	7-17	41	+6.58	1-2	50	+1.75	6-15	40	+4.83	0-0	-	+0.00
Catterick	4-9	44	-2.49	3-7	43	-1.93	1-2	50	-0.56	0-0	-	+0.00
Chelmsfd (AW)	28-99	28	+10.98	10-36	28	-4.37	14-50	28	+11.23	4-13	31	+4.13
Chepstow	9-23	39	+3.40	1-9	11	-7.47	7-12	58	+8.86	1-2	50	+2.00
Chester	9-29	31	-3.98	3-4	75	+7.30	5-19	26	-7.12	1-6	17	-4.17
Doncaster	20-94	21	-15.42	10-24	42	+24.44	7-57	12	-37.46	3-13	23	-2.40
Epsom	2-21	10	-3.50	0-3	-	-3.00	2-12	17	+5.50	0-6	-	-6.00
Ffos Las	3-7	43	-0.93	1-1	100	+0.62	1-4	25	-2.17	1-2	50	+0.63
Goodwood	16-75	21	-14.92	2-12	17	-8.00	12-46	26	+2.83	2-17	12	-9.75
Hamilton	3-8	38	-0.10	0-0	-	+0.00	2-7	29	-3.60	1-1	100	+3.50
Haydock	29-94	31	+11.33	6-21	29	+0.28	17-52	33	+5.98	6-21	29	+5.07
Kempton (AW)	27-135	20	-22.92	8-53	15	-24.43	15-61	25	+2.76	4-21	19	-1.25
Leicester	6-52	12	-33.11	2-24	8	-17.36	4-25	16	-12.75	0-3	-	-3.00
Lingfield	20-41	49	+41.80	10-18	56	+31.58	10-21	48	+12.21	0-2	-	-2.00
Lingfield (AW)	36-125	29	+6.58	10-40	25	+4.78	18-64	28	-6.82	8-21	38	+8.63
Musselburgh	8-22	36	+15.42	3-4	75	+1.96	5-16	31	+15.46	0-2	-	-2.00
Newbury	24-131	18	-14.78	8-52	15	-28.49	11-61	18	+2.21	5-18	28	+11.50
Newcastle	2-10	20	-4.25	0-0	-	+0.00	2-6	33	-0.25	0-4	-	-4.00
N'castle (AW)	12-33	36	+5.81	5-15	33	+4.62	5-14	36	+2.42	2-4	50	-1.22
Newmarket	16-157	10	-47.47	3-68	4	-31.13	10-71	14	-19.84	3-18	17	+3.50
Newmarket (J)	20-121	17	-30.60	4-32	13	-13.13	14-68	21	-16.73	2-21	10	-0.75
Nottingham	10-60	17	-8.05	2-23	9	-16.64	7-30	23	+6.58	1-7	14	+2.00
Pontefract	7-34	21	-5.14	2-15	13	-9.84	5-17	29	+6.70	0-2	-	-2.00
Redcar	10-22	45	+4.70	4-11	36	+0.45	6-11	55	+4.25	0-0	-	+0.00
Ripon	17-39	44	+10.35	3-10	30	-1.92	12-27	44	+10.02	2-2	100	+2.25
Salisbury	9-37	24	-7.03	1-13	8	-10.75	8-23	35	+4.72	0-1	-	-1.00
Sandown	13-54	24	+5.26	4-12	33	+1.42	7-30	23	-3.50	2-12	17	+7.33
South'll (AW)	2-8	25	-0.33	1-3	33	-1.33	1-4	25	+2.00	0-1	-	-1.00
Thirsk	8-26	31	-5.55	4-11	36	+1.50	4-14	29	-6.05	0-1	-	-1.00
Warwick	0-1	-	-1.00	0-0	-	+0.00	0-0	-	+0.00	0-1	-	-1.00
Wetherby	1-4	25	-2.33	0-0	-	+0.00	1-4	25	-2.33	0-0	-	+0.00
Windsor	13-53	25	-16.43	3-19	16	-13.22	9-27	33	+1.04	1-7	14	-4.25
Wolves (AW)	24-98	24	-26.53	10-38	26	-7.28	10-46	22	-19.89	4-14	29	+0.65
Yarmouth	28-97	29	+11.32	9-41	22	-6.89	16-46	35	+12.72	3-10	30	+5.50
York	31-154	20	+24.30	12-45	27	+5.87	7-54	13	-7.25	12-55	22	+25.68

Ten-year summary

	Wins	Runs	%	Win prize-money	Total prize-money	£1
2017	156	582	27	£1,581,585.23	£2,689,295.73	+46.43
2016	137	596	23	£1,423,781.23	£2,127,308.68	-83.29
2015	113	533	21	£1,583,672.69	£2,364,888.31	-127.11
2014	113	520	22	£1,478,038.78	£2,281,869.22	+17.06
2013	107	503	21	£1,133,364.77	£1,896,067.18	-12.27
2012	83	448	19	£748,501.35	£1,257,840.26	-65.35
2011	76	423	18	£848,955.18	£1,228,089.25	-96.35
2010	59	361	16	£942,548.43	£1,181,417.91	-91.16
2009	69	346	20	£793,312.00	£1,320,567.05	-53.39
2008	86	425	20	£793,358.07	£1,056,524.73	+93.92

TASLEET: burst on to the sprinting scene with this Duke of York victory

John Gosden

By month – 2017

	Overall			Two-year-olds			Three-year-olds			Older horses		
	W-R	%	£1	W-R	%	£1	W-R	%	£1	W-R	%	£1
January	4-19	21	-5.14	0-0	-	+0.00	4-19	21	-5.14	0-0	-	+0.00
February	4-17	24	-9.18	0-0	-	+0.00	4-17	24	-9.18	0-0	-	+0.00
March	3-18	17	-8.25	0-0	-	+0.00	3-18	17	-8.25	0-0	-	+0.00
April	19-68	28	+30.42	0-0	-	+0.00	17-56	30	+34.04	2-12	17	-3.63
May	17-80	21	-24.70	1-7	14	-5.47	14-59	24	-13.73	2-14	14	-5.50
June	13-81	16	+0.21	0-11	-	-11.00	12-56	21	+23.41	1-14	7	-12.20
July	11-68	16	-37.99	1-14	7	-12.20	9-38	24	-13.79	1-16	6	-12.00
August	13-55	24	+4.42	5-27	19	-5.75	6-20	30	+4.67	2-8	25	+5.50
September	17-70	24	+9.07	10-30	33	+12.41	5-27	19	-4.58	2-13	15	+1.25
October	18-98	18	-3.76	10-48	21	+2.24	7-36	19	-1.00	1-14	7	-5.00
November	11-65	17	-13.52	9-49	18	-6.52	2-14	14	-5.00	0-2	-	-2.00
December	4-36	11	-24.56	4-30	13	-18.56	0-6	-	-6.00	0-0	-	+0.00

By month – 2016

	Overall			Two-year-olds			Three-year-olds			Older horses		
	W-R	%	£1	W-R	%	£1	W-R	%	£1	W-R	%	£1
January	5-17	29	-3.99	0-0	-	+0.00	4-14	29	-3.09	1-3	33	-0.90
February	1-11	9	-6.00	0-0	-	+0.00	0-6	-	-6.00	1-5	20	+0.00
March	2-8	25	-1.80	0-0	-	+0.00	2-6	33	+0.20	0-2	-	-2.00
April	16-61	26	-3.01	0-0	-	+0.00	14-53	26	-2.84	2-8	25	-0.17
May	14-79	18	-18.66	1-8	13	-3.66	11-56	20	-19.16	2-15	13	+4.00
June	12-89	13	-32.10	4-21	19	+8.42	8-56	14	-28.52	0-12	-	-12.00
July	18-75	24	+22.09	6-21	29	-1.52	10-39	26	+23.61	2-15	13	+0.00
August	16-45	36	+21.59	3-12	25	-5.70	12-29	41	+19.29	1-4	25	+8.00
September	14-69	20	-1.50	7-32	22	-5.90	5-24	21	-1.97	2-13	15	+6.38
October	26-93	28	+34.64	17-53	32	+40.42	8-26	31	+3.22	1-14	7	-9.00
November	11-49	22	-10.38	9-39	23	-5.13	1-5	20	-2.50	1-5	20	-2.75
December	6-17	35	+1.25	6-17	35	+1.25	0-0	-	+0.00	0-0	-	+0.00

By month – 2015

	Overall			Two-year-olds			Three-year-olds			Older horses		
	W-R	%	£1	W-R	%	£1	W-R	%	£1	W-R	%	£1
January	7-20	35	+1.89	0-0	-	+0.00	5-15	33	+1.81	2-5	40	+0.08
February	2-11	18	-2.50	0-0	-	+0.00	1-8	13	-6.00	1-3	33	+3.50
March	4-12	33	-3.61	0-0	-	+0.00	1-6	17	-4.67	3-6	50	+1.06
April	18-60	30	+13.03	0-0	-	+0.00	15-49	31	-1.47	3-11	27	+14.50
May	15-88	17	-20.67	1-6	17	-0.50	11-67	16	-17.67	3-15	20	-2.50
June	13-75	17	-29.46	1-11	9	-5.50	10-54	19	-25.71	2-10	20	+1.75
July	13-53	25	+2.78	3-14	21	+6.88	10-30	33	+4.91	0-9	-	-9.00
August	10-52	19	+22.31	2-14	14	-9.99	8-28	29	+42.30	0-10	-	-10.00
September	23-67	34	+7.75	12-34	35	+3.31	8-27	30	-0.45	3-6	50	+4.89
October	13-77	17	-22.36	10-50	20	-9.97	2-19	11	-11.39	1-8	13	-1.00
November	11-41	27	+19.41	11-33	33	+27.41	0-7	-	-7.00	0-1	-	-1.00
December	4-21	19	-6.10	3-18	17	-4.50	1-3	33	-1.60	0-0	-	+0.00

By race type – 2017

	Overall			Two-year-olds			Three-year-olds			Older horses		
	W-R	%	£1	W-R	%	£1	W-R	%	£1	W-R	%	£1
Handicap	32-191	17	-27.63	3-12	25	+6.63	26-147	18	-23.63	3-32	9	-10.63
Group	20-98	20	+6.41	2-8	25	+5.75	13-49	27	+16.86	5-41	12	-16.20
Maiden	40-168	24	-28.34	5-47	11	-34.30	35-121	29	+5.96	0-0	-	+0.00

By race type – 2016

	Overall			Two-year-olds			Three-year-olds			Older horses		
	W-R	%	£1	W-R	%	£1	W-R	%	£1	W-R	%	£1
Handicap	28-126	22	+35.44	3-14	21	-4.09	23-98	23	+27.03	2-14	14	+12.50
Group	12-84	14	-18.87	1-8	13	-2.00	6-28	21	+2.30	5-48	10	-19.17
Maiden	83-302	27	+10.64	41-148	28	+30.01	39-149	26	-38.47	3-5	60	+19.10

By race type – 2015

	Overall			Two-year-olds			Three-year-olds			Older horses		
	W-R	%	£1	W-R	%	£1	W-R	%	£1	W-R	%	£1
Handicap	24-98	24	-5.60	2-8	25	-2.63	15-71	21	-17.72	7-19	37	+14.75
Group	17-81	21	-11.09	5-10	50	+16.13	8-35	23	-11.46	4-36	11	-15.75
Maiden	66-306	22	-49.39	31-147	21	-4.31	34-156	22	-43.42	1-3	33	-1.67

By jockey – 2017

	Overall			Two-year-olds			Three-year-olds			Older horses		
	W-R	%	£1	W-R	%	£1	W-R	%	£1	W-R	%	£1
Frankie Dettori	37-131	28	+44.96	8-25	32	+14.70	27-84	32	+38.76	2-22	9	-8.50
Robert Tart	19-80	24	+7.30	4-28	14	-12.20	13-48	27	+12.00	2-4	50	+7.50
Robert Havlin	15-106	14	-47.14	12-66	18	-19.14	3-31	10	-19.00	0-9	-	-9.00
James Doyle	10-43	23	-7.27	1-9	11	-7.71	7-22	32	+4.65	2-12	17	-4.20
Nicky Mackay	10-55	18	-17.56	2-24	8	-8.50	8-31	26	-9.06	0-0	-	+0.00
Jim Crowley	9-41	22	-12.40	3-10	30	-2.06	4-19	21	-7.09	2-12	17	-3.25
K Shoemark	7-32	22	-0.09	2-12	17	-1.50	4-16	25	-5.59	1-4	25	+7.00
Andrea Atzeni	5-27	19	-6.72	1-3	33	-0.50	4-20	20	-2.22	0-4	-	-4.00
Jimmy Fortune	4-12	33	+7.38	1-1	100	+7.00	2-8	25	-0.63	1-3	33	+1.00
Oisin Murphy	3-5	60	+7.55	3-5	60	+7.55	0-0	-	+0.00	0-0	-	+0.00
Harry Bentley	3-7	43	+2.75	2-3	67	+4.50	1-4	25	-1.75	0-0	-	+0.00
William Buick	3-35	9	-11.50	0-3	-	-3.00	3-25	12	-1.50	0-7	-	-7.00

By jockey – 2016

	Overall			Two-year-olds			Three-year-olds			Older horses		
	W-R	%	£1	W-R	%	£1	W-R	%	£1	W-R	%	£1
Robert Havlin	55-211	26	+48.38	22-71	31	+14.40	25-105	24	-1.38	8-35	23	+35.35
Frankie Dettori	38-144	26	-2.57	13-43	30	+8.60	22-76	29	+4.46	3-25	12	-15.63
Nicky Mackay	13-63	21	-9.68	3-24	13	-13.02	10-36	28	+6.35	0-3	-	-3.00
James Doyle	11-42	26	+1.45	8-20	40	+5.36	3-19	16	-0.91	0-3	-	-3.00
Paul Hanagan	7-32	22	-12.56	1-6	17	-2.25	5-15	33	-3.65	1-11	9	-6.67
Tom Queally	5-11	45	+6.41	0-0	-	+0.00	5-11	45	+6.41	0-0	-	+0.00
Robert Tart	3-22	14	+12.75	3-12	25	+22.75	0-8	-	-8.00	0-2	-	-2.00
Graham Lee	2-7	29	-2.29	0-3	-	-3.00	2-3	67	+1.71	0-1	-	-1.00
William Buick	2-36	6	-28.75	0-9	-	-9.00	2-21	10	-13.75	0-6	-	-6.00

By jockey – 2015

	Overall			Two-year-olds			Three-year-olds			Older horses		
	W-R	%	£1	W-R	%	£1	W-R	%	£1	W-R	%	£1
Robert Havlin	40-175	23	+32.19	12-62	19	+5.60	22-88	25	+19.84	6-25	24	+6.75
Frankie Dettori	36-134	27	-12.71	13-39	33	+3.48	19-71	27	-12.85	4-24	17	-3.33
Paul Hanagan	13-31	42	+14.72	4-6	67	+2.14	6-21	29	+6.08	3-4	75	+6.50
William Buick	12-52	23	-6.22	3-12	25	-1.67	8-31	26	-0.55	1-9	11	-4.00
Nicky Mackay	12-74	16	-19.51	3-25	12	-5.50	8-44	18	-10.63	1-5	20	-3.39
James Doyle	7-35	20	-10.17	4-11	36	+0.58	2-20	10	-10.50	1-4	25	-0.25
Dane O'Neill	4-15	27	-2.00	0-2	-	-2.00	4-12	33	+1.00	0-1	-	-1.00
Ryan Moore	3-10	30	+3.08	1-2	50	+0.25	1-7	14	-5.17	1-1	100	+8.00
Jimmy Fortune	3-13	23	+11.25	2-6	33	+14.75	1-5	20	-1.50	0-2	-	-2.00

By course – 2014-2017

	Overall			Two-year-olds			Three-year-olds			Older horses		
	W-R	%	£1	W-R	%	£1	W-R	%	£1	W-R	%	£1
Ascot	31-200	16	-2.20	3-18	17	+16.25	17-104	16	-14.70	11-78	14	-3.75
Ayr	1-2	50	-0.92	0-0	-	+0.00	1-1	100	+0.08	0-1	-	-1.00
Bath	0-5	-	-5.00	0-1	-	-1.00	0-4	-	-4.00	0-0	-	+0.00
Beverley	1-6	17	-2.75	0-0	-	+0.00	1-6	17	-2.75	0-0	-	+0.00
Brighton	0-3	-	-3.00	0-1	-	-1.00	0-2	-	-2.00	0-0	-	+0.00
Carlisle	0-2	-	-2.00	0-0	-	+0.00	0-2	-	-2.00	0-0	-	+0.00
Catterick	1-1	100	+0.83	0-0	-	+0.00	1-1	100	+0.83	0-0	-	+0.00
Chelmsfd (AW)	28-120	23	-22.66	6-46	13	-18.13	18-68	26	-13.35	4-6	67	+8.82
Chepstow	3-6	50	+2.91	0-0	-	+0.00	3-6	50	+2.91	0-0	-	+0.00
Chester	7-28	25	-3.54	0-1	-	-1.00	5-22	23	-7.04	2-5	40	+4.50
Doncaster	26-137	19	-44.36	9-36	25	-1.92	17-77	22	-18.45	0-24	-	-24.00
Epsom	11-42	26	-5.57	1-5	20	-3.33	9-31	29	+1.96	1-6	17	-4.20
Goodwood	20-93	22	-11.70	5-16	31	+0.01	10-50	20	-9.78	5-27	19	-1.93
Hamilton	0-1	-	-1.00	0-0	-	+0.00	0-1	-	-1.00	0-0	-	+0.00
Haydock	25-85	29	+45.59	10-26	38	+14.76	9-39	23	+8.83	6-20	30	+22.00
Kempton (AW)	54-239	23	-8.14	25-124	20	-11.10	27-102	26	+12.10	2-13	15	-9.14
Leicester	9-55	16	-17.14	5-22	23	-8.71	2-30	7	-25.68	2-3	67	+17.25
Lingfield	3-23	13	-8.75	0-4	-	-4.00	3-19	16	-4.75	0-0	-	+0.00
Lingfield (AW)	36-198	18	-73.84	9-60	15	-18.39	24-116	21	-44.03	3-22	14	-11.42
Newbury	40-171	23	+17.00	14-52	27	+11.38	23-91	25	+12.13	3-28	11	-6.50
Newcastle	0-9	-	-9.00	0-4	-	-4.00	0-4	-	-4.00	0-1	-	-1.00
N'castle (AW)	14-39	36	+3.37	8-18	44	+8.14	6-21	29	-4.77	0-0	-	+0.00
Newmarket	50-250	20	-3.75	19-89	21	+4.24	26-125	21	+6.63	5-36	14	-14.63
Newmarket (J)	28-167	17	+9.46	8-60	13	-18.59	17-89	19	+19.55	3-18	17	+8.50
Nottingham	21-106	20	+10.89	9-45	20	+4.48	10-52	19	-5.34	2-9	22	+11.75
Pontefract	2-11	18	-1.75	0-2	-	-2.00	1-7	14	-0.50	1-2	50	+0.75
Redcar	0-3	-	-3.00	0-3	-	-3.00	0-0	-	+0.00	0-0	-	+0.00
Ripon	1-2	50	-0.50	0-0	-	+0.00	1-2	50	-0.50	0-0	-	+0.00
Salisbury	11-34	32	+32.89	2-7	29	+2.50	7-23	30	+27.17	2-4	50	+3.23
Sandown	26-121	21	+2.31	6-29	21	-1.67	17-73	23	-2.27	3-19	16	+6.25
South'll (AW)	7-17	41	-4.31	0-1	-	-1.00	5-13	38	-3.74	2-3	67	+0.43
Thirsk	1-4	25	-2.20	1-3	33	-1.20	0-1	-	-1.00	0-0	-	+0.00
Wetherby	1-1	100	+6.00	0-0	-	+0.00	1-1	100	+6.00	0-0	-	+0.00
Windsor	13-63	21	-23.91	3-7	43	+7.38	10-51	20	-26.28	0-5	-	-5.00
Wolves (AW)	46-135	34	+1.89	24-64	38	+12.33	21-68	31	-8.74	1-3	33	-1.70
Yarmouth	14-47	30	+19.71	6-23	26	-2.08	8-23	35	+22.79	0-1	-	-1.00
York	12-63	19	-12.30	0-3	-	-3.00	11-40	28	+6.95	1-20	5	-16.25

Ten-year summary

	Wins	Runs	%	Win prize-money	Total prize-money	£1
2017	134	675	20	£4,541,824.95	£6,163,758.83	-82.98
2016	142	613	23	£1,997,426.28	£3,487,430.77	+7.64
2015	133	577	23	£3,094,711.38	£5,277,650.54	-17.52
2014	132	613	22	£2,876,012.06	£4,241,990.89	-24.63
2013	108	525	21	£1,263,914.58	£2,033,077.64	-24.83
2012	119	629	19	£2,150,284.26	£3,739,407.23	-60.64
2011	99	553	18	£1,828,265.33	£2,529,369.21	-14.31
2010	105	518	20	£1,101,277.72	£1,714,237.43	-28.71
2009	88	516	17	£1,447,841.46	£2,308,709.36	-97.55
2008	95	498	19	£1,843,697.13	£2,596,896.00	+19.30

CRACKSMAN: handled with typical patience by John Gosden

David O'Meara

By month – 2017

	Overall			Two-year-olds			Three-year-olds			Older horses		
	W-R	%	£1	W-R	%	£1	W-R	%	£1	W-R	%	£1
January	4-21	19	+9.25	0-0	-	+0.00	0-3	-	-3.00	4-18	22	+12.25
February	1-25	4	-20.50	0-0	-	+0.00	1-7	14	-2.50	0-18	-	-18.00
March	2-18	11	+10.10	0-0	-	+0.00	1-8	13	-5.90	1-10	10	+16.00
April	6-65	9	-7.63	0-1	-	-1.00	2-21	10	-12.13	4-43	9	+5.50
May	15-137	11	+23.91	1-10	10	-5.50	8-48	17	+62.41	6-79	8	-33.00
June	18-147	12	-5.24	4-19	21	+8.93	9-46	20	+10.58	5-82	6	-24.75
July	9-146	6	-77.48	1-16	6	-14.33	4-46	9	-29.15	4-84	5	-34.00
August	20-165	12	-61.05	1-21	5	-19.43	10-49	20	+5.88	9-95	9	-47.50
September	11-116	9	-40.13	2-21	10	-4.00	5-36	14	+6.75	4-59	7	-42.88
October	9-106	8	-46.88	1-13	8	+0.00	3-33	9	-17.00	5-60	8	-29.88
November	8-71	11	-27.50	1-7	14	-4.00	4-16	25	+8.00	3-48	6	-31.50
December	5-52	10	+0.00	0-9	-	-9.00	1-11	9	-6.00	4-32	13	+15.00

By month – 2016

	Overall			Two-year-olds			Three-year-olds			Older horses		
	W-R	%	£1	W-R	%	£1	W-R	%	£1	W-R	%	£1
January	2-17	12	-2.00	0-0	-	+0.00	0-3	-	-3.00	2-14	14	+1.00
February	0-10	-	-10.00	0-0	-	+0.00	0-2	-	-2.00	0-8	-	-8.00
March	1-10	10	-7.63	0-0	-	+0.00	0-2	-	-2.00	1-8	13	-5.63
April	7-77	9	-24.13	2-3	67	+4.88	0-13	-	-13.00	5-61	8	-16.00
May	15-125	12	-20.42	2-9	22	-2.13	3-20	15	+6.13	10-96	10	-24.42
June	12-151	8	-68.50	3-21	14	+9.75	3-28	11	-15.00	6-102	6	-63.25
July	14-141	10	-65.71	3-22	14	-10.46	2-23	9	-11.00	9-96	9	-44.25
August	14-125	11	-33.17	2-15	13	-3.50	2-26	8	-12.50	10-84	12	-17.17
September	8-125	6	-76.38	0-19	-	-19.00	3-22	14	-4.63	5-84	6	-52.75
October	16-114	14	-22.18	0-13	-	-13.00	5-23	22	+9.00	11-78	14	-18.18
November	7-53	13	-7.02	0-5	-	-5.00	2-16	13	+1.00	5-32	16	-3.02
December	7-27	26	+0.50	0-3	-	-3.00	2-9	22	+0.00	5-15	33	+3.50

By month – 2015

	Overall			Two-year-olds			Three-year-olds			Older horses		
	W-R	%	£1	W-R	%	£1	W-R	%	£1	W-R	%	£1
January	4-22	18	-7.65	0-0	-	+0.00	0-3	-	-3.00	4-19	21	-4.65
February	1-18	6	-14.00	0-0	-	+0.00	1-6	17	-2.00	0-12	-	-12.00
March	5-41	12	-15.25	0-1	-	-1.00	2-16	13	-7.25	3-24	13	-7.00
April	14-71	20	+7.77	0-5	-	-5.00	0-18	-	-18.00	14-48	29	+30.77
May	16-125	13	-10.88	2-7	29	+6.00	3-33	9	-20.13	11-85	13	+3.25
June	18-127	14	+20.84	0-6	-	-6.00	5-40	13	+13.06	13-81	16	+13.78
July	21-135	16	-31.07	2-10	20	+0.00	4-46	9	-33.87	15-79	19	+2.80
August	18-135	13	-44.88	1-11	9	-8.75	11-44	25	+11.63	6-80	8	-47.75
September	7-113	6	-59.17	0-13	-	-13.00	3-34	9	-12.17	4-66	6	-34.00
October	8-81	10	-28.88	0-8	-	-8.00	4-29	14	-11.38	4-44	9	-9.50
November	4-34	12	-15.25	0-10	-	-10.00	3-10	30	+4.75	1-14	7	-10.00
December	6-29	21	+22.10	0-5	-	-5.00	4-11	36	+31.00	2-13	15	-3.90

By race type – 2017

	Overall			Two-year-olds			Three-year-olds			Older horses		
	W-R	%	£1	W-R	%	£1	W-R	%	£1	W-R	%	£1
Handicap	78-795	10	-197.17	1-28	4	-17.00	33-225	15	-1.17	44-542	8	-179.00
Group	0-26	-	-26.00	0-2	-	-2.00	0-1	-	-1.00	0-23	-	-23.00
Maiden	13-97	13	+0.88	1-10	10	-4.00	12-84	14	+7.88	0-3	-	-3.00

By race type – 2016

	Overall			Two-year-olds			Three-year-olds			Older horses		
	W-R	%	£1	W-R	%	£1	W-R	%	£1	W-R	%	£1
Handicap	74-749	10	-230.79	2-25	8	-10.00	14-139	10	-26.50	58-585	10	-194.29
Group	0-37	-	-37.00	0-2	-	-2.00	0-0	-	+0.00	0-35	-	-35.00
Maiden	11-88	13	-47.33	2-39	5	-31.83	6-41	15	-20.50	3-8	38	+5.00

By race type – 2015

	Overall			Two-year-olds			Three-year-olds			Older horses		
	W-R	%	£1	W-R	%	£1	W-R	%	£1	W-R	%	£1
Handicap	91-728	13	-131.73	0-24	-	-24.00	32-229	14	-21.63	59-475	12	-86.11
Group	5-32	16	+17.00	0-0	-	+0.00	0-2	-	-2.00	5-30	17	+19.00
Maiden	13-103	13	-42.47	5-46	11	-20.75	8-49	16	-13.72	0-8	-	-8.00

By jockey – 2017

	Overall			Two-year-olds			Three-year-olds			Older horses		
	W-R	%	£1	W-R	%	£1	W-R	%	£1	W-R	%	£1
D Tudhope	54-389	14	+18.69	4-41	10	-20.15	26-115	23	+96.34	24-233	10	-57.50
Phillip Makin	11-108	10	-15.68	2-29	7	-16.43	7-43	16	-1.25	2-36	6	+2.00
David Nolan	6-73	8	-19.50	1-12	8	+1.00	1-18	6	-12.50	4-43	9	-8.00
Josh Doyle	5-99	5	-38.75	0-4	-	-4.00	2-36	6	-11.00	3-59	5	-23.75
K Shoemark	4-19	21	+4.00	0-1	-	-1.00	1-6	17	-2.00	3-12	25	+7.00
Martin Harley	4-34	12	-12.25	0-3	-	-3.00	1-8	13	-3.00	3-23	13	-6.25
Shelley Birkett	4-64	6	-25.50	0-0	-	+0.00	2-30	7	-9.00	2-34	6	-16.50
Patrick Vaughan	4-72	6	-19.75	0-1	-	-1.00	1-11	9	-8.25	3-60	5	-10.50
Adam Kirby	3-25	12	-11.25	0-0	-	+0.00	1-4	25	+0.50	2-21	10	-11.75
Sam James	3-29	10	-8.00	1-9	11	+3.00	2-9	22	+0.00	0-11	-	-11.00
Andrea Atzeni	2-6	33	-1.52	0-0	-	+0.00	2-5	40	-0.52	0-1	-	-1.00
Harry Bentley	2-13	15	-2.50	0-0	-	+0.00	0-5	-	-5.00	2-8	25	+2.50

By jockey – 2016

	Overall			Two-year-olds			Three-year-olds			Older horses		
	W-R	%	£1	W-R	%	£1	W-R	%	£1	W-R	%	£1
D Tudhope	47-343	14	-85.09	5-39	13	-18.58	11-62	18	+13.88	31-242	13	-80.38
Josh Doyle	9-119	8	-68.52	1-8	13	-4.00	2-21	10	-8.00	6-90	7	-56.52
Phillip Makin	8-79	10	-24.13	1-15	7	-12.13	1-17	6	-13.50	6-47	13	+1.50
G Gibbons	7-44	16	-5.25	1-5	20	-1.50	3-16	19	+7.00	3-23	13	-10.75
Shelley Birkett	7-57	12	+14.25	0-2	-	-2.00	0-9	-	-9.00	7-46	15	+25.25
David Nolan	5-77	6	-38.38	0-2	-	-2.00	1-7	14	-4.38	4-68	6	-32.00
Sam James	4-83	5	-50.25	3-21	14	+1.75	0-19	-	-19.00	1-43	2	-33.00
Martin Harley	3-9	33	+3.00	0-0	-	+0.00	0-0	-	+0.00	3-9	33	+3.00
Harry Bentley	3-14	21	+19.00	1-4	25	+11.00	0-3	-	-3.00	2-7	29	+11.00

By jockey – 2015

	Overall			Two-year-olds			Three-year-olds			Older horses		
	W-R	%	£1	W-R	%	£1	W-R	%	£1	W-R	%	£1
D Tudhope	49-301	16	-53.32	3-25	12	-9.75	19-97	20	-14.92	27-179	15	-28.65
Sam James	19-181	10	-62.38	1-18	6	-15.00	5-60	8	-17.25	13-103	13	-30.13
David Nolan	15-97	15	-10.51	0-6	-	-6.00	5-33	15	-4.78	10-58	17	+0.28
Josh Doyle	14-122	11	-30.00	0-9	-	-9.00	7-38	18	+11.00	7-75	9	-32.00
Phillip Makin	8-45	18	+9.23	0-4	-	-4.00	1-8	13	-6.27	7-33	21	+19.50
Miss R H'stall	3-6	50	+5.50	0-0	-	+0.00	0-1	-	-1.00	3-5	60	+6.50
G Gibbons	3-22	14	+2.75	0-3	-	-3.00	1-9	11	+6.00	2-10	20	-0.25
Shelley Birkett	3-33	9	+20.00	0-3	-	-3.00	1-11	9	+10.00	2-19	11	+13.00
James Doyle	2-7	29	+28.50	0-0	-	+0.00	0-2	-	-2.00	2-5	40	+30.50

By course – 2014-2017

	Overall			Two-year-olds			Three-year-olds			Older horses		
	W-R	%	£1	W-R	%	£1	W-R	%	£1	W-R	%	£1
Ascot	6-120	5	-4.50	0-6	-	-6.00	1-16	6	-11.50	5-98	5	+13.00
Ayr	27-170	16	-37.71	0-18	-	-18.00	6-33	18	-7.17	21-119	18	-12.54
Bath	0-1	-	-1.00	0-0	-	+0.00	0-0	-	+0.00	0-1	-	-1.00
Beverley	32-215	15	-12.54	1-39	3	-32.00	12-73	16	-7.29	19-103	18	+26.75
Carlisle	5-62	8	-27.17	1-9	11	-2.00	2-24	8	-15.17	2-29	7	-10.00
Catterick	16-150	11	-65.93	4-25	16	-14.19	5-53	9	-18.61	7-72	10	-33.13
Chelmsfd (AW)	9-120	8	-68.80	0-10	-	-10.00	2-27	7	-16.50	7-83	8	-42.30
Chester	3-56	5	-26.50	0-6	-	-6.00	0-12	-	-12.00	3-38	8	-8.50
Doncaster	19-211	9	-77.09	4-10	40	+14.13	3-38	8	-24.38	12-163	7	-66.84
Epsom	4-31	13	-11.40	0-0	-	+0.00	1-4	25	-1.90	3-27	11	-9.50
Goodwood	1-30	3	-26.50	0-0	-	+0.00	0-4	-	-4.00	1-26	4	-22.50
Hamilton	20-108	19	-28.53	1-13	8	-1.00	10-43	23	-9.10	9-52	17	-18.43
Haydock	22-200	11	+8.88	0-6	-	-6.00	7-35	20	+38.50	15-159	9	-23.62
Kempton (AW)	6-55	11	+5.00	1-3	33	+1.50	1-18	6	-1.00	4-34	12	+4.50
Leicester	9-60	15	-23.20	0-5	-	-5.00	4-20	20	-0.50	5-35	14	-17.70
Lingfield	3-9	33	-0.50	0-3	-	-3.00	0-3	-	-3.00	3-3	100	+5.50
Lingfield (AW)	10-72	14	-14.25	0-1	-	-1.00	2-15	13	-0.25	8-56	14	-13.00
Musselburgh	15-121	12	-49.90	3-26	12	-13.43	4-32	13	-10.00	8-63	13	-26.47
Newbury	0-17	-	-17.00	0-2	-	-2.00	0-6	-	-6.00	0-9	-	-9.00
Newcastle	11-74	15	-21.82	3-10	30	+0.10	7-37	19	-3.92	1-27	4	-18.00
N'castle (AW)	17-171	10	-55.65	2-14	14	+9.00	7-62	11	-27.03	8-95	8	-37.63
Newmarket	4-60	7	-34.50	1-2	50	+1.00	1-9	11	-5.00	2-49	4	-30.50
Newmarket (J)	4-38	11	-14.38	0-0	-	+0.00	1-7	14	-0.50	3-31	10	-13.88
Nottingham	4-49	8	-27.63	0-6	-	-6.00	0-15	-	-15.00	4-28	14	-6.63
Pontefract	14-125	11	-27.75	0-10	-	-10.00	5-34	15	-1.38	9-81	11	-16.38
Redcar	34-205	17	+1.23	7-42	17	+3.50	13-76	17	+9.00	14-87	16	-11.27
Ripon	31-225	14	-42.31	3-26	12	-4.63	8-56	14	-18.02	20-143	14	-19.66
Salisbury	0-3	-	-3.00	0-0	-	+0.00	0-0	-	+0.00	0-3	-	-3.00
Sandown	2-17	12	-7.50	0-1	-	-1.00	1-7	14	-2.50	1-9	11	-4.00
South'll (AW)	16-113	14	-17.70	0-7	-	-7.00	5-34	15	-2.90	11-72	15	-7.80
Thirsk	24-182	13	-38.09	5-27	19	-4.33	9-51	18	+7.74	10-104	10	-41.50
Wetherby	3-18	17	+46.50	0-3	-	-3.00	1-6	17	+45.00	2-9	22	+4.50
Windsor	1-11	9	-2.00	0-0	-	+0.00	0-2	-	-2.00	1-9	11	+0.00
Wolves (AW)	39-354	11	-83.39	0-40	-	-40.00	15-111	14	-21.75	24-203	12	-21.64
Yarmouth	4-10	40	+5.14	1-1	100	+0.67	2-3	67	+1.48	1-6	17	+3.00
York	30-354	8	-68.75	0-24	-	-24.00	5-55	9	+6.75	25-275	9	-51.50

Ten-year summary

	Wins	Runs	%	Win prize-money	Total prize-money	£1
2017	108	1069	10	£1,007,942.19	£1,689,956.18	-243.14
2016	103	975	11	£767,371.55	£1,680,593.79	-336.62
2015	122	931	13	£1,024,052.53	£1,580,833.33	-176.30
2014	112	830	13	£1,257,328.64	£1,772,806.65	-102.16
2013	136	905	15	£777,659.87	£1,159,386.21	-121.29
2012	69	542	13	£517,175.66	£709,691.68	-34.43
2011	48	423	11	£297,865.68	£479,370.95	-149.06
2010	25	153	16	£87,754.32	£122,742.04	-29.60

*first runners in 2010

BRAVERY: receiving a well-deserved pat from his trainer for winning the Lincoln

Roger Varian

By month – 2017

	Overall			Two-year-olds			Three-year-olds			Older horses		
	W-R	%	£1	W-R	%	£1	W-R	%	£1	W-R	%	£1
January	0-7	-	-7.00	0-0	-	+0.00	0-1	-	-1.00	0-6	-	-6.00
February	0-0	-	+0.00	0-0	-	+0.00	0-0	-	+0.00	0-0	-	+0.00
March	1-1	100	+0.05	0-0	-	+0.00	0-0	-	+0.00	1-1	100	+0.05
April	15-41	37	+3.17	0-1	-	-1.00	11-27	41	+0.80	4-13	31	+3.38
May	17-68	25	-3.48	2-6	33	+1.13	9-37	24	-1.40	6-25	24	-3.20
June	14-78	18	-34.38	2-6	33	-0.75	9-50	18	-19.88	3-22	14	-13.75
July	19-83	23	-22.38	2-13	15	-6.04	10-45	22	-13.83	7-25	28	-2.51
August	10-94	11	-46.38	1-25	4	-22.25	7-49	14	-11.71	2-20	10	-12.42
September	12-74	16	-16.40	2-24	8	-7.25	8-37	22	-0.88	2-13	15	-8.27
October	13-72	18	+16.09	4-36	11	+2.73	8-27	30	+19.48	1-9	11	-6.13
November	6-30	20	-2.19	4-20	20	-4.94	0-4	-	-4.00	2-6	33	+6.75
December	2-7	29	-1.67	1-5	20	-1.50	1-1	100	+0.83	0-1	-	-1.00

By month – 2016

	Overall			Two-year-olds			Three-year-olds			Older horses		
	W-R	%	£1	W-R	%	£1	W-R	%	£1	W-R	%	£1
January	3-11	27	-3.44	0-0	-	+0.00	3-5	60	+2.56	0-6	-	-6.00
February	6-15	40	-4.11	0-0	-	+0.00	3-6	50	-0.04	3-9	33	-4.07
March	2-10	20	+3.50	0-0	-	+0.00	1-6	17	+3.00	1-4	25	+0.50
April	7-41	17	-22.64	0-0	-	+0.00	5-30	17	-15.08	2-11	18	-7.55
May	15-99	15	-37.00	1-6	17	-4.43	7-62	11	-32.92	7-31	23	+0.35
June	17-93	18	-20.22	2-11	18	-3.83	11-58	19	-1.85	4-24	17	-14.54
July	7-42	17	-16.13	1-9	11	-5.25	5-18	28	+0.62	1-15	7	-11.50
August	5-21	24	+2.38	0-0	-	+0.00	1-10	10	-8.00	4-11	36	+10.38
September	17-78	22	+10.29	7-26	27	+16.93	6-36	17	-18.51	4-16	25	+11.88
October	11-98	11	-44.97	4-57	7	-31.20	7-33	21	-5.77	0-8	-	-8.00
November	5-32	16	+0.63	3-20	15	+6.88	2-10	20	-4.25	0-2	-	-2.00
December	2-14	14	-9.63	0-6	-	-6.00	2-7	29	-2.63	0-1	-	-1.00

By month – 2015

	Overall			Two-year-olds			Three-year-olds			Older horses		
	W-R	%	£1	W-R	%	£1	W-R	%	£1	W-R	%	£1
January	3-12	25	+2.48	0-0	-	+0.00	2-9	22	+1.73	1-3	33	+0.75
February	3-8	38	+6.60	0-0	-	+0.00	1-6	17	-1.50	2-2	100	+8.10
March	1-4	25	+1.00	0-0	-	+0.00	0-2	-	-2.00	1-2	50	+3.00
April	5-38	13	-18.00	0-1	-	-1.00	3-29	10	-16.25	2-8	25	-0.75
May	6-51	12	-27.59	0-10	-	-10.00	3-26	12	-13.59	3-15	20	-4.00
June	14-62	23	-12.29	2-10	20	-6.52	10-38	26	+2.61	2-14	14	-8.38
July	27-76	36	+27.44	5-15	33	+2.50	19-46	41	+26.03	3-15	20	-1.09
August	11-68	16	-22.08	1-14	7	-10.50	10-43	23	-0.58	0-11	-	-11.00
September	16-69	23	+27.18	5-25	20	-8.70	7-33	21	+21.38	4-11	36	+14.50
October	4-51	8	-14.00	2-29	7	-4.00	2-19	11	-7.00	0-3	-	-3.00
November	6-21	29	+8.38	0-8	-	-8.00	3-7	43	+6.38	3-6	50	+10.00
December	4-14	29	-0.70	3-6	50	+1.30	0-4	-	-4.00	1-4	25	+2.00

By race type – 2017

	Overall			Two-year-olds			Three-year-olds			Older horses		
	W-R	%	£1	W-R	%	£1	W-R	%	£1	W-R	%	£1
Handicap	49-228	21%	-12.32	0-7	-	-7.00	29-132	22%	+15.79	20-89	22%	-21.11
Group	2-34	6%	-5.38	1-6	17%	+20.00	1-13	8%	-10.38	0-15	-	-15.00
Maiden	30-145	21%	-70.62	2-35	6%	-29.13	26-104	25%	-38.92	2-6	33%	-2.58

By race type – 2016

	Overall			Two-year-olds			Three-year-olds			Older horses		
	W-R	%	£1	W-R	%	£1	W-R	%	£1	W-R	%	£1
Handicap	37-228	16	-75.33	2-11	18	+7.75	21-131	16	-56.04	14-86	16	-27.04
Group	4-34	12	-5.40	0-3	-	-3.00	0-7	-	-7.00	4-24	17	+4.60
Maiden	41-229	18	-42.23	13-102	13	-21.40	25-123	20	-24.59	3-4	75	+3.77

By race type – 2015

	Overall			Two-year-olds			Three-year-olds			Older horses		
	W-R	%	£1	W-R	%	£1	W-R	%	£1	W-R	%	£1
Handicap	51-223	23	+28.06	3-21	14	+9.50	31-139	22	-0.17	17-63	27	+18.73
Group	3-28	11	+3.83	0-4	-	-4.00	2-11	18	+16.33	1-13	8	-8.50
Maiden	39-188	21	-56.40	15-88	17	-45.42	24-100	24	-10.98	0-0	-	+0.00

By jockey – 2017

	Overall			Two-year-olds			Three-year-olds			Older horses		
	W-R	%	£1	W-R	%	£1	W-R	%	£1	W-R	%	£1
Andrea Atzeni	51-218	23	-3.60	9-54	17	+12.44	29-101	29	+4.75	13-63	21	-20.79
S De Sousa	21-78	27	-5.03	2-16	13	-10.63	15-46	33	+10.74	4-16	25	-5.15
Jack Mitchell	18-93	19	-6.93	5-35	14	-16.44	10-37	27	+19.63	3-21	14	-10.13
Harry Bentley	6-52	12	-37.51	0-11	-	-11.00	4-29	14	-19.81	2-12	17	-6.70
Cameron Noble	3-12	25	-1.50	0-0	-	+0.00	1-5	20	-1.50	2-7	29	+0.00
Jim Crowley	3-25	12	-4.75	1-7	14	-3.25	1-15	7	-7.50	1-3	33	+6.00
Dane O'Neill	2-9	22	-4.90	1-5	20	-3.00	1-3	33	-0.90	0-1	-	-1.00
Daniel Tudhope	1-3	33	+0.75	0-0	-	+0.00	0-2	-	-2.00	1-1	100	+2.75
Ryan Moore	1-3	33	-1.09	0-0	-	+0.00	0-0	-	+0.00	1-3	33	-1.09
Fran Berry	1-4	25	+3.00	0-2	-	-2.00	0-1	-	-1.00	1-1	100	+6.00
James Doyle	1-4	25	-2.00	0-0	-	+0.00	1-2	50	+0.00	0-2	-	-2.00
David Egan	1-26	4	-23.00	0-3	-	-3.00	1-21	5	-18.00	0-2	-	-2.00

By jockey – 2016

	Overall			Two-year-olds			Three-year-olds			Older horses		
	W-R	%	£1	W-R	%	£1	W-R	%	£1	W-R	%	£1
Andrea Atzeni	52-242	21	-5.88	12-70	17	+4.75	21-107	20	-29.29	19-65	29	+18.66
Harry Bentley	16-95	17	-22.07	1-12	8	+3.00	13-64	20	-11.40	2-19	11	-13.67
Jack Mitchell	16-103	16	-41.93	3-24	13	-12.46	11-53	21	-15.97	2-26	8	-13.50
Paul Hanagan	3-25	12	-10.25	1-6	17	-0.50	2-13	15	-3.75	0-6	-	-6.00
Joe Fanning	2-4	50	+0.71	0-1	-	-1.00	2-3	67	+1.71	0-0	-	+0.00
Frederik Tylicki	2-10	20	+1.50	0-2	-	-2.00	2-8	25	+3.50	0-0	-	+0.00
Dane O'Neill	2-14	14	-9.20	1-5	20	-3.70	1-7	14	-3.50	0-2	-	-2.00
William Buick	1-3	33	-1.17	0-1	-	-1.00	1-1	100	+0.83	0-1	-	-1.00
Jim Crowley	1-5	20	-3.50	0-2	-	-2.00	0-1	-	-1.00	1-2	50	-0.50

By jockey – 2015

	Overall			Two-year-olds			Three-year-olds			Older horses		
	W-R	%	£1	W-R	%	£1	W-R	%	£1	W-R	%	£1
Jack Mitchell	20-69	29	+49.83	6-24	25	+7.80	13-41	32	+40.03	1-4	25	+2.00
Andrea Atzeni	15-81	19	-25.51	3-23	13	-15.45	9-46	20	-5.59	3-12	25	-4.47
Frederik Tylicki	13-78	17	-12.65	0-18	-	-18.00	8-44	18	-0.25	5-16	31	+5.60
Paul Hanagan	11-45	24	+0.15	4-17	24	-3.68	7-26	27	+5.83	0-2	-	-2.00
Graham Lee	9-45	20	-15.65	1-5	20	-1.00	4-22	18	-13.15	4-18	22	-1.50
Jim Crowley	7-22	32	+9.91	1-4	25	-2.00	3-9	33	+3.91	3-9	33	+8.00
William Buick	5-22	23	-6.79	0-5	-	-5.00	3-10	30	-2.29	2-7	29	+0.50
James Doyle	4-14	29	-1.75	1-4	25	-1.50	3-9	33	+0.75	0-1	-	-1.00
Joe Fanning	3-5	60	+21.00	1-2	50	+8.00	1-2	50	+7.00	1-1	100	+6.00

By course – 2014-2017

	Overall			Two-year-olds			Three-year-olds			Older horses		
	W-R	%	£1	W-R	%	£1	W-R	%	£1	W-R	%	£1
Ascot	12-101	12	-30.18	2-16	13	+1.00	7-39	18	-2.42	3-46	7	-28.75
Ayr	4-7	57	+2.24	0-0	-	+0.00	2-2	100	+3.91	2-5	40	-1.67
Bath	5-19	26	-4.03	2-6	33	+1.50	2-9	22	-4.78	1-4	25	-0.75
Beverley	6-20	30	+4.98	4-7	57	+13.50	2-9	22	-4.52	0-4	-	-4.00
Brighton	4-35	11	-12.92	0-8	-	-8.00	4-22	18	+0.08	0-5	-	-5.00
Carlisle	1-8	13	-5.75	0-1	-	-1.00	1-6	17	-3.75	0-1	-	-1.00
Catterick	1-8	13	-5.13	0-1	-	-1.00	1-7	14	-4.13	0-0	-	+0.00
Chelmsfd (AW)	16-85	19	-20.47	2-16	13	-1.50	11-48	23	-7.41	3-21	14	-11.57
Chepstow	1-10	10	-7.75	0-4	-	-4.00	1-5	20	-2.75	0-1	-	-1.00
Chester	7-35	20	-1.29	1-4	25	-2.09	5-20	25	+8.30	1-11	9	-7.50
Doncaster	29-120	24	+38.95	3-26	12	-8.09	15-56	27	+20.08	11-38	29	+26.97
Epsom	8-30	27	+9.88	0-3	-	-3.00	5-15	33	+10.15	3-12	25	+2.73
Ffos Las	3-6	50	+0.05	1-2	50	-0.70	1-3	33	-1.50	1-1	100	+2.25
Goodwood	9-61	15	-19.38	3-11	27	-1.38	2-25	8	-12.00	4-25	16	-6.00
Hamilton	2-6	33	-2.35	0-0	-	+0.00	2-5	40	-1.35	0-1	-	-1.00
Haydock	15-89	17	-28.76	2-21	10	-15.27	10-47	21	-3.31	3-21	14	-10.18
Kempton (AW)	32-170	19	-26.99	13-74	18	-2.45	14-70	20	-17.58	5-26	19	-6.96
Leicester	13-68	19	-14.16	2-24	8	-19.55	9-36	25	+6.52	2-8	25	-1.13
Lingfield	9-42	21	-12.62	2-12	17	-2.75	6-23	26	-6.12	1-7	14	-3.75
Lingfield (AW)	19-95	20	-11.93	3-13	23	-7.75	11-56	20	-6.23	5-26	19	+2.05
Musselburgh	1-6	17	-2.00	0-0	-	+0.00	1-3	33	+1.00	0-3	-	-3.00
Newbury	10-86	12	-33.75	3-28	11	-14.13	5-42	12	-17.13	2-16	13	-2.50
Newcastle	1-3	33	-0.50	1-2	50	+0.50	0-0	-	+0.00	0-1	-	-1.00
N'castle (AW)	10-53	19	-23.87	2-17	12	-12.40	6-26	23	-8.47	2-10	20	-3.00
Newmarket	13-149	9	-56.00	5-49	10	+11.00	7-74	9	-44.00	1-26	4	-23.00
Newmarket (J)	8-78	10	-39.09	1-21	5	-17.50	4-39	10	-14.00	3-18	17	-7.59
Nottingham	14-85	16	-21.03	2-32	6	-10.00	5-35	14	-16.00	7-18	39	+4.97
Pontefract	1-20	5	-14.50	0-1	-	-1.00	1-14	7	-8.50	0-5	-	-5.00
Redcar	2-19	11	-8.50	1-5	20	+0.50	1-10	10	-5.00	0-4	-	-4.00
Ripon	9-35	26	-9.51	1-7	14	-4.25	7-20	35	-0.26	1-8	13	-5.00
Salisbury	11-52	21	+10.06	2-10	20	-3.27	9-37	24	+18.33	0-5	-	-5.00
Sandown	15-62	24	-4.38	1-13	8	-10.25	11-37	30	+9.63	3-12	25	-3.75
South'll (AW)	3-11	27	-5.15	0-1	-	-1.00	3-7	43	-1.15	0-3	-	-3.00
Thirsk	3-23	13	-12.63	0-3	-	-3.00	3-18	17	-7.63	0-2	-	-2.00
Warwick	0-2	-	-2.00	0-0	-	+0.00	0-2	-	-2.00	0-0	-	+0.00
Wetherby	0-2	-	-2.00	0-0	-	+0.00	0-2	-	-2.00	0-0	-	+0.00
Windsor	30-90	33	+32.42	1-13	8	-10.50	20-57	35	+14.01	9-20	45	+28.91
Wolves (AW)	28-118	24	+5.74	4-31	13	-8.68	17-68	25	+13.36	7-19	37	+1.06
Yarmouth	19-72	26	+4.73	8-25	32	+1.42	8-33	24	+8.58	3-14	21	-5.27
York	10-76	13	-31.65	1-13	8	-11.27	2-21	10	-11.50	7-42	17	-8.88

Ten-year summary

	Wins	Runs	%	Win prize-money	Total prize-money	£1
2017	109	555	20	£1,217,847.83	£1,897,248.44	-114.57
2016	97	554	18	£1,788,831.62	£2,394,852.99	-141.34
2015	100	474	21	£887,554.86	£1,541,464.56	-21.60
2014	78	471	17	£1,374,851.71	£2,252,219.09	-80.70
2013	89	402	22	£921,239.74	£1,332,296.98	+19.63
2012	72	398	18	£532,154.46	£877,983.27	-55.48
2011	53	272	19	£387,237.31	£702,386.72	+56.94

*first runners in 2011

DEFOE: climbed his way through the ranks for Roger Varian last year

Charlie Appleby

By month – 2017

	Overall			Two-year-olds			Three-year-olds			Older horses		
	W-R	%	£1	W-R	%	£1	W-R	%	£1	W-R	%	£1
January	3-4	75	+3.60	0-0	-	+0.00	1-2	50	+1.00	2-2	100	+2.60
February	1-4	25	-2.09	0-0	-	+0.00	1-1	100	+0.91	0-3	-	-3.00
March	0-3	-	-3.00	0-0	-	+0.00	0-2	-	-2.00	0-1	-	-1.00
April	6-29	21	+0.83	1-1	100	+3.33	5-22	23	+3.50	0-6	-	-6.00
May	17-48	35	+24.08	6-10	60	+9.65	8-27	30	+14.43	3-11	27	+0.00
June	7-48	15	-2.63	2-13	15	-8.38	2-18	11	-8.25	3-17	18	+14.00
July	17-54	31	+14.13	6-21	29	-2.42	8-21	38	+19.19	3-12	25	-2.64
August	12-55	22	-14.44	7-21	33	-2.07	4-20	20	-1.88	1-14	7	-10.50
September	17-47	36	-5.91	15-33	45	+2.59	1-12	8	-9.13	1-2	50	+0.63
October	10-33	30	+8.84	8-25	32	+1.84	2-7	29	+8.00	0-1	-	-1.00
November	8-19	42	+9.77	6-13	46	+7.77	1-5	20	-1.00	1-1	100	+3.00
December	4-12	33	+3.75	3-10	30	+2.25	1-2	50	+1.50	0-0	-	+0.00

By month – 2016

	Overall			Two-year-olds			Three-year-olds			Older horses		
	W-R	%	£1	W-R	%	£1	W-R	%	£1	W-R	%	£1
January	1-4	25	-1.00	0-0	-	+0.00	0-2	-	-2.00	1-2	50	+1.00
February	0-3	-	-3.00	0-0	-	+0.00	0-0	-	+0.00	0-3	-	-3.00
March	0-3	-	-3.00	0-0	-	+0.00	0-0	-	+0.00	0-3	-	-3.00
April	6-15	40	+24.10	0-0	-	+0.00	5-10	50	+16.10	1-5	20	+8.00
May	9-33	27	+29.63	2-5	40	+0.25	6-20	30	+16.38	1-8	13	+13.00
June	11-53	21	-1.58	4-10	40	+1.40	5-23	22	-4.98	2-20	10	+2.00
July	18-75	24	-1.41	9-27	33	+4.90	5-22	23	+5.63	4-26	15	-11.94
August	7-43	16	-19.60	5-25	20	-9.70	1-8	13	-5.90	1-10	10	-4.00
September	9-53	17	-18.25	6-32	19	-12.13	1-15	7	-12.63	2-6	33	+6.50
October	6-42	14	-24.70	3-26	12	-19.45	2-13	15	-5.75	1-3	33	+0.50
November	3-7	43	+2.85	3-6	50	+3.85	0-1	-	-1.00	0-0	-	+0.00
December	0-0	-	+0.00	0-0	-	+0.00	0-0	-	+0.00	0-0	-	+0.00

By month – 2015

	Overall			Two-year-olds			Three-year-olds			Older horses		
	W-R	%	£1	W-R	%	£1	W-R	%	£1	W-R	%	£1
January	16-45	36	+2.93	0-0	-	+0.00	10-32	31	-3.07	6-13	46	+6.00
February	12-47	26	-15.98	0-0	-	+0.00	9-35	26	-11.08	3-12	25	-4.90
March	19-40	48	+7.81	0-0	-	+0.00	12-30	40	-0.96	7-10	70	+8.77
April	19-64	30	-4.51	0-4	-	-4.00	15-51	29	-3.21	4-9	44	+2.70
May	13-61	21	-19.67	3-13	23	-5.48	8-41	20	-15.69	2-7	29	+1.50
June	12-73	16	-7.95	4-27	15	+4.75	7-39	18	-13.20	1-7	14	+0.50
July	10-70	14	-26.99	5-28	18	-12.65	5-37	14	-9.34	0-5	-	-5.00
August	20-89	22	-12.54	14-47	30	+9.53	5-38	13	-22.40	1-4	25	+0.33
September	10-82	12	-58.26	7-56	13	-41.86	2-24	8	-16.90	1-2	50	+0.50
October	8-39	21	-8.49	3-29	10	-19.93	5-10	50	+11.43	0-0	-	+0.00
November	5-22	23	-7.25	2-12	17	-6.25	3-7	43	+2.00	0-3	-	-3.00
December	7-31	23	-2.04	3-19	16	-1.00	4-8	50	+2.96	0-4	-	-4.00

By race type – 2017

	Overall			Two-year-olds			Three-year-olds			Older horses		
	W-R	%	£1	W-R	%	£1	W-R	%	£1	W-R	%	£1
Handicap	20-104	19	+2.20	4-9	44	+2.74	11-67	16	-10.54	5-28	18	+10.00
Group	7-54	13	-31.25	2-16	13	-9.88	2-13	15	-8.38	3-25	12	-13.00
Maiden	36-77	47	+77.62	15-30	50	+20.43	21-47	45	+57.19	0-0	-	+0.00

By race type – 2016

	Overall			Two-year-olds			Three-year-olds			Older horses		
	W-R	%	£1	W-R	%	£1	W-R	%	£1	W-R	%	£1
Handicap	21-123	17	+6.40	4-11	36	+3.50	9-61	15	-23.00	8-51	16	+25.90
Group	6-43	14	-9.38	2-18	11	-7.63	2-9	22	+4.50	2-16	13	-6.25
Maiden	31-114	27	-9.73	19-77	25	-20.08	12-36	33	+11.34	0-1	-	-1.00

By race type – 2015

	Overall			Two-year-olds			Three-year-olds			Older horses		
	W-R	%	£1	W-R	%	£1	W-R	%	£1	W-R	%	£1
Handicap	81-315	26	-37.88	9-49	18	-19.72	55-214	26	-22.26	17-52	33	+4.10
Group	4-22	18	-9.39	2-7	29	-2.38	0-8	-	-8.00	2-7	29	+1.00
Maiden	54-267	20	-80.90	28-169	17	-48.13	26-98	27	-32.77	0-0	-	+0.00

By jockey – 2017

	Overall			Two-year-olds			Three-year-olds			Older horses		
	W-R	%	£1	W-R	%	£1	W-R	%	£1	W-R	%	£1
William Buick	49-159	31	+53.55	24-54	44	+23.57	18-68	26	+23.36	7-37	19	+6.62
James Doyle	25-83	30	-7.73	18-48	38	+0.27	4-18	22	-1.38	3-17	18	-6.63
Adam Kirby	11-39	28	-6.05	6-17	35	+1.85	2-12	17	-6.50	3-10	30	-1.40
Martin Lane	8-38	21	+3.41	1-12	8	-7.50	6-23	26	+10.41	1-3	33	+0.50
Phillip Makin	3-9	33	+2.24	1-4	25	-2.64	2-5	40	+4.88	0-0	-	+0.00
C O'Donoghue	2-6	33	+1.25	2-5	40	+2.25	0-1	-	-1.00	0-0	-	+0.00
George Wood	1-1	100	+1.20	1-1	100	+1.20	0-0	-	+0.00	0-0	-	+0.00
Jack Mitchell	1-1	100	+4.00	0-0	-	+0.00	1-1	100	+4.00	0-0	-	+0.00
Tom Marquand	1-2	50	+1.50	0-0	-	+0.00	1-2	50	+1.50	0-0	-	+0.00
Jamie Spencer	1-5	20	-3.43	1-3	33	-1.43	0-2	-	-2.00	0-0	-	+0.00
Franny Norton	0-1	-	-1.00	0-0	-	+0.00	0-0	-	+0.00	0-1	-	-1.00
Hayley Turner	0-1	-	-1.00	0-0	-	+0.00	0-1	-	-1.00	0-0	-	+0.00

By jockey – 2016

	Overall			Two-year-olds			Three-year-olds			Older horses		
	W-R	%	£1	W-R	%	£1	W-R	%	£1	W-R	%	£1
William Buick	35-161	22	+4.25	14-74	19	-28.60	17-54	31	+35.35	4-33	12	-2.50
James Doyle	15-68	22	-19.76	8-30	27	-8.57	2-15	13	-4.75	5-23	22	-6.44
J McDonald	8-33	24	+10.88	5-11	45	+5.50	2-10	20	+0.38	1-12	8	+5.00
Adam Kirby	4-16	25	+17.85	3-3	100	+9.85	0-5	-	-5.00	1-8	13	+13.00
Martin Lane	4-30	13	-18.52	1-6	17	-3.63	2-20	10	-13.90	1-4	25	-1.00
Jim Crowley	1-1	100	+0.57	1-1	100	+0.57	0-0	-	+0.00	0-0	-	+0.00
Tom Eaves	1-1	100	+1.10	0-0	-	+0.00	1-1	100	+1.10	0-0	-	+0.00
Jack Mitchell	1-2	50	+5.00	0-0	-	+0.00	0-1	-	-1.00	1-1	100	+6.00
Phillip Makin	1-6	17	-4.33	0-1	-	-1.00	1-2	50	-0.33	0-3	-	-3.00

By jockey – 2015

	Overall			Two-year-olds			Three-year-olds			Older horses		
	W-R	%	£1	W-R	%	£1	W-R	%	£1	W-R	%	£1
William Buick	51-229	22	-59.69	23-96	24	-21.18	21-111	19	-39.21	7-22	32	+0.70
Adam Kirby	29-97	30	+12.22	5-35	14	-3.80	14-44	32	+2.73	10-18	56	+13.28
Shane Gray	14-50	28	-19.14	0-5	-	-5.00	12-41	29	-13.81	2-4	50	-0.33
Kevin Stott	12-59	20	-20.76	4-24	17	-11.27	5-25	20	-7.99	3-10	30	-1.50
James Doyle	10-57	18	-17.50	2-25	8	-18.75	8-28	29	+5.25	0-4	-	-4.00
Phillip Makin	9-31	29	-3.11	2-12	17	-6.88	7-17	41	+5.76	0-2	-	-2.00
Martin Lane	9-54	17	-26.75	1-16	6	-9.00	7-32	22	-14.75	1-6	17	-3.00
Ryan Moore	4-6	67	+2.10	0-1	-	-1.00	3-3	100	+2.35	1-2	50	+0.75
J McDonald	4-16	25	+7.20	2-5	40	+8.50	1-9	11	-6.80	1-2	50	+5.50

By course – 2014-2017

	Overall			Two-year-olds			Three-year-olds			Older horses		
	W-R	%	£1	W-R	%	£1	W-R	%	£1	W-R	%	£1
Ascot	15-129	12	-27.48	6-27	22	-9.60	7-59	12	-16.88	2-43	5	-1.00
Ayr	0-2	-	-2.00	0-0	-	+0.00	0-1	-	-1.00	0-1	-	-1.00
Bath	1-10	10	-7.13	0-1	-	-1.00	1-7	14	-4.13	0-2	-	-2.00
Beverley	3-15	20	-5.75	1-11	9	-8.38	2-4	50	+2.63	0-0	-	+0.00
Brighton	3-16	19	-0.97	2-11	18	+2.20	1-5	20	-3.17	0-0	-	+0.00
Carlisle	0-2	-	-2.00	0-1	-	-1.00	0-1	-	-1.00	0-0	-	+0.00
Catterick	1-3	33	+1.00	0-2	-	-2.00	1-1	100	+3.00	0-0	-	+0.00
Chelmsfd (AW)	17-80	21	-28.79	6-32	19	-11.68	8-38	21	-16.61	3-10	30	-0.50
Chester	5-21	24	+0.08	1-4	25	-1.00	4-12	33	+6.08	0-5	-	-5.00
Doncaster	21-102	21	+0.51	9-48	19	-26.72	8-37	22	+14.23	4-17	24	+13.00
Epsom	4-27	15	-12.78	2-9	22	-6.28	0-12	-	-12.00	2-6	33	+5.50
Ffos Las	1-6	17	-4.00	1-4	25	-2.00	0-2	-	-2.00	0-0	-	+0.00
Goodwood	19-93	20	+0.08	10-31	32	+6.50	5-36	14	-4.92	4-26	15	-1.50
Hamilton	2-6	33	-2.23	0-0	-	+0.00	2-6	33	-2.23	0-0	-	+0.00
Haydock	10-70	14	-44.32	4-32	13	-24.60	4-27	15	-14.09	2-11	18	-5.64
Kempton (AW)	57-201	28	-0.58	35-116	30	+7.31	19-73	26	-1.86	3-12	25	-6.03
Leicester	8-43	19	-20.39	5-25	20	-12.76	3-15	20	-4.63	0-3	-	-3.00
Lingfield	6-28	21	+1.01	3-17	18	-6.14	2-8	25	+8.75	1-3	33	-1.60
Lingfield (AW)	45-145	31	+3.09	8-32	25	-2.54	25-75	33	+6.83	12-38	32	-1.20
Musselburgh	0-1	-	-1.00	0-0	-	+0.00	0-1	-	-1.00	0-0	-	+0.00
Newbury	10-55	18	-15.43	3-15	20	-0.94	5-30	17	-10.40	2-10	20	-4.09
Newcastle	0-5	-	-5.00	0-3	-	-3.00	0-2	-	-2.00	0-0	-	+0.00
N'castle (AW)	5-12	42	+14.11	1-4	25	-0.25	3-4	75	+1.36	1-4	25	+13.00
Newmarket	39-154	25	+58.25	14-64	22	+19.90	17-63	27	+31.23	8-27	30	+7.13
Newmarket (J)	35-175	20	-34.47	23-90	26	-6.13	8-64	13	-29.68	4-21	19	+1.33
Nottingham	6-44	14	-12.50	3-19	16	-10.00	3-22	14	+0.50	0-3	-	-3.00
Pontefract	11-31	35	+0.57	4-12	33	-1.88	6-16	38	+1.44	1-3	33	+1.00
Redcar	7-22	32	-3.94	4-12	33	-1.14	2-8	25	-4.30	1-2	50	+1.50
Ripon	1-10	10	-3.00	0-4	-	-4.00	1-4	25	+3.00	0-2	-	-2.00
Salisbury	2-23	9	-16.50	0-8	-	-8.00	1-11	9	-7.75	1-4	25	-0.75
Sandown	10-60	17	-8.32	6-22	27	+5.05	4-30	13	-5.38	0-8	-	-8.00
South'll (AW)	1-3	33	-1.00	0-0	-	+0.00	1-2	50	+1.00	0-1	-	-1.00
Thirsk	6-20	30	+0.98	2-7	29	-2.40	4-12	33	+4.38	0-1	-	-1.00
Wetherby	0-1	-	-1.00	0-0	-	+0.00	0-1	-	-1.00	0-0	-	+0.00
Windsor	9-43	21	-10.58	1-6	17	-3.90	7-29	24	-3.18	1-8	13	-3.50
Wolves (AW)	52-156	33	-19.58	14-58	24	-9.13	31-83	37	-13.05	7-15	47	+2.60
Yarmouth	6-32	19	-15.18	5-19	26	-3.43	1-8	13	-6.75	0-5	-	-5.00
York	11-58	19	-11.70	5-12	42	+4.25	4-19	21	+1.80	2-27	7	-17.75

Ten-year summary

	Wins	Runs	%	Win prize-money	Total prize-money	£1
2017	102	356	29	£1,181,335.00	£2,041,610.48	+36.93
2016	70	331	21	£1,307,474.07	£1,979,285.87	-15.97
2015	151	663	23	£1,493,288.17	£2,156,859.81	-152.93
2014	102	549	19	£924,235.69	£1,493,782.48	-113.14
2013	60	304	20	£693,520.24	£970,334.52	-17.07

*first runners in 2013

SOUND AND SILENCE: a tough and consistent juvenile for Charlie Appleby

Andrew Balding

By month – 2017

	Overall			Two-year-olds			Three-year-olds			Older horses		
	W-R	%	£1	W-R	%	£1	W-R	%	£1	W-R	%	£1
January	4-31	13	-1.88	0-0	-	+0.00	0-8	-	-8.00	4-23	17	+6.13
February	7-35	20	-0.97	0-0	-	+0.00	2-10	20	-5.84	5-25	20	+4.88
March	5-25	20	-11.37	0-0	-	+0.00	3-8	38	-2.62	2-17	12	-8.75
April	6-52	12	-19.63	0-0	-	+0.00	4-27	15	-9.63	2-25	8	-10.00
May	13-85	15	+15.88	0-5	-	-5.00	8-45	18	-3.13	5-35	14	+24.00
June	10-74	14	-13.25	0-10	-	-10.00	6-46	13	-12.63	4-18	22	+9.38
July	10-83	12	+22.35	4-16	25	+5.75	4-48	8	-26.40	2-19	11	+43.00
August	13-89	15	+3.81	3-22	14	+2.06	8-43	19	-12.25	2-24	8	+14.00
September	16-87	18	-6.18	1-28	4	-23.00	7-33	21	-7.88	8-26	31	+24.70
October	6-66	9	-19.50	1-24	4	-11.00	4-28	14	-3.50	1-14	7	-5.00
November	3-35	9	-21.67	1-17	6	-13.00	1-10	10	-5.00	1-8	13	-3.67
December	0-10	-	-10.00	0-4	-	-4.00	0-4	-	-4.00	0-2	-	-2.00

By month – 2016

	Overall			Two-year-olds			Three-year-olds			Older horses		
	W-R	%	£1	W-R	%	£1	W-R	%	£1	W-R	%	£1
January	4-35	11	-18.25	0-0	-	+0.00	1-6	17	-1.50	3-29	10	-16.75
February	1-20	5	-15.00	0-0	-	+0.00	0-7	-	-7.00	1-13	8	-8.00
March	7-33	21	-7.38	0-0	-	+0.00	3-11	27	-2.25	4-22	18	-5.13
April	5-50	10	-25.50	0-0	-	+0.00	2-28	7	-18.00	3-22	14	-7.50
May	9-104	9	-42.00	2-12	17	+14.00	5-60	8	-35.00	2-32	6	-21.00
June	21-109	19	+4.98	2-14	14	-4.25	14-57	25	+18.32	5-38	13	-9.09
July	21-119	18	+5.53	6-30	20	-0.10	15-66	23	+28.63	0-23	-	-23.00
August	13-79	16	-1.50	6-18	33	+8.25	7-38	18	+13.25	0-23	-	-23.00
September	14-85	16	-18.75	6-27	22	+1.75	7-42	17	-7.25	1-16	6	-13.25
October	8-65	12	+29.38	4-27	15	+12.38	2-20	10	-9.00	2-18	11	+26.00
November	4-24	17	-6.25	2-10	20	+0.75	1-6	17	-2.75	1-8	13	-4.25
December	0-8	-	-8.00	0-4	-	-4.00	0-3	-	-3.00	0-1	-	-1.00

By month – 2015

	Overall			Two-year-olds			Three-year-olds			Older horses		
	W-R	%	£1	W-R	%	£1	W-R	%	£1	W-R	%	£1
January	2-17	12	-10.93	0-0	-	+0.00	1-5	20	-3.43	1-12	8	-7.50
February	4-19	21	+10.75	0-0	-	+0.00	2-6	33	+0.25	2-13	15	+10.50
March	5-22	23	-3.30	0-0	-	+0.00	2-9	22	-3.00	3-13	23	-0.30
April	9-54	17	-10.24	0-0	-	+0.00	3-27	11	-5.59	6-27	22	-4.65
May	8-93	9	-50.67	0-1	-	-1.00	3-46	7	-28.75	5-46	11	-20.92
June	13-98	13	-40.30	0-6	-	-6.00	8-53	15	-25.50	5-39	13	-8.80
July	20-103	19	+12.33	2-18	11	+13.00	11-47	23	+0.75	7-38	18	-1.42
August	10-101	10	-58.42	3-26	12	-8.05	3-41	7	-33.37	4-34	12	-17.00
September	11-95	12	-44.94	3-28	11	-10.50	8-41	20	-8.44	0-26	-	-26.00
October	3-63	5	-38.75	1-24	4	-16.00	1-19	5	-15.75	1-20	5	-7.00
November	7-50	14	-13.97	2-19	11	-10.20	3-17	18	-5.52	2-14	14	+1.75
December	3-40	8	-24.50	0-13	-	-13.00	3-14	21	+1.50	0-13	-	-13.00

By race type – 2017

	Overall			Two-year-olds			Three-year-olds			Older horses		
	W-R	%	£1	W-R	%	£1	W-R	%	£1	W-R	%	£1
Handicap	50-376	13	-18.59	1-13	8	-8.00	24-184	13	-68.28	25-179	14	+57.68
Group	6-48	13	+14.13	0-7	-	-7.00	2-21	10	-15.88	4-20	20	+37.00
Maiden	21-125	17	-61.77	2-28	7	-21.94	16-84	19	-36.21	3-13	23	-3.63

By race type – 2016

	Overall			Two-year-olds			Three-year-olds			Older horses		
	W-R	%	£1	W-R	%	£1	W-R	%	£1	W-R	%	£1
Handicap	59-410	14	-82.87	0-13	-	-13.00	43-205	21	+29.85	16-192	8	-99.72
Group	4-28	14	+7.25	2-9	22	+1.75	0-5	-	-5.00	2-14	14	+10.50
Maiden	34-204	17	-21.58	20-81	25	+17.83	14-120	12	-36.40	0-3	-	-3.00

By race type – 2015

	Overall			Two-year-olds			Three-year-olds			Older horses		
	W-R	%	£1	W-R	%	£1	W-R	%	£1	W-R	%	£1
Handicap	52-429	12	-154.05	1-13	8	-6.00	20-192	10	-99.00	31-224	14	-49.05
Group	2-31	6	-7.00	0-2	-	-2.00	1-6	17	+7.00	1-23	4	-12.00
Maiden	33-222	15	-77.42	10-108	9	-31.75	22-111	20	-45.17	1-3	33	-0.50

By jockey – 2017

	Overall			Two-year-olds			Three-year-olds			Older horses		
	W-R	%	£1	W-R	%	£1	W-R	%	£1	W-R	%	£1
David Probert	30-213	14	-54.91	5-57	9	-33.94	15-86	17	-16.48	10-70	14	-4.50
Oisin Murphy	27-145	19	+8.59	3-25	12	+7.50	18-71	25	+0.24	6-49	12	+0.85
Joshua Bryan	8-41	20	-2.63	0-3	-	-3.00	3-15	20	+0.00	5-23	22	+0.38
Rob Hornby	8-75	11	-6.50	0-21	-	-21.00	5-38	13	-17.50	3-16	19	+32.00
William Cox	5-31	16	+0.58	1-4	25	-1.75	0-7	-	-7.00	4-20	20	+9.33
P J McDonald	3-8	38	+21.50	0-0	-	+0.00	0-3	-	-3.00	3-5	60	+24.50
Liam Keniry	3-40	8	-22.88	0-5	-	-5.00	3-23	13	-5.88	0-12	-	-12.00
Jim Crowley	2-5	40	+24.00	0-1	-	-1.00	1-2	50	+6.00	1-2	50	+19.00
Jimmy Quinn	2-23	9	-5.00	1-3	33	+7.00	0-13	-	-13.00	1-7	14	+1.00
Jimmy Fortune	1-1	100	+14.00	0-0	-	+0.00	0-0	-	+0.00	1-1	100	+14.00
William Carver	1-1	100	+4.00	0-0	-	+0.00	1-1	100	+4.00	0-0	-	+0.00
Ryan Moore	1-2	50	+0.75	0-0	-	+0.00	1-1	100	+1.75	0-1	-	-1.00

By jockey – 2016

	Overall			Two-year-olds			Three-year-olds			Older horses		
	W-R	%	£1	W-R	%	£1	W-R	%	£1	W-R	%	£1
Oisin Murphy	31-201	15	-40.33	12-49	24	+27.08	12-86	14	-36.65	7-66	11	-30.75
David Probert	28-191	15	-57.45	7-38	18	+2.45	18-102	18	-25.90	3-51	6	-34.00
Rob Hornby	17-74	23	+16.75	6-11	55	+28.25	9-37	24	+5.50	2-26	8	-17.00
E Greatrex	9-57	16	+27.00	0-6	-	-6.00	8-32	25	+43.00	1-19	5	-10.00
Liam Keniry	7-51	14	+11.41	1-15	7	-10.50	3-22	14	+7.25	3-14	21	+14.66
Jimmy Quinn	5-14	36	+25.75	0-0	-	+0.00	5-12	42	+27.75	0-2	-	-2.00
Jim Crowley	4-15	27	+5.38	1-1	100	+7.00	1-3	33	+1.50	2-11	18	-3.13
Graham Lee	2-3	67	+20.75	0-0	-	+0.00	0-0	-	+0.00	2-3	67	+20.75
Luke Morris	1-1	100	+1.00	0-0	-	+0.00	1-1	100	+1.00	0-0	-	+0.00

By jockey – 2015

	Overall			Two-year-olds			Three-year-olds			Older horses		
	W-R	%	£1	W-R	%	£1	W-R	%	£1	W-R	%	£1
David Probert	40-317	13	-127.91	5-61	8	-34.75	26-152	17	-36.34	9-104	9	-56.82
Oisin Murphy	15-117	13	-65.24	3-32	9	-19.20	8-47	17	-18.07	4-38	11	-27.97
E Greatrex	12-51	24	+39.81	2-4	50	+27.20	3-21	14	-9.38	7-26	27	+21.99
Rob Hornby	6-47	13	-6.00	0-7	-	-7.00	1-12	8	-4.00	5-28	18	+5.00
Liam Keniry	6-60	10	-25.03	1-12	8	+1.00	2-32	6	-22.00	3-16	19	-4.03
Andrea Atzeni	3-14	21	-4.68	0-2	-	-2.00	3-11	27	-1.68	0-1	-	-1.00
Jim Crowley	3-29	10	-20.64	0-4	-	-4.00	3-12	25	-3.64	0-13	-	-13.00
Mr H Hunt	2-5	40	+0.50	0-0	-	+0.00	0-0	-	+0.00	2-5	40	+0.50
Cathy Gannon	2-15	13	-5.00	0-3	-	-3.00	1-10	10	-6.50	1-2	50	+4.50

By course – 2014-2017

	Overall			Two-year-olds			Three-year-olds			Older horses		
	W-R	%	£1	W-R	%	£1	W-R	%	£1	W-R	%	£1
Ascot	8-139	6	-78.50	0-13	-	-13.00	5-53	9	-20.50	3-73	4	-45.00
Ayr	2-11	18	-2.50	1-1	100	+2.00	1-3	33	+2.50	0-7	-	-7.00
Bath	15-82	18	-0.34	2-9	22	+14.25	6-48	13	-15.50	7-25	28	+0.91
Beverley	2-8	25	-2.13	0-1	-	-1.00	2-6	33	-0.13	0-1	-	-1.00
Brighton	10-53	19	+0.35	2-11	18	-5.44	5-25	20	+4.53	3-17	18	+1.25
Carlisle	3-11	27	-1.75	0-1	-	-1.00	3-9	33	+0.25	0-1	-	-1.00
Catterick	0-2	-	-2.00	0-0	-	+0.00	0-2	-	-2.00	0-0	-	+0.00
Chelmsfd (AW)	16-119	13	-49.06	0-10	-	-10.00	11-48	23	+2.33	5-61	8	-41.39
Chepstow	19-91	21	+1.43	3-14	21	-0.80	8-54	15	-4.75	8-23	35	+6.98
Chester	33-140	24	+73.56	5-22	23	+7.50	16-69	23	+12.38	12-49	24	+53.68
Doncaster	8-69	12	-9.88	4-12	33	+23.13	2-22	9	-7.00	2-35	6	-26.00
Epsom	12-89	13	+12.83	3-13	23	+24.50	3-37	8	-22.50	6-39	15	+10.83
Ffos Las	14-45	31	+40.85	2-8	25	+5.00	9-28	32	+32.85	3-9	33	+3.00
Goodwood	14-130	11	-36.39	2-29	7	-16.25	7-50	14	-21.14	5-51	10	+1.00
Hamilton	1-7	14	-4.50	1-1	100	+1.50	0-4	-	-4.00	0-2	-	-2.00
Haydock	11-82	13	-25.30	4-12	33	+1.20	3-41	7	-21.50	4-29	14	-5.00
Kempton (AW)	39-300	13	-83.49	4-58	7	-31.64	27-152	18	-12.66	8-90	9	-39.20
Leicester	7-57	12	-21.63	0-6	-	-6.00	7-34	21	+1.38	0-17	-	-17.00
Lingfield	8-41	20	-8.50	1-6	17	+0.00	4-20	20	-9.75	3-15	20	+1.25
Lingfield (AW)	38-239	16	-48.90	3-22	14	+12.80	17-110	15	-53.70	18-107	17	-8.00
Musselburgh	1-4	25	+0.50	0-0	-	+0.00	1-4	25	+0.50	0-0	-	+0.00
Newbury	14-128	11	-36.83	2-39	5	-31.25	9-64	14	-23.58	3-25	12	+18.00
Newcastle	0-1	-	-1.00	0-0	-	+0.00	0-0	-	+0.00	0-1	-	-1.00
N'castle (AW)	2-17	12	-10.38	1-3	33	+1.00	0-4	-	-4.00	1-10	10	-7.38
Newmarket	12-118	10	-48.78	2-35	6	-23.75	7-38	18	+5.13	3-45	7	-30.15
Newmarket (J)	11-71	15	+14.35	2-17	12	+6.00	8-28	29	+26.35	1-26	4	-18.00
Nottingham	8-44	18	+9.46	2-17	12	-6.13	3-18	17	+7.25	3-9	33	+8.33
Pontefract	1-15	7	-7.00	1-3	33	+5.00	0-7	-	-7.00	0-5	-	-5.00
Redcar	1-7	14	-4.50	0-3	-	-3.00	1-3	33	-0.50	0-1	-	-1.00
Ripon	1-5	20	-2.50	0-0	-	+0.00	1-2	50	+0.50	0-3	-	-3.00
Salisbury	22-140	16	-41.45	7-39	18	-3.43	9-67	13	-28.50	6-34	18	-9.52
Sandown	12-135	9	-29.68	2-35	6	-21.75	6-72	8	-31.68	4-28	14	+23.75
South'll (AW)	26-89	29	+1.03	2-7	29	+9.50	17-45	38	+3.21	7-37	19	-11.68
Thirsk	1-4	25	+13.00	0-0	-	+0.00	1-4	25	+13.00	0-0	-	+0.00
Wetherby	1-5	20	-3.50	0-0	-	+0.00	1-2	50	-0.50	0-3	-	-3.00
Windsor	18-128	14	-47.85	7-21	33	+2.47	10-68	15	-14.20	1-39	3	-36.13
Wolves (AW)	15-109	14	-50.32	0-14	-	-14.00	10-49	20	-22.17	5-46	11	-14.15
Yarmouth	3-20	15	-8.75	0-1	-	-1.00	3-13	23	-1.75	0-6	-	-6.00
York	8-76	11	+19.00	1-16	6	-14.00	0-20	-	-20.00	7-40	18	+53.00

Ten-year summary

	Wins	Runs	%	Win prize-money	Total prize-money	£1
2017	93	672	14	£1,702,065.55	£2,565,904.52	-62.39
2016	107	731	15	£1,038,999.35	£1,672,623.97	-102.74
2015	95	755	13	£837,267.45	£1,548,715.65	-272.93
2014	119	659	18	£1,335,198.23	£2,035,497.26	-35.60
2013	99	713	14	£873,940.78	£1,356,742.43	-13.36
2012	93	712	13	£779,847.73	£1,365,377.42	-155.54
2011	70	543	13	£620,393.39	£971,676.62	-59.07
2010	78	511	15	£707,996.22	£1,116,809.38	-11.81
2009	68	498	14	£460,056.19	£783,172.54	-38.44
2008	67	436	15	£510,631.82	£865,416.84	+12.56

DONJUAN TRIUMPHANT: transformed after his switch to Andrew Balding

Michael Stoute

By month – 2017

	Overall			Two-year-olds			Three-year-olds			Older horses		
	W-R	%	£1	W-R	%	£1	W-R	%	£1	W-R	%	£1
January	0-1	-	-1.00	0-0	-	+0.00	0-1	-	-1.00	0-0	-	+0.00
February	1-2	50	+4.50	0-0	-	+0.00	0-0	-	+0.00	1-2	50	+4.50
March	0-0	-	+0.00	0-0	-	+0.00	0-0	-	+0.00	0-0	-	+0.00
April	8-41	20	-12.53	0-0	-	+0.00	4-31	13	-20.63	4-10	40	+8.10
May	17-64	27	+48.23	0-1	-	-1.00	11-41	27	+39.63	6-22	27	+9.60
June	9-62	15	-28.99	1-3	33	+4.00	7-43	16	-18.99	1-16	6	-14.00
July	9-51	18	-1.50	0-6	-	-6.00	6-30	20	-7.50	3-15	20	+12.00
August	23-92	25	-7.03	5-22	23	-8.38	11-42	26	-6.16	7-28	25	+7.50
September	10-61	16	-13.56	5-23	22	+1.44	4-22	18	-8.00	1-16	6	-7.00
October	2-48	4	-41.25	2-32	6	-25.25	0-7	-	-7.00	0-9	-	-9.00
November	1-10	10	-4.00	0-9	-	-9.00	1-1	100	+5.00	0-0	-	+0.00
December	0-4	-	-4.00	0-4	-	-4.00	0-0	-	+0.00	0-0	-	+0.00

By month – 2016

	Overall			Two-year-olds			Three-year-olds			Older horses		
	W-R	%	£1	W-R	%	£1	W-R	%	£1	W-R	%	£1
January	0-0	-	+0.00	0-0	-	+0.00	0-0	-	+0.00	0-0	-	+0.00
February	0-0	-	+0.00	0-0	-	+0.00	0-0	-	+0.00	0-0	-	+0.00
March	0-0	-	+0.00	0-0	-	+0.00	0-0	-	+0.00	0-0	-	+0.00
April	13-57	23	+1.26	0-0	-	+0.00	9-46	20	-6.49	4-11	36	+7.75
May	17-73	23	-15.09	0-0	-	+0.00	15-61	25	-8.84	2-12	17	-6.25
June	18-73	25	+39.48	1-5	20	-1.00	14-56	25	+32.23	3-12	25	+7.25
July	15-68	22	-19.14	0-5	-	-5.00	13-50	26	-6.48	2-13	15	-7.67
August	21-73	29	-7.67	5-14	36	+7.04	15-48	31	-5.72	1-11	9	-9.00
September	16-82	20	-5.36	5-34	15	-0.08	10-44	23	-3.38	1-4	25	-1.90
October	9-59	15	-27.95	7-26	27	-6.45	2-28	7	-16.50	0-5	-	-5.00
November	2-16	13	+13.00	2-13	15	+16.00	0-3	-	-3.00	0-0	-	+0.00
December	0-4	-	-4.00	0-3	-	-3.00	0-1	-	-1.00	0-0	-	+0.00

By month – 2015

	Overall			Two-year-olds			Three-year-olds			Older horses		
	W-R	%	£1	W-R	%	£1	W-R	%	£1	W-R	%	£1
January	0-0	-	+0.00	0-0	-	+0.00	0-0	-	+0.00	0-0	-	+0.00
February	0-0	-	+0.00	0-0	-	+0.00	0-0	-	+0.00	0-0	-	+0.00
March	0-0	-	+0.00	0-0	-	+0.00	0-0	-	+0.00	0-0	-	+0.00
April	5-51	10	-27.55	0-0	-	+0.00	3-45	7	-26.60	2-6	33	-0.95
May	15-67	22	+6.32	0-1	-	-1.00	12-50	24	+12.70	3-16	19	-5.39
June	17-66	26	+7.39	1-3	33	+3.00	14-51	27	+1.39	2-12	17	+3.00
July	11-65	17	+2.00	0-11	-	-11.00	10-42	24	+10.00	1-12	8	+3.00
August	14-79	18	-19.93	3-27	11	-4.75	11-44	25	-7.18	0-8	-	-8.00
September	8-70	11	-31.28	4-35	11	-16.88	4-28	14	-7.40	0-7	-	-7.00
October	7-44	16	+3.76	6-29	21	+9.76	1-11	9	-2.00	0-4	-	-4.00
November	2-12	17	-8.72	2-10	20	-6.72	0-2	-	-2.00	0-0	-	+0.00
December	0-1	-	-1.00	0-1	-	-1.00	0-0	-	+0.00	0-0	-	+0.00

By race type – 2017

	Overall			Two-year-olds			Three-year-olds			Older horses		
	W-R	%	£1	W-R	%	£1	W-R	%	£1	W-R	%	£1
Handicap	32-171	19	-0.31	0-4	-	-4.00	22-117	19	-13.17	10-50	20	+16.85
Group	12-62	19	-0.75	1-4	25	-1.25	1-11	9	-8.50	10-47	21	+9.00
Maiden	20-92	22	-12.35	4-17	24	-4.88	16-73	22	-5.48	0-2	-	-2.00

By race type – 2016

	Overall			Two-year-olds			Three-year-olds			Older horses		
	W-R	%	£1	W-R	%	£1	W-R	%	£1	W-R	%	£1
Handicap	40-202	20	-23.75	1-5	20	+16.00	35-166	21	-22.25	4-31	13	-17.50
Group	12-59	20	-2.67	0-5	-	-5.00	4-28	14	-9.52	8-26	31	+11.85
Maiden	48-200	24	+6.98	17-84	20	-4.12	31-112	28	+15.10	0-4	-	-4.00

By race type – 2015

	Overall			Two-year-olds			Three-year-olds			Older horses		
	W-R	%	£1	W-R	%	£1	W-R	%	£1	W-R	%	£1
Handicap	28-175	16	-33.38	0-6	-	-6.00	27-141	19	-14.38	1-28	4	-13.00
Group	4-40	10	-14.25	0-3	-	-3.00	0-10	-	-10.00	4-27	15	-1.25
Maiden	43-210	20	-5.50	16-104	15	-15.58	26-105	25	+9.79	1-1	100	+0.30

By jockey – 2017

	Overall			Two-year-olds			Three-year-olds			Older horses		
	W-R	%	£1	W-R	%	£1	W-R	%	£1	W-R	%	£1
Ryan Moore	29-137	21	-28.76	5-26	19	-6.00	13-69	19	-30.55	11-42	26	+7.79
Jim Crowley	14-58	24	+4.95	3-6	50	+1.94	4-24	17	-9.40	7-28	25	+12.41
Andrea Atzeni	5-21	24	-2.00	1-5	20	-2.25	2-7	29	-1.25	2-9	22	+1.50
R Kingscote	4-13	31	+4.25	0-1	-	-1.00	3-9	33	-0.75	1-3	33	+6.00
Ted Durcan	4-71	6	-50.75	1-37	3	-29.00	3-23	13	-10.75	0-11	-	-11.00
David Probert	3-11	27	+2.50	0-4	-	-4.00	3-7	43	+6.50	0-0	-	+0.00
Daniel Tudhope	2-6	33	+1.75	1-1	100	+1.75	1-3	33	+2.00	0-2	-	-2.00
Joe Fanning	2-6	33	-0.32	0-0	-	+0.00	2-5	40	+0.68	0-1	-	-1.00
K Shoemark	2-7	29	+23.50	0-2	-	-2.00	2-5	40	+25.50	0-0	-	+0.00
Dane O'Neill	2-9	22	-2.25	0-3	-	-3.00	2-5	40	+1.75	0-1	-	-1.00
Frankie Dettori	2-11	18	-5.75	1-1	100	+1.38	1-2	50	+0.88	0-8	-	-8.00
William Buick	2-11	18	+13.00	0-3	-	-3.00	1-6	17	+7.00	1-2	50	+9.00

By jockey – 2016

	Overall			Two-year-olds			Three-year-olds			Older horses		
	W-R	%	£1	W-R	%	£1	W-R	%	£1	W-R	%	£1
Ryan Moore	32-129	25	-17.19	5-30	17	-11.58	18-73	25	-13.19	9-26	35	+7.58
Ted Durcan	25-130	19	-35.85	6-22	27	+5.64	18-92	20	-29.99	1-16	6	-11.50
Andrea Atzeni	8-28	29	-3.24	1-5	20	-2.25	7-19	37	+3.01	0-4	-	-4.00
G Gibbons	8-30	27	+29.88	2-10	20	+19.00	6-20	30	+10.88	0-0	-	+0.00
Paul Hanagan	6-28	21	-7.84	2-11	18	+0.50	4-12	33	-3.34	0-5	-	-5.00
Jim Crowley	4-10	40	+4.30	1-2	50	-0.43	2-6	33	+4.63	1-2	50	+0.10
William Buick	3-5	60	+16.00	0-1	-	-1.00	3-4	75	+17.00	0-0	-	+0.00
Dane O'Neill	3-12	25	+7.91	0-2	-	-2.00	3-7	43	+12.91	0-3	-	-3.00
R Kingscote	3-14	21	-7.04	0-3	-	-3.00	3-11	27	-4.04	0-0	-	+0.00

By jockey – 2015

	Overall			Two-year-olds			Three-year-olds			Older horses		
	W-R	%	£1	W-R	%	£1	W-R	%	£1	W-R	%	£1
Ted Durcan	26-153	17	+3.47	8-53	15	-8.96	17-86	20	+11.43	1-14	7	+1.00
Ryan Moore	22-105	21	-33.38	3-15	20	-7.74	14-60	23	-12.01	5-30	17	-13.64
Paul Hanagan	8-21	38	+13.07	2-5	40	+13.62	6-13	46	+2.45	0-3	-	-3.00
Stevie Donohoe	8-44	18	+22.41	3-19	16	-0.50	5-25	20	+22.91	0-0	-	+0.00
Graham Gibbons	3-16	19	-1.25	0-4	-	-4.00	3-12	25	+2.75	0-0	-	+0.00
Dane O'Neill	2-16	13	-12.90	0-1	-	-1.00	1-12	8	-10.20	1-3	33	-1.70
Hayley Turner	1-1	100	+1.10	0-0	-	+0.00	1-1	100	+1.10	0-0	-	+0.00
Tom Eaves	1-1	100	+0.36	0-0	-	+0.00	1-1	100	+0.36	0-0	-	+0.00
Graham Lee	1-2	50	-0.78	0-0	-	+0.00	1-2	50	-0.78	0-0	-	+0.00

By course – 2014-2017

	Overall			Two-year-olds			Three-year-olds			Older horses		
	W-R	%	£1	W-R	%	£1	W-R	%	£1	W-R	%	£1
Ascot	16-124	13	-8.75	2-6	33	+10.00	8-63	13	-12.50	6-55	11	-6.25
Ayr	0-5	-	-5.00	0-1	-	-1.00	0-3	-	-3.00	0-1	-	-1.00
Bath	4-19	21	-6.54	0-1	-	-1.00	4-18	22	-5.54	0-0	-	+0.00
Beverley	1-16	6	-8.00	1-2	50	+6.00	0-14	-	-14.00	0-0	-	+0.00
Brighton	2-10	20	-3.88	0-2	-	-2.00	2-8	25	-1.88	0-0	-	+0.00
Carlisle	5-8	63	+0.70	1-1	100	+1.38	4-7	57	-0.67	0-0	-	+0.00
Catterick	3-7	43	-1.63	0-0	-	+0.00	3-6	50	-0.63	0-1	-	-1.00
Chelmsfd (AW)	20-93	22	+3.40	3-27	11	+8.25	13-59	22	-13.10	4-7	57	+8.25
Chepstow	1-3	33	-0.25	0-0	-	+0.00	1-3	33	-0.25	0-0	-	+0.00
Chester	10-42	24	-14.04	1-3	33	-0.38	6-25	24	-7.32	3-14	21	-6.34
Doncaster	21-62	34	+48.22	3-16	19	-1.75	13-36	36	+35.10	5-10	50	+14.88
Epsom	3-22	14	-11.25	0-1	-	-1.00	1-10	10	-5.50	2-11	18	-4.75
Ffos Las	2-3	67	+17.25	0-0	-	+0.00	2-3	67	+17.25	0-0	-	+0.00
Goodwood	19-99	19	-30.83	2-6	33	-1.58	14-63	22	-7.75	3-30	10	-21.50
Hamilton	1-1	100	+0.36	0-0	-	+0.00	1-1	100	+0.36	0-0	-	+0.00
Haydock	10-49	20	-0.63	1-6	17	-2.00	8-24	33	+11.38	1-19	5	-10.00
Kempton (AW)	26-161	16	-59.19	13-78	17	-31.27	9-72	13	-26.44	4-11	36	-1.48
Leicester	15-68	22	-20.33	3-27	11	-20.14	12-38	32	+2.81	0-3	-	-3.00
Lingfield	3-17	18	-4.50	1-8	13	-6.00	2-8	25	+2.50	0-1	-	-1.00
Lingfield (AW)	18-57	32	+20.30	6-16	38	+11.80	10-38	26	+2.90	2-3	67	+5.60
Musselburgh	0-4	-	-4.00	0-0	-	+0.00	0-4	-	-4.00	0-0	-	+0.00
Newbury	15-99	15	-26.52	5-25	20	+17.38	6-47	13	-28.01	4-27	15	-15.89
Newcastle	4-6	67	+13.35	3-4	75	+13.25	1-2	50	+0.10	0-0	-	+0.00
N'castle (AW)	5-13	38	+19.73	3-3	100	+22.48	1-7	14	-4.25	1-3	33	+1.50
Newmarket	16-142	11	-20.50	3-43	7	-20.50	8-69	12	-29.00	5-30	17	+7.50
Newmarket (J)	13-116	11	-70.71	3-41	7	-30.58	7-55	13	-29.00	3-20	15	-11.13
Nottingham	15-74	20	+5.83	2-17	12	-12.97	13-56	23	+19.80	0-1	-	-1.00
Pontefract	10-47	21	-15.39	0-6	-	-6.00	8-32	25	-4.23	2-9	22	-5.17
Redcar	1-5	20	-3.43	1-2	50	-0.43	0-2	-	-2.00	0-1	-	-1.00
Ripon	2-10	20	+3.00	0-1	-	-1.00	2-9	22	+4.00	0-0	-	+0.00
Salisbury	10-68	15	-20.99	1-18	6	-14.00	8-46	17	-6.49	1-4	25	-0.50
Sandown	26-108	24	+8.19	2-17	12	-11.13	19-71	27	+4.56	5-20	25	+14.75
South'll (AW)	0-1	-	-1.00	0-0	-	+0.00	0-1	-	-1.00	0-0	-	+0.00
Thirsk	6-15	40	+1.34	1-2	50	+0.25	5-12	42	+2.09	0-1	-	-1.00
Warwick	1-1	100	+1.38	0-0	-	+0.00	1-1	100	+1.38	0-0	-	+0.00
Wetherby	0-1	-	-1.00	0-0	-	+0.00	0-1	-	-1.00	0-0	-	+0.00
Windsor	7-69	10	-47.63	1-7	14	-4.25	6-56	11	-37.38	0-6	-	-6.00
Wolves (AW)	10-69	14	-18.04	2-31	6	-22.33	7-36	19	+4.99	1-2	50	-0.70
Yarmouth	12-54	22	-14.24	4-25	16	-11.56	6-24	25	-1.38	2-5	40	-1.31
York	18-89	20	+9.83	2-4	50	+7.00	8-41	20	+2.96	8-44	18	-0.13

Ten-year summary

	Wins	Runs	%	Win prize-money	Total prize-money	£1
2017	80	436	18	£2,338,227.15	£3,823,039.61	-61.12
2016	111	505	22	£1,491,547.82	£2,525,773.73	-25.48
2015	79	455	17	£988,868.57	£1,696,525.96	-69.01
2014	81	461	18	£1,293,230.34	£2,211,794.30	-131.27
2013	87	398	22	£1,167,720.87	£1,687,826.91	-69.86
2012	69	363	19	£609,776.18	£1,022,421.28	-30.99
2011	53	366	14	£596,991.20	£1,554,607.39	-130.34
2010	73	465	16	£2,245,094.20	£3,027,131.17	-141.94
2009	99	429	23	£2,077,608.50	£3,421,892.26	-64.76
2008	88	467	19	£1,511,579.51	£2,760,173.51	-100.52

CRYSTAL OCEAN: a typical Sir Michael Stoute colt who may still be improving

Top trainers by winners (Turf)

All runs				First time out			Horses		
Won	Ran	%	Trainer	Won	Ran	%	Won	Ran	%
156	977	16	**Mark Johnston**	31	217	14	116	217	53
151	1360	11	**Richard Fahey**	38	298	13	140	298	47
144	985	15	**Richard Hannon**	34	268	13	134	268	50
109	458	24	**William Haggas**	38	160	24	107	160	67
89	470	19	**John Gosden**	38	225	17	101	225	45
84	307	27	**Charlie Appleby**	44	139	32	80	139	58
82	434	19	**Roger Varian**	33	162	20	75	162	46
78	752	10	**David O'Meara**	25	174	14	68	174	39
78	833	9	**Tim Easterby**	5	146	3	52	146	36
71	585	12	**Keith Dalgleish**	15	129	12	46	129	36
66	461	14	**Andrew Balding**	21	160	13	67	160	42
62	332	19	**Sir Michael Stoute**	21	135	16	57	135	42
60	486	12	**Kevin Ryan**	10	124	8	57	124	46
54	367	15	**Michael Dods**	6	74	8	34	74	46
52	294	18	**Clive Cox**	16	103	16	44	103	43
52	430	12	**K R Burke**	9	129	7	49	129	38
51	464	11	**Charles Hills**	9	142	6	49	142	35
48	463	10	**Mick Channon**	10	108	9	40	108	37
45	276	16	**Eve Johnson Houghton**	11	74	15	30	74	41
44	325	14	**John Quinn**	8	76	11	38	76	50
41	466	9	**David Evans**	7	112	6	49	112	44
40	215	19	**Roger Charlton**	21	90	23	42	90	47
40	257	16	**Michael Bell**	14	76	18	32	76	42
39	348	11	**Tom Dascombe**	11	109	10	37	109	34
38	325	12	**Ralph Beckett**	16	135	12	49	135	36
38	307	12	**Hugo Palmer**	18	134	13	57	134	43
38	377	10	**Ruth Carr**	6	51	12	31	51	61
35	301	12	**David Simcock**	22	129	17	47	129	36
34	382	9	**Michael Appleby**	16	145	11	55	145	38
33	293	11	**Richard Hughes**	8	93	9	44	93	47
32	165	19	**A P O'Brien**	16	75	21	26	75	35
32	278	12	**Iain Jardine**	7	70	10	29	70	41
31	225	14	**Hughie Morrison**	8	71	11	27	71	38
31	281	11	**David Barron**	14	78	18	37	78	47
31	172	18	**Luca Cumani**	4	56	7	25	56	45
30	167	18	**Saeed bin Suroor**	24	93	26	42	93	45
30	302	10	**Paul Midgley**	1	46	2	21	46	46
30	296	10	**Ed Dunlop**	5	105	5	36	105	34
29	166	17	**Henry Candy**	5	55	9	24	55	44
27	190	14	**Robert Cowell**	9	70	13	26	70	37
27	317	9	**Michael Easterby**	12	78	15	27	78	35
26	226	12	**Ed Walker**	8	89	9	36	89	40
26	266	10	**Roger Fell**	3	51	6	24	51	47
25	292	9	**Jim Goldie**	1	43	2	21	43	49
25	154	16	**Simon Crisford**	11	77	14	29	77	38
24	120	20	**Owen Burrows**	6	53	11	19	53	36
23	209	11	**Brian Meehan**	5	57	9	19	57	33

Top trainers by prize-money (Turf)

Total prize-money	Trainer	Win prize-money	Wins	Class 1-3 Won	Ran	%	Class 4-6 Won	Ran	%
£8,335,028	**A P O'Brien**	£5,563,606	32	31	162	19	1	3	33
£5,860,009	**John Gosden**	£4,348,218	89	46	278	17	43	192	22
£3,661,034	**Richard Fahey**	£2,065,696	151	40	569	7	111	791	14
£3,441,167	**Sir Michael Stoute**	£2,008,230	62	34	191	18	28	141	20
£2,897,554	**Mark Johnston**	£1,998,311	156	65	453	14	91	524	17
£2,644,723	**Richard Hannon**	£1,646,285	144	39	334	12	105	651	16
£2,328,014	**Andrew Balding**	£1,573,442	66	26	241	11	40	220	18
£2,202,995	**William Haggas**	£1,179,245	109	46	230	20	63	228	28
£2,003,522	**Charlie Appleby**	£1,152,787	84	36	178	20	48	129	37
£1,580,985	**Roger Varian**	£967,561	82	34	209	16	48	225	21
£1,434,924	**Clive Cox**	£907,794	52	18	110	16	34	184	18
£1,336,922	**David O'Meara**	£806,520	78	19	261	7	59	491	12
£1,259,134	**David Simcock**	£613,106	35	19	167	11	16	134	12
£1,162,397	**Tim Easterby**	£761,900	78	27	263	10	51	570	9
£1,083,517	**Charles Hills**	£629,538	51	17	172	10	34	292	12
£1,040,526	**Roger Charlton**	£577,438	40	18	100	18	22	115	19
£921,377	**K R Burke**	£693,497	52	14	105	13	38	325	12
£893,101	**Kevin Ryan**	£511,934	60	20	172	12	40	314	13
£881,617	**Michael Bell**	£560,368	40	12	78	15	28	179	16
£850,770	**Ralph Beckett**	£408,659	38	14	139	10	24	186	13
£809,244	**Saeed bin Suroor**	£352,581	30	17	97	18	13	70	19
£743,270	**Hugo Palmer**	£323,104	38	14	158	9	24	149	16
£713,207	**Dean Ivory**	£575,755	17	5	44	11	12	126	10
£684,146	**James Fanshawe**	£477,943	17	5	72	7	12	90	13
£673,215	**Keith Dalgleish**	£432,004	71	10	132	8	61	453	13
£579,491	**Eve Johnson Houghton**	£387,701	45	9	84	11	36	192	19
£559,621	**Henry Candy**	£258,455	29	6	56	11	23	110	21
£529,304	**Iain Jardine**	£424,138	32	8	54	15	24	224	11
£491,932	**Sir Mark Prescott**	£274,276	16	2	26	8	14	88	16
£487,004	**Brian Meehan**	£336,013	23	9	72	13	14	137	10
£486,773	**Michael Dods**	£300,184	54	7	77	9	47	290	16
£478,191	**Tom Dascombe**	£301,831	39	11	110	10	28	238	12
£477,004	**David Elsworth**	£270,636	15	7	67	10	8	53	15
£464,815	**Owen Burrows**	£307,135	24	7	45	16	17	75	23
£433,951	**Paul Midgley**	£309,353	30	10	122	8	20	180	11
£430,048	**Martyn Meade**	£259,826	11	6	28	21	5	32	16
£418,682	**Hughie Morrison**	£246,086	31	8	80	10	23	145	16
£412,242	**Ruth Carr**	£261,488	38	7	66	11	31	311	10
£403,219	**Michael Appleby**	£244,056	34	9	94	10	25	288	9
£402,874	**Ian Williams**	£231,138	22	10	85	12	12	107	11
£397,010	**Wesley A Ward**	£272,208	2	2	13	15	0	0	—
£388,194	**Mick Channon**	£214,050	48	5	135	4	43	328	13
£383,868	**Robert Cowell**	£223,688	27	10	91	11	17	99	17
£377,602	**John Quinn**	£245,895	44	10	62	16	34	263	13
£366,012	**David Evans**	£209,945	41	7	91	8	34	375	9
£352,729	**David Barron**	£245,049	31	8	84	10	23	197	12
£335,316	**Luca Cumani**	£205,305	31	5	38	13	26	134	19

Top trainers by winners (AW)

	All runs			First time out			Horses		
Won	Ran	%	Trainer	Won	Ran	%	Won	Ran	%
58	392	15	Mark Johnston	31	217	14	116	217	53
56	459	12	Michael Appleby	16	145	11	55	145	38
49	130	38	William Haggas	38	160	24	107	160	67
47	357	13	Richard Hannon	34	268	13	134	268	50
46	371	12	Richard Fahey	38	298	13	140	298	47
46	213	22	John Gosden	38	225	17	101	225	45
40	404	10	David Evans	7	112	6	49	112	44
39	185	21	Hugo Palmer	18	134	13	57	134	43
39	280	14	Jamie Osborne	10	88	11	36	88	41
34	154	22	Archie Watson	10	48	21	30	48	63
33	108	31	Saeed bin Suroor	24	93	26	42	93	45
32	168	19	Sir Mark Prescott	8	60	13	25	60	42
30	318	9	David O'Meara	25	174	14	68	174	39
29	213	14	David Simcock	22	129	17	47	129	36
29	195	15	Ian Williams	6	69	9	33	69	48
29	223	13	Richard Hughes	8	93	9	44	93	47
28	194	14	Marco Botti	6	97	6	30	97	31
28	137	20	Ralph Beckett	16	135	12	49	135	36
28	161	17	Ed Walker	8	89	9	36	89	40
27	121	22	Roger Varian	33	162	20	75	162	46
27	211	13	Andrew Balding	21	160	13	67	160	42
27	211	13	John Butler	8	58	14	23	58	40
24	104	23	Roger Charlton	21	90	23	42	90	47
22	180	12	Ed Dunlop	5	105	5	36	105	34
22	67	33	Charlie Appleby	44	139	32	80	139	58
22	184	12	Derek Shaw	1	39	3	12	39	31
22	174	13	K R Burke	9	129	7	49	129	38
21	212	10	Dean Ivory	6	54	11	24	54	44
20	151	13	Tom Dascombe	11	109	10	37	109	34
19	184	10	Stuart Williams	1	61	2	24	61	39
19	144	13	David Barron	14	78	18	37	78	47
19	113	17	James Tate	7	54	13	25	54	46
18	104	17	Sir Michael Stoute	21	135	16	57	135	42
18	120	15	Charles Hills	9	142	6	49	142	35
18	272	7	Tony Carroll	4	104	4	24	104	23
18	147	12	Iain Jardine	7	70	10	29	70	41
18	167	11	Richard Guest	7	42	17	17	42	40
18	154	12	Gary Moore	6	72	8	26	72	36
18	235	8	Daniel Mark Loughnane	5	61	8	13	61	21
17	111	15	James Fanshawe	5	66	8	27	66	41
16	104	15	Robert Cowell	9	70	13	26	70	37
16	169	9	Michael Easterby	12	78	15	27	78	35
16	96	17	Simon Crisford	11	77	14	29	77	38
15	162	9	Kevin Ryan	10	124	8	57	124	46
15	86	17	William Muir	3	45	7	22	45	49
15	113	13	Ivan Furtado	5	37	14	16	37	43
15	141	11	Michael Attwater	5	39	13	13	39	33

Top trainers by prize-money (AW)

Total prize-money	Trainer	Win prize-money	Wins	Class 1-3 Won	Ran	%	Class 4-6 Won	Ran	%
£611,947	**Mark Johnston**	£403,602	58	17	98	17	41	294	14
£557,625	**Richard Fahey**	£388,275	46	10	72	14	36	299	12
£498,716	**William Haggas**	£412,043	49	11	26	42	38	104	37
£381,872	**Sir Michael Stoute**	£329,997	18	6	16	38	12	88	14
£361,594	**Marco Botti**	£239,909	28	9	54	17	19	140	14
£353,034	**David O'Meara**	£201,422	30	9	79	11	21	239	9
£330,761	**Michael Appleby**	£236,400	56	6	46	13	48	405	12
£324,761	**Richard Hannon**	£183,256	47	3	33	9	44	323	14
£316,263	**Roger Varian**	£250,287	27	10	27	37	17	94	18
£314,639	**Saeed bin Suroor**	£227,853	33	8	27	30	25	81	31
£314,315	**Hugo Palmer**	£250,630	39	7	29	24	32	156	21
£309,208	**John Gosden**	£196,841	46	3	29	10	43	184	23
£285,213	**David Simcock**	£184,967	29	8	47	17	21	166	13
£284,403	**Archie Watson**	£180,978	34	5	26	19	29	126	23
£274,567	**James Fanshawe**	£178,324	17	3	30	10	14	81	17
£263,382	**David Evans**	£147,652	40	4	32	13	36	367	10
£262,673	**Stuart Williams**	£165,604	19	5	63	8	14	120	12
£259,453	**Jamie Osborne**	£156,637	39	3	56	5	36	223	16
£240,461	**Kevin Ryan**	£133,150	15	4	37	11	11	125	9
£237,891	**Andrew Balding**	£128,624	27	3	49	6	24	160	15
£233,106	**Ralph Beckett**	£172,861	28	6	25	24	22	112	20
£214,464	**Ian Williams**	£158,213	29	3	25	12	26	169	15
£201,503	**Roger Charlton**	£165,600	24	4	19	21	20	85	24
£195,552	**Sir Mark Prescott**	£148,401	32	4	9	44	28	159	18
£187,955	**Dean Ivory**	£121,041	21	3	30	10	18	182	10
£170,092	**Richard Hughes**	£95,612	29	0	20	—	29	200	14
£169,972	**David Barron**	£104,801	19	1	29	3	18	114	16
£165,563	**Robert Cowell**	£93,971	16	3	24	13	13	78	17
£162,196	**James Tate**	£119,835	19	4	14	29	15	99	15
£161,898	**Ed Dunlop**	£106,296	22	2	19	11	20	161	12
£152,488	**Michael Easterby**	£65,665	16	2	37	5	14	132	11
£150,988	**Charlie Appleby**	£121,538	22	4	17	24	18	50	36
£146,016	**Derek Shaw**	£113,046	22	1	30	3	21	151	14
£140,759	**Ruth Carr**	£120,383	9	1	5	20	8	88	9
£131,559	**Charlie Fellowes**	£89,639	13	4	21	19	9	61	15
£127,910	**K R Burke**	£90,609	22	3	22	14	19	151	13
£125,099	**Ed Walker**	£80,617	28	0	12	—	27	148	18
£118,927	**Charles Hills**	£86,679	18	3	11	27	15	109	14
£116,939	**Simon Crisford**	£84,647	16	1	11	9	15	85	18
£116,500	**Michael Bell**	£57,089	13	1	14	7	12	73	16
£113,149	**William Knight**	£76,441	13	4	23	17	9	67	13
£112,532	**John Butler**	£82,589	27	0	6	—	27	203	13
£111,154	**Keith Dalgleish**	£59,674	14	1	21	5	13	202	6
£104,087	**Tony Carroll**	£55,957	18	0	14	—	17	240	7
£103,255	**Iain Jardine**	£72,930	18	1	5	20	17	141	12
£101,895	**Chris Dwyer**	£51,914	13	0	18	—	13	97	13
£97,598	**Brian Ellison**	£47,709	12	1	18	6	11	116	9

Top jockeys (Turf)

Won	Ran	%	Jockey	Best Trainer	Won	Ran
150	749	20	**Silvestre De Sousa**	Roger Varian	21	78
116	629	18	**Jim Crowley**	Charles Hills	16	81
105	486	22	**Ryan Moore**	Sir Michael Stoute	29	137
95	539	18	**Daniel Tudhope**	David O'Meara	54	389
86	526	16	**Joe Fanning**	Mark Johnston	64	392
82	572	14	**P J McDonald**	Mark Johnston	35	204
79	436	18	**Andrea Atzeni**	Roger Varian	51	218
73	562	13	**Paul Mulrennan**	Michael Dods	31	203
72	312	23	**William Buick**	Charlie Appleby	49	159
69	375	18	**James Doyle**	Charlie Appleby	25	83
68	574	12	**Paul Hanagan**	Richard Fahey	68	453
67	437	15	**Jamie Spencer**	David Simcock	21	119
66	516	13	**Oisin Murphy**	Andrew Balding	27	145
66	428	15	**Adam Kirby**	Clive Cox	35	176
62	559	11	**Graham Lee**	Keith Dalgleish	15	102
61	431	14	**Franny Norton**	Mark Johnston	41	294
58	470	12	**David Allan**	Tim Easterby	39	315
57	473	12	**David Probert**	Andrew Balding	30	213
54	231	23	**Frankie Dettori**	John Gosden	37	131
51	368	14	**Sean Levey**	Richard Hannon	54	368
51	385	13	**Richard Kingscote**	Tom Dascombe	40	273
50	473	11	**Luke Morris**	Sir Mark Prescott	36	200
50	329	15	**Pat Cosgrave**	William Haggas	26	134
50	423	12	**Ben Curtis**	David Barron	18	110
49	446	11	**Tom Marquand**	Richard Hannon	33	275
49	301	16	**Dane O'Neill**	Charles Hills	11	38
47	325	14	**Harry Bentley**	Henry Candy	8	22
47	363	13	**David Egan**	Michael Attwater	8	19
47	386	12	**Phillip Makin**	David Barron	14	94
46	371	12	**Jason Hart**	John Quinn	41	276
45	494	9	**James Sullivan**	Ruth Carr	25	292
43	503	9	**Tom Eaves**	Kevin Ryan	21	179
43	462	9	**Tony Hamilton**	Richard Fahey	36	383
42	471	9	**Fran Berry**	David Evans	18	87
40	285	14	**Kevin Stott**	Kevin Ryan	31	211
38	411	9	**Josephine Gordon**	Hugo Palmer	32	203
38	326	12	**Kieran Shoemark**	Roger Charlton	28	156
37	318	12	**J F Egan**	Mick Channon	12	82
37	258	14	**Charles Bishop**	Eve Johnson Houghton	28	172
35	385	9	**Shane Kelly**	Richard Hughes	36	321
34	262	13	**George Wood**	James Fanshawe	9	78
33	437	8	**Andrew Mullen**	Tom Tate	7	38
33	375	9	**Connor Beasley**	Keith Dalgleish	16	131
30	273	11	**Robert Winston**	Dean Ivory	21	166
29	237	12	**Hollie Doyle**	Richard Hannon	20	124
28	323	9	**Martin Dwyer**	William Muir	11	125
27	189	14	**Callum Rodriguez**	Michael Dods	16	102
26	212	12	**Adam McNamara**	Richard Fahey	22	160

Top jockeys (AW)

Won	Ran	%	Jockey	Best Trainer	Won	Ran
126	1023	12	**Luke Morris**	Sir Mark Prescott	36	200
78	462	17	**Adam Kirby**	Clive Cox	35	176
68	492	14	**Josephine Gordon**	Hugo Palmer	32	203
57	330	17	**Oisin Murphy**	Andrew Balding	27	145
54	311	17	**Joe Fanning**	Mark Johnston	64	392
53	317	17	**Silvestre De Sousa**	Roger Varian	21	78
49	288	17	**Richard Kingscote**	Tom Dascombe	40	273
46	272	17	**Martin Harley**	James Tate	18	94
46	306	15	**P J McDonald**	Mark Johnston	35	204
44	217	20	**Jim Crowley**	Charles Hills	16	81
41	126	33	**James Doyle**	Charlie Appleby	25	83
38	379	10	**Stevie Donohoe**	Charlie Fellowes	19	127
38	361	11	**Dougie Costello**	Jamie Osborne	23	196
37	378	10	**David Probert**	Andrew Balding	30	213
36	308	12	**Robert Winston**	Dean Ivory	21	166
36	374	10	**Tom Marquand**	Richard Hannon	33	275
35	367	10	**Andrew Mullen**	Tom Tate	7	38
31	362	9	**Shane Kelly**	Richard Hughes	36	321
29	253	11	**Ben Curtis**	David Barron	18	110
29	274	11	**Hollie Doyle**	Richard Hannon	20	124
28	77	36	**Ryan Moore**	Sir Michael Stoute	29	137
28	238	12	**Tony Hamilton**	Richard Fahey	36	383
28	407	7	**Liam Keniry**	Ed Walker	16	110
28	144	19	**Lewis Edmunds**	Richard Whitaker	10	45
27	204	13	**Phillip Makin**	David Barron	14	94
27	161	17	**Jack Mitchell**	Roger Varian	18	93
26	211	12	**Daniel Muscutt**	James Fanshawe	17	99
26	186	14	**Daniel Tudhope**	David O'Meara	54	389
26	202	13	**Kieran Shoemark**	Roger Charlton	28	156
26	164	16	**Robert Havlin**	John Gosden	15	106
24	233	10	**Fran Berry**	David Evans	18	87
24	343	7	**Tom Eaves**	Kevin Ryan	21	179
23	127	18	**Paul Hanagan**	Richard Fahey	68	453
23	227	10	**J F Egan**	Mick Channon	12	82
23	137	17	**Martin Lane**	Derek Shaw	10	44
22	198	11	**Sean Levey**	Richard Hannon	54	368
22	251	9	**Franny Norton**	Mark Johnston	41	294
22	123	18	**Jamie Spencer**	David Simcock	21	119
22	129	17	**George Baker**	J R Jenkins	4	14
20	186	11	**Adam Beschizza**	Ed Vaughan	8	26
20	167	12	**Jane Elliott**	George Margarson	11	68
19	130	15	**Kevin Stott**	Kevin Ryan	31	211
18	187	10	**Graham Lee**	Keith Dalgleish	15	102
18	172	10	**William Carson**	Tony Carroll	5	30
18	227	8	**Charlie Bennett**	Hughie Morrison	15	108
18	118	15	**Ben Robinson**	Brian Ellison	16	124
17	172	10	**Connor Beasley**	Keith Dalgleish	16	131
17	85	20	**Nicky Mackay**	John Gosden	10	55

Est. 1909
**RACING &
FOOTBALL** **OUTLOOK**

Group 1 records

Year	Winner	Age (if appropriate)	Trainer	Jockey	SP	draw/ran

2,000 Guineas (1m) Newmarket

Year	Winner	Trainer	Jockey	SP	draw/ran
2008	**Henrythenavigator**	A O'Brien	J Murtagh	11-1	6/15
2009	**Sea The Stars**	J Oxx	M Kinane	8-1	15/15
2010	**Makfi**	M Delzangles	C-P Lemaire	33-1	5/19
2011	**Frankel**	Sir H Cecil	T Queally	1-2f	1/13
2012	**Camelot**	A O'Brien	J O'Brien	15-8f	12/18
2013	**Dawn Approach**	J Bolger	K Manning	11-8f	6/13
2014	**Night Of Thunder**	R Hannon	K Fallon	40-1	3/14
2015	**Gleneagles**	A O'Brien	R Moore	4-1f	16/18
2016	**Galileo Gold**	H Palmer	F Dettori	14-1	1/13
2017	**Churchill**	A O'Brien	R Moore	6-4f	3/10

THIS IS a specialist miler's race rather than a stepping stone to the Derby despite the recent success of Camelot and Sea The Stars – prior to the latter there had been a 20-year wait for a horse to do the double. Most winners had proved themselves at two, with 17 of the last 26 having won a Group race including 12 at the highest level. Seven of those (Churchill, Dawn Approach, Frankel, Rock Of Gibraltar, Pennekamp, Zafonic and Rodrigo De Triano) had won the Dewhurst, which tends to be a far better guide than the Racing Post Trophy, with Camelot the only horse to complete that double since High Top in 1973. Favourites had a desperate record until five of the last seven winners hit back for punters. There have been just four British-trained winners in 13 years, with only Frankel and Haafhd following up victory in one of the domestic trials since Mystiko in 1991.

1,000 Guineas (1m) Newmarket

Year	Winner	Trainer	Jockey	SP	draw/ran
2008	**Natagora**	P Bary	C Lemaire	11-4f	3/15
2009	**Ghanaati**	B Hills	R Hills	20-1	7/14
2010	**Special Duty**	C Head-Maarek	S Pasquier	9-2f	18/17
2011	**Blue Bunting**	M Al Zarooni	F Dettori	16-1	16/18
2012	**Homecoming Queen**	A O'Brien	R Moore	25-1	16/17
2013	**Sky Lantern**	R Hannon Sr	R Hughes	9-1	7/15
2014	**Miss France**	A Fabre	M Guyon	7-1	4/17
2015	**Legatissimo**	D Wachman	R Moore	13-2	13/13
2016	**Minding**	A O'Brien	R Moore	11-10f	8/16
2017	**Winter**	A O'Brien	W Lordan	9-1	7/14

COURSE FORM is the key factor in this race and is likely to become even more vital with the Fillies' Mile run at Newmarket for the first time in 2011. The 2016 winner Minding followed up victory in that race, while five of the last 16 winners came via the Rockfel; four of the last 15 had been first or second in the Cheveley Park; 2006 winner Speciosa won the Nell Gwyn, in which Sky Lantern was second; Miss France landed the Oh So Sharp Stakes; and Blue Bunting won a Listed race over course and distance the previous October. Punters have hit back a little in recent years, but still ten of the last 20 winners have been priced in double figures. French fillies have a good record, with seven winners since 1993 and Miss France the only one of those not to have Group 1 form as a juvenile.

Lockinge Stakes (1m) Newbury

2008	Creachadoir	4	S bin Suroor	F Dettori	3-1f	7/11
2009	Virtual	4	J Gosden	J Fortune	6-1	10/11
2010	Paco Boy	5	R Hannon Sr	R Hughes	8-11f	3/9
2011	Canford Cliffs	4	R Hannon Sr	R Hughes	4-5f	4/7
2012	Frankel	4	Sir H Cecil	T Queally	2-7f	6/6
2013	Farhh	5	S bin Suroor	S de Sousa	10-3	5/12
2014	Olympic Glory	4	R Hannon	F Dettori	11-8f	3/8
2015	Night Of Thunder	4	R Hannon	J Doyle	11-4jf	3/16
2016	Belardo	4	R Varian	A Atzeni	8-1	6/12
2017	Ribchester	4	R Fahey	W Buick	7-4f	5/8

IT'S ESSENTIAL to look for horses who have already shown themselves to be Group 1 milers as 19 of the last 23 winners had won at the top level, all but one over the trip, and three of the exceptions had been second. Consequently it has been straightforward to identify the winner as 11 of the last 15 favourites have obliged and two of the exceptions were second in the market. Four-year-olds have by far the strongest record, accounting for 22 of the last 31 winners, and fillies can also do well with three winners in the last 12 years. The Sandown Mile is a popular prep race yet Belardo was only the second horse to do the double with 20 other Sandown winners failing.

Coronation Cup (1m4f) Epsom

2008	Soldier Of Fortune	4	A O'Brien	J Murtagh	9-4	7/11
2009	Ask	6	Sir M Stoute	R Moore	5-1	8/8
2010	Fame And Glory	4	A O'Brien	J Murtagh	5-6f	8/9
2011	St Nicholas Abbey	4	A O'Brien	R Moore	Evsf	1/5
2012	St Nicholas Abbey	5	A O'Brien	J O'Brien	8-11f	4/6
2013	St Nicholas Abbey	6	A O'Brien	J O'Brien	3-10f	3/5
2014	Cirrus Des Aigles	8	C Barande-Barbe	C Soumillon	10-11f	7/7
2015	Pether's Moon	5	R Hannon	P Dobbs	11-1	5/4
2016	Postponed	5	R Varian	A Atzeni	8-11f	3/8
2017	Highland Reel	5	A O'Brien	R Moore	9-4f	3/10

AIDAN O'BRIEN has trained eight of the last 13 winners, led by St Nicholas Abbey's hat-trick. That horse was favourite on every occasion, as were Highland Reel, Postponed, Cirrus Des Aigles and Fame And Glory in the last eight years, although history shows that the traditionally small field can produce plenty of upsets, which was the case again in 2015 with Pether's Moon. The key is to oppose four-year-olds as youngsters are often well fancied yet none have won since 2011, making it just four in 15 years overall.

The Oaks (1m4f) Epsom

2008	**Look Here**	R Beckett	S Sanders	33-1	13/16
2009	**Sariska**	M Bell	J Spencer	9-4f	5/10
2010	**Snow Fairy**	E Dunlop	R Moore	9-1	15/15
2011	**Dancing Rain**	W Haggas	J Murtagh	20-1	7/13
2012	**Was**	A O'Brien	S Heffernan	20-1	10/12
2013	**Talent**	R Beckett	R Hughes	20-1	3/11
2014	**Taghrooda**	J Gosden	P Hanagan	5-1	9/17
2015	**Qualify**	A O'Brien	C O'Donoghue	50-1	2/11
2016	**Minding**	A O'Brien	R Moore	10-11f	4/9
2017	**Enable**	J Gosden	F Dettori	6-1	9/10

GUARANTEED STAMINA is more important than proven top-class form for this race, which can make things tricky for punters with five of the last ten winners priced at least 20-1. Aidan O'Brien has won two of the last three runnings with horses who came via the Guineas, but they are the only winners not to have been tried beyond a mile since Casual Look in 2003. It therefore follows that the 1,000 Guineas has become a weaker guide than was once the case, with Minding the only winner to follow up since Kazzia in 2002 and four failures in that time. Nine of the last 11 winners had never been tried in a Group 1 and seven of them had triumphed over at least 1m2f, although none of the trials stands above any other and too much is often made of the Musidora winner, with three beaten favourites since 2008 and Sariska the only one to double up since Reams Of Verse in 1997.

The Derby (1m4f) Epsom

2008	**New Approach**	J Bolger	K Manning	5-1	3/16
2009	**Sea The Stars**	J Oxx	M Kinane	11-4	4/12
2010	**Workforce**	Sir M Stoute	R Moore	6-1	8/12
2011	**Pour Moi**	A Fabre	M Barzalona	4-1	7/13
2012	**Camelot**	A O'Brien	J O'Brien	8-13f	5/9
2013	**Ruler Of The World**	A O'Brien	R Moore	7-1	10/12

HIGHLAND REEL: Aidan O'Brien's eighth Coronation Cup winner in 13 years

DUBAI MILLENNIUM: wins the first Prince of Wales's Stakes run as a Group 1, since when 12 winners had struck at the top level outside Britain and Ireland

2014	**Australia**	A O'Brien	J O'Brien	11-8f	12/16
2015	**Golden Horn**	J Gosden	F Dettori	13-8f	8/12
2016	**Harzand**	D Weld	P Smullen	13-2	9/16
2017	**Wings Of Eagles**	A O'Brien	P Beggy	40-1	14/18

MANY HIGH-CLASS colts are beaten here due to lack of stamina and it's important to have a top-class staying sire (12 of the last 14 winners had one with a stamina index of at least 1m1f) plus more stamina on the dam's side. Australia, Camelot and Sea The Stars came via the 2,000 Guineas, but they all had middle-distance pedigrees and 15 of the last 21 winners warmed up in one of the recognised trials – five Dante winners (Golden Horn, Authorized, Motivator, North Light and Benny The Dip) and a runner-up (Workforce), four Leopardstown winners (Harzand, High Chaparral, Galileo and Sinndar), three Chester winners (Ruler Of The World, Kris Kin and Oath) and a runner-up (Wings Of Eagles) plus one Lingfield winner (High-Rise). Despite the 40-1 success of Wings Of Eagles, this is a race for fancied runners as he was the biggest-priced winner in more than 40 years, with the previous 12 coming from the first three in the betting including three of the last six favourites.

Queen Anne Stakes (1m) Royal Ascot

2008	**Haradasun**	5	A O'Brien	J Murtagh	5-1	2/11
2009	**Paco Boy**	4	R Hannon Sr	R Hughes	10-3	7/9
2010	**Goldikova**	5	F Head	O Peslier	11-8f	10/10
2011	**Canford Cliffs**	4	R Hannon Sr	R Hughes	11-8	6/7
2012	**Frankel**	4	Sir H Cecil	T Queally	1-10f	8/11
2013	**Declaration Of War**	4	A O'Brien	J O'Brien	15-2	6/13
2014	**Toronado**	4	R Hannon	R Hughes	4-5f	8/10
2015	**Solow**	5	F Head	M Guyon	11-8f	4/8
2016	**Tepin**	5	M Casse	J Leparoux	11-2	12/13
2017	**Ribchester**	4	R Fahey	W Buick	11-10f	1/16

FOUR-YEAR-OLDS once considered Classic contenders fit the bill and this age group has taken 22 of the last 29 runnings. No horse older than five has triumphed since 1976 with Goldikova among some top-class ones to fail when defending her crown in 2011.

Seven of the last 11 winners ran in the Lockinge at Newbury, which is obviously the key trial – Ribchester, Frankel and Canford Cliffs all did the double – and 13 of the last 14 winners had previously won a Group 1 at some stage. Toronado is the only horse to ever win the race first time out.

St James's Palace Stakes (1m) Royal Ascot

2008	**Henrythenavigator**	A O'Brien	J Murtagh	4-7f	3/8
2009	**Mastercraftsman**	A O'Brien	J Murtagh	5-6f	3/10
2010	**Canford Cliffs**	R Hannon Sr	R Hughes	11-4j	4/9
2011	**Frankel**	Sir H Cecil	T Queally	3-10f	5/9
2012	**Most Improved**	B Meehan	K Fallon	9-1	15/16
2013	**Dawn Approach**	J Bolger	K Manning	5-4f	5/9
2014	**Kingman**	J Gosden	J Doyle	8-11f	7/7
2015	**Gleneagles**	A O'Brien	R Moore	8-15f	5/5
2016	**Galileo Gold**	H Palmer	F Dettori	6-1	7/7
2017	**Barney Roy**	R Hannon	J Doyle	5-2	4/8

GUINEAS FORM holds the key to this prize and ten of the last 13 winners had come out on top in one of the Classics. The Curragh is just about the best guide as six Irish 2,000 Guineas winners have followed up in that time compared to five from Newmarket and one from Longchamp. Gleneagles and Henrythenavigator had won at Newmarket and the Curragh and Frankel is the only Newmarket winner to follow up without a run in between since Bolkonski in 1975, although Barney Roy came straight from his Guineas second when winning last year. Most Improved is the only winner to have skipped the Classics altogether since Dr Fong in 1998 and the last winner not to have previously run in a Group 1 at all was Shavian in 1990.

Prince of Wales's Stakes (1m2f) Royal Ascot

2008	**Duke Of Marmalade**	4	A O'Brien	J Murtagh	Evsf	1/12
2009	**Vision D'Etat**	4	E Libaud	O Peslier	4-1	2/8
2010	**Byword**	4	A Fabre	M Guyon	5-2f	5/12
2011	**Rewilding**	4	M Al Zarooni	F Dettori	17-2	6/7
2012	**So You Think**	6	A O'Brien	J O'Brien	4-5f	7/11
2013	**Al Kazeem**	5	R Charlton	J Doyle	11-4	9/11
2014	**The Fugue**	5	J Gosden	W Buick	11-2	7/8
2015	**Free Eagle**	4	D Weld	P Smullen	5-2f	4/9
2016	**My Dream Boat**	4	C Cox	A Kirby	16-1	3/6
2017	**Highland Reel**	5	A O'Brien	R Moore	9-4	6/8

A RACE that has altered hugely since gaining Group 1 status in 2000 when Dubai Millennium provided one of the outstanding moments in Royal Ascot history. The race now attracts an international field and 12 of the last 18 winners had won a Group 1 outside Britain and Ireland. That also shows the quality required as three of the six exceptions had won a Group 1 at home, with only My Dream Boat, Free Eagle and Byword not successful at the highest level. Only four of the last 13 winners were trained in Britain as traditional trials such as the Brigadier Gerard Stakes and the Gordon Richards Stakes have waned in influence, although My Dream Boat followed up victory in the latter in 2016. The Tattersalls Gold Cup is the best pointer with four of the last seven horses to try it managing to complete the double (Decorated Knight last year was the first to do so since Al Kazeem in 2013 and came second).

Gold Cup (2m4f) Royal Ascot

2008	Yeats	7	A O'Brien	J Murtagh	11-8f	7/10
2009	Yeats	8	A O'Brien	J Murtagh	6-4f	4/9
2010	Rite Of Passage	6	D Weld	P Smullen	20-1	1/12
2011	Fame And Glory	5	A O'Brien	J Spencer	11-8f	3/15
2012	Colour Vision	4	S Bin Suroor	F Dettori	6-1	5/9
2013	Estimate	4	Sir M Stoute	R Moore	7-2f	5/14
2014	Leading Light	4	A O'Brien	J O'Brien	10-11f	14/13
2015	Trip To Paris	4	E Dunlop	G Lee	12-1	13/12
2016	Order Of St George	4	A O'Brien	R Moore	10-11f	10/17
2017	Big Orange	6	M Bell	J Doyle	5-1	7/14

A HALF-MILE longer than any other British or Irish Group 1, this race understandably attracts plenty of real specialists, with Royal Rebel, Kayf Tara, Drum Taps and Sadeem all dual winners since 1988 before Yeats became the first ever four-time winner in 2009. His trainer Aidan O'Brien remains the trainer to follow as he has since won with Order Of St George, Leading Light and Fame And Glory, as well as finishing second with Order Of St George, Age Of Aquarius and Kingfisher, and five of his last six winners started their year in the Vintage Crop Stakes at Navan. The other strong trials are the Sagaro Stakes, which has come back into vogue with Estimate and Colour Vision winning both races to match Celeric, Double Trigger, Sadeem, Longboat and Gildoran since the mid-1980s, and the Henry II Stakes, the route taken by eight of the 13 winners prior to Yeats's reign plus Big Orange and Trip To Paris in the last three years. Wherever it's been, 15 of the last 18 winners had been successful over 2m. Four-year-olds have won five of the last six renewals and any older horse has to have proved themselves at the top level already as eight of the last 11 older winners had previously landed a Group 1 (plus last year's winner Big Orange had won the last two runnings of the Goodwood Cup before it was upgraded to a Group 1).

Coronation Stakes (1m) Royal Ascot

2008	Lush Lashes	J Bolger	K Manning	5-1	9/11
2009	Ghanaati	B Hills	R Hills	2-1f	5/10
2010	Lillie Langtry	A O'Brien	J Murtagh	7-2f	3/13
2011	Immortal Verse	R Collet	G Mosse	8-1	11/12
2012	Fallen For You	J Gosden	W Buick	12-1	11/10
2013	Sky Lantern	R Hannon Sr	R Hughes	9-2jf	16/17
2014	Rizeena	C Brittain	R Moore	11-2	7/12
2015	Ervedya	J-C Rouget	C Soumillon	3-1	7/9
2016	Qemah	J-C Rouget	G Benoist	6-1	11/13
2017	Winter	A O'Brien	R Moore	4-9f	7/7

A CHAMPIONSHIP race for three-year-old fillies. The 1,000 Guineas at Newmarket is much the best guide as ten of the last 15 winners had run on the Rowley Mile, with nine achieving a top-seven finish including five fillies who did the double (Winter, Sky Lantern, Ghanaati, Attraction and Russian Rhythm). It's generally best to have been off the track since then, though, as just three of the last 24 winners ran in the Newmarket Classic and the Irish 1,000 Guineas at the Curragh, which often counts against many in the field. Any horse who has been stepped up in trip can be opposed as Lush Lashes is the only winner in the last 23 years to have raced over further.

Diamond Jubilee Stakes (6f) Royal Ascot

2008	Kingsgate Native	3	J Best	S Sanders	33-1	15/17
2009	Art Connoisseur	3	M Bell	T Queally	20-1	11/14
2010	Starspangledbanner	4	A O'Brien	J Murtagh	13-2j	21/24
2011	Society Rock	4	J Fanshawe	P Cosgrave	25-1	3/16
2012	Black Caviar	5	P Moody	L Nolen	1-6f	15/14
2013	Lethal Force	4	C Cox	A Kirby	11-1	15/18
2014	Slade Power	5	E Lynam	W Lordan	7-2f	4/14
2015	Undrafted	5	W Ward	F Dettori	14-1	6/15
2016	Twilight Son	4	H Candy	R Moore	7-2	3/9
2017	The Tin Man	5	J Fanshawe	T Queally	9-2	3/19

A RACE whose profile has been steadily on the rise and reached fever pitch with its inauguration into the Global Sprint Challenge alongside the King's Stand Stakes, attracting the best sprinters from around the world, most notably the legendary Black Caviar in 2012. Yet despite Black Caviar and the American winner Undrafted in 2015, the percentage call is to side with domestic talent as they are the only winners trained outside Britain and Ireland since Cape Of Good Hope in 2005, during which time several fancied foreign raiders – Takeover Target (twice), J J The Jet Plane, Sacred Kingdom, Star Witness and Brazen Beau – have been beaten at 4-1 or shorter. In contrast, course form remains critical because, of the last 18 winners at Ascot, nine had already been successful at the course and the same number had managed a top-four finish at Royal Ascot. The race throws up more than its share of shocks, with four winners priced 20-1 or bigger in the last ten years, but two of those were among a host of unfancied three-year-olds to run well from very few representatives – including five places at 40-1 or bigger from 2003 to 2014 – and that age group is now barred from running because of the Commonwealth Cup.

Coral-Eclipse (1m2f) Sandown

2008	Mount Nelson	4	A O'Brien	J Murtagh	7-2	8/8
2009	Sea The Stars	3	J Oxx	M Kinane	4-7f	6/10
2010	Twice Over	5	H Cecil	T Queally	13-8f	1/5
2011	So You Think	5	A O'Brien	S Heffernan	4-6f	3/5
2012	Nathaniel	4	J Gosden	W Buick	7-2	4/9
2013	Al Kazeem	5	R Charlton	J Doyle	15-8f	2/7
2014	Mukhadram	5	W Haggas	P Hanagan	14-1	10/9
2015	Golden Horn	3	J Gosden	F Dettori	4-9f	1/5
2016	Hawkbill	3	C Appleby	W Buick	6-1	3/7
2017	Ulysses	4	Sir M Stoute	J Crowley	8-1	6/9

TRADITIONALLY THE first clash of the generations. It has suffered a little in recent times from a lack of three-year-old representation, but the tide may be turning again, helped by Golden Horn and Sea The Stars following up Derby victories after the previous four to take their chance – Authorized, Motivator, Benny The Dip and Erhaab – were all beaten. Indeed, following Golden Horn's win, Hawkbill and The Gurkha provided a one-two for three-year-olds in 2016 and Barney Roy was just touched off last year. Fillies are to be avoided as Pebbles in 1985 is the only one to succeed since the 19th century, since when Bosra Sham and Ouija Board were beaten favourites. Royal Ascot form is the key, particularly the Prince of Wales's Stakes, although Al Kazeem was the first to do the double since Mtoto 26 years earlier with many horses beaten at Ascot – most recently Ulysses, Mukhadram, So You Think, Twice Over and David Junior – improving on that form.

165

July Cup (6f) Newmarket

2008	**Marchand d'Or**	5	F Head	D Bonilla	5-2f	5/13
2009	**Fleeting Spirit**	4	J Noseda	T Queally	12-1	5/13
2010	**Starspangledbanner**	4	A O'Brien	J Murtagh	2-1f	4/14
2011	**Dream Ahead**	3	D Simcock	H Turner	7-1	2/16
2012	**Mayson**	4	R Fahey	P Hanagan	20-1	11/12
2013	**Lethal Force**	4	C Cox	A Kirby	9-2	4/11
2014	**Slade Power**	5	E Lynam	W Lordan	7-4f	13/13
2015	**Muhaarar**	3	C Hills	P Hanagan	2-1jf	7/14
2016	**Limato**	4	H Candy	H Bentley	9-2f	16/18
2017	**Harry Angel**	3	C Cox	A Kirby	9-2	6/10

FIVE OF the last 12 winners were following up victories over the same trip at Royal Ascot – four in the Diamond Jubilee Stakes before Muhaarar from the inaugural Commonwealth Cup, in which last year's winner Harry Angel had also been second – but surprisingly it pays to ignore Group 1 form in other races as ten of the other 12 winners since 2001 were scoring for the first time at the top level. Indeed, this is a race in which stars are often born with 41 of the 50 winners being aged three or four. Often that's because horses are dropping into sprints having been tried over further as stamina is an important asset on this stiff uphill finish. Greats like Ajdal and Soviet Song are memorable for that many years ago and more recently the likes of Limato, Muhaarar and Dream Ahead had run over a mile earlier in the season.

King George VI and Queen Elizabeth Stakes (1m4f) Ascot

2008	**Duke Of Marmalade**	4	A O'Brien	J Murtagh	4-6f	5/8
2009	**Conduit**	4	Sir M Stoute	R Moore	13-8f	8/9
2010	**Harbinger**	4	Sir M Stoute	O Peslier	4-1	1/6
2011	**Nathaniel**	3	J Gosden	W Buick	11-2	3/5
2012	**Danedream**	4	P Schiergen	A Starke	9-1	4/10
2013	**Novellist**	4	A Wohler	J Murtagh	13-2	3/8
2014	**Taghrooda**	3	J Gosden	P Hanagan	7-2	7/8
2015	**Postponed**	4	L Cumani	A Atzeni	6-1	9/7

THE GURKHA: a typical fit for a Sussex Stakes winner as a glamorous three-year-old sent off favourite – certainly more so than last year's winner!

2016	Highland Reel	4	A O'Brien	R Moore	13-8f	3/7
2017	Enable	3	J Gosden	F Dettori	5-4f	7/10

THIS RACE has suffered from a lack of three-year-old representation in recent years, with Enable, Taghrooda, Nathaniel, Alamshar and Galileo the only horses of that age to come out on top since Lammtarra in 1995. Taghrooda was an even bigger trends-buster as she became the first British-trained three-year-old filly to win any Group 1 over this trip against older males in the worldwide history of the sport – it therefore makes it all the more astonishing that Enable matched her just three years later. Still, it generally pays to look for a four-year-old (the age of 11 of the last 14 winners) proven at the top level and the trip because since Belmez in 1990 just four winners hadn't previously landed a Group 1 and just five hadn't been first or second in a Group 1 over 1m4f. The Coronation Cup is a poor guide, though, with only Opera House and Daylami doing the double in more than 40 years.

Sussex Stakes (1m) Goodwood

2008	Henrythenavigator	3	A O'Brien	J Murtagh	4-11f	4/6
2009	Rip Van Winkle	3	A O'Brien	J Murtagh	6-4f	7/8
2010	Canford Cliffs	3	R Hannon Sr	R Hughes	4-6f	7/7
2011	Frankel	3	Sir H Cecil	T Queally	8-13f	3/4
2012	Frankel	4	Sir H Cecil	T Queally	1-20f	3/4
2013	Toronado	3	R Hannon Sr	R Hughes	11-4	7/7
2014	Kingman	3	J Gosden	J Doyle	2-5f	4/4
2015	Solow	5	F Head	M Guyon	2-5f	5/8
2016	The Gurkha	3	A O'Brien	R Moore	11-8f	1/10
2017	Here Comes When	7	A Balding	J Crowley	20-1	7/7

THIS IS a great race for glamorous three-year-olds as that age group has provided 29 of the 43 winners since it was opened to all ages in 1975. Nine of the last 12 triumphant three-year-olds were favourites and 11 of the last 13 had been first or second in the St James's Palace Stakes, which is the key trial. Seven of the last ten successful older horses had contested the Queen Anne Stakes, with Solow, Frankel and Ramonti doing the double since 2007. With Royal Ascot form holding up so well, it's perhaps little wonder that eight of the last ten favourites have obliged, six of them at odds-on.

Nassau Stakes (1m1f192yds) Goodwood

2008	Halfway To Heaven	3	A O'Brien	J Murtagh	5-1	6/9
2009	Midday	3	H Cecil	T Queally	11-2	10/10
2010	Midday	4	H Cecil	T Queally	15-8f	6/7
2011	Midday	5	Sir H Cecil	T Queally	6-4f	6/6
2012	The Fugue	3	J Gosden	R Hughes	11-4	7/8
2013	Winsili	3	J Gosden	W Buick	20-1	15/14
2014	Sultanina	4	J Gosden	W Buick	11-2	2/6
2015	Legatissimo	3	D Wachman	W Lordan	2-1f	8/9
2016	Minding	3	A O'Brien	R Moore	1-5f	1/5
2017	Winter	3	A O'Brien	R Moore	10-11f	6/6

THIS IS another fantastic race for punters as 22 of the last 24 winners emerged from the top three in the market including 14 favourites. The key is to side with a top-class three-year-old as the Classic generation have provided 33 of the 43 winners since the race was opened to older fillies in 1975, despite Midday's best efforts in racking up a hat-trick.

Preferably they should be dropping down in trip rather than stepping up as Winter and Halfway To Heaven are the only winners to have had their previous runs over a mile since 2004, during which time Minding has followed up victory in the Oaks while Legatissimo, The Fugue, Midday and Peeping Fawn all improved on placed efforts at Epsom.

Juddmonte International Stakes (1m2f85yds) York

2008	Duke Of Marmalade	4	A O'Brien	J Murtagh	4-6f	4/9*
2009	Sea The Stars	3	J Oxx	M Kinane	1-4f	3/4
2010	Rip Van Winkle	4	A O'Brien	J Murtagh	7-4f	7/9
2011	Twice Over	6	Sir H Cecil	I Mongan	11-2	4/5
2012	Frankel	4	Sir H Cecil	T Queally	1-10f	7/9
2013	Declaration Of War	4	A O'Brien	J O'Brien	7-1	2/6
2014	Australia	3	A O'Brien	J O'Brien	8-13f	6/6
2015	Arabian Queen	3	D Elsworth	S De Sousa	50-1	5/7
2016	Postponed	5	R Varian	A Atzeni	15-8f	6/12
2017	Ulysses	4	Sir M Stoute	J Crowley	4-1	3/7

*Note – this race and following two York races all run at Newmarket in 2008

FAMOUS FOR its many upsets since Brigadier Gerard suffered his only defeat to Roberto in 1972, this race rediscovered its teeth in 2015 when 50-1 shot Arabian Queen stunned the mighty Golden Horn. Otherwise, though, it has turned in punters' favour in recent times with no other winner returned bigger than 8-1 since Ezzoud in 1993 and seven of the last 11 favourites winning. Older horses have dominated the three-year-olds with just six younger horses triumphing since 1984, all of whom were recent Group 1 winners apart from Arabian Queen with the previous three being Derby winners. The best trial is the Coral-Eclipse, which has provided nine of the last 23 winners, with Ulysses the seventh to complete the double in that time.

Yorkshire Oaks (1m3f195yds) York

2008	Lush Lashes	3	J Bolger	K Manning	Evsf	2/6*
2009	Dar Re Mi	4	J Gosden	J Fortune	11-2	4/6
2010	Midday	4	H Cecil	T Queally	11-4	6/8
2011	Blue Bunting	3	M Al Zarooni	F Dettori	11-4f	6/8
2012	Shareta	4	A de Royer-Dupre	C Lemaire	2-1	7/6
2013	The Fugue	4	J Gosden	W Buick	2-1f	6/7
2014	Tapestry	3	A O'Brien	R Moore	8-1	6/7
2015	Pleascach	3	J Bolger	K Manning	8-1	8/11
2016	Seventh Heaven	3	A O'Brien	C O'Donoghue	10-3	10/12
2017	Enable	3	J Gosden	F Dettori	1-4f	1/6

ALWAYS A top-class race, this has been won by the Classic generation 12 times in the last 18 years, including each of the last four. However, Enable was the first Oaks winner to follow up since Alexandrova in 2005, with four beaten in that time – Taghrooda, Was, Snow Fairy and Sariska – three of them when favourite. Significantly, Enable and Alexandrova had won the Irish Oaks in between because that has been a better guide – the last six Curragh winners to take their chance have finished 1221211, while 2014 heroine Tapestry had finished second in Ireland.

Nunthorpe Stakes (5f) York

2008	Borderlescott	6	R Bastiman	P Cosgrave	12-1	12/14

ULYSSES: the seventh horse since 1995 to do the Eclipse/Juddmonte double

2009	**Borderlescott**	7	R Bastiman	N Callan	9-1	2/16
2010	**Sole Power**	3	E Lynam	W Lordan	100-1	11/12
2011	**Margot Did**	3	M Bell	H Turner	20-1	11/15
2012	**Ortensia**	7	P Messara	W Buick	7-2jf	8/19
2013	**Jwala**	4	R Cowell	S Drowne	40-1	8/17
2014	**Sole Power**	7	E Lynam	R Hughes	11-4f	10/13
2015	**Mecca's Angel**	4	M Dods	P Mulrennan	15-2	10/19
2016	**Mecca's Angel**	5	M Dods	P Mulrennan	9-2	7/19
2017	**Marsha**	4	Sir M Prescott	L Morris	8-1	8/11

THIS HAS become a real race for upsets, none bigger than Sole Power at 100-1 in 2010, and there have also been 20-1 and 40-1 winners since then. The main reason is that the race isn't often won by a proven top-level sprinter, with eight of the last 16 winners never having previously landed a Group race, let alone a Group 1 race, and the King's Stand is less influential than many might think as only Sole Power has done the double since 2000. It's therefore little wonder that progressive younger horses have tended to hold sway, although all six winners older than five since 1945 have come in the last 20 years.

Sprint Cup (6f) Haydock

2008	**African Rose**	3	Mme C Head	S Pasquier	7-2f	12/15
2009	**Regal Parade**	5	D Nicholls	A Nicholls	14-1	13/14
2010	**Markab**	7	H Candy	P Cosgrave	12-1	14/13
2011	**Dream Ahead**	3	D Simcock	W Buick	4-1f	9/16
2012	**Society Rock**	5	J Fanshawe	K Fallon	10-1	3/13
2013	**Gordon Lord Byron**	5	T Hogan	J Murtagh	7-2	2/13
2014	**G Force**	3	D O'Meara	D Tudhope	11-1	10/17
2015	**Twilight Son**	3	H Candy	F Sweeney	10-1	5/15
2016	**Quiet Reflection**	3	K Burke	D Costello	7-2f	4/14
2017	**Harry Angel**	3	C Cox	A Kirby	2-1f	8/11

THREE-YEAR-OLDS have taken a firm grip on this race in recent times, winning four in a row and six of the last ten runnings in all at more than double the strike-rate of their older rivals. That has turned the tide back in punters' favour – four of those winning three-year-olds were favourites – but this has also provided plenty of upsets, with midsummer form often misleading on much softer ground. Ten of the last 16 winners were returned in double figures, including 33-1 Red Clubs in 2007, and the same number were making their breakthrough at the highest level, with Dream Ahead and Harry Angel the only July Cup winners since Ajdal in 1987 and six others beaten in the meantime.

St Leger (1m6f132yds) Doncaster

2008	Conduit		Sir M Stoute	F Dettori	8-1	5/14
2009	Mastery		S bin Suroor	T Durcan	14-1	7/8
2010	Arctic Cosmos		J Gosden	W Buick	12-1	8/10
2011	Masked Marvel		J Gosden	W Buick	15-2	3/9
2012	Encke		M Al Zarooni	M Barzalona	25-1	1/9
2013	Leading Light		A O'Brien	J O'Brien	7-2f	7/11
2014	Kingston Hill		R Varian	A Atzeni	9-4f	4/12
2015	Simple Verse		R Beckett	A Atzeni	8-1	1/7
2016	Harbour Law		L Mongan	G Baker	22-1	9/9
2017	Capri		A O'Brien	R Moore	3-1f	9/11

TOP-CLASS horses are increasingly being kept to shorter trips and Capri was an unusual winner last year given he already had an Irish Derby in the bag, making him the first Curragh winner to follow up since Nijinsky. No Derby winner has followed up since Reference Point in 1987 – Camelot is the only one to even try in 2012 – and, while 17 of the last 20 winners had won a Group race, their progress tends to have been steady rather than spectacular. Five of the eight winners to come via the Derby since 1997 finished outside the places at Epsom and even three of the eight to have warmed up in the Great Voltigeur in that time were beaten there. The Gordon Stakes has been the other key trial in this period, with four horses doing the double, though none since Conduit in 2008. Kingston Hill is the only winner in more than 25 years to have had his prep run over just 1m2f, though during that time only Leading Light warmed up beyond the Leger distance. Simple Verse is the only filly to prevail since User Friendly in 1992.

Prix de l'Arc de Triomphe (1m4f) Longchamp

2008	Zarkava	3	A de Royer-Dupre	C Soumillon	13-8f	1/16
2009	Sea The Stars	3	J Oxx	M Kinane	4-6f	6/19
2010	Workforce	3	Sir M Stoute	R Moore	6-1	8/19
2011	Danedream	3	P Schiergen	A Starke	20-1	2/16
2012	Solemia	4	C Laffon-Parias	O Peslier	33-1	6/18
2013	Treve	3	C Head-Maarek	T Jarnet	9-2	15/17
2014	Treve	4	C Head-Maarek	T Jarnet	11-1	3/20
2015	Golden Horn	3	J Gosden	F Dettori	9-2	14/17
2016	Found	4	A O'Brien	R Moore	6-1	12/16*
2017	Enable	3	J Gosden	F Dettori	10-11f	2/18*

*Run at Chantilly in 2016 and 2017.

THE PREMIER middle-distance championship of Europe is generally one for the French, with 17 of the last 28 winners trained at home, although the tide is turning. There hasn't been a successful French-trained colt since Rail Link in 2006 and seven of the subsequent 11 winners came from abroad, while three of the last eight runners-up were Japanese and it's surely a matter of time before they break their duck. It follows that the big domestic trials have a poor record, with the Prix Niel, having thrown up ten winners in 13 years up to 2006, drawing a blank since then and the Prix Foy enduring an even worse run, with no winner since Subotica in 1992. Fillies are enjoying a remarkable period, with seven of the last ten renewals going to the girls. Only four horses older than four have won since the Second World War and the losers include two recent favourites in Orfevre and Treve.

Queen Elizabeth II Stakes (1m) Ascot

2008	Raven's Pass	3	J Gosden	J Fortune	3-1	7/7
2009	Rip Van Winkle	3	A O'Brien	J Murtagh	8-13f	4/4
2010	Poet's Voice	3	S Bin Suroor	F Dettori	9-2	7/8
2011	Frankel	3	Sir H Cecil	T Queally	4-11f	2/8
2012	Excelebration	4	A O'Brien	J O'Brien	10-11f	6/8
2013	Olympic Glory	3	R Hannon Sr	R Hughes	11-2	7/12
2014	Charm Spirit	3	F Head	O Peslier	5-1	7/11
2015	Solow	5	F Head	M Guyon	11-10f	2/9
2016	Minding	3	A O'Brien	R Moore	7-4f	8/13
2017	Persuasive	4	J Gosden	F Dettori	8-1	6/15

THE MILE championship of Europe in which the Classic generation has held sway, with seven victories in the last ten years extending a long period of superiority. That said, the time of year makes this a tough date for 2,000 Guineas winners, with Frankel and George Washington the only ones to do the double from nine to try in the last 15 years. Similarly, only Frankel and Bahri have followed up St James's Palace Stakes wins since 1995, although seven of the last 15 successful three-year-olds ran in that race before progressing subsequently. Winners tend to be proven at the highest level, with 12 of the last 15 having already won a Group 1, and as a result last year's winner Persuasive was the first not to come from the first three in the market since 2001. Fillies have won each of the last two runnings, although they are the only ones to come out on top since 1987.

Champion Stakes (1m2f) Ascot

2008	New Approach	3	J Bolger	K Manning	6-5f	2/11
2009	Twice Over	4	H Cecil	T Queally	14-1	6/14
2010	Twice Over	5	H Cecil	T Queally	7-2	4/10
2011	Cirrus Des Aigles	5	C Barande-Barbe	C Soumillon	12-1	1/12
2012	Frankel	4	Sir H Cecil	T Queally	2-11f	6/8
2013	Farhh	5	S Bin Suroor	S de Sousa	11-4	5/10
2014	Noble Mission	5	Lady Cecil	J Doyle	7-1	5/9
2015	Fascinating Rock	4	D Weld	P Smullen	10-1	7/13
2016	Almanzor	3	J-C Rouget	C Soumillon	11-8f	1/10
2017	Cracksman	3	J Gosden	F Dettori	13-8f	4/10

Run at Newmarket until 2011.

THE SUBJECT of a big-money makeover when switched to Ascot in 2011. Older horses have increasingly come to the fore, accounting for seven winners in a row up to 2015 including four five-year-olds. While Almanzor and Cracksman have since stopped the rot, that's a trend likely to grow stronger because, among the 18 successful three-year-olds since 1980, mile form has proved a lot more influential than form over further – 12 of those 18 had won a Classic with New Approach the only one since Time Charter in 1982 to have done it over 1m4f – yet top milers now have the option of the QEII on the same day. This has been the best British Group 1 for French horses, with four winners in the last 12 years extending a long tradition of success.

Est. 1909
RACING & FOOTBALL OUTLOOK

Big handicap records

Lincoln (1m) Doncaster

Year	Winner	Age	Weight	Trainer	Jockey	SP	Draw/ran
2008	**Smokey Oakey**	4	8-9	M Tompkins	J Quinn	10-1	12/21
2009	**Expresso Star**	4	8-12	J Gosden	J Fortune	10-3f	9/20
2010	**Penitent**	4	9-2	W Haggas	J Murtagh	3-1f	1/21
2011	**Sweet Lightning**	6	9-4	M Dods	J Murtagh	16-1	16/21*
2012	**Brae Hill**	6	9-1	R Fahey	T Hamilton	25-1	12/22
2013	**Levitate**	5	8-7	J Quinn	D Egan (3)	20-1	3/22
2014	**Ocean Tempest**	5	9-3	J Ryan	A Kirby	20-1	3/17
2015	**Gabrial**	6	9-0	R Fahey	T Hamilton	12-1	15/22
2016	**Secret Brief**	4	9-4	C Appleby	W Buick	12-1	22/22
2017	**Bravery**	4	9-1	D O'Meara	D Tudhope	20-1	1/22

*Run at Newcastle in 2011.

AS WITH all big handicaps, the rating required to get a run gets higher and higher, so long-standing trends about siding with a progressive horse on a low weight have been rendered obsolete. Even so, a big weight is still a huge disadvantage as the last winner to carry more than 9st 4lb was Babodana in 2004. Older horses have come to the fore – only two of the last seven winners were aged four after a run of nine in 16 years for that age group – and the switch hasn't been good news for punters, with every winner in that time priced at least 12-1. It's common for runners to come via the all-weather or Dubai, but 12 of the last 16 winners were having their first run of the season and it's wise to side with trainers who have a proven track record of getting one ready as four of the last nine winning trainers – Richard Fahey, John Quinn, William Haggas and Mark Tompkins – had also won the race within the previous seven years. A high draw is a concern as ten of the last 11 winners at Doncaster came from a stall no higher than 16.

Royal Hunt Cup (1m) Royal Ascot

2008	**Mr Aviator**	4	9-5	R Hannon Sr	R Hughes	25-1	26/29
2009	**Forgotten Voice**	4	9-1	J Noseda	J Murtagh	4-1f	25/25
2010	**Invisible Man**	4	8-9	S Bin Suroor	F Dettori	28-1	7/29
2011	**Julienas**	4	8-8	W Swinburn	E Ahern	12-1	24/28
2012	**Prince Of Johanne**	6	9-1	T Tate	J Fahy	16-1	33/30
2013	**Belgian Bill**	5	8-11	G Baker	J Doyle	33-1	6/28
2014	**Field Of Dream**	7	9-1	J Osborne	A Kirby	20-1	33/28
2015	**GM Hopkins**	4	9-3	J Gosden	R Moore	8-1	11/30
2016	**Portage**	4	9-5	M Halford	J Doyle	10-1	4/28

| 2017 | Zhui Feng | 4 | 9-0 | A Perrett | M Dwyer | 25-1 | 26/29 |

A REAL puzzle for punters with Forgotten Voice in 2009 the only winning favourite in the last 20 years. A common mistake is to side with a lightly raced improver because experience is in fact a vital commodity – 18 of the last 20 winners had run at least eight times, which is more than many of the beaten favourites. Weight trends had changed markedly even before the further condensing of the handicap caused by the demise of the Buckingham Palace Stakes, with fewer runners getting in below the 9st barrier, so it's telling that Portage (with just 9st 5lb) was the first to carry more than 9st 3lb since 2008, making it just three in 29 years to have defied a greater burden. A high draw is generally essential, with only three of the last 15 winners at Ascot overcoming a single-figure berth.

Wokingham (6f) Royal Ascot

2008	**Big Timer**	4	9-2	Miss L Perrett	T Eaves	20-1	1/27
2009	**High Standing**	4	8-12	W Haggas	R Moore	6-1	4/26
2010	**Laddies Poker Two**	5	8-11	J Noseda	J Murtagh	9-2f	26/27
2011	**Deacon Blues**	4	8-13	J Fanshawe	J Murtagh	15-2	11/25
2012	**Dandy Boy**	6	9-8	D Marnane	P Dobbs	33-1	15/28
2013	**York Glory**	5	9-2	K Ryan	J Spencer	14-1	22/26
2014	**Baccarat**	5	9-5	R Fahey	G Chaloner (3)	9-1	27/28
2015	**Interception**	5	9-3	D Lanigan	G Baker	10-1	21/25
2016	**Outback Traveller**	5	9-1	R Cowell	M Harley	10-1	28/28
2017	**Out Do**	8	8-13	D O'Meara	D Tudhope	25-1	1/27

THIS RACE is run at such a furious gallop that stamina comes to the fore and, while 13 of the last 14 winners had already triumphed over the big-race trip, the exception had done his winning over further – in all nine of those 14 had a 7f victory to their name and 2015 winner Interception had been placed four times at 7f, including in a Listed race. Therefore the Victoria Cup, run over 7f at the same track in May, is one of the key trials, along with the 6f handicaps at Newmarket's Guineas meeting and York's Dante meeting. Fresh horses are preferred, with 11 of the last 16 winners having run no more than twice that year, which is remarkable for a sprint handicap in June. There's nothing to fear about a big weight, but only two winners have been older than five since 1999.

BABODANA: the last Lincoln winner to carry more than 9st 4lb

BALLET CONCERTO: put youngsters back on top in the John Smith's Cup

Northumberland Plate (2m) Newcastle

2008	**Arc Bleu**	7	8-2	A Martin	A Nicholls	14-1	6/18
2009	**Som Tala**	6	8-8	M Channon	T Culhane	16-1	4/17
2010	**Overturn**	6	8-7	D McCain	E Ahern	14-1	21/19
2011	**Tominator**	4	8-8	R Hollinshead	P Pickard (3)	25-1	14/19
2012	**Ile De Re**	6	9-3	D McCain	J Crowley	5-2f	9/16
2013	**Tominator**	6	9-10	J O'Neill	G Lee	8-1	4/18
2014	**Angel Gabrial**	5	9-1	R Fahey	G Chaloner (3)	4-1f	1/19
2015	**Quest For More**	5	9-4	R Charlton	G Baker	15-2	3/19
2016	**Antiquarium**	4	9-5	C Appleby	J McDonald	16-1	3/20
2017	**Higher Power**	5	9-9	J Fanshawe	T Queally	11-2	13/20

WITH SO much of the season revolving around Royal Ascot and Newcastle's biggest day of the summer generally coming just a week later, this provides a good opportunity for horses laid out for the race rather than coming here as an afterthought. Just two of the last 15 winners had run at Royal Ascot despite several fancied runners in that time, including four beaten favourites, coming from the royal meeting. Older horses have increasingly come to the fore, with five of the last ten winners aged at least six and two eight-year-olds among the previous eight to triumph. The first bend comes shortly after the start, so those drawn high can be disadvantaged, with 12 of the last 19 winners drawn seven or lower, and Overturn used controversial tactics to overcome that in 2010. The Chester Cup is traditionally a strong guide and that has been reinforced recently with Ile De Re doing the double before Tominator and Angel Gabrial stepped up on placed efforts at Chester. Ten of the last 15 winners were opening their account for the season.

Bunbury Cup (7f) Newmarket

2008	**Little White Lie**	4	9-0	J Jenkins	D Holland	14-1	1/18
2009	**Plum Pudding**	6	9-10	R Hannon Sr	R Moore	12-1	15/19
2010	**St Moritz**	4	9-1	M Johnston	F Dettori	4-1f	4/19
2011	**Brae Hill**	5	9-1	R Fahey	B McHugh	11-1	2/20

2012	**Bonnie Brae**	5	9-9	D Elsworth	R Moore	13-2	12/15
2013	**Field Of Dream**	6	9-7	J Osborne	A Kirby	14-1	20/19
2014	**Heaven's Guest**	4	9-3	R Fahey	T Hamilton	12-1	9/13
2015	**Rene Mathis**	5	9-1	R Fahey	P Hanagan	16-1	10/17
2016	**Golden Steps**	5	9-0	M Botti	F Dettori	7-1jf	14/16
2017	**Above The Rest**	6	9-1	D Barron	C Lee (5)	12-1	19/18

IT'S REMARKABLE how often this race is won by a horse carrying a big weight. Mine, a three-time winner between 2002 and 2006, twice defied a burden of at least 9st 9lb and has been emulated by Bonnie Brae and Plum Pudding since then. Despite that only one of the last 24 winners had won more than once that year – 17 hadn't won at all, including all of the last eight – so the key is clearly to find a horse slipping down the weights but classy enough to still be near the top of the handicap. This is run over a specialist trip and Golden Steps is the only winner not to have already won a handicap over the distance since 2002.

John Smith's Cup (1m2f85yds) York

2008	**Flying Clarets**	5	8-12	R Fahey	F Tylicki (7)	12-1	12/16
2009	**Sirvino**	4	8-8	T Brown	N Brown (3)	16-1	16/18
2010	**Wigmore Hall**	3	8-5	M Bell	M Lane (3)	5-1	13/19
2011	**Green Destiny**	4	8-13	W Haggas	A Beschizza (3)	6-1	17-19
2012	**King's Warrior**	5	8-9	P Chapple-Hyam	R Havlin	33-1	19/18
2013	**Danchai**	4	8-11	W Haggas	A Atzeni	10-1	16/19
2014	**Farraaj**	5	9-11	R Varian	A Atzeni	6-1	22/16
2015	**Master Carpenter**	4	9-4	R Millman	P Makin	14-1	1/17
2016	**Educate**	7	9-8	I Mohammed	T Brown	18-1	14/19
2017	**Ballet Concerto**	4	9-3	Sir M Stoute	J Doyle	8-1	11/20

YOUTH SEEMS to be the key to this race, with Educate the only winner older than five – and just three of that age successful – since Vintage Premium in 2002 despite three-year-olds struggling desperately to get a run. Indeed, subsequent Grade 1 winner Wigmore Hall was the only three-year-old when successful in 2010 and none have made the field since. Like the Northumberland Plate, this is another handicap in which missing Royal Ascot helps, in keeping with ten of the last 15 winners whereas 13 of the last 16 beaten favourites registered a top-four finish there. This is run on one of the best Saturdays of the summer and, with many top jockeys engaged elsewhere, it provides an opportunity for some younger riders as six of the last 12 winners were partnered by an apprentice.

Stewards' Cup (6f) Goodwood

2008	**Conquest**	4	8-9	W Haggas	D O'Neill	40-1	13/26
2009	**Genki**	5	9-1	R Charlton	S Drowne	14-1	17/26
2010	**Evens And Odds**	6	9-1	D Nicholls	B Cray (5)	20-1	11/28
2011	**Hoof It**	4	10-0	M Easterby	K Fallon	13-2jf	18/27
2012	**Hawkeyethenoo**	6	9-9	J Goldie	G Lee	9-1	4/27
2013	**Rex Imperator**	4	9-4	W Haggas	N Callan	12-1	26/27
2014	**Intrinsic**	4	8-11	R Cowell	R Hughes	6-1	22/24
2015	**Magical Memory**	3	8-12	C Hills	F Dettori	6-1f	1/27
2016	**Dancing Star**	3	8-12	A Balding	D Probert	9-2f	4/27
2017	**Lancelot Du Lac**	7	9-5	D Ivory	F Dettori	25-1	15/26

THIS IS a major betting heat with a strong ante-post market and the betting has become a good guide as nine winners at single-figure odds in 15 years, plus three more not a lot bigger, is a fine record given the size of the field. This is a race for established sprint handicappers and even the two three-year-old winners in the last two years had landed the big 6f handicap for that age group at Newmarket's July meeting. Fifteen of the last 20 older winners came via the Wokingham, though none of them had won at Royal Ascot and all but two had another run in between. That run tends to have been a good one as nine of the last 15 winners finished first or second in their prep race, which is amazing given the competitiveness of sprint handicaps. Only two winners since 1984 carried more than 9st 7lb, while the last winner to have warmed up in Pattern company was Crews Hill in 1981.

Ebor (1m6f) York

2008	**All The Good**	5	9-0	S Bin Suroor	D O'Neill	25-1	7/20*
2009	**Sesenta**	5	8-8	W Mullins	G Carroll (5)	25-1	16/19
2010	**Dirar**	5	9-1	G Elliott	J Spencer	14-1	22/20
2011	**Moyenne Corniche**	6	8-13	B Ellison	D Swift (3)	25-1	10/20
2012	**Willing Foe**	5	9-2	S Bin Suroor	F Dettori	12-1	16/19
2013	**Tiger Cliff**	4	9-0	Lady Cecil	T Queally	5-1	18/14
2014	**Mutual Regard**	5	9-9	J Murtagh	L Steward (5)	20-1	16/19
2015	**Litigant**	7	9-1	J Tuite	O Murphy	33-1	6/19
2016	**Heartbreak City**	6	9-6	T Martin	A McNamara (5)	15-2	15/20
2017	**Nakeeta**	6	9-5	I Jardine	C Rodriguez (5)	12-1	18/19

Run at Newbury as the Newburgh Handicap in 2008

ONE OF the oldest and most famous handicaps, first run in 1847, this has an extremely strong ante-post market and was moved to a Saturday in 2011 to boost its profile further. Sea Pigeon brought the house down when lumping top-weight home in 1979, but low weights are massively favoured and, once taking into account jockeys' claims, just three winners have carried more than 9st 2lb since 1998 and none more than 9st 4lb despite the handicap becoming more and more condensed. A shrewd trainer will use a claimer to bring the weight down, with five of the last nine winners partnered by such a rider. Watch out for three-year-olds as they had a tremendous record around the turn of the century and have simply found it increasingly tough to get a run since then, with two of the four to run since 2006, Honolulu and Changingoftheguard, finishing second. Indeed, progressive horses are always preferred with just five winners older than five since Sea Pigeon and ten of the last 15 having raced no more than nine times on the Flat in Britain or Ireland.

Ayr Gold Cup (6f) Ayr

2008	**Regal Parade**	4	8-10	D Nicholls	W Carson (5)	18-1	20/27
2009	**Jimmy Styles**	5	9-2	C Cox	F Dettori	14-1	15/26
2010	**Redford**	5	9-2	D Nicholls	F Dettori	14-1	17/26
2011	**Our Jonathan**	4	9-6	K Ryan	F Norton	11-1	12/26
2012	**Captain Ramius**	6	9-0	K Ryan	P Smullen	16-1	8/26
2013	**Highland Colori**	5	9-4	A Balding	O Murphy (5)	20-1	19/26
2014	**Louis The Pious**	6	9-4	D O'Meara	J Doyle	10-1	19/27
2015	**Don't Touch**	3	9-1	R Fahey	T Hamilton	6-1f	8/25
2016	**Brando**	4	9-10	K Ryan	T Eaves	11-1	8/23
2017	**Donjuan Triumphant**	4	9-10	A Balding	PJ McDonald	13-2	4/17*

Run at Haydock as the 32Red Gold Cup in 2017

A HISTORIC race first run in 1804, but punters are still struggling to get to grips with it –

DOLPHIN VISTA: crucially, the shock Cambridgeshire winner had form over further, becoming the 11th winner in 16 years with a win over 1m2f

Don't Touch is the only successful favourite in the last 20 years with Donjuan Triumphant the only other winner priced in single figures in that time. The key is to ignore winning form as that can mean too much weight, with eight of the last 15 winners having not won in any of their four most recent outings. Nine of the last 12 runnings have gone to major northern yards, with Kevin Ryan leading the way with four victories. The effect of the draw can be gleaned from the consolation races – the Bronze Cup was run for the first time in 2009 and is now on the Friday of the meeting, with the Silver Cup preceding the big one.

Cambridgeshire (1m1f) Newmarket

2008	**Tazeez**	4	9-2	J Gosden	R Hills	25-1	8/28
2009	**Supaseus**	6	9-1	H Morrison	T Block	16-1	7/32
2010	**Credit Swap**	5	8-7	M Wigham	J Crowley	14-1	3/35
2011	**Prince Of Johanne**	5	8-12	T Tate	J Fahy (3)	40-1	31/32
2012	**Bronze Angel**	3	8-8	M Tregoning	W Buick	9-1	21/33
2013	**Educate**	4	9-9	I Mohammed	J Murtagh	8-1f	4/33
2014	**Bronze Angel**	5	8-13	M Tregoning	L Steward (5)	14-1	11/31
2015	**Third Time Lucky**	3	8-4	R Fahey	A Beschizza	14-1	7/34
2016	**Spark Plug**	5	9-4	B Meehan	J Fortune	12-1	28/31
2017	**Dolphin Vista**	4	8-10	M Meade	G Wood (3)	50-1	29/34

THE FIRST leg of the Autumn Double. Because of its unusual distance and its straight course, this has thrown up a number of specialists down the years, with dual winner Bronze Angel being the most obvious recent example, so consider horses who have run well in the race before. Many of the runners are milers racing over an extra furlong, but stronger stayers often come to the fore and 11 of the last 16 winners had triumphed over 1m2f while Spark Plug had been second in a Listed race at the trip. Experience of a big field is vital and 13 of the last 14 winners had won a race of at least 13 runners, 11 of them in a handicap. Big weights spell trouble as Educate is the only horse to carry more than 9st 4lb to victory since Beauchamp Pilot in 2002.

Cesarewitch (2m2f) Newmarket

2008	Caracciola	11	9-6	N Henderson	E Ahern	50-1	22/32
2009	Darley Sun	3	8-6	D Simcock	A Atzeni (3)	9-2f	8/32
2010	Aaim To Prosper	7	8-2	B Meehan	L-P Beuzelin (3)	16-1	3/32
2011	Never Can Tell	4	8-11	J Osborne	F Dettori	25-1	36/33
2012	Aaim To Prosper	8	9-10	B Meehan	K Fallon	66-1	1/34
2013	Scatter Dice	4	8-8	M Johnston	S de Sousa	66-1	18/33
2014	Big Easy	7	8-7	P Hobbs	T Queally	10-1	2/33
2015	Grumeti	7	8-2	A King	A Beschizza	50-1	15/34
2016	Sweet Selection	4	8-8	H Morrison	S de Sousa	7-1	23/33
2017	Withhold	4	8-8	R Charlton	S de Sousa	5-1f	24/34

THE SECOND leg of the Autumn Double. This is another race in which the draw is far more important than you would think from the trip, with only three winners drawn higher than 18 since 1997, the latest – Withhold – in a year when much quicker ground on the stands rail led to the whole field switching sides. Generally punters are too swayed by a young improver as Darley Sun is one of only two winning three-year-olds in 24 years and he was the only favourite to win in the last ten years during a spell that has seen winners returned twice at 66-1 and twice at 50-1 – St Michel was the latest losing favourite from the Classic generation in 2016. One of the big-priced winners, Aaim To Prosper, reinforced the significance of previous form in the race as he followed up his victory two years earlier. Scatter Dice is the only winner since 1995 not to have already been successful over at least 2m and the success of jumps yards reinforces the importance of proven stamina as just four of the last 22 runnings didn't have a recognised hurdler in the first two. The Northumberland Plate is the best trial having thrown up nine of the last 23 winners.

November Handicap (1m4f) Doncaster

2008	Tropical Strait	5	8-13	D Arbuthnot	M Dwyer	20-1	22/21
2009	Charm School	4	8-12	J Gosden	J Fortune	17-2	14/23
2010	Times Up	4	8-13	J Dunlop	D O'Neill	14-1	9/22
2011	Zuider Zee	4	8-13	J Gosden	R Havlin	8-1	20/23
2012	Art Scholar	5	8-7	M Appleby	F Norton	20-1	9/23
2013	Conduct	6	9-2	W Haggas	S Sanders	8-1	21/23
2014	Open Eagle	5	8-12	D O'Meara	D Tudhope	15-2f	18/23
2015	Litigant	7	9-10	J Tuite	G Baker	10-1	12/22
2016	Prize Money	3	9-1	S bin Suroor	G Wood (5)	4-1	12/15
2017	Saunter	4	8-13	I Williams	J Crowley	6-1	14/23

THE LAST big betting heat of the season and one that has changed in recent years due to the lack of three-year-olds able to get a run. When Malt Or Mash won in 2007 that age group had won 14 of the last 24 renewals and three-year-olds still have to be feared if getting in, as Prize Money proved in 2016 – bear in mind he had run just once as a two-year-old and four of the previous eight had been unraced so all were therefore late developers. However, four of the last six winners were at least five, a massive change given just five of the previous 32 had been older than four. A big weight remains a drawback as nine of the last 11 winners carried less than 9st once taking into account jockeys' claims. Favourites have a desperate record, with Open Eagle the only one to oblige since 1995.

Big-Race Dates, Fixtures and Track Facts

Fixtures

Key - Flat, **Jumps**

March

24	Sat	Doncaster, **Bangor**, Lingfield, Wolverhampton, **Newbury**
25	Sun	Doncaster, **Ascot**
26	Mon	**Huntingdon, Taunton, Market Rasen**
27	Tue	Newcastle, **Hereford**, Southwell
28	Wed	Newcastle, **Warwick, Wincanton**, Wolverhampton
29	Thu	**Wetherby, Towcester**, Chelmsford City, Wolverhampton
30	Fri	Newcastle, Bath, Lingfield
31	Sat	**Carlisle**, Chelmsford City, **Haydock**, Kempton, Musselburgh, **Newton Abbot**

April

1	Sun	Southwell, **Ffos Las, Plumpton**
2	Mon	Redcar, **Fakenham, Chepstow, Huntingdon, Plumpton, Market Rasen**, Wolverhampton
3	Tue	Pontefract, Lingfield, **Wincanton**
4	Wed	Catterick, Southwell, Kempton, Lingfield
5	Thu	Musselburgh, **Warwick**, Chelmsford City, Wolverhampton
6	Fri	**Wetherby**, Chelmsford City, **Fontwell**, Lingfield
7	Sat	**Kelso, Stratford**, Kempton, **Uttoxeter**, Wolverhampton
8	Sun	**Carlisle, Exeter**
9	Mon	**Ludlow, Kempton**, Wolverhampton
10	Tue	**Hexham, Southwell**, Wolverhampton
11	Wed	**Market Rasen**, Kempton, Nottingham, Lingfield
12	Thu	**Aintree**, Southwell, Chelmsford City, **Taunton**
13	Fri	**Aintree**, Leicester, Kempton, **Sedgefield**
14	Sat	**Aintree**, Wolverhampton, **Chepstow, Newcastle**, Lingfield
15	Sun	**Ffos Las, Plumpton**
16	Mon	**Kelso**, Windsor, Redcar
17	Tue	**Carlisle**, Newmarket, **Exeter**
18	Wed	Beverley, **Cheltenham**, Kempton, Newmarket
19	Thu	Newcastle, **Cheltenham**, Ripon, Newmarket
20	Fri	**Ayr, Southwell**, Bath, **Fontwell**, Newbury
21	Sat	**Ayr, Bangor**, Newbury, Thirsk, Nottingham, Wolverhampton
22	Sun	**Stratford, Wincanton**
23	Mon	**Hexham, Newton Abbot**, Pontefract, Windsor, **Sedgefield**
24	Tue	**Huntingdon**, Brighton, **Ludlow, Exeter**, Yarmouth
25	Wed	Catterick, Epsom, **Perth**, Lingfield, **Taunton**
26	Thu	Beverley, **Warwick**, Chelmsford City, **Perth, Kempton**
27	Fri	Doncaster, **Towcester, Chepstow, Perth**, Sandown
28	Sat	Doncaster, Leicester, **Sandown**, Haydock, Wolverhampton, Ripon
29	Sun	Wetherby, Salisbury
30	Mon	Ayr, Southwell, Salisbury, Thirsk, Windsor

May

1 Tue .... Ayr, Nottingham, Brighton, Yarmouth, Kempton
2 Wed.............................Pontefract, Wolverhampton, Ascot, Bath, Brighton
3 Thu................ Musselburgh, Southwell, Chelmsford City, Redcar, Lingfield
4 Fri.................Musselburgh, **Cheltenham**, Chepstow, Newcastle, Lingfield
5 Sat...........Doncaster, Newmarket, Goodwood, **Hexham**, **Uttoxeter**, Thirsk
6 Sun...Hamilton, Newmarket
7 Mon.....................................Beverley, **Warwick**, Bath, **Kempton**, Windsor
8 Tue .... Wetherby, **Fakenham**, Brighton, **Ludlow**, **Exeter**
9 Wed...............**Kelso**, Chester, **Fontwel**l, Wolverhampton, **Newton Abbot**
10 Thu..........Chester, Chelmsford City, **Huntingdon**, **Wincanton**, **Worcester**
11 Fri.................Ripon, Chester, Ascot, **Market Rasen**, Lingfield, Nottingham
12 Sat......**Haydock**, Nottingham, Ascot, **Hexham**, **Warwick**, Lingfield, Thirsk
13 Sun.. Ludlow, Plumpton
14 Mon.................Catterick, **Towcester**, **Kempton**, Wolverhampton, Windsor
15 Tue ....Beverley, **Southwell**, Chepstow, **Sedgefield**, **Wincanton**
16 Wed............................**Perth**, Yarmouth, Bath, York, **Newton Abbot**
17 Thu .... **Perth**, Newmarket, **Fontwell**, York, Salisbury
18 Fri...**Aintree**, Newmarket, Newbury, Hamilton, York
19 Sat................ Doncaster, **Bangor**, Newbury, Thirsk, Newmarket, **Uttoxeter**
20 Sun...Ripon, **Market Rasen**, **Stratford**
21 Mon................................ Carlisle, Leicester, Windsor, Redcar, **Towcester**
22 Tue ....Ayr, **Huntingdon**, Chepstow, **Hexham**, Nottingham
23 Wed...........................Ayr, **Southwell**, Kempton, **Warwick**, Yarmouth
24 Thu.................Catterick, Chelmsford City, Goodwood, Lingfield, Sandown
25 Fri.................................. Haydock, **Worcester**, Bath, Pontefract, Goodwood
26 Sat......**Cartmel**, Chester, **Ffos Las**, Haydock, Goodwood, York, Salisbury
27 Sun..**Kelso**, **Uttoxeter**, **Fontwell**
28 Mon...**Cartmel**, **Huntingdon**, Chelmsford City, Redcar, Leicester, Windsor
29 Tue ....Redcar, Leicester, Brighton, Wolverhampton, Lingfield
30 Wed.................................. Beverley, Nottingham, **Cartmel**, **Warwick**, Ripon
31 Thu..........Hamilton, Wolverhampton, Chelmsford City, **Ffos Las**, Lingfield

June

1 Fri.............Catterick, **Market Rasen**, Bath, Doncaster, Epsom, Goodwood
2 Sat..... Doncaster, **Worcester**, Chepstow, **Hexham**, Epsom, Musselburgh,
....Lingfield
3 Sun...**Perth**, **Fakenham**
4 Mon................................... Ayr, Leicester, **Newton Abbot**, Windsor
5 Tue ....Newcastle, **Bangor**, **Fontwell**, **Southwell**
6 Wed..................Hamilton, **Uttoxeter**, Kempton, Wetherby, Wolverhampton
7 Thu...................................... Carlisle, Yarmouth, Sandown, Haydock, Ripon
8 Fri.....Carlisle, **Stratford**, Brighton, Haydock, Wolverhampton, Goodwood
9 Sat............ Beverley, Newmarket, Lingfield, Catterick, **Stratford**, Haydock,
....Musselburgh
10 Sun..Nottingham, Goodwood
11 Mon........................Pontefract, **Worcester**, Brighton, Windsor
12 Tue ....Thirsk, **Southwell**, Lingfield, Salisbury
13 Wed................. Hamilton, Yarmouth, Chelmsford City, Haydock, Kempton

14 Thu.......................... Haydock, Nottingham, Newbury, **Uttoxeter**, Yarmouth
15 Fri............**Aintree**, Chepstow, York, Goodwood, **Newton Abbot**, Sandown
16 Sat................ **Hexham**, Chester, Bath, York, Leicester, **Fontwell**, Sandown
17 Sun.. Doncaster, Salisbury
18 Mon... Ayr, Nottingham, Windsor, Carlisle
19 Tue .... Royal Ascot, Beverley, **Stratford**, Thirsk, Brighton
20 Wed.................. Royal Ascot, Hamilton, **Uttoxeter**, Ripon, Chelmsford City
21 Thu...................... Royal Ascot, Ripon, Chelmsford City, **Ffos Las**, Lingfield
22 Fri........... Royal Ascot, Ayr, **Market Rasen**, Redcar, Newmarket, Wetherby
23 Sat......... Royal Ascot, Ayr, Newmarket, Haydock, Lingfield, **Perth**, Redcar
24 Sun.. **Hexham**, **Worcester**, Pontefract
25 Mon................................... **Southwell**, Chepstow, Wolverhampton, Windsor
26 Tue .... Beverley, Brighton, Newbury, **Newton Abbot**
27 Wed...............................Carlisle, **Worcester**, Bath, Kempton, Salisbury
28 Thu .... Hamilton, Leicester, Newcastle, Newmarket, Nottingham
29 Fri........... **Cartmel**, Chester, Doncaster, Newmarket, Newcastle, Yarmouth
30 Sat... Doncaster, Chester, Lingfield, Newcastle, Newmarket, Windsor, York

July

 1 Sun...**Cartmel**, **Uttoxeter**, Windsor
 2 Mon......................................Hamilton, Wolverhampton, Windsor, Pontefract
 3 Tue .... Hamilton, **Stratford**, Brighton, Chepstow
 4 Wed.........................Musselburgh, **Worcester**, Bath, Thirsk, Kempton
 5 Thu....................... Haydock, Yarmouth, Epsom, **Perth**, Newbury
 6 Fri.......... Beverley, Chelmsford City, Doncaster, **Newton Abbot**, Haydock,
 .... Sandown
 7 Sat................... Beverley, Leicester, Chelmsford City, Carlisle, Nottingham,
 ....Sandown, Haydock
 8 Sun..Ayr, **Market Rasen**
 9 Mon.. Ayr, **Worcester**, Windsor, Ripon
10 Tue ....Pontefract, **Uttoxeter**, Brighton, Wolverhampton
11 Wed..............................Catterick, Yarmouth, Bath, Kempton, Lingfield
12 Thu.............................Carlisle, Newmarket, Epsom, Doncaster, Newbury
13 Fri.......................... York, Chester, Ascot, Newmarket, Chepstow, **Ffos Las**
14 Sat................ Hamilton, Chester, Ascot, York, Newmarket, **Newton Abbot**,
 ....Salisbury
15 Sun... **Perth**, **Southwell**, **Stratford**
16 Mon.. Ayr, Wolverhampton, Windsor, Ripon
17 Tue .... Beverley, **Worcester**, Bath, Thirsk
18 Wed.................. Catterick, **Uttoxeter**, Lingfield, Wolverhampton, Yarmouth
19 Thu .... Doncaster, Leicester, Chepstow, Hamilton, Epsom
20 Fri....... Hamilton, Newmarket, Newbury, Haydock, Nottingham, Pontefract
21 Sat.... **Cartmel**, **Market Rasen**, Lingfield, Haydock, Newmarket, Newbury,
 .... Ripon
22 Sun.....................................Redcar, **Stratford**, **Newton Abbot**
23 Mon... Ayr, Windsor, Beverley, **Cartmel**
24 Tue ....Musselburgh, Nottingham, Chelmsford City, Ffos Las
25 Wed.............................Catterick, Leicester, Bath, Lingfield, Sandown
26 Thu......................... Doncaster, **Worcester**, Newbury, Yarmouth, Sandown
27 Fri ....Thirsk, Newmarket, Ascot, York, **Uttoxeter**, Chepstow

28 Sat.........Newcastle, Chester, Ascot, York, Newmarket, Lingfield, Salisbury
29 Sun.. Pontefract, **Uttoxeter**
30 Mon................................Ayr, Wolverhampton, **Newton Abbot**, Windsor
31 Tue .... Beverley, **Worcester**, Goodwood, **Perth**, Yarmouth

August

1 Wed...................................**Perth**, Leicester, Goodwood, Redcar, Sandown
2 Thu ....Nottingham, Epsom, **Stratford**, Ffos Las, Goodwood
3 Fri.................Musselburgh, **Bangor**, Bath, Thirsk, Newmarket, Goodwood
4 Sat...........Doncaster, Newmarket, Chelmsford City, Hamilton, Goodwood,
....Thirsk, Lingfield
5 Sun... Chester, **Market Rasen**
6 Mon..Carlisle, **Newton Abbot**, Ripon, Windsor
7 Tue ....Ayr, Nottingham, Newbury, Catterick
8 Wed............................... Pontefract, Yarmouth, Bath, Brighton, Kempton
9 Thu............................ Haydock, Yarmouth, Brighton, Newcastle, Sandown
10 Fri............Haydock, Newmarket, Brighton, Musselburgh, Wolverhampton,
.... Chelmsford City
11 Sat... Ayr, Newmarket, Ascot, Haydock, Chelmsford City, Redcar, Lingfield
12 Sun..Leicester, Windsor
13 Mon................................. Ayr, Wolverhampton, Windsor, Ripon
14 Tue .... Thirsk, Nottingham, Chelmsford City, Ffos Las
15 Wed.................Beverley, **Worcester**, Kempton, **Newton Abbot**, Salisbury
16 Thu................... Beverley, Wolverhampton, Chepstow, Yarmouth, Salisbury
17 Fri.............. Catterick, Newmarket, Chelmsford City, Nottingham, Newbury,
....Wolverhampton
18 Sat.. Doncaster, **Market Rasen**, Bath, **Perth**, Newmarket, Newbury, Ripon
19 Sun...Pontefract, **Southwell**
20 Mon.................................... Thirsk, **Bangor**, Windsor, Leicester
21 Tue .... Hamilton, Yarmouth, Brighton, Kempton, **Newton Abbot**
22 Wed..............................Carlisle, **Worcester**, Bath, York, Kempton
23 Thu.......................York, **Stratford**, Chepstow, Wolverhampton, **Fontwell**
24 Fri......York, Newmarket, Chelmsford City, Ffos Las, Goodwood, Salisbury
25 Sat........**Cartmel**, Newmarket, Chelmsford City, Redcar, Goodwood, York,
....Windsor
26 Sun.. Beverley, Yarmouth, Goodwood
27 Mon..................................**Cartmel**, Southwell, Chepstow, Ripon, Epsom
28 Tue ....Ripon, **Stratford**, Bath, Epsom
29 Wed.....................Catterick, **Worcester**, Kempton, Musselburgh, Lingfield
30 Thu............ Carlisle, Chelmsford City, Musselburgh, **Fontwell**, **Sedgefield**
31 Fri..........Hamilton, **Bangor**, Sandown, Newcastle, Wolverhampton, Thirsk

September

1 Sat.............. Beverley, Chester, Chelmsford City, Wolverhampton, Lingfield,
....**Newton Abbot**, Sandown
2 Sun..**Worcester**, Brighton
3 Mon................................. Newcastle, Brighton, Chepstow, Windsor
4 Tue ....Leicester, Goodwood, **Stratford**, Kempton
5 Wed..........................**Southwell**, Bath, Wolverhampton, Ffos Las, Lingfield
6 Thu...................Carlisle, Chelmsford City, Haydock, Salisbury, **Sedgefield**

AYR: will its big day go ahead on September 22 after last year's abandonment?

7	Fri	Haydock, Ascot, Musselburgh, Kempton, Newcastle
8	Sat	Haydock, **Stratford**, Ascot, Thirsk, Wolverhampton, Kempton
9	Sun	York, **Fontwell**
10	Mon	**Perth**, Brighton, Chelmsford City, **Newton Abbot**
11	Tue	Catterick, Leicester, Salisbury, **Worcester**
12	Wed	Carlisle, **Uttoxeter**, Kempton, Doncaster
13	Thu	Doncaster, Chepstow, Hamilton, Epsom
14	Fri	Doncaster, Chester, Salisbury, Sandown
15	Sat	Doncaster, Chester, Bath, Musselburgh, Chelmsford City, Lingfield
16	Sun	Bath, Ffos Las
17	Mon	**Hexham**, **Worcester**, Brighton, Kempton
18	Tue	Redcar, Yarmouth, Chepstow, Kempton
19	Wed	Beverley, Yarmouth, Sandown, **Kelso**
20	Thu	Ayr, Yarmouth, Chelmsford City, Pontefract
21	Fri	Ayr, Newbury, Newcastle, **Newton Abbot**
22	Sat	Ayr, Newmarket, Chelmsford City, Catterick, Wolverhampton, Newbury
23	Sun	Hamilton, **Uttoxeter**, **Plumpton**
24	Mon	Hamilton, Leicester, Kempton, Newcastle
25	Tue	Beverley, **Warwick**, Chelmsford City, Lingfield
26	Wed	**Perth**, Wolverhampton, Goodwood, Redcar
27	Thu	**Perth**, Newmarket, Kempton, Pontefract
28	Fri	Haydock, Newmarket, Newcastle, **Worcester**

29 Sat................. Haydock, Chester, Chelmsford City, Ripon, **Market Rasen**,
.... Newmarket
30 Sun... Musselburgh, Epsom

October

1 Mon... Catterick, Bath, Kempton, **Newton Abbot**
2 Tue .... Ayr, **Southwell**, Kempton, **Sedgefield**
3 Wed............................ Newcastle, **Bangor**, Salisbury, Nottingham
4 Thu.................... **Huntingdon**, Chelmsford City, **Warwick**, Lingfield
5 Fri.............................. **Hexham**, Wolverhampton, Ascot, **Fontwell**
6 Sat........................ Redcar, Newmarket, Ascot, Wolverhampton, **Fontwell**
7 Sun.. **Kelso**, **Uttoxeter**
8 Mon..............................Pontefract, **Stratford**, Kempton, Windsor
9 Tue .... Catterick, Leicester, Brighton, Newcastle
10 Wed.............................**Ludlow**, Kempton, Nottingham, **Towcester**
11 Thu.............................Ayr, **Worcester**, Chelmsford City, **Exeter**
12 Fri..........................York, Newmarket, **Newton Abbot**, Wolverhampton
13 Sat...................**Hexham**, Newmarket, Chelmsford City, York, **Chepstow**
14 Sun.. **Chepstow**, Goodwood
15 Mon.............................Musselburgh, Yarmouth, Kempton, Windsor
16 Tue ....**Hereford**, Kempton, **Huntingdon**, Leicester
17 Wed............................Newcastle, Nottingham, Bath, **Wetherby**
18 Thu........................**Carlisle**, **Uttoxeter**, Brighton, Chelmsford City
19 Fri.......................... Haydock, **Fakenham**, **Wincanton**, Newcastle, Redcar
20 Sat....................... Catterick, **Market Rasen**, Ascot, **Stratford**, **Ffos Las**,
.... Wolverhampton
21 Sun...**Sedgefield**, **Kempton**
22 Mon............................... Pontefract, Kempton, **Plumpton**, Windsor
23 Tue ....Newcastle, Yarmouth, **Exeter**, Kempton
24 Wed............................ Newcastle, Newmarket, **Fontwell**, **Worcester**
25 Thu............................**Carlisle**, **Ludlow**, Chelmsford City, **Southwell**
26 Fri............................ Doncaster, **Cheltenham**, Kempton, Newbury
27 Sat........................ Doncaster, **Cheltenham**, Kempton, **Kelso**, Newbury
28 Sun...**Aintree**, **Wincanton**
29 Mon..................................**Ayr**, Leicester, Chelmsford City, Redcar
30 Tue .... Catterick, **Bangor**, **Chepstow**, Wolverhampton
31 Wed............................ **Fakenham**, Kempton, Nottingham, **Taunton**

November

1 Thu............................ **Sedgefield**, **Stratford**, Lingfield, Wolverhampton
2 Fri................................ **Wetherby**, Newmarket, Kempton, **Uttoxeter**
3 Sat.......................... **Ayr**, Newmarket, **Ascot**, Newcastle, **Wetherby**
4 Sun.. **Carlisle**, **Huntingdon**
5 Mon...**Hereford**, Kempton, **Plumpton**
6 Tue ....Redcar, Wolverhampton, **Exeter**, Kempton
7 Wed........................**Musselburgh**, Nottingham, **Chepstow**, Newcastle
8 Thu........................ **Sedgefield**, **Market Rasen**, Chelmsford City, **Newbury**
9 Fri...**Hexham**, **Warwick**, **Fontwell**, Newcastle
10 Sat........................**Aintree**, Chelmsford City, Doncaster, **Wincanton**, **Kelso**
11 Sun..**Ffos Las**, **Sandown**

12	Mon	....**Carlisle**, Southwell, **Kempton**
13	Tue	...........................**Hereford**, Chelmsford City, **Huntingdon**, **Lingfield**
14	Wed	....**Ayr**, **Bangor**, **Exeter**, Kempton
15	Thu	.................................**Ludlow**, Chelmsford City, Southwell, **Taunton**
16	Fri	.... **Newcastle**, **Cheltenham**, Lingfield, Wolverhampton
17	Sat	.... **Wetherby**, **Cheltenham**, Lingfield, **Uttoxeter**, Wolverhampton
18	Sun	....**Cheltenham**, **Fontwell**
19	Mon	....**Leicester**, Kempton, **Plumpton**
20	Tue	....................................**Fakenham**, Lingfield, **Southwell**
21	Wed	...............................**Hexham**, **Warwick**, **Chepstow**, Kempton
22	Thu	...................Newcastle, **Market Rasen**, **Wincanton**, Wolverhampton
23	Fri	...................................**Catterick**, **Ascot**, **Ffos Las**, Kempton
24	Sat	...................**Haydock**, **Huntingdon**, **Ascot**, Wolverhampton, Lingfield
25	Sun	....**Uttoxeter**, **Exeter**
26	Mon	...................................**Musselburgh**, **Ludlow**, **Kempton**
27	Tue	.................................**Sedgefield**, Southwell, **Lingfield**
28	Wed	.... Newcastle, **Hereford**, **Wetherby**, Wolverhampton
29	Thu	...............................**Ayr**, **Towcester**, Chelmsford City, **Taunton**
30	Fri	...................................**Doncaster**, Southwell, **Newbury**, Newcastle

December

1	Sat	.... **Doncaster**, **Bangor**, **Newbury**, **Newcastle**, Wolverhampton
2	Sun	....**Carlisle**, **Leicester**
3	Mon	...............................**Musselburgh**, Wolverhampton, **Plumpton**
4	Tue	...................................**Fakenham**, Lingfield, **Southwell**
5	Wed	...............................**Haydock**, **Ludlow**, Kempton, Lingfield
6	Thu	......................**Leicester**, Chelmsford City, **Market Rasen**, **Wincanton**
7	Fri	...............................**Sedgefield**, **Exeter**, Kempton, **Sandown**
8	Sat	...................**Aintree**, Wolverhampton, **Chepstow**, **Wetherby**, **Sandown**
9	Sun	....**Kelso**, **Huntingdon**
10	Mon	...............................**Musselburgh**, Wolverhampton, **Lingfield**
11	Tue	.... Southwell, **Fontwell**, **Uttoxeter**
12	Wed	...............................**Hexham**, **Leicester**, Kempton, Lingfield
13	Thu	...................**Newcastle**, **Warwick**, Chelmsford City, **Taunton**
14	Fri	...................**Doncaster**, **Bangor**, Kempton, **Cheltenham**
15	Sat	.... **Doncaster**, **Cheltenham**, Newcastle, **Hereford**, Wolverhampton
16	Sun	....**Carlisle**, **Southwell**
17	Mon	...........................Wolverhampton, **Ffos Las**, **Plumpton**
18	Tue	....**Catterick**, **Fakenham**, Southwell
19	Wed	.... Newcastle, **Ludlow**, Lingfield, **Newbury**
20	Thu	.... Southwell, Chelmsford City, **Towcester**, **Exeter**
21	Fri	.... Southwell, **Ascot**, **Uttoxeter**, Wolverhampton
22	Sat	...............................**Haydock**, **Ascot**, **Newcastle**, Lingfield
26	Wed	.........**Sedgefield**, **Huntingdon**, **Fontwell**, **Wetherby**, **Market Rasen**,
		....**Kempton**, Wolverhampton, **Wincanton**
27	Thu	....................**Wetherby**, Wolverhampton, **Chepstow**, **Kempton**
28	Fri	.... **Catterick**, **Leicester**, Lingfield
29	Sat	...................................**Doncaster**, Southwell, **Newbury**, **Kelso**
30	Sun	....**Haydock**, Lingfield, **Taunton**
31	Mon	....**Uttoxeter**, Lingfield, **Warwick**

Big-race dates

March

24 Mar	Doncaster	Lincoln (Heritage Handicap)
30 Mar	Lingfield	All-Weather Championship Finals

April

17 Apr	Newmarket	Nell Gwyn Stakes (Group 3)
18 Apr	Newmarket	Earl of Sefton Stakes (Group 3)
19 Apr	Newmarket	Craven Stakes (Group 3)
21 Apr	Newbury	Fred Darling Stakes (Group 3)
21 Apr	Newbury	Greenham Stakes (Group 3)
21 Apr	Newbury	John Porter Stakes (Group 3)
27 Apr	Sandown	Gordon Richards Stakes (Group 3)
27 Apr	Sandown	bet365 Mile (Group 2)

May

2 May	Ascot	Sagaro Stakes (Group 3)
5 May	Newmarket	2,000 Guineas (Group 1)
5 May	Newmarket	Dahlia Stakes (Group 3)
6 May	Newmarket	1,000 Guineas (Group 1)
6 May	Newmarket	Jockey Club Stakes (Group 2)
9 May	Chester	Chester Cup (Heritage Handicap)
10 May	Chester	Chester Vase (Group 3)
10 May	Chester	Huxley Stakes (Group 3)
11 May	Chester	Ormonde Stakes (Group 3)
12 May	Ascot	Victoria Cup (Heritage Handicap)
12 May	Lingfield	Derby Trial (Group 3)
16 May	York	Duke of York Stakes (Group 2)
16 May	York	Musidora Stakes (Group 3)
17 May	York	Dante Stakes (Group 2)
17 May	York	Middleton Stakes (Group 3)
18 May	York	Yorkshire Cup (Group 2)
19 May	Newbury	Lockinge Stakes (Group 1)
24 May	Sandown	Henry II Stakes (Group 2)
24 May	Sandown	Brigadier Gerard Stakes (Group 3)
26 May	Haydock	Temple Stakes (Group 2)
26 May	Haydock	Sandy Lane Stakes (Group 2)

June

1 Jun	Epsom	The Oaks (Group 1)
1 Jun	Epsom	Princess Elizabeth Stakes (Group 3)
2 Jun	Epsom	The Derby (Group 1)
2 Jun	Epsom	Coronation Cup (Group 1)
9 Jun	Haydock	John of Gaunt Stakes (Group 3)
9 Jun	Haydock	Pinnacle Stakes (Group 3)
19 Jun	Royal Ascot	King's Stand Stakes (Group 1)
19 Jun	Royal Ascot	Queen Anne Stakes (Group 1)
19 Jun	Royal Ascot	St James's Palace Stakes (Group 1)
19 Jun	Royal Ascot	Coventry Stakes (Group 2)
20 Jun	Royal Ascot	Prince of Wales's Stakes (Group 1)
20 Jun	Royal Ascot	Queen Mary Stakes (Group 2)
20 Jun	Royal Ascot	Duke of Cambridge Stakes (Group 2)
20 Jun	Royal Ascot	Jersey Stakes (Group 3)

20 Jun	Royal Ascot	Royal Hunt Cup (Heritage Handicap)
21 Jun	Royal Ascot	Gold Cup (Group 1)
21 Jun	Royal Ascot	Ribblesdale Stakes (Group 2)
21 Jun	Royal Ascot	Norfolk Stakes (Group 2)
22 Jun	Royal Ascot	Coronation Stakes (Group 1)
22 Jun	Royal Ascot	Commonwealth Cup (Group 1)
22 Jun	Royal Ascot	King Edward VII Stakes (Group 2)
22 Jun	Royal Ascot	Albany Stakes (Group 3)
23 Jun	Royal Ascot	Diamond Jubilee Stakes (Group 1)
23 Jun	Royal Ascot	Hardwicke Stakes (Group 2)
23 Jun	Royal Ascot	Wokingham (Heritage Handicap)
30 Jun	Newcastle	Northumberland Plate (Heritage Handicap)
30 Jun	Newcastle	Chipchase Stakes (Group 3)
30 Jun	Newmarket	Criterion Stakes (Group 3)

July

7 Jul	Sandown	Coral-Eclipse Stakes (Group 1)
7 Jul	Haydock	Lancashire Oaks (Group 2)
12 Jul	Newmarket	Princess of Wales's Stakes (Group 2)
12 Jul	Newmarket	July Stakes (Group 2)
13 Jul	Newmarket	Falmouth Stakes (Group 1)
13 Jul	Newmarket	Duchess of Cambridge Stakes (Group 2)
13 Jul	York	Summer Stakes (Group 3)
14 Jul	Newmarket	July Cup (Group 1)
14 Jul	Newmarket	Superlative Stakes (Group 2)
14 Jul	Newmarket	Bunbury Cup (Heritage Handicap)
14 Jul	York	John Smith's Cup (Heritage Handicap)
21 Jul	Newbury	Hackwood Stakes (Group 3)
28 Jul	Ascot	King George VI and Queen Elizabeth Stakes (Group 1)
28 Jul	Ascot	Summer Mile (Group 2)
28 Jul	York	York Stakes (Group 2)
31 Jul	Goodwood	Goodwood Cup (Group 2)
31 Jul	Goodwood	Lennox Stakes (Group 2)
31 Jul	Goodwood	Vintage Stakes (Group 2)

August

1 Aug	Goodwood	Sussex Stakes (Group 1)
1 Aug	Goodwood	Molecomb Stakes (Group 3)
2 Aug	Goodwood	Nassau Stakes (Group 1)
2 Aug	Goodwood	Richmond Stakes (Group 2)
3 Aug	Goodwood	Betfred Mile (Heritage Handicap)
3 Aug	Goodwood	King George Stakes (Group 2)
3 Aug	Goodwood	Oak Tree Stakes (Group 3)
4 Aug	Goodwood	Stewards' Cup (Heritage Handicap)
4 Aug	Goodwood	Gordon Stakes (Group 3)
11 Aug	Ascot	Shergar Cup Day
11 Aug	Haydock	Rose of Lancaster Stakes (Group 3)
11 Aug	Newmarket	Sweet Solera Stakes (Group 3)
16 Aug	Salisbury	Sovereign Stakes (Group 3)
18 Aug	Newbury	Hungerford Stakes (Group 2)
18 Aug	Newbury	Geoffrey Freer Stakes (Group 3)
22 Aug	York	Juddmonte International (Group 1)
22 Aug	York	Great Voltigeur Stakes (Group 2)
22 Aug	York	Acomb Stakes (Group 3)
23 Aug	York	Yorkshire Oaks (Group 1)
23 Aug	York	Lowther Stakes (Group 2)
24 Aug	York	Nunthorpe Stakes (Group 1)

24 Aug	York	Lonsdale Cup (Group 2)
25 Aug	York	Ebor (Heritage Handicap)
25 Aug	York	Lonsdale Cup (Group 2)
25 Aug	Goodwood	Celebration Mile (Group 2)
25 Aug	Goodwood	Prestige Stakes (Group 3)
25 Aug	Windsor	Winter Hill Stakes (Group 3)
26 Aug	Goodwood	Supreme Stakes (Group 3)

September

1 Sep	Sandown	Solario Stakes (Group 3)
8 Sep	Haydock	Sprint Cup (Group 1)
8 Sep	Kempton	Sirenia Stakes (Group 3)
8 Sep	Kempton	September Stakes (Group 3)
13 Sep	Doncaster	May Hill Stakes (Group 2)
13 Sep	Doncaster	Park Hill Stakes (Group 2)
14 Sep	Doncaster	Doncaster Cup (Group 2)
14 Sep	Doncaster	Flying Childers Stakes (Group 2)
15 Sep	Doncaster	St Leger (Group 1)
15 Sep	Doncaster	Park Stakes (Group 2)
15 Sep	Doncaster	Champagne Stakes (Group 2)
15 Sep	Doncaster	Portland (Heritage Handicap)
22 Sep	Ayr	Ayr Gold Cup (Heritage Handicap)
22 Sep	Ayr	Firth Of Clyde Stakes (Group 3)
22 Sep	Newbury	Mill Reef Stakes (Group 2)
22 Sep	Newbury	World Trophy (Group 3)
22 Sep	Newbury	Arc Trial (Group 3)
27 Sep	Newmarket	Somerville Tattersall Stakes (Group 3)
28 Sep	Newmarket	Rockfel Stakes (Group 2)
28 Sep	Newmarket	Joel Stakes (Group 2)
29 Sep	Newmarket	Cambridgeshire (Heritage Handicap)
29 Sep	Newmarket	Middle Park Stakes (Group 1)
29 Sep	Newmarket	Cheveley Park Stakes (Group 1)
29 Sep	Newmarket	Royal Lodge Stakes (Group 2)

October

6 Oct	Newmarket	Sun Chariot Stakes (Group 1)
6 Oct	Ascot	Cumberland Lodge Stakes (Group 3)
6 Oct	Ascot	Bengough Stakes (Group 3)
12 Oct	Newmarket	Fillies' Mile (Group 1)
12 Oct	Newmarket	Challenge Stakes (Group 2)
12 Oct	Newmarket	Cornwallis Stakes (Group 3)
12 Oct	Newmarket	Oh So Sharp Stakes (Group 3)
13 Oct	Newmarket	Cesarewitch (Heritage Handicap)
13 Oct	Newmarket	Dewhurst Stakes (Group 1)
13 Oct	Newmarket	Autumn Stakes (Group 3)
13 Oct	Newmarket	Darley Stakes (Group 3)
20 Oct	Ascot	Queen Elizabeth II Stakes (Group 1)
20 Oct	Ascot	Champion Stakes (Group 1)
20 Oct	Ascot	Champions Sprint (Group 1)
20 Oct	Ascot	Champions Filly & Mare Stakes (Group 1)
20 Oct	Ascot	Champions Long Distance Cup (Group 1)
27 Oct	Doncaster	Racing Post Trophy (Group 1)
27 Oct	Newbury	Horris Hill Stakes (Group 3)
27 Oct	Newbury	St Simon Stakes (Group 3)

November

10 Nov	Doncaster	November (Heritage Handicap)

Track Facts

WANT TO size up the layout and undulations of the course where your fancy's about to line up? Over the next 30-odd pages, we bring you three-dimensional maps of all Britain's Flat tracks, allowing you to see at a glance the task facing your selection. The maps come to you courtesy of the Racing Post's website (www.racingpost.com).

We've listed the top dozen trainers and jockeys at each course, ranked by strike-rate, with a breakdown of their relevant statistics over the last four years. We've also included addresses, phone numbers, directions and fixture lists for each track, together with Racing Post standard times for all you clock-watchers.

ASCOT..................................192	LINGFIELD (AW)......................211
AYR......................................193	MUSSELBURGH..........................212
BATH....................................194	NEWBURY..............................213
BEVERLEY 195	NEWCASTLE............................214
BRIGHTON 196	NEWMARKET (ROWLEY)..............215
CARLISLE 197	NEWMARKET (JULY) 216
CATTERICK.............................198	NOTTINGHAM 218
CHELMSFORD...........................199	PONTEFRACT 219
CHEPSTOW..............................200	REDCAR...............................220
CHESTER................................201	RIPON................................221
DONCASTER 202	SALISBURY 222
EPSOM..................................203	SANDOWN..............................223
FFOS LAS..............................204	SOUTHWELL............................224
GOODWOOD..............................205	THIRSK 225
HAMILTON 206	WETHERBY.............................226
HAYDOCK...............................207	WINDSOR..............................227
KEMPTON 208	WOLVERHAMPTON........................228
LEICESTER.............................209	YARMOUTH 229
LINGFIELD (TURF) 210	YORK.................................230

ASCOT

Ascot, Berkshire SL5 7JX
Tel 0870 7227 227

How to get there Road: M4 junction 6 or M3 junction 3 on to A332. Rail: Frequent service from Reading or Waterloo

Features RH, stiff climb for final mile on round course

2018 Fixtures May 2, 11-12, June 19-23, July 13-14, 27-28, August 11, September 7-8, October 5-6, 20

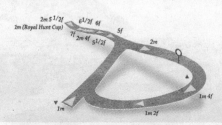

○ Winning Post
▲ Startpoint
▲ Highest Point
▼ Lowest Point
〜 Open ditch
〜 Water jump
∕ Fence

Racing Post standard times

5f	59.5	1m2f	2min5
6f	1min12.4	1m4f	2min28.9
7f	1min25.6	2m	3min22
1m (str)	1min38.8	2m4f	4min20
1m (rnd)	1min39.8	2m5f159yds	4min45

Trainers	Wins-Runs	%	2yo	3yo+	£1 level stks
John Gosden	31-200	16	3-18	28-182	-2.20
Richard Hannon	25-298	8	15-103	10-195	-124.95
A P O'Brien	24-139	17	7-23	17-116	+18.66
William Haggas	21-161	13	4-30	17-131	-32.19
Mark Johnston	18-199	9	6-54	12-145	-63.88
Sir Michael Stoute	16-124	13	2-6	14-118	-8.75
Charlie Appleby	15-129	12	6-27	9-102	-27.48
Saeed bin Suroor	13-92	14	3-13	10-79	-16.79
Roger Varian	12-101	12	2-16	10-85	-30.18
Roger Charlton	10-58	17	2-9	8-49	-6.25
Marco Botti	9-70	13	2-9	7-61	-18.00
Richard Fahey	8-154	5	0-20	8-134	-49.40
Andrew Balding	8-139	6	0-13	8-126	-78.00

Jockeys	Wins-Rides	%	£1 level stks	Best Trainer	W-R
Ryan Moore	45-217	21	-24.14	A P O'Brien	19-70
William Buick	34-198	17	+15.72	Charlie Appleby	8-70
Frankie Dettori	24-145	17	-13.33	John Gosden	10-41
Jamie Spencer	20-176	11	+5.57	Jamie Osborne	3-4
James Doyle	16-142	11	-38.02	Saeed bin Suroor	3-33
Martin Harley	14-119	12	+19.25	Marco Botti	5-26
Andrea Atzeni	13-144	9	-60.50	Roger Varian	5-41
Silvestre De Sousa	13-133	10	-8.05	Mark Johnston	3-20
Adam Kirby	12-146	8	-28.09	Clive Cox	6-49
Richard Hughes	12-102	12	-31.83	Richard Hannon	7-55
Jim Crowley	9-155	6	-91.50	Marcus Tregoning	1-1
Tom Queally	9-84	11	+8.83	James Fanshawe	4-19
George Baker	9-74	12	+1.50	Jamie Osborne	2-2

Favourites

2yo	42.2%	+10.13	3yo	33.3%	-5.46	TOTAL	32.7%	+7.49

Whitletts Road Ayr KA8 0JE.
Tel 01292 264 179

AYR

How to get there
Road: south from
Glasgow on A77
or A75, A70, A76.
Rail: Ayr, bus
service from
station on big
race days

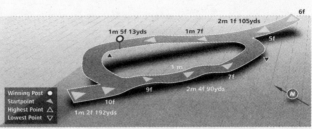

Features LH

2018 Fixtures
April 30, May 1, 22-23, June 4, 18,
22-23, July 8-9, 16, 23, 30, August 7,
11, 13, September 20-22, October
2, 11

Racing Post standard times

5f	57.7	1m2f192yds	2min17.5
6f	1min10	1m5f13yds	2min47
7f50yds	1min28	1m7f	3min15
1m	1min38	2m1f105yds	3min49
1m1f20yds	1min51	2m4f90yds	4min31
1m2f	2min6		

Trainers	Wins-Runs	%	2yo	3yo+	£1 level stks
Jim Goldie	48-514	9	0-13	48-501	-116.04
Keith Dalgleish	46-363	13	10-69	36-294	+5.71
David O'Meara	27-170	16	0-18	27-152	-37.71
Richard Fahey	25-299	8	5-70	20-229	-116.74
Michael Dods	25-220	11	7-41	18-179	+1.88
K R Burke	23-105	22	9-31	14-74	+1.86
Linda Perratt	21-294	7	0-9	21-285	-77.25
Ruth Carr	20-150	13	0-0	20-150	+7.70
Iain Jardine	15-117	13	1-11	14-106	-17.25
Adrian Paul Keatley	15-66	23	0-2	15-64	+36.88
Mark Johnston	14-113	12	8-49	6-64	-58.25
John Quinn	13-83	16	4-21	9-62	+9.38
R Mike Smith	12-105	11	0-0	12-105	-11.25

Jockeys	Wins-Rides	%	£1 level stks	Best Trainer	W-R
Daniel Tudhope	35-187	19	+9.12	David O'Meara	16-90
Paul Mulrennan	34-238	14	-22.66	Michael Dods	13-103
Phillip Makin	34-168	20	+70.10	Keith Dalgleish	19-96
Graham Lee	31-241	13	+47.53	Jim Goldie	9-75
P J McDonald	25-225	11	-37.68	R Mike Smith	8-31
James Sullivan	24-190	13	+16.03	Ruth Carr	18-109
Joe Fanning	22-181	12	-63.58	Mark Johnston	9-63
Jason Hart	17-104	16	+25.83	Shaun Harris	4-9
Tom Eaves	15-177	8	-21.00	Keith Dalgleish	4-46
Fergal Lynch	12-107	11	+6.00	Jim Goldie	8-85
Connor Beasley	11-139	8	-64.88	Michael Dods	3-48
Jack Garritty	11-96	11	+0.00	Richard Fahey	5-34
Joey Haynes	10-83	12	-31.29	K R Burke	8-30

Favourites

2yo	32.9% -16.41		3yo	27.2% -30.52		TOTAL	28.4% -103.06

BATH

Lansdown, Bath, Glos BA1 9BU
Tel 01291 622 260

How to get there
Road: M4, Jctn
18, then A46
south.
Rail: Bath Spa,
special bus
service to course
on race days

Features LH
uphill 4f straight

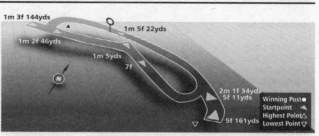

2018 Fixtures March 30, April 20,
May 2, 7, 16, 25, June 1, 16, 27, July
4, 11, 17, 25, August 3, 8, 18, 22, 28,
September 5, 15-16, October 1, 17

Racing Post standard times

5f11yds	1min0.8	1m3f144yds	2min28
5f161yds	1min9.6	1m5f22yds	2min48.5
1m5yds	1min39	2m1f34yds	3min40
1m2f46yds	2min8		

Trainers	Wins-Runs	%	2yo	3yo+	£1 level stks
Malcolm Saunders	28-129	22	0-6	28-123	+15.16
Richard Hannon	26-146	18	13-68	13-78	-35.96
Clive Cox	21-100	21	7-21	14-79	-16.58
Mick Channon	17-139	12	4-37	13-102	-49.55
Charles Hills	17-72	24	5-20	12-52	+21.51
Andrew Balding	15-82	18	2-9	13-73	-0.34
Roger Charlton	15-48	31	4-9	11-39	+18.29
Brian Meehan	15-47	32	4-18	11-29	+64.48
Rod Millman	14-77	18	1-9	13-68	+40.88
Ronald Harris	12-135	9	3-21	9-114	-28.75
Marcus Tregoning	12-40	30	1-4	11-36	+7.46
David Evans	11-123	9	5-43	6-80	-44.60
Tony Carroll	11-120	9	0-5	11-115	-25.00

Jockeys	Wins-Rides	%	£1 level stks	Best Trainer	W-R
Luke Morris	25-175	14	-52.55	Sir Mark Prescott	10-29
Steve Drowne	22-158	14	+21.63	Charles Hills	6-17
George Baker	21-66	32	+5.42	Roger Charlton	3-12
Adam Kirby	20-81	25	+21.91	Clive Cox	10-35
Martin Dwyer	16-116	14	-2.33	Sylvester Kirk	2-4
Silvestre De Sousa	16-82	20	-8.39	Mick Channon	4-17
Dane O'Neill	16-77	21	+11.55	Richard Hannon	2-2
David Probert	15-102	15	-26.25	Andrew Balding	6-35
Tom Marquand	13-67	19	+28.37	Richard Hannon	4-14
Jimmy Fortune	13-48	27	+18.68	Brian Meehan	4-17
Josephine Gordon	12-77	16	+15.67	Malcolm Saunders	3-11
Pat Cosgrave	12-69	17	-3.42	William Haggas	4-10
Oisin Murphy	11-81	14	+16.58	Andrew Balding	3-10

Favourites

2yo	45.1% +6.53	3yo	35.8% -36.10	TOTAL	34.2% -66.70

York Road, Beverley, E Yorkshire
HU17 8QZ. Tel 01482 867 488

BEVERLEY

How to get there
Road: Course is
signposted from
the M62. Rail:
Beverley, bus
service to course
on race days

Features RH,
uphill finish

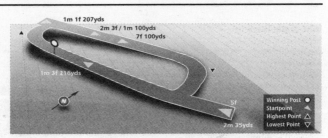

2018 Fixtures
April 18, 26, May 7, 15, 30, June 9, 19,
26, July 6-7, 17, 23, 31, August 15-16,
26, September 1, 19, 25

Racing Post standard times

5f	1min1	1m4f16yds	2min34.2
7f100yds	1min30	2m35yds	3min30
1m100yds	1min43	2m3f100yds	4min17
1m1f207yds	2min1.3		

Trainers	Wins-Runs	%	2yo	3yo+	£1 level stks
Richard Fahey	47-283	17	20-108	27-175	-68.08
Mark Johnston	43-226	19	13-70	30-156	-22.03
David O'Meara	32-215	15	1-39	31-176	-12.54
Tim Easterby	25-258	10	4-78	21-180	-97.25
Kevin Ryan	15-142	11	6-48	9-94	+11.66
Brian Ellison	14-117	12	8-29	6-88	-42.56
Ollie Pears	14-109	13	1-24	13-85	+55.25
Richard Guest	14-68	21	2-9	12-59	+48.50
Michael Dods	13-65	20	9-30	4-35	+6.00
Bryan Smart	11-75	15	4-35	7-40	+0.00
John Quinn	10-80	13	4-27	6-53	-24.65
William Haggas	10-26	38	3-8	7-18	+4.04
Les Eyre	9-85	11	1-11	8-74	-25.50

Jockeys	Wins-Rides	%	£1 level stks	Best Trainer	W-R
Joe Fanning	39-211	18	-8.65	Mark Johnston	28-132
Daniel Tudhope	29-125	23	+45.94	David O'Meara	16-89
David Allan	28-229	12	-56.13	Tim Easterby	14-109
Paul Mulrennan	28-181	15	-16.23	Michael Dods	9-36
Tony Hamilton	25-151	17	-34.44	Richard Fahey	19-105
Graham Lee	18-158	11	-59.20	Bryan Smart	3-7
P J McDonald	17-190	9	-105.88	Ann Duffield	8-60
Ben Curtis	16-103	16	-25.02	Brian Ellison	5-25
Paul Hanagan	16-76	21	-8.09	Richard Fahey	11-45
Tom Eaves	13-184	7	-72.09	Brian Ellison	4-23
Barry McHugh	11-140	8	+49.20	Tony Coyle	7-68
Graham Gibbons	11-125	9	-50.80	David Barron	3-20
Phillip Makin	11-107	10	-53.03	Keith Dalgleish	3-16

Favourites

2yo	35.2%	-21.03		3yo	38.4%	-7.07		TOTAL	31.9%	-85.10

BRIGHTON

Freshfield Road, Brighton, E Sussex
BN2 2XZ. Tel 01273 603 580

How to get there
Road:
Signposted from
A23 London
Road and A27.
Rail: Brighton,
bus to course on
race days

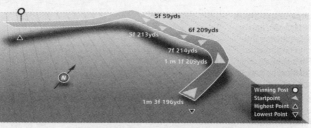

Features LH,
undulating, sharp

2018 Fixtures April 24, May 1-2, 8, 29,
June 8, 11, 19, 26, July 3, 10, August
8-10, 21, September 2-3, 10, 17,
October 9, 18

Racing Post standard times

5f59yds	1min0.4	7f214yds	1min33
5f213yds	1min8.4	1m1f209yds	1min59.4
6f209yds	1min20.5	1m3f196yds	2min28.8

Trainers	*Wins-Runs*	%	*2yo*	*3yo+*	*£1 level stks*
Gary Moore	30-161	19	5-16	25-145	+40.10
Richard Hannon	26-117	22	15-56	11-61	+3.72
Tony Carroll	23-146	16	0-4	23-142	+17.60
Mick Channon	19-119	16	7-37	12-82	+31.45
John Bridger	18-129	14	0-3	18-126	-6.04
John Gallagher	15-75	20	1-7	14-68	+38.75
Mark Johnston	14-67	21	5-26	9-41	-8.86
Eve Johnson Houghton	14-58	24	0-16	14-42	+9.42
George Baker	12-73	16	2-8	10-65	+67.50
Philip Hide	12-57	21	1-4	11-53	+1.78
Sylvester Kirk	11-67	16	4-14	7-53	+2.33
Richard Hughes	11-61	18	0-12	11-49	-8.00
Paul Cole	11-31	35	4-9	7-22	+25.60

Jockeys	*Wins-Rides*	%	*£1 level stks*	*Best Trainer*	*W-R*
Jim Crowley	37-156	24	-5.58	Paul Cole	3-4
Luke Morris	24-139	17	-17.98	John Spearing	5-15
Adam Kirby	24-86	28	+16.85	Clive Cox	8-16
David Probert	23-109	21	+40.25	Paul Cole	3-4
William Carson	22-166	13	-18.83	John Bridger	16-86
Silvestre De Sousa	22-116	19	-7.40	Mark Johnston	3-17
Pat Cosgrave	18-98	18	+28.49	Jim Boyle	4-16
Richard Hughes	17-61	28	+2.82	Richard Hannon	7-20
George Baker	16-72	22	+7.85	Gary Moore	3-17
Hector Crouch	15-119	13	+14.25	Gary Moore	12-77
J F Egan	15-72	21	+38.25	John Berry	5-9
Shane Kelly	14-114	12	-51.50	Richard Hughes	7-34
Fergus Sweeney	14-91	15	+18.75	John Gallagher	4-13

Favourites

2yo	41.9%	-17.44		3yo	28%	-63.28		TOTAL	32.1%	-111.37

Durdar Road, Carlisle, Cumbria,
CA2 4TS. Tel 01228 554 700

CARLISLE

How to get there
Road: M6 Jctn
42, follow signs
on Dalston Road.
Rail: Carlisle, 66
bus to course on
race days

Features RH,
undulating, uphill
finish

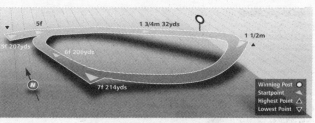

2018 Fixtures May 21, June 7-8,
18, 27, July 7, 12, August 6, 22, 30,
September 6, 12

Racing Post standard times

5f	1min	1m1f61yds	1min55.2
5f193yds	1min12.2	1m3f107yds	2min23.5
6f192yds	1min25.7	1m6f32yds	3min2.5
7f200yds	1min38.5	2m1f52yds	3min46

Trainers	Wins-Runs	%	2yo	3yo+	£1 level stks
Keith Dalgleish	32-221	14	2-42	30-179	-27.83
Richard Fahey	25-207	12	9-81	16-126	-77.68
Tim Easterby	21-171	12	3-47	18-124	-19.52
Mark Johnston	20-123	16	7-38	13-85	-27.18
K R Burke	18-85	21	13-39	5-46	+26.70
Kevin Ryan	13-81	16	5-32	8-49	-12.90
Michael Dods	12-98	12	7-31	5-67	-36.63
Alan Swinbank	9-60	15	0-5	9-55	+15.75
Ann Duffield	8-68	12	6-33	2-35	-8.02
David Barron	8-34	24	2-9	6-25	+26.28
Karen Tutty	7-45	16	0-2	7-43	+1.00
David Nicholls	7-20	35	0-0	7-20	+28.50
William Haggas	7-17	41	1-2	6-15	+6.58

Jockeys	Wins-Rides	%	£1 level stks	Best Trainer	W-R
Ben Curtis	27-97	28	+141.39	Alan Swinbank	6-20
Paul Mulrennan	25-137	18	-23.88	Michael Dods	10-42
Graham Lee	20-121	17	+8.27	Keith Dalgleish	4-13
Tony Hamilton	16-111	14	-28.14	Richard Fahey	12-80
Phillip Makin	16-94	17	+5.32	Keith Dalgleish	11-53
Joe Fanning	14-123	11	-37.80	Mark Johnston	11-62
P J McDonald	10-104	10	-43.41	Ann Duffield	4-39
David Allan	10-72	14	-19.90	Tim Easterby	7-50
Franny Norton	9-62	15	-26.38	Mark Johnston	6-38
Rachel Richardson	9-62	15	+16.00	Tim Easterby	7-39
Jack Garritty	8-64	13	-1.88	John Quinn	2-5
Daniel Tudhope	8-52	15	-12.71	K R Burke	2-4
Tom Eaves	7-136	5	-93.92	Keith Dalgleish	5-44

Favourites

2yo	46.6% +7.86	3yo	39.7% +9.55	TOTAL	33.1% -36.05

CATTERICK

Catterick Bridge, Richmond, N Yorks
DL10 7PE. Tel 01748 811 478

How to get there
Road: A1, exit 5m south of Scotch Corner. Rail: Darlington or Northallerton and bus

Features LH,
undulating, tight

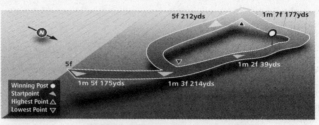

2018 Fixtures
April 4, 25, May 14, 24, June 1, 9, July 11, 18, 25, August 7, 17, 29, September 11, 22, October 1, 9, 20, 30

Racing Post standard times

5f	58.3	1m3f214yds	2min33
5f212yds	1min11.3	1m5f175yds	2min57
7f	1min23.3	1m7f177yds	3min23

Trainers	Wins-Runs	%	2yo	3yo+	£1 level stks
Richard Fahey	37-172	22	20-69	17-103	+4.17
John Quinn	25-131	19	6-38	19-93	+14.71
Mark Johnston	24-121	20	13-58	11-63	-20.26
Tim Easterby	17-149	11	2-33	15-116	-37.88
David O'Meara	16-150	11	4-25	12-125	-65.93
Ruth Carr	16-107	15	1-4	15-103	-19.50
Brian Ellison	14-84	17	2-10	12-74	-11.60
Michael Easterby	13-116	11	0-20	13-96	-27.38
Keith Dalgleish	13-73	18	4-27	9-46	-11.50
Scott Dixon	11-97	11	0-8	11-89	+9.50
Michael Appleby	11-82	13	1-7	10-75	-0.79
David Nicholls	11-81	14	1-3	10-78	+5.00
Kevin Ryan	11-80	14	3-20	8-60	-12.87

Jockeys	Wins-Rides	%	£1 level stks	Best Trainer	W-R
P J McDonald	28-171	16	+13.06	Ann Duffield	8-45
James Sullivan	18-148	12	-48.63	Ruth Carr	12-77
David Allan	18-135	13	+31.03	Tim Easterby	7-58
Daniel Tudhope	18-106	17	-29.65	David O'Meara	11-66
Paul Mulrennan	18-103	17	-23.89	Conor Dore	3-5
Joe Fanning	17-121	14	-9.17	Mark Johnston	9-55
Graham Lee	16-133	12	-60.15	A J Martin	1-1
Jason Hart	14-92	15	+3.55	John Quinn	9-44
Ben Curtis	13-102	13	-45.42	Brian Ellison	5-25
Phillip Makin	13-101	13	-40.48	Keith Dalgleish	5-25
Tony Hamilton	13-91	14	-45.41	Richard Fahey	11-58
Jack Garritty	12-74	16	+6.38	Richard Fahey	4-15
Joe Doyle	12-58	21	+42.00	John Quinn	4-9

Favourites

2yo	48%	+5.19	3yo	33.3%	-22.10	TOTAL	33.7%	-49.14

Great Leighs, CM3 1QP.
Tel 01245 362 412

CHELMSFORD

How to get there
Road: M11 Jctn 8, A120 towards Chelmsford, signposted from A131. Rail: Chelmsford, bus to course on racedays

○ Winning Post
◁ Startpoint
▲ Highest Point
▼ Lowest Point
✒ Open ditch
⌇ Water jump
✒ Fence

Features LH, Polytrack, 1m circuit with wide sweeping bends

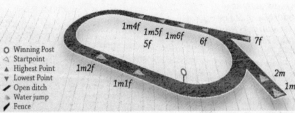

2018 Fixtures March 29, 31, April 5-6, 12, 26, May 3, 10, 24, 28, 31, June 13, 20-21, July 6-7, 24, August 4, 10-11, 14, 17, 24-25, 30, September 1, 6, 10, 15, 20, 22, 25, 29, October 4, 11, 13, 18, 25, 29, November 8, 10, 13, 15, 29, December 6, 13, 20

Racing Post standard times

5f	59.6
6f	1min12.3
1m	1min39
1m2f	2min6.5
1m6f	3min0.6
2m	3min28

Trainers	Wins-Runs	%	2yo	3yo+	£1 level stks
Mark Johnston	36-257	14	18-93	18-164	-88.21
Saeed bin Suroor	33-94	35	9-22	24-72	+2.98
Stuart Williams	31-195	16	5-16	26-179	+20.13
Marco Botti	30-209	14	10-62	20-147	-21.55
Chris Dwyer	30-171	18	2-22	28-149	+44.16
Derek Shaw	29-221	13	1-23	28-198	+5.04
David Simcock	29-139	21	4-18	25-121	+22.16
Michael Appleby	28-279	10	0-11	28-268	-109.22
John Gosden	28-120	24	6-46	22-74	-22.66
William Haggas	28-99	28	10-36	18-63	+10.98
Richard Hannon	26-204	13	13-91	13-113	-57.80
Jamie Osborne	22-160	14	5-48	17-112	-10.95
Sir Mark Prescott	21-113	19	5-40	16-73	-29.48

Jockeys	Wins-Rides	%	£1 level stks	Best Trainer	W-R
Luke Morris	63-552	11	-208.80	Sir Mark Prescott	20-86
Silvestre De Sousa	47-235	20	+3.42	Chris Dwyer	15-58
Jim Crowley	45-212	21	+24.74	Hugo Palmer	6-13
Adam Kirby	42-256	16	-69.01	Ian Williams	4-7
Martin Harley	35-252	14	-35.20	David Simcock	4-14
Martin Lane	32-187	17	+38.03	Derek Shaw	11-53
Ryan Moore	31-76	41	+31.41	Sir Michael Stoute	10-26
Oisin Murphy	30-198	15	-34.49	Andrew Balding	7-34
Josephine Gordon	24-254	9	-93.72	Phil McEntee	8-69
Kieren Fox	23-119	19	+59.83	John Best	12-60
Joe Fanning	21-158	13	-59.37	Mark Johnston	15-89
Pat Cosgrave	19-163	12	-66.90	Saeed bin Suroor	5-5
Robert Havlin	19-116	16	-35.25	John Gosden	11-45

Favourites

2yo	41.8% +2.05		3yo	34.4% -81.98	TOTAL	35.5% -114.21

CHEPSTOW

Chepstow, Monmouthshire,
NP16 6BE. Tel 01291 622 260

How to get there

Road: M4 Jct 22 on west side of Severn Bridge, A48 north, A446. Rail: Chepstow, bus to course on race days

Features LH, undulating

2018 Fixtures May

4, 15, 22, June 2, 15, 25, July 3, 13, 19, 27, August 16, 23, 27, September 3, 13, 18

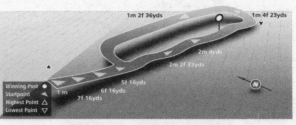

Racing Post standard times

5f16yds	58.3	1m2f36yds	2min6.5
6f16yds	1min9.8	1m4f23yds	2min34
7f16yds	1min21.5	2m49yds	3min28
1m14yds	1min33.5	2m2f	3min52

Trainers	Wins-Runs	%	2yo	3yo+	£1 level stks
Richard Hannon	25-132	19	15-53	10-79	-33.96
David Evans	19-180	11	6-61	13-119	+0.27
Andrew Balding	19-91	21	3-14	16-77	+1.43
Eve Johnson Houghton	15-54	28	5-19	10-35	+13.68
Ralph Beckett	14-48	29	2-14	12-34	-3.56
Bernard Llewellyn	13-105	12	0-0	13-105	+11.67
John O'Shea	12-100	12	0-0	12-100	-16.13
Clive Cox	12-45	27	4-12	8-33	+11.89
Ronald Harris	11-149	7	1-27	10-122	-36.75
Mick Channon	11-74	15	1-26	10-48	-6.90
Richard Price	11-70	16	0-1	11-69	-16.18
Ed de Giles	10-40	25	0-4	10-36	+19.25
John Flint	9-41	22	0-0	9-41	+18.50

Jockeys	Wins-Rides	%	£1 level stks	Best Trainer	W-R
David Probert	22-137	16	-27.01	Patrick Chamings	5-12
Tom Marquand	20-116	17	+6.13	Richard Price	7-21
Franny Norton	16-77	21	+27.05	Paul Henderson	4-7
Luke Morris	14-142	10	-35.50	John O'Shea	4-21
Oisin Murphy	14-83	17	-3.34	Andrew Balding	4-19
Pat Dobbs	12-62	19	-18.17	Richard Hannon	5-25
John Fahy	12-61	20	+5.88	Eve Johnson Houghton	5-15
Dane O'Neill	11-70	16	-9.96	Richard Hannon	2-3
Adam Kirby	11-44	25	+17.28	Clive Cox	6-12
Liam Keniry	10-85	12	-23.40	Neil Mulholland	2-2
Fergus Sweeney	10-60	17	-0.92	David Simcock	4-5
Edward Greatrex	9-103	9	-47.05	Andrew Balding	4-15
Jim Crowley	9-38	24	+23.75	Ed de Giles	3-4

Favourites

2yo	42.5% -2.71	3yo	38.1% -9.28	TOTAL	36.4% -17.91

Steam Mill Street, Chester, CH1 2LY
Tel 01244 304 600

CHESTER

How to get there
Road: Inner Ring
Road and A458
Queensferry
Road.
Rail: Chester
General, bus to
city centre

Features LH, flat,
very sharp

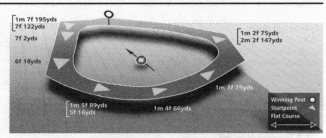

1m 7f 195yds
7f 122yds
7f 2yds
6f 18yds
1m 2f 75yds
2m 2f 147yds
1m 3f 79yds
Winning Post
Startpoint
Flat Course
1m 5f 89yds
5f 16yds
1m 4f 66yds

2018 Fixtures May 9-11, 26, June
16, 29-30, July 13-14, 28, August 5,
September 1, 14-15, 29

Racing Post standard times

5f16yds	59.6	1m3f79yds	2min22.7
5f110yds	1min5.6	1m4f66yds	2min34.6
6f18yds	1min13.1	1m5f89yds	2min48
7f2yds	1min24.3	1m7f195yds	3min24
7f122yds	1min31.4	2m2f147yds	4min1
1m2f75yds	2min7.9		

Trainers	Wins-Runs	%	2yo	3yo+	£1 level stks
Richard Fahey	52-405	13	12-70	40-335	-52.63
Mark Johnston	33-218	15	12-64	21-154	-59.67
Andrew Balding	33-140	24	5-22	28-118	+73.56
Tom Dascombe	31-233	13	15-86	16-147	-80.10
Kevin Ryan	13-66	20	5-13	8-53	+6.91
Tim Easterby	12-88	14	2-11	10-77	-20.25
Richard Hannon	11-81	14	9-36	2-45	-24.61
Sir Michael Stoute	10-42	24	1-3	9-39	-14.04
William Haggas	9-29	31	3-4	6-25	-3.98
A P O'Brien	9-23	39	0-0	9-23	+0.45
Brian Ellison	8-60	13	0-4	8-56	-8.50
Roger Varian	7-35	20	1-4	6-31	-1.29
John Gosden	7-28	25	0-1	7-27	-3.54

Jockeys	Wins-Rides	%	£1 level stks	Best Trainer	W-R
Franny Norton	39-236	17	-63.82	Mark Johnston	22-127
Richard Kingscote	35-177	20	+3.31	Tom Dascombe	24-119
David Probert	15-94	16	-16.00	Andrew Balding	12-59
Ryan Moore	14-45	31	+3.78	A P O'Brien	8-14
J F Egan	10-90	11	+0.50	David Evans	3-30
Patrick Mathers	10-65	15	+13.75	Richard Fahey	10-50
David Nolan	9-86	10	-13.50	Richard Fahey	7-67
Graham Gibbons	9-47	19	+6.88	David Barron	3-16
Oisin Murphy	8-51	16	+5.38	Andrew Balding	8-23
Graham Lee	8-40	20	+21.85	Andrew Balding	1-1
Adam McNamara	8-32	25	+11.17	Richard Fahey	8-30
Paul Hanagan	7-50	14	-16.28	Richard Fahey	3-31
David Allan	7-45	16	-0.50	Tim Easterby	6-30

Favourites

2yo	36.5% -14.88	3yo	30.6% -32.90	TOTAL	30.6% -65.75

DONCASTER

Leger Way, Doncaster
DN2 6BB. Tel 01302 320066/7

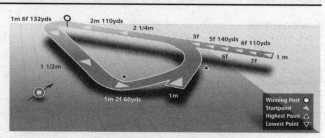

How to get there
Road: M18 Jct 3,
A638, A18 to Hull.
Rail: Doncaster
Central

Features LH, flat

2018 Fixtures
March 24-25,
April 27-28, May
5, 19, June 1-2,
17, 29-30, July 6, 12, 19, 26, August 4,
18, September 12-15, October 26-27,
November 10

Racing Post standard times

5f	57.9	1m (Rnd)	1min36.2
5f140yds	1min6.2	1m2f60yds	2m6
6f	1min10.5	1m4f	2min29
6f110yds	1min17	1m6f132yds	3min3
7f	1min23.3	2m110yds	3min33
1m (Str)	1min36	2m2f	3min52

Trainers	Wins-Runs	%	2yo	3yo+	£1 level stks
Richard Fahey	34-384	9	10-110	24-274	-91.99
Richard Hannon	33-243	14	14-118	19-125	-5.40
Roger Varian	29-120	24	3-26	26-94	+38.95
John Gosden	26-137	19	9-36	17-101	-44.36
Charlie Appleby	21-102	21	9-48	12-54	+0.51
Sir Michael Stoute	21-62	34	3-16	18-46	+48.22
William Haggas	20-94	21	10-24	10-70	-15.42
David O'Meara	19-211	9	4-10	15-201	-77.09
Luca Cumani	18-75	24	1-9	17-66	+1.50
Mark Johnston	17-137	12	8-60	9-77	-34.60
David Simcock	17-75	23	2-15	15-60	+29.83
Saeed bin Suroor	15-50	30	3-11	12-39	-0.39
Ralph Beckett	12-88	14	3-25	9-63	-21.99

Jockeys	Wins-Rides	%	£1 level stks	Best Trainer	W-R
Andrea Atzeni	42-158	27	+111.84	Roger Varian	14-49
Jamie Spencer	28-140	20	+34.70	David Simcock	9-26
Ryan Moore	25-113	22	-5.40	Sir Michael Stoute	9-23
William Buick	24-135	18	-27.69	Charlie Appleby	10-48
Paul Hanagan	20-165	12	-59.09	Richard Hannon	4-8
Daniel Tudhope	18-139	13	-0.50	David O'Meara	5-76
Silvestre De Sousa	17-107	16	-20.02	Mark Johnston	3-11
Graham Lee	16-171	9	-54.75	Jedd O'Keeffe	2-17
James Doyle	16-116	14	-61.31	Charlie Appleby	4-15
Oisin Murphy	16-103	16	-31.44	Ralph Beckett	5-13
Tony Hamilton	15-125	12	+1.41	Richard Fahey	11-99
P J McDonald	14-115	12	+35.63	Mark Johnston	4-13
Frankie Dettori	13-68	19	-12.53	John Gosden	6-27

Favourites

2yo	44.9%	+11.72	3yo	36.2%	-2.32	TOTAL	33.8%	-37.33

Epsom Downs, Surrey, KT18 5LQ
Tel 01372 726 311

EPSOM

How to get there
Road: M25 Jct 8
(A217) or 9 (A24),
2m south of
Epsom on B290.
Rail: Epsom
and bus, Epsom
Downs or
Tattenham
Corner

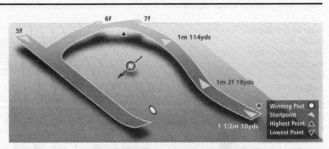

Features LH,
undulating

2018 Fixtures April 25, June 1-2,
July 5, 12, 19, August 2, 27-28,
September 13, 30

Racing Post standard times

5f	54.9	1m114yds	1min41.8
6f	1min7	1m2f18yds	2min5.3
7f	1min20	1m4f10yds	2min33.6

Trainers	Wins-Runs	%	2yo	3yo+	£1 level stks
Mark Johnston	17-113	15	9-25	8-88	-22.48
Mick Channon	13-56	23	2-16	11-40	+22.03
Andrew Balding	12-89	13	3-13	9-76	+12.83
Richard Hannon	12-81	15	7-30	5-51	-23.54
Richard Fahey	11-97	11	1-17	10-80	-21.13
John Gosden	11-42	26	1-5	10-37	-5.57
George Baker	9-37	24	2-4	7-33	+45.75
Roger Varian	8-30	27	0-3	8-27	+9.88
Ralph Beckett	7-42	17	1-5	6-37	-6.18
Eve Johnson Houghton	7-30	23	0-4	7-26	+15.25
Pat Phelan	6-44	14	0-6	6-38	-2.38
Sylvester Kirk	5-42	12	0-7	5-35	+3.25
John Bridger	5-37	14	0-4	5-33	-11.25

Jockeys	Wins-Rides	%	£1 level stks	Best Trainer	W-R
Silvestre De Sousa	31-113	27	+32.78	Mark Johnston	7-33
Charles Bishop	12-24	50	+45.91	Mick Channon	8-17
Jim Crowley	10-66	15	-27.60	Charlie Appleby	1-1
Ryan Moore	8-59	14	-18.59	Sir Michael Stoute	2-9
James Doyle	8-44	18	-14.00	Mark Johnston	2-6
Frankie Dettori	7-32	22	-9.17	John Gosden	6-15
Franny Norton	7-32	22	+12.43	Mark Johnston	5-20
Oisin Murphy	6-75	8	-22.50	John Berry	1-1
Andrea Atzeni	6-58	10	-33.12	Roger Varian	4-14
David Probert	6-54	11	-30.50	Andrew Balding	3-33
Pat Cosgrave	6-34	18	+3.25	George Baker	4-10
Pat Dobbs	6-32	19	+18.38	Richard Hannon	2-11
Edward Greatrex	6-27	22	+32.46	Andrew Balding	4-9

Favourites

2yo	40.9%	-4.09	3yo	36%	-0.53	TOTAL 33%	-30.89

FFOS LAS

Trimsaran, Carmarthenshire, SA17 4DE
Tel: 01554 811092

How to get there
Road: M4 Jctn
48 and follow the
A4138 to Llanelli.
Rail: Llanelli,
Kidwelly or
Carmarthen

Features LH, flat,
galloping

2018 Fixtures
July 24, August 2, 14, 24,
September 5, 16

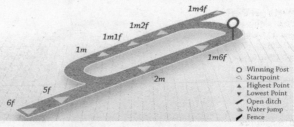

O Winning Post
◁ Startpoint
▲ Highest Point
▼ Lowest Point
∕ Open ditch
↝ Water jump
∕ Fence

Racing Post standard times

5f	57	1m4f	2min34
6f	1min8.5	1m6f	3min
1m	1min38	2m	3min28.5
1m2f	2min6		

Trainers	Wins-Runs	%	2yo	3yo+	£1 level stks
David Evans	17-110	15	7-36	10-74	+49.25
Andrew Balding	14-45	31	2-8	12-37	+40.85
William Muir	7-34	21	4-13	3-21	+13.75
Rod Millman	6-32	19	2-13	4-19	-8.00
Richard Hannon	6-28	21	5-18	1-10	-3.00
Tony Carroll	5-27	19	0-1	5-26	+6.00
William Knight	5-19	26	1-4	4-15	+2.50
Roger Charlton	5-14	36	2-3	3-11	-1.53
Hughie Morrison	4-14	29	0-0	4-14	+8.00
Peter Makin	4-9	44	0-0	4-9	+12.17
Ed de Giles	3-21	14	0-3	3-18	-8.80
Richard Price	3-21	14	0-2	3-19	-6.25
David Simcock	3-20	15	0-3	3-17	-7.38

Jockeys	Wins-Rides	%	£1 level stks	Best Trainer	W-R
David Probert	12-51	24	+30.73	Andrew Balding	7-22
Liam Keniry	10-55	18	+23.50	Andrew Balding	3-12
Steve Drowne	8-53	15	+43.50	Peter Makin	3-7
Oisin Murphy	7-37	19	-5.63	Dominic Ffrench Davis	1-1
Kieran Shoemark	7-30	23	+3.13	David Evans	2-4
Jim Crowley	7-19	37	+15.88	David Evans	2-3
William Twiston-Davies	6-43	14	+0.00	Nigel Twiston-Davies	2-5
Martin Dwyer	6-39	15	+3.25	William Muir	5-16
Shane Kelly	6-29	21	-4.25	Richard Hughes	2-10
George Baker	5-27	19	-11.65	Roger Charlton	2-5
Fran Berry	5-20	25	+3.41	David Evans	3-4
Tom Marquand	5-18	28	+15.23	Ali Stronge	1-1
Declan Bates	4-20	20	-0.46	David Evans	2-12

Favourites

2yo	40.9%	-7.29	3yo	25.3%	-41.21	TOTAL	32%	-52.38

Chichester, W Sussex,
PO18 0PS. Tel 01243 755 022

GOODWOOD

How to get there
Road: signposted
from A27 south
and A285 north.
Rail: Chichester,
bus to course on
race days

Features RH,
undulating

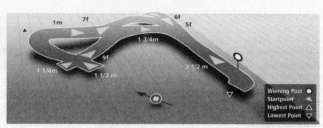

Winning Post ●
Startpoint ▲
Highest Point △
Lowest Point ▽

2018 Fixtures
May 5, 24-26, June 1, 8, 10, 15, July
31, August 1-4, 24-26, September 4,
26, October 14

Racing Post standard times

5f	57	1m3f	2min21
6f	1min9.7	1m4f	2min34
7f	1min24	1m6f	2min58.5
1m	1min36.7	2m	3min21
1m1f	1min51.4	2m4f	4min14
1m1f192yds	2min4		

Trainers	Wins-Runs	%	2yo	3yo+	£1 level stks
Richard Hannon	40-338	12	21-142	19-196	-101.60
Mark Johnston	36-238	15	12-76	24-162	+93.50
Mick Channon	20-172	12	12-60	8-112	-15.13
John Gosden	20-93	22	5-16	15-77	-11.70
Sir Michael Stoute	19-99	19	2-6	17-93	-30.83
Charlie Appleby	19-93	20	10-31	9-62	+0.58
William Haggas	16-75	21	2-12	14-63	-14.42
David Simcock	15-96	16	1-7	14-89	+32.50
Andrew Balding	14-130	11	2-29	12-101	-36.39
Gary Moore	12-83	14	2-15	10-68	+117.71
Charles Hills	10-100	10	4-42	6-58	-48.90
Henry Candy	10-55	18	2-11	8-44	-2.58
Amanda Perrett	9-152	6	0-12	9-140	-87.75

Jockeys	Wins-Rides	%	£1 level stks	Best Trainer	W-R
Jim Crowley	31-210	15	-43.08	David Simcock	5-18
William Buick	26-104	25	+74.63	Charlie Appleby	12-40
Richard Hughes	25-125	20	-15.06	Richard Hannon	13-70
Ryan Moore	23-125	18	-50.85	Sir Michael Stoute	7-32
James Doyle	22-148	15	-12.83	Saeed bin Suroor	3-24
Andrea Atzeni	21-115	18	+60.83	Roger Varian	6-31
Silvestre De Sousa	17-118	14	+14.90	Mick Channon	8-28
Joe Fanning	17-113	15	+32.28	Mark Johnston	15-84
Frankie Dettori	15-90	17	-0.23	John Gosden	5-25
Adam Kirby	13-99	13	-1.67	Luca Cumani	3-13
Pat Cosgrave	11-66	17	+7.75	William Haggas	6-20
Pat Dobbs	10-143	7	-67.92	Richard Hannon	5-59
Oisin Murphy	10-121	8	-68.50	David Simcock	3-11

Favourites

2yo	39.3%	-9.05		3yo	34.3%	-6.46		TOTAL	33.9%	-32.28

HAMILTON

Bothwell Road, Hamilton, Lanarkshire
ML3 0DW. Tel 01698 283 806

How to get there
Road: M74 Jct 5,
off the A74. Rail:
Hamilton West

Features RH,
undulating, dip
can become
testing in wet
weather

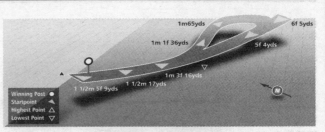

2018 Fixtures
May 6, 18, 31, June 6, 13, 20, 28,
July 2-3, 14, 19-20, August 4, 21, 31,
September 13, 23-24

Racing Post standard times

5f4yds	58.2	1m3f16yds	2min20
6f5yds	1min10	1m4f17yds	2min33.7
1m65yds	1min45	1m5f9yds	2min47.5
1m1f36yds	1min55.5		

Trainers	*Wins-Runs*	%	*2yo*	*3yo+*	*£1 level stks*
Keith Dalgleish	51-371	14	8-64	43-307	-45.28
Mark Johnston	34-172	20	18-56	16-116	-30.37
Richard Fahey	26-221	12	6-67	20-154	-86.18
Kevin Ryan	26-124	21	7-33	19-91	+16.33
David O'Meara	20-108	19	1-13	19-95	-28.53
John Patrick Shanahan	20-104	19	0-5	20-99	-1.23
Jim Goldie	15-167	9	0-4	15-163	-36.35
Iain Jardine	15-95	16	1-7	14-88	+74.75
Michael Dods	13-56	23	3-10	10-46	+1.32
Alan Swinbank	10-72	14	0-0	10-72	-32.58
Alan Berry	9-87	10	0-1	9-86	+55.00
Alistair Whillans	9-85	11	0-2	9-83	-27.75
K R Burke	9-75	12	4-25	5-50	-33.61

Jockeys	*Wins-Rides*	%	*£1 level stks*	*Best Trainer*	*W-R*
Joe Fanning	40-226	18	-43.39	Mark Johnston	26-116
Graham Lee	31-188	16	-49.47	Mick Channon	3-5
Paul Mulrennan	23-159	14	-3.40	Michael Dods	6-21
P J McDonald	20-158	13	-29.38	Ann Duffield	5-41
Phillip Makin	20-119	17	-9.05	Keith Dalgleish	12-70
Connor Beasley	19-143	13	-17.75	Keith Dalgleish	8-37
Daniel Tudhope	18-82	22	+12.75	David O'Meara	9-37
Tom Eaves	13-176	7	-87.95	Keith Dalgleish	3-39
James Sullivan	13-123	11	+9.50	Ruth Carr	3-50
Joey Haynes	12-66	18	+37.08	K R Burke	5-22
Shane Gray	11-71	15	+9.41	Kevin Ryan	5-32
Fergal Lynch	11-52	21	+43.63	Jim Goldie	5-30
Kevin Stott	11-40	28	+13.91	Kevin Ryan	7-20

Favourites

2yo	35.2% -16.81	3yo	44.6% +35.44	TOTAL	33.8% -47.76

Newton-Le-Willows, Merseyside
WA12 0HQ. Tel 01942 725 963

HAYDOCK

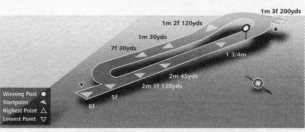

How to get there
Road: M6 Jct 23,
A49 to Wigan.
Rail: Wigan & 320
bus or Newton-le-
Willows

Features LH, flat,
easy turns, suits
the galloping type

2018 Fixtures
April 28, May 25-26, June 7-9, 13-14,
23, July 5-7, 20-21, August 9-11,
September 6-8, 28-29, October 19

Racing Post standard times

5f	58.5	1m2f95yds	2min9
5f (Inner)	58	1m3f200yds	2min26.5
6f	1min11	1m6f	2min54
6f (Inner)	1min10.3	2m45yds	3min24
7f	1min26	2m1f130yds	3min51
1m	1min38		

Trainers	Wins-Runs	%	2yo	3yo+	£1 level stks
Tom Dascombe	48-268	18	12-95	36-173	+136.20
Richard Fahey	29-315	9	10-81	19-234	-142.22
William Haggas	29-94	31	6-21	23-73	+11.33
Mark Johnston	28-188	15	11-66	17-122	-11.83
John Gosden	25-85	29	10-26	15-59	+45.59
David O'Meara	22-200	11	0-6	22-194	+8.88
Richard Hannon	21-182	12	9-76	12-106	-39.15
K R Burke	18-168	11	4-55	14-113	-24.42
Tim Easterby	16-170	9	4-35	12-135	-12.00
Roger Varian	15-89	17	2-21	13-68	-28.76
Kevin Ryan	13-129	10	6-45	7-84	-43.25
Hugo Palmer	12-39	31	7-13	5-26	+3.60
Charles Hills	11-82	13	3-23	8-59	-9.93

Jockeys	Wins-Rides	%	£1 level stks	Best Trainer	W-R
Richard Kingscote	53-262	20	+82.73	Tom Dascombe	38-190
Daniel Tudhope	26-172	15	+36.19	David O'Meara	17-96
Paul Hanagan	24-139	17	-26.29	Richard Fahey	7-35
Graham Lee	18-157	11	-47.96	Kevin Ryan	5-13
Franny Norton	17-137	12	-28.25	Mark Johnston	13-77
William Buick	16-71	23	+3.09	Charlie Appleby	5-26
Joe Fanning	15-73	21	+59.29	Mark Johnston	7-42
Ryan Moore	14-51	27	-6.50	Sir Michael Stoute	3-14
Frankie Dettori	14-46	30	-0.30	John Gosden	5-12
Adam Kirby	13-84	15	-8.58	Clive Cox	7-15
Pat Cosgrave	13-56	23	+5.24	William Haggas	10-26
Sean Levey	12-88	14	+11.88	Richard Hannon	9-59
Jamie Spencer	11-102	11	-55.73	Kevin Ryan	3-24

Favourites

2yo	35.6%	-24.29	3yo	36.3%	-12.35	TOTAL 32.4%	-90.65

KEMPTON

Staines Rd East, Sunbury-On-Thames
TW16 5AQ. Tel 01932 782 292

How to get there
Road: M3 Jct 1,
A308 to Kingston-
on-Thames. Rail:
Kempton Park
from Waterloo

Features RH,
Polytrack, sharp

2018 Fixtures
March 31, April
4, 7, 11, 13, 18, May 1, 23, June 6, 13,
27, July 4, 11, August 8, 15, 21-22,
29, September 4, 7-8, 12, 17-18, 24,
27, October 1-2, 8, 10, 15-16, 22-23,
26-27, 31, November 2, 5-6, 14, 19,
21, 23, December 5, 7, 12, 14

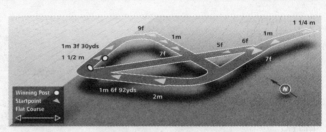

Racing Post standard times

5f	58.8	1m2f	2min4
6f	1min10.6	1m3f	2min17
7f	1min23.7	1m4f	2min30
1m	1min36.6	2m	3min22.5

Trainers	Wins-Runs	%	2yo	3yo+	£1 level stks
Richard Hannon	57-498	12	29-253	28-245	-156.43
Charlie Appleby	57-201	28	35-116	22-85	-0.58
John Gosden	54-239	23	25-124	29-115	-8.14
James Fanshawe	48-253	19	6-43	42-210	-22.89
Andrew Balding	39-300	13	4-58	35-242	-83.49
Ralph Beckett	37-239	15	20-103	17-136	+24.93
Saeed bin Suroor	37-145	26	12-58	25-87	-10.20
Tony Carroll	33-434	8	0-18	33-416	-213.50
Roger Varian	32-170	19	13-74	19-96	-26.99
Gary Moore	31-264	12	3-29	28-235	-73.08
Jeremy Noseda	30-108	28	9-30	21-78	+1.27
Roger Charlton	29-174	17	9-67	20-107	+11.20
Mark Johnston	28-227	12	11-77	17-150	-91.04

Jockeys	Wins-Rides	%	£1 level stks	Best Trainer	W-R
Luke Morris	83-848	10	-182.42	Sir Mark Prescott	15-97
Adam Kirby	83-611	14	-192.42	Charlie Appleby	14-41
Jim Crowley	82-632	13	-176.40	Ralph Beckett	7-23
George Baker	78-442	18	-31.75	Gary Moore	12-63
James Doyle	65-266	24	-15.76	Saeed bin Suroor	10-36
William Buick	51-204	25	-45.19	Charlie Appleby	27-77
Oisin Murphy	44-369	12	-57.17	Andrew Balding	7-63
Tom Queally	43-354	12	-66.31	James Fanshawe	10-66
Liam Keniry	42-560	8	-213.89	Neil Mulholland	8-41
Pat Cosgrave	41-356	12	-20.26	William Haggas	7-39
Martin Harley	41-313	13	-33.22	Marco Botti	7-47
Richard Kingscote	39-245	16	+44.23	Ralph Beckett	8-38
Silvestre De Sousa	39-231	17	-35.46	William Knight	5-15

Favourites

2yo	40.7% -28.30		3yo	36.9% -39.18		TOTAL	35.7% -103.99

London Road, Oadby, Leicester,
LE2 4QH. Tel 0116 271 6515

LEICESTER

How to get there
Road: M1 Jct 21,
A6, 2m south of
city. Rail:
Leicester, bus

Features RH,
straight mile is
downhill for first
4f, then uphill to
finish

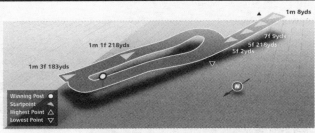

2018 Fixtures April 13, 28, May 21,
28-29, June 4, 16, 28, July 7, 19, 25,
August 1, 12, 20, September 4, 11, 24,
October 9, 16, 29

Racing Post standard times

5f2yds	59	1m60yds	1min42.5
5f218yds	1min10.5	1m1f218yds	2min4.5
7f9yds	1min23	1m3f183yds	2min29.3
1m8yds	1min41		

Trainers	Wins-Runs	%	2yo	3yo+	£1 level stks
Richard Fahey	28-134	21	12-52	16-82	+30.89
Richard Hannon	25-165	15	14-79	11-86	-37.08
Mark Johnston	24-117	21	8-51	16-66	-9.31
Mick Channon	18-80	23	8-33	10-47	+37.30
Sir Michael Stoute	15-68	22	3-27	12-41	-20.33
Charles Hills	14-66	21	6-32	8-34	-0.90
David Evans	13-121	11	4-48	9-73	-12.25
Roger Varian	13-68	19	2-24	11-44	-14.16
Hughie Morrison	10-41	24	0-7	10-34	+26.13
David O'Meara	9-60	15	0-5	9-55	-23.20
John Gosden	9-55	16	5-22	4-33	-17.14
Henry Candy	9-52	17	1-10	8-42	-9.57
Charlie Appleby	8-43	19	5-25	3-18	-20.39

Jockeys	Wins-Rides	%	£1 level stks	Best Trainer	W-R
Silvestre De Sousa	31-125	25	+31.49	Mark Johnston	7-27
Paul Hanagan	31-114	27	+65.78	Richard Fahey	10-26
Adam Kirby	16-120	13	-44.61	Clive Cox	4-36
Ryan Moore	14-91	15	-51.35	Sir Michael Stoute	6-27
James Doyle	14-61	23	+51.12	Saeed bin Suroor	4-10
Jim Crowley	12-83	14	-11.38	Charles Hills	3-7
Andrea Atzeni	12-81	15	-38.46	Roger Varian	8-32
William Buick	12-64	19	-27.06	Charlie Appleby	6-23
Oisin Murphy	10-87	11	-46.08	Alison Hutchinson	1-1
Sean Levey	10-58	17	+6.38	Richard Hannon	8-39
Martin Dwyer	9-83	11	-28.50	Marcus Tregoning	2-9
Jamie Spencer	9-67	13	-24.71	Michael Bell	3-8
Liam Keniry	9-54	17	+17.13	Sylvester Kirk	2-3

Favourites

2yo	40.1% -14.74		3yo	38.2% +1.96		TOTAL	35.8% -35.77

LINGFIELD Turf

Racecourse Road, Lingfield
RH7 6PQ. Tel 01342 834 800

How to get there
Road: M25 Jctn 6, south on A22, then B2029. Rail: Lingfield from London Bridge or Victoria

Features LH, undulating

2018 Fixtures
May 11-12, 24, 31, June 2, 9, 12, 23, 30, July 11, 18, 21, 25, 28, August 4, 11, 29, September 15

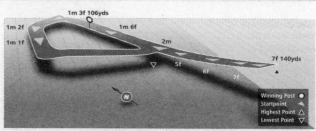

Racing Post standard times

5f	56.9	1m2f	2min6.7
6f	1min9.4	1m3f106yds	2min27
7f	1min21	1m6f	3min
7f140yds	1min28	2m	3min27.5
1m1f	1min53		

Trainers	Wins-Runs	%	2yo	3yo+	£1 level stks
William Haggas	20-41	49	10-18	10-23	+41.80
Richard Hannon	19-116	16	8-48	11-68	-0.12
John Bridger	12-98	12	2-14	10-84	+5.88
Gary Moore	9-70	13	1-8	8-62	-12.75
Jim Boyle	9-44	20	1-8	8-36	+24.50
Roger Varian	9-42	21	2-12	7-30	-12.62
David Evans	8-57	14	5-26	3-31	+10.20
Richard Hughes	8-42	19	3-12	5-30	-6.26
Andrew Balding	8-41	20	1-6	7-35	-8.50
John Best	7-46	15	1-11	6-35	-5.52
Ed Dunlop	7-37	19	2-14	5-23	+0.75
Patrick Chamings	7-27	26	1-3	6-24	+27.33
Ed Vaughan	7-26	27	0-4	7-22	+1.82

Jockeys	Wins-Rides	%	£1 level stks	Best Trainer	W-R
Pat Cosgrave	21-93	23	-12.44	William Haggas	10-20
Jim Crowley	19-82	23	-8.86	David Evans	2-2
Silvestre De Sousa	19-76	25	-18.27	Ed Dunlop	3-5
Luke Morris	14-94	15	-36.68	Sir Mark Prescott	4-10
Oisin Murphy	14-77	18	-24.16	Andrew Balding	3-10
Richard Hughes	13-48	27	+2.95	Richard Hannon	4-14
Adam Kirby	11-64	17	-13.53	Charlie Appleby	1-1
David Probert	10-64	16	+25.05	Andrew Balding	4-15
Harry Bentley	10-36	28	+25.13	Ed Vaughan	5-9
Shane Kelly	9-83	11	-37.61	Richard Hughes	5-28
James Doyle	9-38	24	-14.05	Charlie Appleby	2-3
Andrea Atzeni	8-45	18	-14.58	Roger Varian	5-15
George Baker	8-44	18	+6.00	Roger Charlton	2-4

Favourites

2yo	44.3% -2.80	3yo	31.9% -46.03	TOTAL	36.9% -40.93

LINGFIELD AW

Features LH, Polytrack, tight

2018 Fixtures
March 24, 30, April 3-4, 6, 11, 14, 25, May 3-4, 29, June 21, September 1, 5, 25, October 4, November 1, 16-17, 20, 24, December 4-5, 12, 19, 22, 28, 30-31

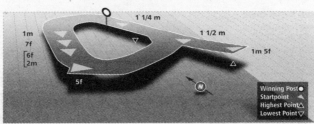

Racing Post standard times

5f	57.5	1m2f	2min1.8
6f	1min9.6	1m4f	2min28
7f	1min22.2	1m5f	2min40.5
1m	1min35.3	2m	3min16

Trainers	Wins-Runs	%	2yo	3yo+	£1 level stks
Richard Hannon	59-332	18	22-99	37-233	+22.07
Mark Johnston	50-286	17	6-41	44-245	-48.99
Charlie Appleby	45-145	31	8-32	37-113	+3.09
Andrew Balding	38-239	16	3-22	35-217	-48.90
David Evans	37-312	12	7-42	30-270	-135.59
William Haggas	36-125	29	10-40	26-85	+6.58
John Gosden	36-198	18	9-60	27-138	-73.84
Ralph Beckett	35-136	26	7-25	28-111	-1.16
Simon Dow	31-239	13	4-23	27-216	-7.56
David Simcock	29-167	17	1-9	28-158	+2.62
Gary Moore	28-264	11	0-14	28-250	-79.25
Lee Carter	27-323	8	0-3	27-320	-127.88
Tony Carroll	27-217	12	2-5	25-212	-75.40

Jockeys	Wins-Rides	%	£1 level stks	Best Trainer	W-R
Adam Kirby	129-673	19	-95.17	Charlie Appleby	17-46
Luke Morris	108-829	13	-248.24	Sir Mark Prescott	22-97
George Baker	94-489	19	-41.95	Gary Moore	12-82
Jim Crowley	77-433	18	-72.72	Amanda Perrett	10-33
Joe Fanning	53-280	19	+7.93	Mark Johnston	34-154
Oisin Murphy	46-278	17	+25.10	Andrew Balding	10-52
Liam Keniry	43-441	10	-26.30	Conor Dore	5-28
Shane Kelly	42-403	10	-162.95	Richard Hughes	9-80
James Doyle	39-143	27	+38.47	Saeed bin Suroor	8-18
David Probert	36-335	11	-125.18	Andrew Balding	14-88
Pat Cosgrave	34-263	13	-64.71	William Haggas	12-38
William Carson	32-374	9	-114.77	John Bridger	8-129
Robert Havlin	32-338	9	-119.43	John Gosden	16-80

Favourites

2yo	38.5% -31.83	3yo	38.1% -86.39	TOTAL	37.3% -126.57

MUSSELBURGH

Linkfield Road EH21 7RG
Tel 0131 665 2859

How to get there
Road: M8 Jct 2,
A8 east, follow
Ring Road, A1
east. Rail:
Musselburgh
from Edinburgh
Waverley

Features RH, flat,
tight

2018 Fixtures March 31, April 5, May
3-4, June 2, 9, July 4, 24, August
3, 10, 29-30, September 7, 15, 30,
October 15

Racing Post standard times

5f	58	1m3f32yds	2min22
7f30yds	1min26.8	1m4f100yds	2min40
1m	1min38.8	1m6f	1min59.2
1m1f	1min51.1	2m	3min25

Trainers	Wins-Runs	%	2yo	3yo+	£1 level stks
Mark Johnston	41-212	19	14-67	27-145	-30.77
Keith Dalgleish	39-317	12	11-67	28-250	-52.50
Richard Fahey	35-191	18	12-53	23-138	+40.18
Jim Goldie	24-281	9	0-6	24-275	-67.97
Kevin Ryan	18-89	20	6-24	12-65	+19.50
David O'Meara	15-121	12	3-26	12-95	-49.90
Tim Easterby	14-119	12	3-21	11-98	-29.30
Iain Jardine	14-116	12	1-9	13-107	-48.36
Michael Easterby	12-61	20	1-4	11-57	+18.75
Linda Perratt	11-201	5	0-3	11-198	-48.50
Ruth Carr	11-86	13	0-0	11-86	-12.00
John Quinn	11-62	18	4-20	7-42	-6.97
Alistair Whillans	10-96	10	0-3	10-93	-37.29

Jockeys	Wins-Rides	%	£1 level stks	Best Trainer	W-R
Joe Fanning	51-264	19	-41.72	Mark Johnston	36-142
Connor Beasley	27-128	21	+70.33	Richard Guest	5-15
Paul Mulrennan	25-173	14	-35.54	Alistair Whillans	4-13
Phillip Makin	24-140	17	-12.16	Keith Dalgleish	13-61
Graham Lee	19-148	13	-59.78	Jim Goldie	6-26
David Allan	17-89	19	+37.38	Tim Easterby	8-49
P J McDonald	14-156	9	-50.25	Linda Perratt	3-29
James Sullivan	14-118	12	+8.25	Ruth Carr	7-51
Tony Hamilton	13-81	16	-0.63	Richard Fahey	11-56
Tom Eaves	12-171	7	-70.81	Kevin Ryan	4-25
Fergal Lynch	11-55	20	+38.50	Jim Goldie	6-36
Jason Hart	10-103	10	-47.00	John Quinn	3-20
Daniel Tudhope	10-54	19	+3.95	David O'Meara	6-34

Favourites

2yo	31.8%	-18.14	3yo	40%	+0.57	
					TOTAL 32.6%	-53.67

Newbury, Berkshire, RG14 7NZ
Tel: 01635 400 15 or 01635 550 354

NEWBURY

How to get there
Road: M4 Jct 13
and A34 south.
Rail: Newbury
Racecourse

Features LH,
wide, flat

2018 Fixtures
April 20-21, May
18-19, June 14,
26, July 5, 12, 20-21, 26, August 7,
17-18, September 21-22, October
26-27

Racing Post standard times

5f34yds	59.6	1m1f	1min50
6f8yds	1min10.5	1m2f6yds	2min3
7f	1min22.8	1m3f5yds	2min17
7f64yds	1min28	1m4f4yds	2min30.3
1m	1min35.8	1m5f61yds	2min47.5
1m7yds	1min36.5	2m	3min23.5

Trainers	Wins-Runs	%	2yo	3yo+	£1 level stks
Richard Hannon	45-422	11	25-232	20-190	-123.30
John Gosden	40-171	23	14-52	26-119	+17.00
William Haggas	24-131	18	8-52	16-79	-14.78
Charles Hills	15-161	9	7-76	8-85	-24.38
Ralph Beckett	15-111	14	4-41	11-70	-11.21
Sir Michael Stoute	15-99	15	5-25	10-74	-26.52
Brian Meehan	14-142	10	5-80	9-62	-18.25
Andrew Balding	14-128	11	2-39	12-89	-36.83
Luca Cumani	14-56	25	0-3	14-53	+23.50
Roger Charlton	12-96	13	3-32	9-64	-15.55
Roger Varian	10-86	12	3-28	7-58	-33.75
Eve Johnson Houghton	10-75	13	2-29	8-46	+28.88
Charlie Appleby	10-55	18	3-15	7-40	-15.43

Jockeys	Wins-Rides	%	£1 level stks	Best Trainer	W-R
Frankie Dettori	29-113	26	+33.02	John Gosden	14-46
Ryan Moore	26-146	18	-35.30	Sir Michael Stoute	10-48
Jim Crowley	23-177	13	-23.26	Ralph Beckett	3-14
James Doyle	22-161	14	-47.26	Saeed bin Suroor	3-14
Paul Hanagan	22-111	20	+21.98	John Gosden	4-7
William Buick	22-107	21	+17.66	Charlie Appleby	7-17
Richard Hughes	20-109	18	-22.27	Richard Hannon	11-72
Jamie Spencer	15-107	14	-14.63	Luca Cumani	4-11
Andrea Atzeni	14-117	12	-8.28	Roger Varian	5-32
George Baker	14-95	15	+15.13	Roger Charlton	3-24
Pat Dobbs	13-151	9	-39.25	Richard Hannon	6-73
Adam Kirby	12-157	8	-72.50	Luca Cumani	3-11
Silvestre De Sousa	12-136	9	-49.75	David Evans	2-5

Favourites

2yo	31.3%	-22.38	3yo	28.6%	-32.73	TOTAL 30%	-64.34

NEWCASTLE

High Gosforth Park NE3 5HP
Tel: 0191 236 2020 or 236 5508

How to get there
Road:
Signposted from
A1. Rail:
Newcastle
Central, metro to
Regent Centre or
Four Lane End
and bus

○ **Winning Post**
◁ **Startpoint**
▲ **Highest Point**
▼ **Lowest Point**

Features LH,
Tapeta, easy bends with uphill straight

2018 Fixtures March 27-28, 30, April
19, May 4, June 5, 28-30, July 28,
August 9, 31, September 3, 7, 21, 24,
28, October 3, 9, 17, 19, 23-24,
November 3, 7, 9, 22, 28, 30,
December 15, 19

Racing Post standard times

5f	58	1m4f98yds	2min36.5
6f	1min10.2	2m56yds	3min27
7f	1min24		
1m	1min36.5		
1m2f	2min6		

Trainers	Wins-Runs	%	2yo	3yo+	£1 level stks
Richard Fahey	30-265	11	12-90	18-175	-44.50
Mark Johnston	20-152	13	9-71	11-81	-13.81
Kevin Ryan	18-126	14	5-28	13-98	+4.31
David O'Meara	17-171	10	2-14	15-157	-55.65
Michael Easterby	17-120	14	2-16	15-104	+12.96
Iain Jardine	14-139	10	0-8	14-131	+9.50
Richard Guest	14-128	11	0-14	14-114	-28.68
K R Burke	14-111	13	5-41	9-70	+35.45
James Bethell	14-72	19	1-14	13-58	+26.70
Hugo Palmer	14-55	25	8-28	6-27	+1.03
Jim Goldie	13-133	10	1-4	12-129	-29.13
David Barron	13-111	12	2-12	11-99	-45.15
John Gosden	14-39	36	8-18	6-21	+3.37

Jockeys	Wins-Rides	%	£1 level stks	Best Trainer	W-R
P J McDonald	29-229	13	-20.53	James Bethell	6-25
Luke Morris	25-180	14	-37.33	Sir Mark Prescott	11-35
Josephine Gordon	23-116	20	-11.44	Hugo Palmer	9-31
Joe Fanning	22-155	14	-2.50	Mark Johnston	7-57
Ben Curtis	19-182	10	-11.44	K R Burke	5-17
Phillip Makin	18-135	13	-27.18	David Barron	6-29
Kevin Stott	18-93	19	-9.07	Kevin Ryan	6-35
Paul Mulrennan	17-222	8	-61.95	Michael Dods	5-58
Nathan Evans	16-125	13	-14.88	Michael Easterby	10-53
Paul Hanagan	16-109	15	-29.68	Richard Fahey	9-53
Tom Eaves	15-245	6	-116.59	David Simcock	3-20
Connor Beasley	15-210	7	-113.63	Richard Guest	5-41
Andrew Mullen	15-176	9	-49.42	Tom Tate	6-14

Favourites

2yo	43.4% +7.48	3yo	39.4% +7.94	TOTAL	35.1% -27.34

Westfield House, The Links,
Newmarket, Suffolk. CB8 0TG

NEWMARKET

Rowley Mile

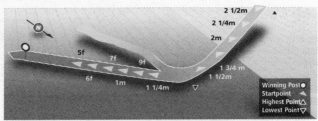

How to get there
Road: from
south M11 Jct
9, then A11,
otherwise A14
and A11. Rail:
Newmarket

Features RH, wide, galloping,
uphill finish

2018 Fixtures April 17-19, May 5-6,
17-19, September 22, 27-29, October
6, 12-13, 24, November 2-3

Racing Post standard times

5f	57.5	1m2f	2min0.5
6f	1min10.1	1m4f	2min28
7f	1min22.5	1m6f	2min53.5
1m	1min35.1	2m	3min19
1m1f	1min47.8	2m2f	3min45

Trainers	Wins-Runs	%	2yo	3yo+	£1 level stks
John Gosden	50-250	20	19-89	31-161	-3.75
Charlie Appleby	39-154	25	14-64	25-90	+58.25
Richard Hannon	34-278	12	13-120	21-158	-20.46
Saeed bin Suroor	26-132	20	11-42	15-90	+11.88
A P O'Brien	24-96	25	13-53	11-43	+35.02
Mark Johnston	21-199	11	13-79	8-120	-30.87
William Haggas	16-157	10	3-68	13-89	-47.47
Sir Michael Stoute	16-142	11	3-43	13-99	-42.00
Roger Varian	13-149	9	5-49	8-100	-56.00
Richard Fahey	12-154	8	3-43	9-111	-58.95
Charles Hills	12-136	9	4-56	8-80	-70.43
Andrew Balding	12-118	10	2-35	10-83	-48.78
Mick Channon	11-82	13	2-34	9-48	-13.88

Jockeys	Wins-Rides	%	£1 level stks	Best Trainer	W-R
Ryan Moore	48-279	17	-66.64	A P O'Brien	19-59
William Buick	44-244	18	+35.35	Charlie Appleby	23-89
Frankie Dettori	38-182	21	+61.18	John Gosden	24-76
James Doyle	26-199	13	-74.03	Saeed bin Suroor	10-44
Andrea Atzeni	23-239	10	-46.59	Roger Varian	7-81
Paul Hanagan	23-197	12	-96.06	John Gosden	6-13
Jim Crowley	22-175	13	-35.30	Martyn Meade	2-3
Silvestre De Sousa	21-156	13	-20.58	Roger Varian	3-5
Adam Kirby	16-141	11	-27.90	Charlie Appleby	5-15
Jamie Spencer	12-141	9	-47.00	Kevin Ryan	4-18
Pat Cosgrave	12-105	11	-40.67	William Haggas	6-39
Joe Fanning	11-148	7	-2.00	Mark Johnston	7-87
Richard Hughes	10-84	12	-21.18	Richard Hannon	6-43

Favourites

2yo	37.8% -13.42	3yo	31.2% -30.40	TOTAL	32.4% -52.96

NEWMARKET

Westfield House, The Links,
Newmarket, Suffolk. CB8 0TG

July Course

How to get there
See previous
page

Features RH,
wide, galloping,
uphill finish

2018 Fixtures
June 9, 22-23,
28-30, July 12-14,
20-21, 27-28,
August 3-4,
10-11, 17-18,
24-25

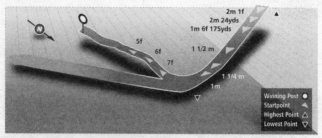

Racing Post standard times

5f	57.2	1m110yds	1min43	1m6f175yds	3min3
6f	1min10.1	1m2f	2min1.5	2m24yds	3min20
7f	1min23	1m4f	2min26.5		
1m	1min36	1m5f	2min40		

Trainers	*Wins-Runs*	%	2yo	3yo+	£1 level stks
Richard Hannon	45-331	14	32-182	13-149	-43.78
Mark Johnston	38-185	21	12-60	26-125	+16.27
Charlie Appleby	35-175	20	23-90	12-85	-34.47
John Gosden	28-167	17	8-60	20-107	+9.46
William Haggas	20-121	17	4-32	16-89	-30.60
Richard Fahey	19-148	13	5-39	14-109	+16.50
Saeed bin Suroor	18-88	20	5-27	13-61	+0.05
Charles Hills	15-138	11	3-46	12-92	-65.92
Ralph Beckett	15-79	19	2-25	13-54	-11.38
Sir Michael Stoute	13-116	11	3-41	10-75	-70.71
Marco Botti	11-76	14	4-25	7-51	+13.54
Andrew Balding	11-71	15	2-17	9-54	+14.35
Chris Wall	10-51	20	0-7	10-44	+14.75

Jockeys	*Wins-Rides*	%	£1 level stks	*Best Trainer*	W-R
James Doyle	43-185	23	+37.74	Charlie Appleby	7-27
William Buick	27-160	17	-40.39	Charlie Appleby	10-58
Ryan Moore	27-131	21	-35.52	A P O'Brien	7-16
Silvestre De Sousa	24-173	14	-71.33	Saeed bin Suroor	6-11
Harry Bentley	24-124	19	+7.41	Ralph Beckett	3-7
Jim Crowley	24-114	21	+18.98	Mark Johnston	4-12
Dane O'Neill	23-137	17	+11.60	Mark Johnston	5-17
Adam Kirby	18-121	15	-36.58	Charlie Appleby	7-14
Frankie Dettori	17-110	15	-31.18	John Gosden	6-25
Paul Hanagan	14-124	11	-42.13	Richard Fahey	3-22
Sean Levey	13-117	11	-35.29	Richard Hannon	12-88
Ted Durcan	13-83	16	+34.50	Chris Wall	5-10
Joe Fanning	13-81	16	-14.63	Mark Johnston	7-47

Favourites

2yo	43.7% +17.01	3yo 34.9% -20.49	TOTAL	37.6% +19.72

HAWKBILL: another July Course winner for James Doyle in the Godolphin blue

NOTTINGHAM

Colwick Park, Nottingham,
NG2 4BE. Tel 0115 958 0620

How to get there
Road: M1 Jct 25,
A52 east to B686,
signs for Trent
Bridge, then
Colwick Park.
Rail:
Nottingham

Features LH, flat,
easy turns

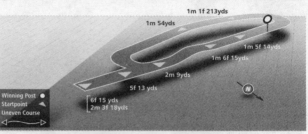

2018 Fixtures April 11, 21,
May 1, 11-12, 22, 30, June
10, 14, 18, 28, July 7, 20,
24, August 2, 7, 14, 17,
October 3, 10, 17, 31

Racing Post standard times

5f13yds	58.4	1m2f50yds (Inner)	2min8.6
5f13yds (Inner)	59.8	1m6f15yds	2min57
6f15yds	1min12.2	2m9yds	3min24
1m75yds	1min42	2m9yds (Inner)	3min32
1m75yds (Inner)	1min43.5	2m2f18yds	3min55
1m2f50yds	2min6		

Trainers	Wins-Runs	%	2yo	3yo+	£1 level stks
Richard Fahey	32-175	18	12-58	20-117	+29.93
Michael Appleby	30-203	15	0-15	30-188	+35.75
Richard Hannon	21-133	16	11-63	10-70	-19.78
John Gosden	21-106	20	9-45	12-61	+10.89
Clive Cox	18-81	22	4-24	14-57	+10.45
Sir Michael Stoute	15-74	20	2-17	13-57	+5.83
Roger Varian	14-85	16	2-32	12-53	-21.03
Mick Channon	13-115	11	7-42	6-73	+23.74
Mark Johnston	13-102	13	9-51	4-51	-40.92
K R Burke	13-71	18	2-11	11-60	+33.00
Ralph Beckett	11-67	16	3-26	8-41	+3.45
James Fanshawe	11-66	17	1-15	10-51	+6.26
Richard Guest	10-98	10	0-10	10-88	-12.50

Jockeys	Wins-Rides	%	£1 level stks	Best Trainer	W-R
Silvestre De Sousa	25-124	20	+20.42	Mick Channon	3-17
Andrew Mullen	21-127	17	+79.00	Michael Appleby	15-82
Paul Hanagan	18-76	24	+11.28	Richard Fahey	9-22
Jim Crowley	18-62	29	+55.38	Sir Michael Stoute	2-2
Adam Kirby	16-88	18	-14.13	Clive Cox	8-30
William Buick	16-51	31	+21.71	John Gosden	5-12
Luke Morris	15-132	11	-9.29	Sir Mark Prescott	3-26
Frederik Tylicki	15-64	23	+23.97	James Fanshawe	5-17
Graham Lee	14-129	11	-34.34	Robert Cowell	2-3
Oisin Murphy	13-87	15	+10.04	Ralph Beckett	3-12
Andrea Atzeni	13-63	21	-1.09	Roger Varian	6-27
James Doyle	12-51	24	-3.57	John Gosden	3-8
Tony Hamilton	11-94	12	+3.50	Richard Fahey	9-58

Favourites

2yo 38.1% -16.02	3yo 33.5% -22.22		TOTAL 33.1% -57.87

33 Ropergate, Pontefract,
WF8 1LE. Tel 01977 703 224

PONTEFRACT

How to get there
Road: M62 Jct
32, then A539.
Rail: Pontefract
Monkhill or
Pontefract Baghill
from Leeds

Features LH,
undulating, sharp
home turn, last
half-mile all uphill

2018 Fixtures April 3, 23, May 2, 25,
June 11, 24, July 2, 10, 20, 29, August
8, 19, September 20, 27, October 8,
22

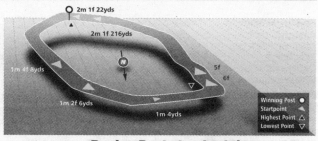

Racing Post standard times

5f	1min1.8	1m4f8yds	2min35.5
6f	1min14.6	2m1f22yds	3min41
1m4yds	1min42.6	2m1f216yds	3min51
1m2f6yds	2min9.4	2m5f122yds	4min41

Trainers	Wins-Runs	%	2yo	3yo+	£1 level stks
Richard Fahey	41-238	17	14-77	27-161	+16.30
Mark Johnston	28-157	18	12-52	16-105	-50.12
Tim Easterby	20-140	14	2-37	18-103	+9.00
David O'Meara	14-125	11	0-10	14-115	-27.75
Kevin Ryan	11-87	13	4-26	7-61	+2.88
Charlie Appleby	11-31	35	4-12	7-19	+0.57
Micky Hammond	10-120	8	1-8	9-112	-30.50
Michael Dods	10-102	10	1-17	9-85	-43.33
Sir Michael Stoute	10-47	21	0-6	10-41	-15.39
Michael Easterby	9-76	12	0-7	9-69	-17.42
Mick Channon	9-46	20	5-19	4-27	+28.75
Richard Whitaker	9-44	20	2-6	7-38	+12.83
David Barron	8-43	19	2-7	6-36	-1.25

Jockeys	Wins-Rides	%	£1 level stks	Best Trainer	W-R
Silvestre De Sousa	27-129	21	-27.06	Mark Johnston	11-36
Graham Lee	22-186	12	-13.00	Jedd O'Keeffe	4-16
Tony Hamilton	18-127	14	-40.34	Richard Fahey	18-90
David Allan	18-100	18	+60.00	Tim Easterby	12-65
Paul Mulrennan	17-148	11	-35.33	Michael Dods	8-50
P J McDonald	16-147	11	-37.26	Micky Hammond	4-51
Daniel Tudhope	16-114	14	-19.50	David O'Meara	10-64
Franny Norton	15-93	16	-9.00	Mark Johnston	11-58
Paul Hanagan	13-74	18	+8.08	Richard Fahey	6-36
Graham Gibbons	12-92	13	-32.05	David Barron	4-26
Phillip Makin	11-69	16	-13.68	Charlie Appleby	3-7
Richard Kingscote	11-58	19	+1.94	Tom Dascombe	5-30
Ben Curtis	10-81	12	-8.67	Alan Swinbank	3-18

Favourites

2yo	41.3%	+6.88		3yo	34.9%	-17.74		TOTAL	33.5%	-25.90

REDCAR

Redcar, Teesside,
TS10 2BY. Tel 01642 484 068

How to get there
Road: A1, A168,
A19, then A174.
Rail: Redcar
Central from
Darlington

Features LH, flat,
galloping

2018 Fixtures
April 2, 16, May 3,
21, 28-29, June 22-23, July 22, August
1, 11, 25, September 18, 26, October
6, 19, 29, November 6

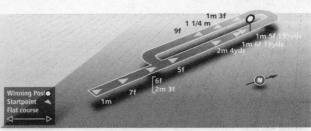

Racing Post standard times

5f	57	1m3f	2min16
6f	1min9.5	1m5f135yds	2min51
7f	1min22	1m6f19yds	2min57.5
1m	1min35	2m4yds	3min22
1m1f	1min48	2m3f	4min8
1m2f	2min3		

Trainers	Wins-Runs	%	2yo	3yo+	£1 level stks
Richard Fahey	44-263	17	20-122	24-141	+3.28
David O'Meara	34-205	17	7-42	27-163	+1.23
Michael Dods	23-169	14	6-55	17-114	-19.09
Tim Easterby	21-324	6	2-98	19-226	-163.17
Kevin Ryan	17-128	13	8-52	9-76	-49.53
Mark Johnston	16-101	16	5-38	11-63	-9.80
David Barron	13-87	15	3-19	10-68	+49.63
Ruth Carr	12-135	9	0-3	12-132	-53.00
Michael Easterby	10-125	8	0-30	10-95	-58.50
William Haggas	10-22	45	4-11	6-11	+4.70
John Quinn	9-93	10	2-44	7-49	-59.99
Brian Ellison	8-111	7	0-13	8-98	-79.04
Nigel Tinkler	8-96	8	1-28	7-68	+1.33

Jockeys	Wins-Rides	%	£1 level stks	Best Trainer	W-R
Graham Lee	29-190	15	-34.30	Paul Midgley	5-25
Paul Mulrennan	28-221	13	-85.29	Michael Dods	11-62
Daniel Tudhope	26-119	22	+48.48	David O'Meara	16-72
Tony Hamilton	25-155	16	-26.99	Richard Fahey	23-93
David Allan	24-236	10	-17.04	Tim Easterby	13-128
Phillip Makin	19-145	13	-45.64	David O'Meara	4-17
Graham Gibbons	17-104	16	+31.93	David Barron	5-27
Jason Hart	16-126	13	-16.14	John Quinn	4-14
P J McDonald	13-189	7	-96.25	Ann Duffield	3-44
Ben Curtis	13-136	10	-75.85	William Haggas	3-3
Joe Fanning	13-81	16	+9.75	Mark Johnston	5-31
Paul Hanagan	12-64	19	-10.80	Richard Fahey	5-31
Tom Eaves	11-172	6	-91.03	Kevin Ryan	4-23

Favourites

2yo	38.6%	-6.09	3yo	34.5%	-4.31	TOTAL	34.6%	+6.10

77 North Street, Ripon, N Yorkshire
HG4 1DS. Tel 01765 602 156 or 01765 603 696

RIPON

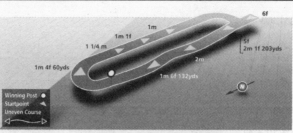

How to get there
Road: A1, then B6265. Rail: Harrogate, bus to Ripon centre, 1m walk

Features RH, sharp

2018 Fixtures
April 19, 28, May 11, 20, 30, June 7, 20-21, July 9, 16, 21, August 6, 13, 18, 27-28, September 29

Racing Post standard times

5f	58	1m2f	2min4.5
6f	1min10.3	1m4f10yds	2min33.4
1m	1min38.1	2m	3min26.5
1m1f	1min52	2m1f203yds	3min53
1m1f170yds	2min1.3		

Trainers	Wins-Runs	%	2yo	3yo+	£1 level stks
Tim Easterby	33-319	10	6-88	27-231	-71.06
David O'Meara	31-225	14	3-26	28-199	-42.31
Richard Fahey	30-270	11	9-82	21-188	-113.34
Mark Johnston	29-176	16	13-55	16-121	-0.13
William Haggas	17-39	44	3-10	14-29	+10.35
Richard Whitaker	11-69	16	1-8	10-61	+35.25
Ann Duffield	10-76	13	8-38	2-38	-8.21
Paul Midgley	10-66	15	2-13	8-53	+8.38
Kevin Ryan	9-99	9	1-20	8-79	-36.00
David Barron	9-96	9	2-10	7-86	-37.40
Micky Hammond	9-92	10	0-6	9-86	+15.00
Ruth Carr	9-80	11	0-0	9-80	+34.75
Roger Varian	9-35	26	1-7	8-28	-9.51

Jockeys	Wins-Rides	%	£1 level stks	Best Trainer	W-R
David Allan	26-194	13	-34.25	Tim Easterby	19-156
Daniel Tudhope	26-119	22	+2.83	David O'Meara	17-86
Paul Mulrennan	25-129	19	+5.73	Paul Midgley	4-15
P J McDonald	20-162	12	-22.58	Ann Duffield	7-42
Tony Hamilton	19-127	15	-19.77	Richard Fahey	14-94
Silvestre De Sousa	19-55	35	+16.49	Mark Johnston	6-14
Graham Lee	17-110	15	-1.57	William Haggas	3-3
Franny Norton	17-98	17	+10.67	Mark Johnston	13-69
Phillip Makin	13-115	11	-32.00	Keith Dalgleish	6-25
Graham Gibbons	12-94	13	-36.72	William Haggas	5-9
Jason Hart	11-79	14	-2.67	John Quinn	3-20
George Chaloner	9-78	12	-22.75	Richard Whitaker	7-34
Rachel Richardson	9-70	13	+6.88	Tim Easterby	9-60

Favourites

2yo	37.9%	-8.88	3yo	40.5% +7.65	TOTAL	35.9% -2.40

SALISBURY

Netherhampton, Salisbury, Wilts
SP2 8PN. Tel 01722 326 461

How to get there
Road: 2m west
of Salisbury on
A3094. Rail:
Salisbury, bus

Features RH,
uphill finish

2018 Fixtures
April 29-30, May
17, 26, June 12,
17, 27, July 14, 28, August 15-16, 24,
September 6, 11, 14, October 3

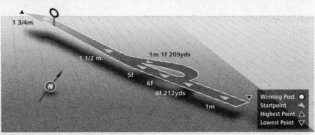

Racing Post standard times

5f	59.8	1m1f198yds	2min5.8
6f	1min12.3	1m4f	2min33
6f212yds	1min26.5	1m6f21yds	3min
1m	1min39.5		

Trainers	Wins-Runs	%	2yo	3yo+	£1 level stks
Richard Hannon	49-330	15	32-163	17-167	-17.29
Andrew Balding	22-140	16	7-39	15-101	-41.45
Ralph Beckett	20-122	16	6-47	14-75	-12.21
Clive Cox	16-92	17	6-32	10-60	-13.90
Rod Millman	11-120	9	6-43	5-77	-28.95
Roger Charlton	11-59	19	3-19	8-40	-24.16
Roger Varian	11-52	21	2-10	9-42	+10.06
John Gosden	11-34	32	2-7	9-27	+32.89
David Evans	10-96	10	6-47	4-49	+12.66
Charles Hills	10-77	13	0-29	10-48	-34.27
Sir Michael Stoute	10-68	15	1-18	9-50	-20.99
Eve Johnson Houghton	9-70	13	3-32	6-38	-6.69
William Haggas	9-37	24	1-13	8-24	-7.03

Jockeys	Wins-Rides	%	£1 level stks	Best Trainer	W-R
Pat Dobbs	20-148	14	-34.38	Richard Hannon	11-68
Jim Crowley	18-126	14	+37.54	Harry Dunlop	2-4
Oisin Murphy	15-129	12	+2.13	Ralph Beckett	3-9
Tom Marquand	14-97	14	+30.54	Richard Hannon	6-37
Richard Hughes	13-77	17	-22.20	Richard Hannon	8-44
David Probert	12-95	13	-42.45	Andrew Balding	9-53
Andrea Atzeni	12-52	23	+9.39	Roger Varian	3-14
Dane O'Neill	11-88	13	+3.95	Henry Candy	3-21
Sean Levey	11-84	13	-26.13	Richard Hannon	11-72
George Baker	11-58	19	+11.13	Ed Walker	3-8
Ryan Moore	11-52	21	-21.23	Sir Michael Stoute	4-19
Paul Hanagan	11-46	24	+0.48	David Loughnane	2-2
James Doyle	11-44	25	+4.92	Roger Charlton	3-7

Favourites

2yo	35.2%	-23.73		3yo	32.2%	-25.54		TOTAL	34%	-43.08

Esher, Surrey, KT10 9AJ.
Tel 01372 463 072 or 01372 464 348

SANDOWN

How to get there
Road: M25 Jct 10
then A3. Rail:
Esher from
Waterloo

Features RH, last
7f uphill

2018 Fixtures
April 27, May 24,
June 7, 15-16,
July 6-7, 25-26, August 1, 9, 31,
September 1, 14, 19

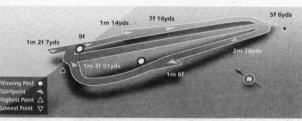

Racing Post standard times

5f6yds	59.8	1m2f7yds	2min5.8
7f16yds	1min27	1m3f91yds	2min23
1m14yds	1min39.9	1m6f	2min58.3
1m1f	1min52.9	2m78yds	3min34

Trainers	Wins-Runs	%	2yo	3yo+	£1 level stks
Richard Hannon	32-241	13	16-98	16-143	-29.00
John Gosden	26-121	21	6-29	20-92	+2.81
Sir Michael Stoute	26-108	24	2-17	24-91	+8.19
Clive Cox	15-89	17	3-20	12-69	+23.40
Roger Varian	15-62	24	1-13	14-49	-4.38
Roger Charlton	13-57	23	2-13	11-44	-8.27
William Haggas	13-54	24	4-12	9-42	+5.26
Andrew Balding	12-135	9	2-35	10-100	-29.68
Mark Johnston	12-89	13	7-27	5-62	-39.54
Charlie Appleby	10-60	17	6-22	4-38	-8.32
Brian Meehan	9-62	15	2-22	7-40	-12.77
Ralph Beckett	8-67	12	1-13	7-54	-19.55
Charles Hills	8-64	13	3-18	5-46	-9.00

Jockeys	Wins-Rides	%	£1 level stks	Best Trainer	W-R
Ryan Moore	39-178	22	+5.05	Sir Michael Stoute	17-57
James Doyle	23-128	18	-34.88	Roger Charlton	4-11
William Buick	21-122	17	-24.99	John Gosden	7-32
Andrea Atzeni	21-104	20	-23.70	Roger Varian	7-21
Jim Crowley	19-145	13	+3.10	David Menuisier	2-3
Oisin Murphy	16-119	13	-4.88	Joseph Tuite	3-4
Silvestre De Sousa	16-85	19	-8.57	Mark Johnston	5-17
Richard Hughes	15-68	22	+4.10	Richard Hannon	9-43
Frankie Dettori	13-75	17	-14.65	John Gosden	4-31
Adam Kirby	12-114	11	-59.96	Clive Cox	6-35
George Baker	11-53	21	-3.84	Roger Charlton	3-5
Dane O'Neill	10-70	14	-27.42	John Gosden	3-7
Pat Dobbs	8-106	8	-32.42	Richard Hannon	5-54

Favourites

2yo	42.5% -1.71	3yo	38% +4.44	TOTAL	38.2% +6.89

SOUTHWELL

Rolleston, Newark, Notts
NG25 0TS. Tel 01636 814 481

How to get there Road: A1 to Newark, then A617 or M1 to Nottingham, then A612. Rail: Rolleston

Features LH, Fibresand, sharp

Please note there are no turf fixtures scheduled for 2017 Stats relate to all-weather only

2018 Fixtures March 27, April 1, 4, 12, 30, May 3, August 27, November 12, 15, 27, 30, December 11, 18, 20-21, 29

Inside Lane: Turf Course
Outside Lane: All Weather
Winning Post ●
Startpoint ▲
Flat Course

Racing Post standard times

5f	58	1m4f	2min35
6f	1min14	1m5f	2min50.5
7f	1min27	1m6f	3min2
1m	1min39.8	2m	3min34
1m3f	2min22.3	2m2f	4min4

Trainers	Wins-Runs	%	2yo	3yo+	£1 level stks
Michael Appleby	97-601	16	1-31	96-570	-143.60
Scott Dixon	42-434	10	2-40	40-394	+29.15
Derek Shaw	30-214	14	0-4	30-210	+57.05
Richard Fahey	30-159	19	8-34	22-125	-18.49
David Evans	27-175	15	3-26	24-149	-2.46
Andrew Balding	26-89	30	2-7	24-82	+1.03
Roy Bowring	22-157	14	0-2	22-155	-3.40
Conor Dore	22-150	15	2-4	20-146	+4.63
Keith Dalgleish	20-130	15	1-11	19-119	-11.12
K R Burke	20-95	21	3-16	17-79	+69.29
J R Jenkins	19-208	9	0-2	19-206	-0.90
Mark Johnston	19-112	17	3-20	16-92	-30.79
John Balding	17-138	12	0-1	17-137	-17.75

Jockeys	Wins-Rides	%	£1 level stks	Best Trainer	W-R
Luke Morris	53-371	14	-135.72	Scott Dixon	12-78
Andrew Mullen	46-349	13	-127.25	Michael Appleby	30-205
Ben Curtis	40-257	16	+51.46	Alan McCabe	6-23
Alistair Rawlinson	34-192	18	-0.47	Michael Appleby	28-150
Tom Eaves	30-286	10	-27.43	Keith Dalgleish	10-30
Joe Fanning	29-228	13	-87.28	Mark Johnston	14-66
Tony Hamilton	25-173	14	+29.80	Richard Fahey	10-60
Daniel Tudhope	25-130	19	-12.71	David O'Meara	10-49
Robert Winston	23-131	18	+3.74	Marjorie Fife	4-16
Paul Mulrennan	20-171	12	-48.62	Conor Dore	7-35
J F Egan	20-112	18	+9.08	David Evans	9-44
Graham Lee	18-133	14	-26.21	James Given	3-18
Silvestre De Sousa	18-83	22	+9.55	Chris Dwyer	5-17

Favourites

2yo	32.4% -25.23	3yo	39.3% -26.07	TOTAL	36.4% -101.44

Station Road, Thirsk, N Yorkshire,
YO7 1QL. Tel 01845 522 276

THIRSK

How to get there
Road: A61 from
A1 in the west
or A19 in the
east. Rail: Thirsk,
10min walk

Features LH,
sharp, tight turns

2018 Fixtures
April 21, 30, May
5, 12, 19, June 12, 19, July 4, 17, 27,
August 3-4, 14, 20, 31, September 8

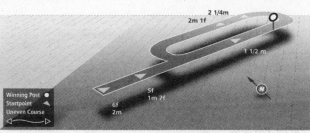

Racing Post standard times

5f	58	1m	1min36.5
6f	1min10.6	1m4f	2min32
7f	1min24	2m	3min23

Trainers	Wins-Runs	%	2yo	3yo+	£1 level stks
Richard Fahey	40-241	17	13-91	27-150	-2.38
David O'Meara	24-182	13	5-27	19-155	-38.09
Tim Easterby	23-279	8	5-89	18-190	-58.48
Michael Dods	22-183	12	4-39	18-144	-15.63
Kevin Ryan	20-168	12	8-45	12-123	-29.46
Ruth Carr	13-144	9	0-3	13-141	-25.30
Michael Easterby	10-120	8	0-25	10-95	-43.25
Brian Ellison	10-100	10	1-17	9-83	+4.00
John Quinn	10-76	13	3-26	7-50	-4.05
Michael Appleby	9-49	18	1-3	8-46	+111.25
Paul Midgley	8-74	11	0-12	8-62	-18.50
Alan Swinbank	8-57	14	0-2	8-55	+7.63
Keith Dalgleish	8-44	18	4-18	4-26	+1.75

Jockeys	Wins-Rides	%	£1 level stks	Best Trainer	W-R
Paul Mulrennan	34-210	16	+27.16	Michael Dods	13-88
David Allan	23-185	12	-24.60	Tim Easterby	9-106
Daniel Tudhope	20-113	18	-24.47	David O'Meara	15-72
Tony Hamilton	17-166	10	-56.21	Richard Fahey	15-100
Tom Eaves	17-166	10	+3.32	Kevin Ryan	3-30
Ben Curtis	17-128	13	+8.75	Alan Swinbank	5-27
Graham Gibbons	17-110	15	-27.85	Ralph Beckett	3-3
Graham Lee	16-161	10	-62.81	Mick Channon	2-7
P J McDonald	14-190	7	-63.05	Ann Duffield	4-30
Phillip Makin	14-116	12	-38.83	Sir Michael Stoute	2-2
Jason Hart	13-106	12	+14.48	John Quinn	4-22
James Sullivan	12-189	6	-60.80	Ruth Carr	9-113
Connor Beasley	10-112	9	-38.10	Bryan Smart	3-18

Favourites

2yo	44.2% +6.95	3yo	35.4% -22.34	TOTAL	35.9% +1.78

WETHERBY

York Road, Wetherby, West Yorks
L22 5EJ. Tel: 01937 582 035

How to get there Road: A1, A58 from Leeds, B1224 from York. Rail: Leeds, Harrogate, York.

Features LH, 1m4f circuit

2018 Fixtures April 29, May 8, June 6, 22

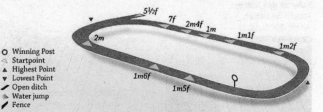

O Winning Post
⌐ Startpoint
▲ Highest Point
▼ Lowest Point
✒ Open ditch
🔥 Water jump
✏ Fence

Racing Post standard times
Insufficient data

Trainers	Wins-Runs	%	2yo	3yo+	£1 level stks
Richard Fahey	4-19	21	2-6	2-13	+1.25
Tim Easterby	3-20	15	0-3	3-17	+0.80
David O'Meara	3-18	17	0-3	3-15	+46.50
Ruth Carr	2-15	13	0-0	2-15	-2.50
Kevin Ryan	2-15	13	1-2	1-13	+23.00
Michael Dods	2-14	14	0-2	2-12	+3.00
Mark Johnston	2-10	20	1-4	1-6	+3.10
Tony Coyle	2-10	20	0-1	2-9	+3.50
Roger Fell	2-8	25	0-1	2-7	+3.00
Eric Alston	2-6	33	0-0	2-6	+17.00
David Loughnane	2-3	67	0-0	2-3	+43.00
George Margarson	2-3	67	1-1	1-2	+18.00
David Brown	2-2	100	0-0	2-2	+26.00

Jockeys	Wins-Rides	%	£1 level stks	Best Trainer	W-R
P J McDonald	6-29	21	+42.50	David Loughnane	2-2
Tony Hamilton	5-26	19	-0.50	Roger Fell	2-8
Paul Mulrennan	5-22	23	+9.10	John Mackie	1-1
David Allan	4-24	17	+2.55	Alan Swinbank	1-1
Phillip Makin	4-19	21	+9.00	David O'Meara	2-4
Tom Eaves	3-24	13	+38.00	David Brown	2-2
Joe Fanning	3-20	15	+21.00	George Margarson	1-1
James Sullivan	3-19	16	+10.50	Ruth Carr	2-10
Daniel Tudhope	3-9	33	+58.50	Luca Cumani	1-1
Barry McHugh	2-18	11	-4.50	Tony Coyle	2-8
Ben Curtis	2-17	12	-4.00	Tom Dascombe	1-2
Paul Hanagan	2-14	14	-6.83	William Haggas	1-2
Cam Hardie	2-7	29	+5.88	John Quinn	1-1

Favourites

2yo	50%	+2.73	3yo	29.6%	-6.28	TOTAL	29.4%	-6.48

WINDSOR

Maidenhead Road, Windsor, Berks
SL4 5JJ. Tel 01753 498 400

How to get there
Road: M4 Jctn 6,
A355, A308. Rail:
Paddington to
Windsor Central/
Waterloo to Wind-
sor Riverside

Features Figure
of eight, flat, long
straight

1m 3f 135yds
1m 2f 7yds
1m 67yds
5f 10yds
5f 217yds

Winning Post
Startpoint
Flat Course

2018 Fixtures April 16, 23, 30, May 7,
14, 21, 28, June 4, 11, 18, 25, 30, July
1-2, 9, 16, 23, 30, August 6, 12-13, 20,
25, September 3, October 8, 15, 22

Racing Post standard times

5f10yds	59.2	1m2f7yds	2min5
6f	1min10.5	1m3f135yds	2min25
1m67yds	1min41.1		

Trainers	Wins-Runs	%	2yo	3yo+	£1 level stks
Richard Hannon	49-327	15	27-143	22-184	-85.69
Clive Cox	32-139	23	11-34	21-105	+19.24
Roger Varian	30-90	33	1-13	29-77	+32.42
David Evans	23-192	12	13-83	10-109	-59.18
Ralph Beckett	22-105	21	5-28	17-77	-4.79
Henry Candy	21-104	20	5-20	16-84	+22.25
Andrew Balding	18-128	14	7-21	11-107	-47.85
Roger Charlton	17-83	20	2-24	15-59	+2.81
Charles Hills	16-107	15	6-42	10-65	-3.25
Ed Walker	16-73	22	3-24	13-49	-1.63
Saeed bin Suroor	14-36	39	3-8	11-28	+8.08
Gary Moore	13-113	12	1-15	12-98	+11.45
John Gosden	13-63	21	3-7	10-56	-23.91

Jockeys	Wins-Rides	%	£1 level stks	Best Trainer	W-R
Adam Kirby	43-213	20	+4.15	Clive Cox	21-71
Andrea Atzeni	30-118	25	+23.04	Roger Varian	14-44
George Baker	27-138	20	+6.52	Ed Walker	5-11
Jamie Spencer	27-134	20	+17.14	Ed Walker	5-12
Jim Crowley	25-173	14	-60.31	Ralph Beckett	6-19
James Doyle	25-132	19	-28.43	Saeed bin Suroor	7-15
Ryan Moore	25-83	30	-5.51	Richard Hannon	6-14
David Probert	23-196	12	-26.18	Andrew Balding	10-66
Oisin Murphy	21-164	13	-40.37	Andrew Balding	6-33
Richard Hughes	20-134	15	-77.80	Richard Hannon	13-70
Harry Bentley	17-66	26	+39.67	Roger Varian	3-8
Pat Cosgrave	16-134	12	-47.91	William Haggas	8-31
Pat Dobbs	16-101	16	-32.29	Ralph Beckett	5-20

Favourites

2yo	51.6%	+16.55	3yo	40%	-3.10	
				TOTAL	40.1%	+1.78

WOLVES

Dunstall Park, Gorsebrook Road, Wolverhampton, West Midlands. WV6 0PE. Tel 08702 202 442

How to get there
Road: A449, close to M6, M42 and M54. Rail: Wolverhampton

Features LH, sharp, relaid with Tapeta in 2014

2018 Fixtures
yyyyy

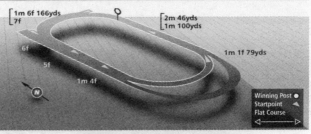

Racing Post standard times

5f20yds	1min0.5	1m1f103yds	1min57.3
5f216yds	1min13.2	1m4f50yds	2min35.3
7f32yds	1min27	1m5f194yds	2min58.5
1m141yds	1min46.7	2m119yds	3min36

Trainers	Wins-Runs	%	2yo	3yo+	£1 level stks
Mark Johnston	71-394	18	13-96	58-298	-75.03
David Evans	68-590	12	12-125	56-465	-155.20
Richard Fahey	62-495	13	8-142	54-353	-56.93
Michael Appleby	55-472	12	0-12	55-460	-125.45
Charlie Appleby	52-156	33	14-58	38-98	-19.58
Daniel Mark Loughnane	49-562	9	0-42	49-520	-157.90
Jamie Osborne	47-296	16	15-92	32-204	-70.49
John Gosden	46-135	34	24-64	22-71	+1.89
Tony Carroll	45-442	10	1-15	44-427	-119.56
Marco Botti	44-253	17	13-72	31-181	-3.31
Tom Dascombe	42-337	12	11-108	31-229	-79.78
David O'Meara	39-354	11	0-40	39-314	-82.89
James Tate	34-204	17	4-45	30-159	-40.42

Jockeys	Wins-Rides	%	£1 level stks	Best Trainer	W-R
Luke Morris	164-1106	15	-193.51	Sir Mark Prescott	24-127
Adam Kirby	127-607	21	-84.64	Charlie Appleby	15-41
Joe Fanning	85-565	15	-83.25	Mark Johnston	39-205
Richard Kingscote	66-394	17	-5.61	Tom Dascombe	30-194
Martin Harley	56-351	16	+11.36	Marco Botti	12-41
Silvestre De Sousa	47-222	21	-22.94	Chris Dwyer	6-18
Stevie Donohoe	46-405	11	-54.13	Ian Williams	16-102
Pat Cosgrave	46-225	20	+50.28	George Baker	9-29
Graham Gibbons	45-334	13	+6.48	Michael Easterby	12-50
George Baker	44-251	18	-84.81	David Lanigan	7-17
Tom Eaves	42-481	9	-115.84	James Given	11-72
Tony Hamilton	42-311	14	-75.63	Richard Fahey	30-195
Robert Winston	41-254	16	-45.96	Dean Ivory	14-60

Favourites

2yo	39%	-35.99	3yo	40.8%	-17.44	TOTAL	37.4% -101.51

North Denes, Great Yarmouth, Norfolk
NR30 4AU. Tel 01493 842 527

YARMOUTH

How to get there
Road: A47 to
end, A1064. Rail:
Great Yarmouth,
bus

Features LH, flat

2018 Fixtures
yyyyy

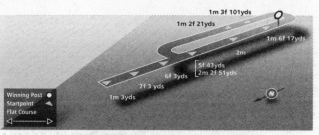

Racing Post standard times

5f43yds	1min0.5	1m2f21yds	2min5
6f3yds	1min11	1m3f101yds	2min23.5
7f3yds	1min23.6	1m6f17yds	2min59
1m3yds	1min36.5	2m	3min24.5
1m1f	1min50	2m2f51yds	3min56

Trainers	*Wins-Runs*	%	*2yo*	*3yo+*	*£1 level stks*
William Haggas	28-97	29	9-41	19-56	+11.32
David Simcock	22-72	31	4-11	18-61	+64.25
Roger Varian	19-72	26	8-25	11-47	+4.73
John Gosden	14-47	30	6-23	8-24	+19.71
Chris Wall	13-64	20	1-10	12-54	-13.29
Sir Michael Stoute	12-54	22	4-25	8-29	-14.24
Luca Cumani	11-54	20	2-14	9-40	+17.32
Mark Johnston	11-53	21	3-14	8-39	+65.77
Chris Dwyer	10-70	14	2-13	8-57	-4.88
James Tate	10-58	17	3-14	7-44	-19.23
John Ryan	9-75	12	1-16	8-59	-13.45
Michael Bell	9-73	12	3-27	6-46	-16.77
Marco Botti	9-63	14	2-21	7-42	-19.23

Jockeys	*Wins-Rides*	%	*£1 level stks*	*Best Trainer*	*W-R*
Silvestre De Sousa	30-133	23	+13.49	Chris Dwyer	6-30
Andrea Atzeni	29-99	29	+6.81	Roger Varian	10-33
Jamie Spencer	26-133	20	+11.57	David Simcock	8-23
Ryan Moore	25-84	30	-10.51	William Haggas	5-16
Martin Harley	16-108	15	-27.03	David Simcock	3-5
Frankie Dettori	13-28	46	+24.65	John Gosden	4-7
Luke Morris	12-137	9	-81.50	Sir Mark Prescott	3-28
Pat Cosgrave	12-81	15	-32.30	William Haggas	6-28
Ted Durcan	11-82	13	-28.47	Chris Wall	7-28
Stevie Donohoe	11-72	15	+9.75	Charlie Fellowes	7-21
Jim Crowley	11-43	26	-4.53	Owen Burrows	4-8
Paul Hanagan	10-53	19	-6.02	Roger Varian	3-5
James Doyle	10-39	26	+5.03	Sir Michael Stoute	2-3

Favourites

2yo	51.7% +12.38	3yo	44.9% +47.47	4yo+	32% -35.04

YORK

Knavesmire Road, York, YO23 1EX
Tel 01904 620 911

How to get there
Road: Course
is south of city.
From north, A1,
A59 to York,
northern bypass
from A19 to A64.
Otherwise, A64.
Rail: York, bus

Features LH, flat

2018 Fixtures yyyyy

Racing Post standard times

5f	57.5	1m208yds	1min49
5f89yds	1min2.7	1m2f88yds	2min7
6f	1min10	1m4f	2min28.1
7f	1min22.3	1m6f	2min57
1m	1min37	2m88yds	3min29

Trainers	Wins-Runs	%	2yo	3yo+	£1 level stks
William Haggas	31-154	20	12-45	19-109	+24.30
David O'Meara	30-354	8	0-24	30-330	-68.75
Richard Fahey	28-508	6	14-166	14-342	-213.50
Kevin Ryan	21-222	9	11-83	10-139	-56.40
Tim Easterby	18-270	7	3-48	15-222	-84.00
Sir Michael Stoute	18-89	20	2-4	16-85	+9.83
Mark Johnston	17-214	8	10-91	7-123	-43.99
John Gosden	12-63	19	0-3	12-60	-12.30
Saeed bin Suroor	11-65	17	2-8	9-57	-0.34
Michael Dods	11-64	17	0-5	11-59	+18.08
Charlie Appleby	11-58	19	5-12	6-46	-11.70
Brian Ellison	10-140	7	0-16	10-124	-12.25
Roger Varian	10-76	13	1-13	9-63	-31.65

Jockeys	Wins-Rides	%	£1 level stks	Best Trainer	W-R
Daniel Tudhope	21-186	11	-14.00	David O'Meara	13-136
Andrea Atzeni	18-124	15	+7.13	Roger Varian	7-34
James Doyle	18-113	16	-14.57	Saeed bin Suroor	5-17
Paul Hanagan	16-179	9	-54.75	Richard Fahey	7-79
Phillip Makin	15-140	11	+0.96	David O'Meara	5-34
Frankie Dettori	15-86	17	-13.97	John Gosden	8-24
P J McDonald	13-112	12	+73.25	Micky Hammond	3-11
William Buick	13-97	13	+7.43	Charlie Appleby	6-25
Paul Mulrennan	12-148	8	-22.67	Michael Dods	6-36
Ryan Moore	12-114	11	-29.28	Sir Michael Stoute	4-29
Jim Crowley	12-97	12	+41.75	Sir Michael Stoute	3-9
Graham Gibbons	11-114	10	-35.01	David Barron	3-38
Silvestre De Sousa	10-123	8	+1.88	Mark Johnston	4-33

Favourites

2yo	28.7%	-26.11		3yo	34.6%	+14.92		TOTAL	28.9%	-23.61

WILLIAM HAGGAS: the Newmarket trainer loves going back to his roots at York

Win – free form!

THIS YEAR'S QUIZ could hardly be more simple, and the prize should prove invaluable to our lucky winner. We're offering a free subscription to The Flat Form Book, the BHA's official form book – every week from May to November, you could be getting the previous week's results in full, together with notebook comments highlighting future winners, adjusted Official Ratings and Racing Post Ratings. The winner will also get a copy of last year's complete form book.

All you have to do is this: identify the three horses pictured on the following pages. And the clue is that all three were Group 1-winning three-year-old fillies for Aidan O'Brien in Britain last season. If you think you know the answer, write their names in the box below in the order in which they appear.

Send your answers along with your details on the entry form below, to:

2018 Flat Annual Competition, Racing & Football Outlook, Floor 7, Vivo Building, South Bank Central, 30 Stamford Street, London, SE1 9LS. Entries must reach us no later than first post on May 3. The winner's name and the right answers will be printed in the RFO's May 8 edition.

Six runners-up will each receive a copy of last year's form book.

Name..

Address..

....

Town...

Postcode..

In the event of more than one correct entry, the winner will be drawn at random from the correct entries. The Editor's decision is final and no correspondence will be entered into.

BETTING CHART

ON	ODDS	AGAINST
50	Evens	50
52.4	11-10	47.6
54.5	6-5	45.5
55.6	5-4	44.4
58	11-8	42
60	6-4	40
62	13-8	38
63.6	7-4	36.4
65.3	15-8	34.7
66.7	2-1	33.3
68	85-40	32
69.2	9-4	30.8
71.4	5-2	28.6
73.4	11-4	26.6
75	3-1	25
76.9	100-30	23.1
77.8	7-2	22.2
80	4-1	20
82	9-2	18
83.3	5-1	16.7
84.6	11-2	15.4
85.7	6-1	14.3
86.7	13-2	13.3
87.5	7-1	12.5
88.2	15-2	11.8
89	8-1	11
89.35	100-12	10.65
89.4	17-2	10.6
90	9-1	10
91	10-1	9
91.8	11-1	8.2
92.6	12-1	7.4
93.5	14-1	6.5
94.4	16-1	5.6
94.7	18-1	5.3
95.2	20-1	4.8
95.7	22-1	4.3
96.2	25-1	3.8
97.2	33-1	2.8
97.6	40-1	2.4
98.1	50-1	1.9
98.5	66-1	1.3
99.0	100-1	0.99

The table above (often known as the 'Field Money Table') shows both bookmakers' margins and how much a backer needs to invest to win £100. To calculate a bookmaker's margin, simply add up the percentages of all the odds on offer. The sum by which the total exceeds 100% gives the 'over-round' on the book. To determine what stake is required to win £100 (includes returned stake) at a particular price, just look at the relevant row, either odds-against or odds-on.

RULE 4 DEDUCTIONS

When a horse is withdrawn before coming under starter's orders, but after a market has been formed, bookmakers are entitled to make the following deductions from win and place returns (excluding stakes) in accordance with Tattersalls' Rule 4(c).

	Odds of withdrawn horse	*Deduction from winnings*
(1)	3-10 or shorter	75p in the £
(2)	2-5 to 1-3	70p in the £
(3)	8-15 to 4-9	65p in the £
(4)	8-13 to 4-7	60p in the £
(5)	4-5 to 4-6	55p in the £
(6)	20-21 to 5-6	50p in the £
(7)	Evens to 6-5	45p in the £
(8)	5-4 to 6-4	40p in the £
(9)	13-8 to 7-4	35p in the £
(10)	15-8 to 9-4	30p in the £
(11)	5-2 to 3-1	25p in the £
(12)	100-30 to 4-1	20p in the £
(13)	9-2 to 11-2	15p in the £
(14)	6-1 to 9-1	10p in the £
(15)	10-1 to 14-1	5p in the £
(16)	longer than 14-1	no deductions

(17) .... When more than one horse is withdrawn without coming under starter's orders, total deductions shall not exceed 75p in the £.

Starting-price bets are affected only when there was insufficient time to form a new market.

Feedback!

If you have any comments or criticism about this book, or suggestions for future editions, please tell us.

Write
Nick Watts/Dylan Hill
2018 Flat Annual
Racing & Football Outlook
Floor 7, Vivo Building, South Bank Central
30 Stamford Street
London SE1 9LS

email
rfo@rfoutlook.com

Horse index

All horses discussed, with page numbers, except for references in the Group 1 and two-year-old form sections (pages 80-111), which have their own indexes

Accidental Agent................................55
Aeolus 54
Al Muffrih 44
Aljazzi 45
Alpha Centauri 25, 51
Altyn Orda...................................27, 45
Amazing Red......................................35
Amedeo Modigliani 23, 28, 48
Arch Villain 35
Arthenia...53
Artieshow...45
Atkinson Grimshaw.............................8
Atty Persse 62
Balgair 46
Barraquero 23, 62
Bartholomeu Dias 53
Battaash 35, 52, 78
Battle Of Jericho...............................36
Beat The Bank...................................64
Bernardo O'Reilly..............................14
Big Country 67, 70
Billesdon Brook.................................61
Blakeney Point 62
Blazing Tunder 55
Bless Him 36
Bombyx 30
Breath Caught 65
Briyouni 75
Brorocco...64
Brother Bear 51
Bubble And Squeak..........................55
Bye Bye Baby.....................................31
Cape Cova 68
Capri..50, 79
Cardsharp 57
Cecchini 64
Chain Of Daisies 55
Charm Spirit......................................18
Chemical Charge 65
Chiara Luna..................................36, 51
Chrisellaine.......................................53
Clemmie.....................25, 36, 49, 77
Club Tropicana..................................14
Code Red 54
Connect...52
Contingent...........................27, 32, 51
Contrapposto 66
Cool Spirit 68
Count Octave 64

Cracksman....................................37, 43, 78
Cross Counter....................................37
Crossing The Line.............................64
Crystal Ocean 37, 79
Cuttin' Edge 54
Dancing Star 64
Danehill Kodiac.................................60
Danzan..64
Danzeno..67
Dark Acclaim 45
Dark Pearl..54
Dee Ex Bee 37, 57
Defoe..44
Delano Roosevelt..............................28
Desert Doctor....................................54
Different League..........................25, 77
Dominating...57
Dragstone Rock.................................14
Dreamboat Annie 54
Duke Of Bronte 63
Duretto..64
Dutch Connection 52
Edge Of Sanity....................................8
Eirene...66
Elarqam 21, 30, 56
Ellthea..58
Emaraaty.......................................21, 30
Eminent..63
Enable 43, 78
Enjazaat..53
Equilateral 53
Euginio...61
Expert Eye....................21, 38, 71, 76
Family Tree....................................23, 28
Fantasy Keeper 75
Fighting Irish 54
Flavius...23, 51
Fleet Review......................................49
Flight Of Fantasy 54
Flux Capacitor...................................14
Fortune's Pearl..................................64
Foxtrot Lady 64
Frank's Legacy..................................69
Free Forum...75
Frontiersman......................................38
Fun Mac 55
Gardens Of Babylon 29
Gavota..27, 62
Gawdawpalin 55

Ghaiyyath	22, 29
Giant Spark	74
Gift In Time	68
Ginger Lady	46
Give And Take	44
Give It Some Teddy	73
Glendevon	24, 54
Glorious Journey	22, 30
Go Fox	46
Gobi Desert	50
Goldrush	50
Gustav Klimt	20, 28, 48
Gustavo Fring	14
Handsome Sansom	15
Happily	25, 31, 50, 77
Harbour Law	66
Harry Angel	38, 52, 78
Havana Grey	58
Heartache	52
Herculean	23, 30, 62
Here Comes When	64
Hey Gaman	45
Hey Jonesy	59
Highgarden	34, 38
Hollander	54
Horseplay	64
Huddersfilly Town	69
Hydrangea	50
I Can Fly	32
Ice Age	55
Idaho	50
Il Primo Sole	39
Invincible Army	45
Isomer	64
Jabbaar	8
Jallota	52
James Cook	23, 29
James Garfield	23, 39
Juliet Capulet	27
Juliet Foxtrot	53
Just Brilliant	46
Kaeso	74
Kenya	23, 39, 48
Kew Gardens	28, 48, 71
Key Victory	24
Keyser Soze	15, 46
Khafoo Shemimi	61
Kinaesthesia	65
Kingman	17
Knight To Behold	54
Kyllachy Dragon	8
Lady Aurelia	78
Lady Of Shalott	34
Laraaib	53
Latrobe	29
Laughton	73
Laurens	27, 33, 58, 71, 77
Lethal Steps	50
Librisa Breeze	65, 79
Limato	55
L'Inganno Felice	9
Liquid Amber	26, 33, 51
Lord Glitters	59
Lubinka	46
Lucky Deal	57
Luminate	33
Luxford	75
Machine Learner	54
Madeline	27
Magic Circle	74
Magic Lily	27, 33, 39
Magical	25, 31, 50
Magical Memory	52
Magnolia Springs	26, 34, 55
Malaspina	69
Marmelo	55
Marnie James	9
Masar	22, 29, 45
Massaat	53
Master Carpenter	63
Mayleaf Shine	9
Mendelssohn	23, 30, 49, 76
Michael's Mount	69
Miracle Of Medinah	54
Mirage Dancer	40
Miss Dd	9
Mjjack	59
Monarchs Glen	40
Moonraker	67
Morando	64
Mount Moriah	65
Mountain Bell	65
Movie Set	15
Mrs Danvers	55
Music Society	55
Musical Art	55
Mutaaqeb	53
Mutakatif	53
My Lord And Master	30
Nakeeta	9
Nawassi	26
Near Gold	30
Nearly Caught	55
Nebo	53
Nelson	23, 28, 40, 48
Nyaleti	27
Occupy	30, 65
Oh This Is Us	61
Oliver Reed	61
Olmedo	23
On To Victory	55
One Master	40

Order Of St George............................41, 50
Oriental Song 53
Orion's Bow...41
Patty Patch...15
Perfect Clarity................................34, 52
Perfect Illusion......................................30
Phijee..54
Philamundo...15
Photographer..30
Plunger..55
Podemos...65
Polydream......................................27, 77
Port Douglas 55
Princess Harley.....................................46
Raheen House 63
Raid...41
Rajasinghe.....................................15, 46
Raydiance.......................................23, 59
Rebel Cause..16
Rebel Streak..64
Rebel Surge 16
Redgrave...54
Regal Reality...24
Rekindling 51
Restive...10
Reverend...44
Rhododendron.......................................50
Ripley...53
River Icon..10
Roaring Lion....................21, 29, 44, 72
Robin Of Navan.....................................54
Rock Of Estonia 53
Sacred Life 23
Salouen 55
Sands Chorus..68
Sands Of Mali..59
Sarrochi...27, 32
Saunter..69
Saxon Warrior 20, 28, 48, 76
Sea Of Flames.......................................16
Second Step 62
September 25, 31, 50
Setting Sail..30
Shabaaby...53
Shabbah...54
She Believes..55
Showroom..30
Sfumato..10
Sharjah Bridge 45
She's Pukka...10
Sheriff Garrett..75
Shrewd...11
Sioux Nation....................................23, 49
Sir Ottoman 69
Smugglers Creek...................................11
Snazzy Jazzy...52

Snowflakes...25
South Seas...64
Speedo Boy 69
Spring Loaded 46
Star Rock..55
Stephensons Rocket..............................54
Stone The Crows 11
Stormy Antarctic....................................53
Stradivarius 72, 79
Stream Song 33
Surrey Hope...54
Sweet Selection 55
Sword Exceed..68
Tabarrak...60
Tabdeed...24, 53
Tajaanus..61
Take Me With You 27
Tawny Port...68
Teppal..26
The Great Wall 67
The King...30
The Pentagon...................23, 28, 41, 48
Thistimenextyear....................................16
Thrave..24, 30
Threading...27, 57
Thundering Blue 66
Tip Two Win 54
Tis Marvellous 52
Tocco D'Amore 42, 51
Topapinion...46
Tor..11
Torcedor...51
Toujours 33
Tuff Rock..54
UAE KIng...42
Unfortunately....................................58, 77
US Navy Flag 20, 49, 76
Velvet Voice...46
Veracious...26
Verbal Dexterity 22, 50
Vintager...66
Wadilsafa..30, 53
Wafy 53
Wells Farhh Go 23, 30, 56
Whirling Dervish 30
Whitefountainfairy 64
Wild Illusion.....................................27, 33, 77
Willie John..24, 30
Wind Chimes..27
Withhold...61
Without Parole..................................24, 29
Wootton..23
Yes You 11
Zilara..42
Zonderland...52
Zwayyan...64